Creditworthy

Columbia Studies in the History of U.S. Capitalism

Columbia Studies in the History of U.S. Capitalism
Series Editors: Devin Fergus, Louis Hyman, Bethany Moreton, and Julia Ott

Capitalism has served as an engine of growth, a source of inequality, and a catalyst for conflict in American history. While remaking our material world, capitalism's myriad forms have altered—and been shaped by—our most fundamental experiences of race, gender, sexuality, nation, and citizenship. This series takes the full measure of the complexity and significance of capitalism, placing it squarely back at the center of the American experience. By drawing insight and inspiration from a range of disciplines and alloying novel methods of social and cultural analysis with the traditions of labor and business history, our authors take history "from the bottom up" all the way to the top.

Capital of Capital: Money, Banking, and Power in New York City, by Steven H. Jaffe and Jessica Lautin
From Head Shops to Whole Foods: The Rise and Fall of Activist Entrepreneurs, by Joshua Clark Davis

Creditworthy

*A History of Consumer Surveillance and
Financial Identity in America*

Josh Lauer

Columbia University Press   New York

Columbia University Press
Publishers Since 1893
New York   Chichester, West Sussex
cup.columbia.edu

Library of Congress Cataloging-in-Publication Data

Names: Lauer, Josh (Professor of communication), author.
Title: Creditworthy : a history of consumer surveillance and financial identity
    in America / Josh Lauer.
Other titles: Credit worthy
Description: New York : Columbia University Press, [2017] | Series: Columbia
    studies in the history of U.S. capitalism | Includes bibliographical
    references and index.
Identifiers: LCCN 2016050103 (print) | LCCN 2017015938 (ebook) | ISBN
    9780231544627 (electronic) | ISBN 9780231168083 (cloth) | ISBN 9780231216630
    (pbk.)
Subjects: LCSH: Credit analysis—United States—History.
Classification: LCC HG3701 (ebook) | LCC HG3701 L35 2017 (print) | DDC
    332.70973—dc23
LC record available at https://lccn.loc.gov/2016050103

Cover design: Milenda Nan Ok Lee
Cover image: Walter Sanders/Life Picture Collection © Getty Images.
Clerks consult credit files at the Credit Bureau of Greater New York, 1953.
Printed and bound by CPI Group (UK) Ltd, Croydon, CR0 4YY

Contents

Acknowledgments *vii*

Introduction 1

1. "A Bureau for the Promotion of Honesty": The Birth of
Systematic Credit Surveillance 26

2. Coming to Terms with Credit: The Nineteenth-Century
Origins of Consumer Credit Surveillance 51

3. Credit Workers Unite: Professionalization and the Rise of a
National Credit Infrastructure 78

4. Running the Credit Gantlet: Extracting, Ordering, and
Communicating Consumer Information 103

5. "You Are Judged by Your Credit": Teaching and Targeting
the Consumer 126

6. "File Clerk's Paradise": Postwar Credit Reporting on the
Eve of Automation 156

7. Encoding the Consumer: The Computerization of
Credit Reporting and Credit Scoring 182

8. Database Panic: Computerized Credit Surveillance and
Its Discontents   212

9. From Debts to Data: Credit Bureaus in the New
Information Economy   242

   Epilogue   269

Notes   277
Selected Bibliography   323
Index   335

Acknowledgments

If one must go into debt, then debts of gratitude are the best to accumulate. It is a pleasure to reckon the long columns of beneficence—institutional, intellectual, and personal—that have underwritten this work.

This project began at the University of Pennsylvania's Annenberg School for Communication, where I had the privilege to study with Joseph Turow, Barbie Zelizer, Oscar Gandy, and Katherine Sender. I was drawn to the Annenberg School by the work of Carolyn Marvin, whose cultural histories of technology inspired my own scholarly ambitions. I am lucky to have had Carolyn as a teacher, mentor, and friend.

I have also been fortunate to land among so many smart, generous colleagues at the University of New Hampshire. I am especially grateful to three department chairs—Lawrence Prelli, Joshua Meyrowitz, and James Farrell—who each went out of their way to help secure time and scarce resources in support of my research.

Financial support for this work was provided by the University of New Hampshire, including a Summer Faculty Fellowship from the Graduate School, a travel stipend from the Research and Engagement Academy, and an invaluable semester-long Center for the Humanities Faculty Fellowship. I also received a travel grant from the DeGolyer Library at Southern

Methodist University to visit the J.C. Penney archives, where I enjoyed the expert assistance of Joan Gosnell. Thanks also to the interlibrary loan staffs at the University of Pennsylvania and the University of New Hampshire, and to Sharon Black at the Annenberg School library.

Portions of this book have been published elsewhere. A version of chapter 1 appeared as "From Rumor to Written Record: Credit Reporting and the Invention of Financial Identity in Nineteenth-Century America," *Technology & Culture* 49, no. 2 (2008). Part of chapter 5 appeared as "Making the Ledgers Talk: Customer Control and the Origins of Retail Data Mining, 1920–1940," in *The Rise of Marketing and Market Research,* edited by Hartmut Berghoff, Philip Scranton, and Uwe Spiekermann (Palgrave Macmillan, 2012). Material from several chapters appears in "The End of Judgment: Consumer Credit Scoring and Managerial Resistance to the Black Boxing of Creditworthiness," in *The Emergence of Routines: Entrepreneurship, Organization, and Business History,* edited by Daniel M.G. Raff and Philip Scranton (Oxford University Press, 2017). Archival material from the R.G. Dun Collection is quoted with permission from Harvard Business School's Baker Library.

My thinking about this project has been enriched by feedback from co-panelists and audiences at many conferences, including those sponsored by the International Communication Association, the National Communication Association, the Business History Conference, the Hagley Museum and Library, the Organization of American Historians, the History of Science Society, and the Economic and Business History Society. I am especially grateful to Claire Lemercier and Claire Zalc for the opportunity to share my work at École Normale Supérieure in Paris; to Daniel Raff and Philip Scranton for including me in a workshop at the University of Pennsylvania's Wharton School; to Robert Hunt for bringing me to the Federal Reserve Bank of Philadelphia; to David Lyon and Sachil Singh for hosting me at Queen's University's Surveillance Studies Centre; to Lana Swartz for involving me in a money-themed symposium at the University of Southern California's Annenberg School for Communication and Journalism; and to Rowena Olegario for including me in a corporate reputation symposium at the University of Oxford's Saïd Business School.

In addition to those already named, many others have guided my thinking and sharpened my arguments through conversations and, in many cases, through their own work. Thank you to Mark Andrejevic, Dan Bouk, Claire Brennecke, Rachel Bunker, Lendol Calder, Roger Chartier, Nora Draper, Marc Flandreau, Tarleton Gillespie, Lisa Gitelman, David Hiley, Chris Jay Hoofnagle, Caley Horan, Jennifer Horner, Daniel Horowitz, Louis Hyman, Richard John, Barbara Kiviat, Jessica Lepler, Kenneth Lipartito, Deborah Lubken, Bill Maurer, Elizabeth Mellyn, Gabriel Mesevage, Jeff Niederdeppe, David Park, John Durham Peters, Jamie Pietruska, Jefferson Pooley, Bill Simon, John Staudenmaier, Sean Vanatta, and Emily West. Extended discussions with two colleagues in particular, Craig Robertson and Richard Popp, introduced me to much valuable scholarship and never failed to buoy my enthusiasm for our peculiar subfields of media history. Thanks also to Charles Brown, Anthony Capaldi, Gary Chandler, Norm Magnuson, Corey Stone, and Chet Wiermanski for generously sharing their first-hand knowledge of the credit industry.

This book, for all of its shortcomings, is much better thanks to the feedback of two anonymous reviewers and the interventions of series editors Louis Hyman, Julia Ott, and Bethany Moreton, who went above and beyond the call of duty. Thanks also to Columbia editor Philip Leventhal for shepherding the work into publication.

Finally, none of this would be possible without the support and welcome diversions of my family. Thank you to my brothers—Deakin, Judd, and Brett—and to my parents, Al Lauer and Anne Fletcher. My deepest gratitude goes to my children, Sebastian and Zadie, whose love and company give me the greatest happiness.

Creditworthy

Introduction

In late November 1913, a dapper old man stopped into a Cleveland department store to do some shopping. On his way out, he gave a young female clerk his name and instructed her to charge several items to his account. The clerk, who did not know the man, insisted on calling the credit department to authorize his purchases. Perhaps the stranger's wig and lack of eyebrows aroused her suspicion. The seventy-four-year-old man suffered from generalized alopecia, a condition that had caused him to lose all of his body hair. After the credit department confirmed the customer's identity and creditworthiness, his charged goods were approved, and he left without incident. This exchange would be completely unremarkable except that the stranger was no average consumer. He was John D. Rockefeller, literally the richest man in the world. The multimillionaire oil baron had been denied access to credit, "at least until the clerk learned that he was 'good.'"[1]

One hundred years later this story still resonates. Twenty-first-century Americans are accustomed to having their identities and creditworthiness tested, often multiple times each day, to see if they are "good." Indeed, whenever we use a bank card to pay for something, we enter into an invisible surveillance network that confirms our identity, records the details of our transaction, and instantly updates our status and legitimacy as a paying consumer. All of this happens in the few seconds that it takes to swipe a plastic card—or just as commonly, in the time it takes for an online purchase to be confirmed. Such speed and ease are hard to argue with. Why fool around with cash when the whole thing can be settled with a signature or code? Rockefeller and many of his fellow Americans would have agreed. For someone like Rockefeller, a charge account was largely a matter of convenience. He had piles of money sitting in the bank. But for many Americans who did not, credit accounts allowed them to walk out of stores with all sorts of things—from furniture and appliances to clothing and food—all on the thin promise of future earnings. Credit was not just a frivolous indulgence, as its critics have long insisted. In many cases, it was a necessary bridge between income and paychecks.

The absurdity of the Rockefeller incident was comic fodder for newspapers throughout the nation. The retired titan of industry took it in stride and even commended the embarrassed clerk for her "caution." He had bigger concerns, such as founding some of the nation's most venerable philanthropic organizations and caring for his ailing wife. Yet the story, for all of its populist mirth, reveals something else: consumer credit surveillance was an established fact of life. It was funny that Rockefeller's credit standing had been questioned, but it was taken for granted that systems for interrogating one's identity and creditworthiness already existed. Rockefeller, like millions of Americans from all walks of life, had a second self, a disembodied financial identity that inhabited the vast files of retail credit departments and local credit bureaus (figure 0.1). No one, not even the wealthy or famous, could escape the gaze of this unseen surveillance apparatus.

How did this happen? How did Americans become faceless names and numbers in an enigmatic network of credit records, scoring systems, and information brokers? How did financial identity become such an important marker of our personal trustworthiness and worth? It is easy to mistake consumer credit surveillance and financial identity for new technological developments, products of late twentieth-century databases and algorithms. The importance of financial identity and credit risk has become a topic of serious public debate. The scourge of so-called identity theft and the 2008 subprime mortgage crisis illustrate the high stakes of credit information in contemporary life. However, systems for monitoring

```
Rock, Clarence A, purch agt, r 6907 Quinby ave..2EP FP
Rock, Henry A, watchman, r 7921 Jones rd.......2EP ES
Rock, Herman A, 2d vice-pres Dan Dorn Iron Wks,
    r 2179 E 89th...........................CP 2DP ES
Rock, Herman A (Mrs), r 2179 E 89th.............2EP
Rock, James ·J, ticket agt, r 2737 E 55th.............2FP
Rock, Joe, 2707 Church ave.......................EP
Rock, John, ret, r 5603 Kinsman rd..........AP DP 2EP
Rock, N, r 44 Champa ave...........................FP
Rock, S E, r 1610 Ansel rd..........................FP
Rock, Wm, engr, r 2329 E 100th..................DP 2EP
Rock, Wm C, fire dept, r 1415 W 81st...........EP ES
Rock, W S, r 1415 W 81st...........................FP
Rockefeller, The, 5105 Woodland ave...........CP DP
Rockefeller, A N (Miss), r Wickliffe, O............2EP
Rockefeller, Frank, 1007 Garfield bldg, Wickliffe, O..
    ..................................AP CP 3DP 2EP
Rockefeller, Frank (Mrs), r Wickliffe, O.........DP EP
Rockefeller, H D, 1052 Euclid......................AP
Rockefeller, H E (Miss), r 1020 Prospect.............2EP
Rockefeller, John D, r Forest Hill E C..............
    .........................2AP 5CP 3DP 2EP FP
Rockefeller, R N, The St Regis.....................EP
Rocker, Henry A, lawyer, r 2546 E 43d..DP DS 2EP 2FP
Rocker Printing Co (Sam'l Rocker), r 1924 Woodland
    ave....................................2DP 2EP ES
```

Figure 0.1 John D. Rockefeller and his family received consumer credit ratings like everyone else. Their names and ratings appeared beside those of fellow citizens from all walks of life, from lawyers to firemen. (*The Credit Rating Book for Cleveland, O[hio]*, Early's Mercantile Agency, January 1909)

consumer credit identities and for judging one's creditworthiness are not new at all. They were central to the ascent of consumer capitalism in the United States. Long before credit cards filled mailboxes in the 1960s, before Americans bought refrigerators on the installment plan, or the first mass-produced and mass-financed Model Ts rolled off assembly lines, consumer credit surveillance systems were already in place. This was the surveillance system that Rockefeller stumbled into when his financial identity—his hidden record of prompt payment and trustworthiness— temporarily trumped his identity as the world's richest man in the flesh.

The history of American consumer credit and its cheerless corollary, debt, has only recently begun to receive serious attention.[2] Compared to the study of capitalism's dazzling material culture and advertising, the history of borrowing and paying bills appears dreary in the extreme. Credit, as Lendol Calder lamented in his pioneering history of the subject, is the "neglected stepchild of consumer culture."[3] Yet borrow and pay we must. The way that Americans manage and spend their money is, paradoxically, so banal and so private that it easily eludes historical analysis. The same taboo that inhibits Americans from discussing personal finance has also made it very difficult for scholars to study it. We flaunt our consumption—our cars, our homes, our fashionable clothing—as proof of self-worth and social membership, but we hide our debts, our mortgages, our overdue bills, and our collection notices.

This secret world of personal finance is essential to our understanding of modern economic life.[4] Its history, as Calder and others have shown, reveals not only the deep nineteenth-century roots of consumer credit and changing American attitudes toward debt, but also the far-reaching effects of the institutionalization of credit. To say that consumer credit comes with strings attached is an understatement. Borrowing forces us into complex, rigid, and often unforgiving relationships with financial institutions and businesses that demand our personal information and ceaselessly collect data about us. It requires that we enter into bureaucratic systems of identification, record-keeping, accounting, marketing, and consumer research. Whenever we promise to pay we become subjects of intensive surveillance.

This book explains how this happened and why it matters today. In *Creditworthy* I detail the rise of consumer credit surveillance in the United States and its ongoing effort to control the behavior of American citizens and to quantify their value in a growing array of contexts, from credit and insurance risk to consumer analytics and target marketing. In short, this book is about how credit surveillance seeks to make American consumers "good"—morally responsible, obedient, predictable, and profitable. This history follows a broad arc, from the development of commercial credit reporting during the 1840s to the growth of algorithmic risk scoring and big corporate data in the 1990s. It also traverses a number of momentous social, economic, and technological shifts over more than a century, from urbanization and mass marketing to post–World War II suburban sprawl and information age computing.

At the center of this story is the consumer credit bureau. The modern credit bureau is one of the most powerful surveillance institutions in American life, yet we know almost nothing about it.[5] The industry is currently dominated by three major bureaus—Equifax, Experian, and TransUnion. Together these private firms track the movements, personal histories, and financial behavior of nearly all adult Americans. Until the late 1960s, when the reporting industry suddenly became a lightning rod in debates over database surveillance and privacy, credit bureaus worked in quiet obscurity. They seemed to come from nowhere during the late twentieth century and to exemplify the frightening new realities of computerized surveillance. Yet many of these bureaus have been around since the 1920s or earlier. In fact, two of the nation's leading bureaus, Equifax and Experian, have roots dating to the 1890s. The consumer credit bureau was a vital information infrastructure upon which American consumer capitalism was built. These surveillance systems supported new consumer lending and financing industries that emerged during the first half of the twentieth century, as automobile makers, department stores, mortgage companies, and banks learned how to turn personal debt into corporate profits.[6] Without this infrastructure, the modern credit economy and today's digital commerce would be inconceivable. More than any other institution, the consumer credit bureau formalized financial identity as an integral dimension of personal identity and established a technological framework for predicting credit risk and extracting debts.

THE RISE OF MODERN CREDIT SURVEILLANCE

While we know quite a bit about the history of consumer culture in the United States—its advertising, its spectacular commodification, its desires and deceits—we know much less about how all of this consumption, much of it done on credit, was even possible to transact. This is no trivial detail. The ascent of consumer capitalism, after all, is inextricably linked to the growth of institutional credit at the turn of the twentieth century. It was nothing new for a local grocer or tailor to trust his well-known customers to pay later. This kind of informal open book credit was pervasive in nineteenth-century America. But how could new institutional lenders—

department stores, mail order houses, installment dealers, finance companies, and, later, banks—trust total strangers, hundreds or thousands of them, to repay a debt? The answer is that they could not. But neither could local grocers or tailors. As eastern cities and upstart interior towns filled with unfamiliar faces after the Civil War, the problem of judging creditworthiness was a problem for everyone, including small shopkeepers who allowed their neighbors to run up debts. In this new world of anonymity and transience, consumers who looked "good"—well dressed, professional occupation, well connected—often turned out to be the worst deadbeats. And just as troubling, some who looked "bad"—shabby clothes, low-skilled job, no references—often turned out to be entirely reliable and loyal customers. How could a merchant identify the "good" consumers and avoid the "bad" ones?

This problem, the confounding task of deciding whom to trust and whom to invest in, led to the development of systematic credit surveillance in the United States. The first to produce such systems were commercial credit reporting firms that emerged during the 1840s.[7] These firms, the predecessors of modern-day business rating agencies such as Dun & Bradstreet, were not concerned with consumers but with *commercial* borrowers—that is, anyone who might borrow money, raw materials, or goods in support of enterprise. As economic relationships became increasingly distant and impersonal during the antebellum market revolution, commercial credit reporting firms played a key role in helping lenders determine the creditworthiness of unknown customers throughout the nation. These agencies sought to compile information about the personal life, habits, property, and financial reputation of all American merchants and entrepreneurs. This confidential information was recorded in massive ledger books and shared only with subscribers who inquired at the agency's office. During the late 1850s, some of these firms began to publish rating books that displayed the creditworthiness of each individual in cryptic alphanumeric codes. In essence, what early commercial reporting firms sought to do was to convert an individual's local reputation into an easily readable, centralized summary of creditworthiness for remote lenders. In the process they did something more profound: they created the modern concept of financial identity.

This book begins with commercial credit reporting because its key features—totalizing surveillance, detailed personal information, quantification, and disembodied financial identity—all became defining aspects of consumer credit reporting. The first organizations devoted to monitoring the creditworthiness of American *consumers*, rather than business borrowers, appeared in New York around 1870. The idea quickly spread. By 1890 consumer reporting organizations could be found in cities and towns across the nation, from New York to San Francisco. These early ventures were a motley array of private agencies and voluntary protective associations. While some produced little more than blacklists of debtors and delinquents, others developed complex identification and rating systems that monitored the lives and fortunes of entire city populations. The most ambitious published annual reference books in which the names, addresses, occupations, marital status (for women), and credit ratings of more than 20,000 individual consumers were listed.

These late nineteenth-century organizations are the origin of the modern credit bureau and the foundation of the national surveillance infrastructure that governs consumer creditworthiness today. During the first decades of the twentieth century, a national association was formed to organize new credit bureaus and to coordinate their activities with hundreds of others that already existed. By 1940 this national association included more than 1,400 independently owned and operated local bureaus, ranging from big-city offices to small-town outfits. Collectively, these bureaus maintained credit records for more than sixty million Americans—around 70 percent of the nation's total adult population. This federation of bureaus was hardly airtight, but it drew Americans into tightening networks of surveillance. The industry remained fragmented until the 1980s, when a small number of computerized bureaus annexed hundreds of local bureaus and consolidated their power. By the end of the decade the leading national bureaus each had databases with more than a hundred million consumer files.

Though the credit bureau occupies center stage throughout this book, the history of consumer credit surveillance cannot be told without highlighting a parallel and equally important development: the rise of professional credit management. During the late nineteenth century a peculiar new business specialist, the credit man, emerged in the back offices of mass retailers. As the volume of credit applications grew in department stores, installment houses, and large specialty dealers, credit men assumed the difficult job of judging an unknown customer's creditworthiness. Even more than local grocers or tailors, retail credit men struggled to separate the good from the bad among the procession of credit-seeking strangers that came to their offices. For this reason, credit men—and, after World War I, a growing number of credit women—had a major stake in the success of local credit bureaus and were deeply involved in the organization of consumer surveillance networks.

While supporting the development of the consumer reporting industry, newly professionalized credit managers also worked to found a "science" of credit management and to systematize the collection of customer information in their own in-house credit departments.[8] By the 1920s credit managers had established sophisticated systems for compiling, analyzing, and rapidly transmitting consumer credit information within their own stores and to the local credit bureau. In this way, credit bureaus and credit departments worked hand in hand to build the consumer surveillance infrastructure that exists today.

RETHINKING THE HISTORY OF MODERN SURVEILLANCE

Given the importance of these surveillance networks for overseeing the vast expansion of credit-fueled consumer capitalism, it might be enough to simply describe their operations. These organizations were information service providers far ahead of their time. In the context of an industrializing economy, one that excelled at churning out physical things, they produced a strange and intangible new commodity: personal information. Credit surveillance was part of a nascent information infrastructure that began to take shape during the nineteenth century.[9] Following the lead of commercial credit reporting firms, consumer credit bureaus and retail credit departments amassed enormous archives in which the lives of American citizens were scrupulously documented and dissected.

While the growth of modern surveillance has attracted intense scholarly interest in recent decades, most of it has been directed at contemporary developments. This is hardly surprising. The proliferation of new data-gathering technologies, many no older than the 1990s, have transformed the nature of privacy, citizenship, and personal identity in alarming ways. Indeed, it has become quite difficult to communicate, search for information, shop, or move through public space without leaving digital evidence about oneself at every turn. The escalation of post-9/11 policing and security has only added to the urgency of studying new surveillance practices.[10] At the same time, the gravity of current events and the speed of technological change have made it difficult to view contemporary surveillance in its broader historical context. By focusing on the impact of recent and emerging technologies—mobile computing, biometrics, and big data, for instance—one might get the impression that modern surveillance is very new. And by foregrounding the expansion of government surveillance, we fail to see the key role that commercial organizations have played in the creation of modern surveillance society.

This book revises several basic assumptions about the rise of modern surveillance in the United States. First among these is that surveillance as we know it—systematic, pervasive, invisible, personal—is a new phenomenon. Though scholars generally agree that surveillance is a fundamental element of modernity, and that the origins of modern surveillance can be traced to the bureaucratic recordkeeping of nineteenth-century nation-states and capitalists, this early history is rarely taken seriously.[11] Instead, surveillance before computing and miniaturized electronics—at the very least, surveillance before World War II—is too often characterized as primitive and inefficient.[12] The history of American credit surveillance forces us to reconsider this shortsighted and misleading perspective. Paper-pushing clerks in early credit reporting agencies and credit departments were not just quaint precursors of our modern surveillance. They operated complex surveillance systems in which millions of Americans were tracked and monitored. This surveillance, moreover, was deeply personal and had real effects. One's reputation as "good pay" or a deadbeat was no longer an isolated local matter; it was inscribed in one's financial identity and transmitted throughout the nation.

In addition to historicizing modern surveillance, this book also challenges assumptions about the institutional origins of mass surveillance in the United States, specifically the primacy of the nation-state. The history of modern surveillance, as it currently exists, is largely the history of government surveillance.[13] Yet the state was not the only source of organized surveillance before World War II. It had powerful rivals in the private sector. This was especially true in the United States, where commercial surveillance systems, including credit reporting organizations, were well established in the nineteenth century and in some cases dwarfed those of the decentralized state. Not only did early credit surveillance networks track thousands of American citizens, but the information that they compiled and sold also dealt with much more than financial facts. Credit records typically included the intimate details of one's domestic arrangements, personality, health, legal and criminal history, and job performance, and sometimes one's physical appearance. In other words, they were comprehensive dossiers. Even after law enforcement and other government agencies grew more powerful during the early twentieth century, the credit reporting industry remained one of the nation's most invasive and omnivorous collectors of personal data. Its files were so rich with confidential information that local police and government agencies, including the Federal Bureau of Investigation and the Internal Revenue Service, often turned to the *credit bureau* for help.

The history of capitalist surveillance has yet to receive the attention that it deserves. Though nineteenth-century capitalism is widely understood as the nation-state's twin partner in the creation of modern surveillance, we have very few specifics about the former.[14] Who were these unnamed "capitalists," and what exactly did they do to advance surveillance as a distinctively "modern" practice? Beyond gestures toward the rise of bureaucracy and economic rationalization, themes taken directly from the sociology of Max Weber, the formation of capitalist surveillance is woefully underhistoricized. This is especially striking given the centrality of private-sector surveillance today. One of the most troubling aspects of contemporary surveillance is the growth of commercial databases and new interactive technologies through which personal data is routinely harvested, often without our consent. These powerful forms of surveillance raise not only privacy issues—especially when commercial data is shared with the state—but also larger concerns about how such data is used to classify individuals, to sort people and populations into categories of risk and preference, and to shape our perception of reality, including which social, economic, and political groups we belong to (and are excluded from). These very issues are the subject of some of the most trenchant and insightful critiques of contemporary surveillance.[15] Yet without a *history* of capitalist surveillance to connect to, recent developments cannot be seen as integral to the calculating logic of capitalism and its commodification of information over a much longer period of time. As this book shows, the roots of extractive "surveillance capitalism" can be traced to nineteenth-century lists and ledgers.[16]

To date, the history of capitalist surveillance has focused on the regulation of labor. As the American economy was industrialized during the nineteenth century, those who owned the means of production—capitalists—faced the problem of mobilizing and disciplining armies of wage laborers. Surveillance, in this context, centered upon the problem of prodding the work force to perform more efficiently and, naturally, more profitably. In this light, Karl Marx's analysis of workplace regimentation and coercion is sometimes viewed as an early critique of capitalist surveillance. "The place of the slave-driver's lash," he observed, "is taken by the overseer's book of penalties."[17] Monetary incentives, in other words, were the gentler but no less exploitative rods that capitalists used to drive wage laborers to do their bidding. The formalization of workplace surveillance, however, is more often associated with Frederick W. Taylor than with Marx.[18] In his famous time-motion studies of the 1890s and 1900s, Taylor deconstructed industrial work routines and promoted new supervisory techniques for controlling laborers and empowering managers. His concept of scientific management was as much a product of its time as it was the invention of its efficiency-obsessed engineer. The search for social order was a hallmark of the American Progressive Era, reflected in similar efforts to rationalize and surveil education, politics, government, and other domains of life.[19] Consumption was one of these domains.

DISCIPLINING THE MODERN CONSUMER

The scientific management of production and the close surveillance of workers had an analogue in the scientific management of consumption.

By the time consultants like Taylor showed up to help shop managers harness the productive labor of their employees, American consumers were also under observation. Mass production required mass consumption to buy up all of the cheap and plentiful goods that flooded the market after the Civil War. The problem of making wage laborers work was mirrored by the problem of making American consumers buy. The most obvious and dramatic response to the latter problem was advertising.

Though much early advertising was designed to appeal to large audiences via mass media—newspapers, magazines, signage, and branded packaging—commercial messaging was far from indiscriminate. List brokers and press clipping agencies were feeding an emergent direct mail industry during the 1880s and 1890s, one that classified and targeted "live" prospects throughout the nation.[20] At the turn of the twentieth century advertising experts also began to take special interest in *differences* among "mass" consumers, at first by gender, class, ethnicity, and geography, giving rise to the new field of market research.[21] At nearly the same time that Taylor was clocking the movements of steel workers, advertising agencies, manufacturers, retailers, and publishers were beginning to subject American consumers to an onslaught of questionnaires, surveys, statistical analysis, and eventually psychological tests. Such surveillance, it was hoped, would unlock the secrets of selling and place the consumer, like the worker, under the thumb of capitalist producers and their sales forces.

Yet getting Americans to buy was only part of the problem. Getting them to pay was another. Advertising sold Americans on the material trappings of happiness and success, but credit was often necessary to bring these things home. This included expensive durable goods such as sewing machines and automobiles as well as cheap household items and even groceries. Though most consumers could be trusted to repay their debts at some point, there were always some who would not or could not. As the volume and impersonality of consumer credit increased after the Civil War, retailers, like commercial creditors before them, were desperate to protect themselves from bad debts. The consumer credit reporting organizations that first emerged during the 1870s served this purpose. These new organizations, like commercial reporting firms before them, were sites of disciplinary surveillance.[22] By monitoring the behaviors of *all* local consumers—the good, the bad, and the middling—and sharing this information among their members, reporting organizations sought to enforce the conduct and morality of creditworthiness. Borrowers who did not settle their accounts, or who did so slowly or erratically, received black marks in their credit record and reduced access to credit, or none at all. Creditworthiness was no longer an informal personal matter between buyers and sellers; it had become an institutional fact. Like the overseer's book of penalties, which disciplined the worker, the credit bureau's book of ratings disciplined the consumer.

During the first half of the twentieth century, credit bureaus worked hard to publicize their disciplinary function in newspapers, media campaigns, and even parades. Credit surveillance was no secret; it was advertised and promoted just like the goods that consumers used credit to buy. It was futile to hide one's private life or past mistakes, as *Time* magazine noted in 1936. The credit bureau would uncover everything. [23] The explicit aim of credit surveillance was to bend the financial behavior of Americans to the will of lenders—that is, to make them play the part of good consumers. Toward this end, credit professionals sought to inculcate norms of prompt payment and to shame consumers into honoring their promises, even while helping them dig themselves further into debt. Americans were urged to "treat their credit as a sacred trust" and to avoid the disgrace of "Q.C." (questionable credit).

This was just the public surface of the disciplinary machinery. The real scientific management of consumer credit took place behind the scenes in the offices of local credit bureaus and credit departments. It was there that the identities of consumers were confirmed, their relationships, reputations, and movements were documented, and their financial behavior was continuously recorded. During the early twentieth century, credit bureaus and credit departments adopted standardized applications and forms, specialized recordkeeping practices, and elaborate systems for coding, updating, and communicating information internally and between one another. These were capitalist bureaucracies par excellence. The basic unit of analysis was the individual file. Each consumer had a master file in the local bureau that contained the details of the subject's biography and financial history. The credit departments of retailers, finance companies, banks, fuel dealers, utility companies, and even hospitals kept similar records and fed the local bureau with a constant stream of new information. Creditors could monitor the financial performance of consumers and calibrate credit access—expanding or curtailing—to maximize profitability. Such surveillance regulated the treadmill of debt for each customer. Before World War II an average credit bureau or credit department maintained thousands of these files, and some had many more. By the mid-1930s, for instance, New York City's largest bureau watched over three million individual files.[24] Together these disparate files—housed in local credit bureaus, credit departments, and merchant ledgers—made up one's financial identity. Though imperfectly aligned and often working at cross purposes, these systems of interchange reflected larger shifts toward bureaucratic rationalization as American capitalism became increasingly centralized and coordinated.

Consumer credit surveillance was not just a metaphorical disciplinary apparatus; it involved actual machinery. From the beginning, credit bureaus and credit departments were eager adopters of new office technologies, from vacuum tube and teletype systems to multiline telephone banks and mechanical filing devices. The most probing and comprehensive credit information was useful only if it could be quickly located and communicated. Speed was crucial when credit managers or sales clerks requested credit checks, often with the customer waiting anxiously nearby. The machinery of credit surveillance was typically operated by women, often rooms full of them, tethered to headsets and switchboards among columns of filing cabinets. In the early 1950s, *Life* magazine marveled at the scale and efficiency of the modern credit bureau, ranking its intelligence-gathering capacity alongside that of the Federal Bureau of Investigation (FBI) and the Soviet KGB.[25] Postwar credit bureaus would add new elevator filing systems, document conveyers, and photoduplicating devices to their array of information-handling technologies.

All of this was soon overshadowed by another machine: the computer. During the mid-1960s the credit reporting industry began to convert its millions of paper files into electronic data, a process that was hastened by the simultaneous adoption of computers among the industry's major subscribers—mass retailers, finance companies, credit card companies, and banks. During the 1970s and 1980s the credit reporting industry was completely reshaped by mergers as a handful of computerized bureaus bought out hundreds of small local bureaus. While computerization accelerated credit surveillance and consolidated the reporting industry's national reach, it also opened the door to new technologies of consumer discipline, most importantly statistical scoring. During the closing decades of the twentieth century, the leading national bureaus became deeply involved in the development of risk scoring and database marketing programs that did more than simply calculate credit risk. They drew upon massive datasets to predict the behaviors, interests, and commercial value of Americans.

CAPITALISM, RISK, AND THE FINANCIALIZATION OF EVERYDAY LIFE

When consumer credit risk is discussed today, it is almost always in the context of credit scoring. Fair Isaac's three-digit FICO score has been the industry standard since the 1990s.[26] Yet this well-known ranking is just one of literally hundreds of commercial risk scores that are used. In addition to "generic" credit scores offered by each of the major national bureaus, specialized models are available for calculating the risk—and differential pricing—of mortgages, credit cards, automobile loans, and insurance policies. There are also screening models for prospective tenants and utilities accounts, and marketing models for predicting an individual's household income, discretionary spending, propensity to respond to credit offers, and profitability as an interest-accruing debtor. This is just a partial list of scoring products offered by the leading credit bureaus and their corporate parents. Many others—including controversial health and social networking models—have been developed by a new breed of unregulated data brokers and analytics firms.[27]

As more of everyday experience is governed by commercial algorithms, there is growing concern that these "black-boxed" filters and decision systems are threatening basic legal rights to privacy and due process. Proprietary algorithms not only determine what we see in our search and news results; they also shape our reputations in the marketplace.[28] Credit scoring has been at the leading edge of these developments. While generating numerical values that are easily comparable, scoring models have also naturalized the quantification of risk itself, turning probabilistic rankings into empirical facts about one's trustworthiness, reliability, and value. An individual may dispute errors in his or her credit file, but there is no arguing with—or even fully understanding—the secret formulas that produce our scores. Significantly, late twentieth-century credit scoring signaled a paradigmatic shift in the treatment of consumers as objectified risks and representatives of risk populations.[29] Where once there were individual borrowers, there are now only statistical approximations of borrowers, stripped of their uniqueness and reduced to a set of demographic features, data points, and calculable behaviors.

While credit scoring technologies have expanded economic opportunities for many Americans, they have also introduced a new category of financial self-knowledge. What began as a backend administrative tool is now a vital personal statistic. Consumers are urged to take an entrepreneurial interest in their credit scores, to view them as a metric of economic performance much like a macroeconomic indicator, and to track their fluctuations with the solicitude of a Wall Street broker. As with a growing array of private affairs, from investing and banking to health care and fitness, the self-mastery of creditworthiness demands that consumers embrace a regime of continuous inspection and accounting. The enlistment of consumers in their own surveillance, and the marketing of credit monitoring services to assist in the management of the economic self, reflect what some see as a broader "financialization" of contemporary life.[30]

This book shares such concerns with the proliferation of financial objectification and risk consciousness. But like credit surveillance itself, economic quantification and risk management are not recent technological phenomena. Nor are they unique to late twentieth-century neoliberalism. They are major themes in the history of American capitalism. The market revolution of the 1820s and 1830s not only changed social relationships, it also changed the way Americans talked about themselves. A new capitalist vernacular emerged, one in which personal identity was conflated with financial success and, more poignantly, failure. As Scott Sandage has shown, men no longer lost their fortunes; they became "losers." They also became "first raters" or "third raters" depending upon the estimation of commercial credit rating firms.[31] In this book I show how credit surveillance fostered new forms of economic self-awareness—or what Foucauld-ians call self-governance—and how this surveillance contributed to the deep penetration of market values in American life. In short, I show how personal identity became financial identity.

At a fundamental level, the development of modern credit surveillance was a response to the problem of risk in an emerging national economy. Where creditors knew little or nothing about prospective borrowers, po-tentially disastrous contingencies entered the financial system. Such risks took many forms, from personal failings to acts of God, and they threat-ened to bring down not just individual firms but the entire economic edi-fice. It was exactly such a national calamity, the panic of 1837, that spurred the formation of the first commercial credit reporting organizations. These early agencies and the consumer credit surveillance networks that followed represented efforts to rationalize and contain such risks. This was accom-plished by centralizing information about borrowers, codifying the ele-ments of credit risk, and inventing a new language of creditworthiness and a science of its analysis.

Like other risk industries that blossomed in the aftermath of 1837, nota-bly life insurance, systematic credit surveillance was an attempt to bring a measure of security—and, it was hoped, predictability—to capitalism's spasms of creative destruction.[32] Credit reporting, like insurance, was a "technology of risk."[33] The underlying aim of this new business institution was to make credit risk calculable. The advantage of such calculations was not their empirical accuracy, which they certainly lacked, but their use as a comparative yardstick. Long before the development of statistical scoring, early credit reporting organizations made credit risk commensurable.[34] In the hierarchy of credit ratings, it was plain to see that a borrower desig-nated A1 was a better risk than one identified as 3½. During the late nine-teenth century, consumer credit reporting organizations developed their own rudimentary coding systems to relate an individual's payment history, or ledger experience, with local merchants. The conceptual parallels between insurance classification and credit reporting were obvious to early credit pro-fessionals. Though their own systems were not quantitative, they looked to the insurance industry for inspiration and dreamt of the day when credit-worthiness, like mortality, could be calculated using actuarial methods.

Statistical techniques for analyzing credit risk were not developed until the late 1930s, and even then they remained out of reach for all but trained mathematicians until the late 1950s. But this did not stop credit professionals from exploring new ways to classify and predict creditworthiness. Since a consumer's income proved to be a highly unreliable marker of credit risk—ironically, those with the means to pay often did not—credit experts looked to other variables, including occupation, neighborhood, nationality, race, and even intelligence. These were not newly "discovered" risk variables. Such prejudicial social sorting was part of the tacit knowledge that had long informed credit decisions. During the 1920s and 1930s, these categories of risk were enumerated in instructional texts and given new intellectual legitimacy through industry reports and academic studies. Occupation in particular emerged as a promising variable for classifying the creditworthiness of populations. Salaried professionals and civil servants, with their stable incomes and sense of social responsibility, usually appeared near the top. Unskilled laborers and those with jobs marked by transience or moral disrepute—actors, salesmen, and waitresses, for example—at the bottom. Though credit evaluation remained a largely subjective process for most of the twentieth century, the drive to formalize socioeconomic classification and to inscribe monetary value within such risk populations was at the forefront of consumer credit management decades before the rise of computerized credit scoring.

Initially, consumer credit surveillance was viewed rather narrowly as a system of prevention—a technique for identifying and quarantining deadbeats. This changed after World War I. Credit information began to circulate in much wider contexts as those who handled such personal data—credit managers and credit bureau operators—began to perceive its surplus value as business intelligence. During the 1920s, for instance, retail credit managers suddenly realized that their voluminous files were not only useful for evaluating credit risk. They also contained detailed information—transactional data—about the demographics, preferences, and spending behavior of their customers. Credit surveillance and the routine recordkeeping that it entailed could thus be used to segment a store's customers and to develop targeted sales promotions. Around the same time, credit bureaus began to actively market ancillary services such as insurance reports, personnel reports, and tenant reports. This allowed them to expand their business by repackaging and commodifying information already in their master files. Even more, during the 1950s and 1960s credit bureaus began to offer credit screening services, to manage charge account programs, and, most importantly, to sell lists of premium customers.

Though credit bureaus had long refrained from selling promotional lists—this, they feared, would tarnish their reputation for impartiality and stir resentment among subscribers (on whom they also depended to furnish consumer information)—by the 1960s the reporting industry had moved far beyond its origins as a mere loss prevention service. It was becoming a major player in the postwar information economy and a leading force behind the financialization of contemporary American life. Credit surveillance not only institutionalized the concept of financial identity; it also contributed to more expansive forms of consumer surveillance that have little or nothing to do with credit. The history of this expansion, from early retail data mining to consumer list marketing, helps us understand the origins and logic of contemporary consumer surveillance and its effort to reduce personal identity to superficial measures of demographic, lifestyle, and financial attributes in the age of big commercial data.

CREDIT MORALITY AND THE PERSISTENCE OF CHARACTER

Creditworthiness, despite its current technocratic aura, feels deeply personal. Counterintuitively, perhaps, it is not simply a matter of having the financial means—the capital—to repay a debt. Wealth, as jilted creditors have often attested, guarantees nothing. Plenty of well-to-do customers have refused to settle their bills out of indifference or arrogance. And conversely, plenty of hard-scrabble debtors have bent over backwards to honor their debts. For this reason, creditworthiness is less about whether one *can* pay and more to do with whether one *will* pay. It hinges upon one's reputation for truthfulness, integrity, consistency, and responsibility. Above all, creditworthiness is a moral judgment. To be denied credit is thus a kind of personal affront. It is to suggest that one is not entirely honest or reliable, that one lacks the self-discipline or maturity to manage one's life and financial affairs. This was the humorous subtext of the Rockefeller incident in 1913.[35] It was not just that a department store clerk had failed to recognize one of the most famous people on earth. It was that she had also questioned his creditworthiness. The clerk had unwittingly humiliated Rockefeller by doubting the rich man's trustworthiness.

When the elements of creditworthiness were codified during the nineteenth century, they were conveniently summarized as the three Cs—character, capital, and capacity (one's work experience and ability to earn a living). This formula served as shorthand for credit evaluation well into the twentieth century. Importantly, the first C in this triumvirate, character, was widely understood to be the most revealing. "More significant than property or income," the author of a 1936 guide to personal finance emphasized, "is the character of the purchaser as evidenced by his reputation for integrity and honesty."[36] As a reflection of one's true inner nature and ethical core, character was seen as the decisive element of creditworthiness. It determined who would repay a debt, even in the face of adversity, and who would dodge or default. "Character activates self-government in credit relationships and produces cooperation rather than conflict, debtor initiative rather than resistance," a prominent business professor explained in a 1967 textbook. "With character, debtors are conscientious, organized, balanced, foresighted, and sensitive to the limit of their ability to discharge debt."[37] The best consumers, in other words, have been socialized to the fiscal and moral imperatives of borrowing and acquiesce to its institutional demands.

Character may have been the most important dimension of creditworthiness, but it was also the most inscrutable. The problem of course is that character is an elusive, subjective quality. It cannot be observed or measured directly. To judge character, creditors thus looked for clues in an individual's outward behaviors and relationships: physical appearance and personality; marital stability (or strife); the condition of one's home; drinking habits; predilections for gambling or philandering; and one's reputation among neighbors, employers, and business associates. Statements regarding character were integral to credit reports well into the 1960s. They appeared in open-ended remarks sections and gridlike rubrics that required bureau investigators to indicate whether the subject was "well regarded as to character, habits, and morals."[38]

While information about one's character circulated in credit reports, the bureau's subscribers also performed their own character inspections.

Whenever a customer applied for credit, whether at a department store or a bank, a credit manager typically met with the individual and coaxed out as much information as possible about the applicant's finances, domestic arrangements, and personal life. During these probing face-to-face interviews, which many consumers came to dread, credit managers also scrutinized the disposition and manner of applicants and made their own judgments about their honesty. Even as credit management shifted toward systematic record-keeping and quantification, the personal interview remained standard practice. And even as credit professionals took on new executive functions, it was their uncanny ability to see through appearances—their superior ability to judge character—that remained their defining skill.

From the vantage of our own time, the notion of character seems to belong to a bygone era. Computerized credit reporting and scoring systems have turned credit evaluation into a thoroughly impersonal affair. Credit-worthiness, refigured as credit risk, appears as a value-free, empirical reality—numbers in, numbers out. Thus cleansed of the human credit managers' whims and prejudices—most importantly, their sexism and racism—consumer credit is now more democratic and objective than ever. There is certainly truth to this. But it is also not that simple. Credit risk, particularly as summarized in credit scores, is hardly an economic indicator devoid of social meaning. Despite the best efforts of statisticians and credit analysts to isolate financial risk—to disentangle the economic and the social—the ghost of the social continues to reappear. In theory one's cred-itworthiness is entirely self-made and self-determined, the summation of one's good or bad personal decisions and financial behavior. In reality, however, it is also shaped by one's race, geography, and class position.[39] Economic lives are always embedded in social structures and relation-ships.[40] It should not surprise us, then, if technologies to measure credit-worthiness also reflect social inequality where inequality actually exists.

Even more, computerized credit reporting and credit scoring cannot eliminate the underlying morality of creditworthiness. To be refused credit, in person or by automated reply, is still insulting. For all of its tech-nological abstraction—its remote data crunching and statistical analysis of anonymous populations and subpopulations—credit evaluation is still a form of moral judgment. This is so because creditworthiness is always a measure of an individual's integrity. It cannot be otherwise, even if masked as the cold calculation of lifeless data. Character has not been removed from credit evaluation; it has been displaced by the more palatable language of risk. Despite this semantic shift, the morality of creditworthiness is easy to detect. It is revealed in the use of credit information in areas unrelated to credit decision making, such as employee screening and automobile insurance. Here, credit information is not consulted to evaluate credit risk—the likelihood of financial default—but to gauge an individual's honesty, responsibility, and overall tendency toward conformity or friction. Likewise, credit scores are not aseptic financial facts; they are proxies for what used to be called character, reflected in the goodness or badness of one's numbers.

Ultimately, creditworthiness is about much more than money. It is about the kind of people we are in the eyes of those who want to transact with us. Our creditors have changed over time, from local merchants to global corporations, but they still want to know the same thing: Are we "good"—obedient, reliable, profitable? Financial identity is a form of moral identity, and consumer credit surveillance—reporting, rating, and scoring—is a form of moral accounting. Rockefeller was declared "good" by the Cleveland department store not just because he had millions of dollars on hand, but because he paid his bills on time and could be counted on to return and buy more.

CREDIT SURVEILLANCE AND THE END OF PRIVACY

Any history of surveillance is implicitly a history of privacy. While tracing the rise of modern consumer surveillance in the United States, this book shows how new business institutions and documentary protocols pried open the personal affairs of American citizens. Beginning in the 1840s, commercial credit reporting organizations took it as their mission to compile, and to sell access to, the reputations and financial standing of the nation's business community. At a time when government contact with individuals was limited and many Americans chafed at the intrusion of census takers, credit reporting agencies breached privacy on an unprecedented scale.[41] Where government could not dare to mount a similar program of comprehensive surveillance—at least not in the nineteenth century—the private sector could and did. The justification lay in the moral authority of the creditor, whose right to information superseded the debtor's right to privacy.

For millennia, religious thinkers and philosophers have condemned debt as a form of bondage. To assume a debt, as America's homespun expert on the subject, Benjamin Franklin, warned, was to surrender one's liberty. Debtors jeopardized not only their physical freedom—they could still be jailed in some states in the 1840s—but also their integrity. This is encapsulated in one of Franklin's best-known proverbs: " 'Tis hard for an empty sack to stand upright." Those who owed money were condemned to a life of sin, not because debt itself was immoral, but because they were constantly dodging and putting off their creditors with false promises. "The second vice is lying," Franklin quipped; "the first is running into debt."[42] Knowing this, creditors were wise to second-guess debtors. And more to the point, they were well within their rights to hound and inquire after them. To go into debt was to forfeit one's moral, if not legal, claim to privacy.

Individual creditors might be excused for nosing into the business of their borrowers, but organized intrusions were a different matter. Even as nineteenth-century commercial credit reporting agencies gained acceptance, they faced a persistent undercurrent of hostility. Resentful merchants accused them of espionage, and those injured by unfavorable reports filed lawsuits, including one that went to the U.S. Supreme Court.[43] These cases and the animosity elicited by such coordinated surveillance place contemporary privacy debates, especially debates about the uses (and abuses) of personal data, in a much longer context. Given this history of resistance, we might expect a similar reaction from consumers when they too came under the gaze of institutional credit surveillance. According to industry accounts, many credit-seeking consumers squirmed, and some protested, when store credit managers pressed for the intimate details of their lives. And in rare instances, communities were scandalized when the contents of a merchant's blacklist—but not the fact of the list's existence—came to light. Yet this seems to be the extent of their opposition. Docility, like Rockefeller's in the face of a skeptical store clerk, was typical.

Why were Americans unfazed by the networks of consumer credit surveillance that encircled them? Such indifference is not only curious to the historian of credit surveillance; it baffled credit bureau officials and credit managers. Despite concerted efforts to advertise the credit bureau's role and to cultivate a popular "credit consciousness," credit professionals were continually frustrated by public ignorance. What did consumers think of credit surveillance? Did they think of it at all? Unfortunately, with so little public comment in the historical record, this book can say little about the consumer's side of the experience. Instead, this is a history told from the perspective of the credit reporting industry, as found in company archives, trade press stories, instructional texts, conference reports, credit bureau publications, and public relations puff. This of course presents certain limitations, including the danger of mistaking prescriptive accounts— idealized versions of how credit surveillance *should* work—with the actual day-to-day operation of credit bureaus and credit offices. But more significantly, there is also the risk of overstating the disciplinary power of the surveillance apparatus that credit professionals operated. In truth, this book cannot answer questions about the efficacy of consumer credit surveillance—that is, whether or not it "worked." Credit professionals were certainly convinced that it did. But without the voices of consumers, it is difficult to gauge the moral or psychological effects, if any, that such surveillance produced.

The notion of consumer privacy, a category of privacy distinct from that concerned with violations by the government or press, did not enter public discourse until the 1960s. Progressive-Era reformers championed "the consumer" and galvanized a new political constituency of citizen shoppers before World War II. But there was one right among many, from fair prices to safe food, that they did not demand: the right to privacy.[44] The first stirrings of unease can be detected in the annoyance that some expressed toward the prodding of survey firms and market researchers during the 1920s. Complaining of the "veritable orgy of investigation" that besieged the American public, one editorialist bristled at the constant request for self-disclosure. "As if it weren't bad enough to have to eat tapioca, you must be able to tell which brand of tapioca you are eating and why you prefer it to other brands."[45] During the 1950s marketing experts came under fresh attack for employing psychological techniques to tap into the unconscious desires of consumers. In *The Hidden Persuaders* (1957), a best-selling exposé of the advertising industry's program of "mass psychoanalysis," journalist Vance Packard assailed the ethics of such manipulation and accused its practitioners of violating "the privacy of our minds."[46] This was the opening salvo in a new front of the consumer movement.

By the time Americans awoke to problem of consumer privacy, however, it was too late. A national credit reporting infrastructure was firmly in place and in the early stages of computerization. The credit bureaus' cumulative surveillance extended to hundreds of millions of citizens, and its data was far more granular than most imagined. At the same time, computers were being used to develop statistical scoring programs that would revolutionize not only credit granting but also risk management and marketing. Though federal legislation was passed during the early 1970s to curb the most egregious abuses of credit reporting and credit scoring, these laws did little to protect Americans from a burgeoning information economy. To this day, new technologies and inventive strategies for collecting and monetizing consumer data continue to outpace the law. This book focuses on the role that capitalism and consumerism played in the formation of the modern surveillance society, and on the threat that such commercial surveillance poses to the future of privacy and the measure of human value.

"A Bureau for the Promotion of Honesty"

THE BIRTH OF SYSTEMATIC CREDIT SURVEILLANCE

"There is, probably, no other country in which credit is so purely personal as in the United States." This was the assessment of Francis J. Grund, an Austrian-born math and language teacher who immigrated to America in the 1820s. After working at private schools in Boston and Philadelphia, he made a name for himself as a political journalist and partisan hack. His observations on credit appeared in *The Americans* (1837), a book written at the same time and in the same spirit as Alexis de Tocqueville's more famous work. Though Grund is best remembered as a political chameleon, one who plied his acid pen in the service of vying Whig and Democratic candidates during the mid-nineteenth century, his admiration for the egalitarian experiment in America remained constant.

Among the many things Grund found remarkable about the young nation was the trust that its citizens invested in one another when granting credit. American creditors, he explained, cared more about a borrower's character and hard work than they did about what he owned. It was the opposite in Europe. There, credit was reserved for men with ample collateral, land, or inherited fortunes, thus reinforcing Old World hierarchies and class-bound distributions of wealth and opportunity. "In America the case is different. Men there are trusted in proportion to their reputation for honesty and adaptation to business. Industry, perseverance, acquaintance with the market, enterprise, in short, every moral qualification of a merchant increases his credit as much as the actual amount of his property." This, Grund concluded, was the true "genius" of the American system of credit.[1]

The liberality of American credit was as much a product of practical necessity as it was of any democratic ideology. During the early decades of the nineteenth century, credit relationships became increasingly far-flung and complex. Grund arrived just as the young nation was entering the throes of the "market revolution," a period of intense commercial and technological change that drew Americans from all walks of life into newly integrated circuits of exchange and finance.[2] The family farm and the small business, once tangential to great flows of mercantile capital, were incorporated into a torrent of economic growth through distant commodity markets, piecework and wage labor, mortgages, insurance contracts, speculative investments, and a new entrepreneurial ethos that privileged profit and risk. This capitalist transformation not only recast traditional systems of production and distribution in the United States; it also reordered American society and monetized new dimensions of work, trade, and human relationships.

Credit was at the heart of this transformation. Borrowing was nothing new, of course. Colonial Americans were inveterate debtors, and the new nation had financed its freedom with international loans.[3] But credit and negotiable financial instruments took on new importance during the early republic. Lengthening inland trade connections, shortages of circulating currency, and burgeoning industrialization all contributed to a proliferation of lending in America. "Credit is the vital air of the system of commerce," Daniel Webster reminded his fellow senators in 1834. "It has run deep and wide into our whole system of social life."[4] A mid-nineteenth-century newspaper illustrated the extent of such financial entanglements in folksy microcosm. "I shall doubtless be able to pay you in a few days—a month at most," a cheerful recipient of credit-bought goods reassured his lender. He would have money as soon as Squire Jones paid his woodcutter, who paid the butcher, who paid the shoemaker, who paid the tanner, who finally paid him. Such interlocking local obligations were at one end of a very long chain that extended to the highest levels of transnational finance at the other.

By the 1840s American-style borrowing was recognized by its own citizens as a de facto economic reality, plainly dubbed the "credit system." Though credit was entrenched in American life, its legitimacy and controlling mechanisms remained at the center of heated public debate throughout the nineteenth century. Webster's defense of credit, after all, was no innocent paean to American ingenuity. It was ammunition for his assault on President Jackson's plan to dismantle the Second Bank of the United States. While many investors and upstart merchants embraced the credit system as an instrument of economic development, others opposed it as a dangerous contrivance, one that gave unfair advantage to the wealthy and, even worse, tempted economic calamity by encouraging speculation. Evidence of such disasters was not difficult to find. The panics of 1819 and 1837 would serve as jarring reminders.

Yet what all sides in the debate understood was that credit, in addition to being an economic phenomenon, was distinctly social. The linchpin of the American credit system, as Grund had marveled, was social trust. In the small worlds of nineteenth-century commerce, this trust was a function of familiarity. Those with a reputation for hard work and honesty could generally count on receiving credit, while those who loafed, lied, or repeatedly bungled their affairs could not. When all was said and done, creditworthiness itself amounted to "little more than public opinion."[5] This view, expressed in *Hunt's Merchant's Magazine*, a leading commercial paper of the time, contained no hint of sarcasm. Creditworthiness and reputation were one and the same.

By the 1830s, however, traditional ways of assessing an individual's creditworthiness had begun to lose their efficacy. As urban concentrations on the seaboard swelled and migration brought growing numbers inland, American society began to exhibit telltale signs of modernity. Chief among them was a breakdown of social trust within the commercial sphere.[6] Though neighborly credit relationships remained unchanged, those who traded regionally or nationally found it increasingly difficult to gauge the trustworthiness of trade partners who were unknown to them and about whom little could be learned from provincial contacts. This was a major problem for city merchants, especially importers, manufacturers, wholesalers, and jobbers who sold to country retailers and tradespeople each spring and fall. During these biannual selling seasons, out-of-town buyers converged on New York and other coastal hubs to buy supplies for their home communities. Merchants and shopkeepers purchased new inventory, and tradespeople, farmers, and others acquired raw materials and equipment. Much of the merchandise was sold through credit arrangements. With so much business at stake, there was considerable pressure to trust people of unknown and unverifiable reputation.

The panic of 1837 underscored the perils of such risk taking. As the crisis unfolded, a cascade of defaulted debts wiped out investments, wrecked business, and crippled the American economy.[7] Though many of the afflicted were victims of structural failure rather than heedless speculation or deceit, the difference was moot to their creditors. Those left holding worthless promissory notes, particularly notes belonging to distant strangers, experienced a sobering case of lender's remorse. One of these rueful creditors was Lewis Tappan, an evangelical Christian and noted abolitionist who ran a silk wholesaling firm in New York with his brother Arthur. Bankrupted by uncollectable debts and looking for a fresh start, Tappan turned his meticulous habits of mind to an ambitious new enterprise: credit reporting. If creditors could no longer trust their own impressions or the reassurances of strangers, then Tappan would assemble the facts for them. In 1841 he launched the Mercantile Agency, an organization devoted to compiling detailed information about business owners in every corner of the nation.

Tappan's agency would mark the birth of a new surveillance institution in the United States, one that would bring thousands of Americans into an expansive network of social monitoring. "This AGENCY," Tappan announced in 1843, "was established . . . for the purpose of procuring by resident and special agents, information respecting the standing, responsibility, &c., of country merchants. . . . It is not a system of espionage, but the same as merchants usually employ—only on an extended plan—to ascertain whether persons applying for credit are worthy of the same and to what extent."[8] Tappan was not the first to hit upon the idea. His own firm was seeded with the records of a prior venture. However, it was Tappan's Mercantile

Agency that quickly became synonymous with commercial credit reporting and served as a model for subsequent ventures.[9]

FROM REPUTATION TO WRITTEN RECORD

Until the early nineteenth century, credit evaluation was an informal, personal practice. In small communities, direct observation provided a measure of security—perhaps illusory—that one knew whom one was dealing with. "The most trifling actions that affect a man's credit are to be regarded," Benjamin Franklin instructed. "The sound of your hammer at five in the morning, or eight at night, heard by the creditor, makes him easy six months longer; but if he sees you at the billiard-table, or hears your voice at a tavern, when you should be at work, he sends for his money the next day."[10] The judicious creditor actively surveilled his neighbors, looking and listening for evidence of integrity or, contrarily, sloth and vice. This information, culled from prying eyes and ears, was distilled in community opinion, which could be tapped as needed.

Knowledge of an individual's property and financial assets was important, but even more useful was insight into his or her character. It was not simply a matter of whether one had the means to repay one's debts, but whether one was the sort of person who felt sufficiently constrained, by conscience or social obligation, to do so. Not everyone did. Legal remedies for collecting debts were imperfect, and efforts to legislate insolvency, beginning with the short-lived Bankruptcy Act of 1841, exposed the difficulty of verifying assets, sorting out claims, and separating "honest" debtors from those who used the law as a sly escape hatch.[11] Not surprisingly, jilted creditors sought more penetrating and reliable information about the financial reputation of would-be borrowers, especially those they did not know.[12]

When credit information could not be obtained personally or through the word of a trusted acquaintance, letters of recommendation were often accepted as surrogates. These open-ended testimonials, written by clergymen, lawyers, bankers, and business associates, vouched for the honesty of their bearer, thus providing a modicum of security in the absence of contradictory evidence.[13] Such letters became more common as the geography of American commerce expanded. Seeking to drum up new business in the South, the Tappans, for instance, advertised their willingness to extend credit terms to all who could produce "respectable letters."[14] Unfortunately, these flimsy endorsements were not difficult to obtain, through persistence or collusion, and the Tappans suffered great losses by trusting a system vulnerable to misrepresentation.

Commissioned investigations were embraced as a more dependable way to sound out distant strangers. Individual storekeepers and lawyers in the South would sometimes provide local credit information to eastern wholesalers, but this was rarely shared or systematic.[15] In the early nineteenth century, some large firms employed traveling reporters to canvass various areas of the country for information about businessmen who sought credit relationships, an approach that was both slow and expensive. One notable exception was Thomas Wren Ward, a retired Boston merchant who worked for Baring Brothers & Company, a London-based financial house.[16] Hired in 1829 to report on the firm's American interests, Ward traveled from Maine to Louisiana to inquire into the standing of local businesses. This labor-intensive endeavor centered almost entirely on personal consultations. "Merchants were averse to writing particulars about their neighbors and competitors," as one historian of nineteenth-century credit reporting noted. "They would tell much more in private conversation, but that method involved constant travel."[17] Ward's good reputation and network of acquaintances gained him access to the candid opinions of his contacts, which he dutifully submitted to Baring Brothers until 1853. His terse reports, the first of their kind, summarized the subject's capital and character. For example, "William Goddard [of Boston]—Safe and handsome property. $60,000 upwards. Very particular—energetic in business—has influence—apt to like strongly and dislike strongly."[18]

THE MERCANTILE AGENCY SYSTEM

Tappan's mercantile agency system represented a revolutionary new technology of capitalist surveillance. To overcome the problem of distance and depersonalization during the 1830s, Tappan and his imitators sought to textualize the absent bodies and personalities of anonymous borrowers.

The mercantile agency, in other words, exerted control over its subjects by making them "legible."[19] At the heart of Tappan's New York office was a library of imposing ledgers in which the identities, assets, and local reputations of all known businessmen, and many businesswomen, were recorded.[20] Within the pages of the agency's books, social relationships were converted into disembodied and increasingly abstract forms of data, and American citizens acquired a new institutional identity, a financial identity, by which they would be known and judged.

Tappan's technical innovation was to transform the business community's collective knowledge into a centralized, subscription-based reporting service. Key to the agency's success was the use of unpaid correspondents instead of lone traveling reporters. Most members of this vast network were attorneys who filed reports in exchange for referrals to prosecute debt collections in their communities. Commenting on the superiority of the local correspondent over the traveling reporter, Tappan wrote that "the local agent . . . having his eye upon every trader of importance in his county, and noting it down as it occurs, every circumstance affecting his credit, favorably or unfavorably, becomes better acquainted with his actual condition than any stranger can be."[21] Tappan's agency had over 300 correspondents in 1844 and nearly 700 in 1846.[22] By the early 1870s this number had soared to more than 10,000.[23] As the business writer Jesse R. Sprague later noted, "Lewis Tappan, it might be said, was first to apply the principles of mass production to credit reporting."[24]

The primary task of the agency correspondent was to convey the local standing of individuals in situ. "Hence," a mid-nineteenth-century writer explained, "the main object with the agency is, to furnish THE HOME STANDING of the merchant obtained from intelligent and reliable sources, THERE. . . . There, and only there, can [w]e learn whether he owns property, and is a man of good character—whether he does a legitimate or a speculative business—and whether he is competent, steady, and attentive, or otherwise."[25] In essence, the correspondent was to extract and reproduce the individual's local reputation for a national audience. Information in the agency's ledgers was tightly controlled. Until coded reference books appeared in the late 1850s, subscribers—wholesalers, merchants, banks, and insurance companies—received it only in the offices of the Mercantile

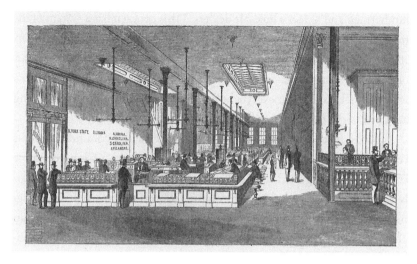

Figure 1.1 The Mercantile Agency's main New York office, as it appeared in the 1860s. Clerks provided credit information to visiting subscribers from behind railed counters. (Vose, *Seventy-Five Years of the Mercantile Agency*)

Agency, and only as read by a discreet clerk who summarized it from the ledgers; copies were not available, and no written traces other than the subscribers' notes could leave the premises (figure 1.1).

Tappan relinquished his stake in the agency in 1854, but his system was continued by several associates, including Robert Graham Dun, who took over in 1859 and ran the firm as R. G. Dun and Company. Though Tappan's agency was the first to achieve wide success, it was not the only one in existence. Its chief rival was the Bradstreet Company, founded in 1849 by John M. Bradstreet, a former dry goods merchant based in Cincinnati, Ohio. In 1855 Bradstreet moved his base of operations to New York City, and the two companies competed aggressively until 1933, when they merged to form Dun & Bradstreet, one of the preeminent commercial credit rating firms in the world today.

By the late nineteenth century, specialized reporting firms were also formed to serve a variety of industries, including manufacturers of iron and steel, jewelry, furniture, shoe and leather, and construction materials.[26] In the lumber trade, for example, the John W. Barry Company published what was known as "Barry's Book," which listed some 35,000 retail lumbermen and 2,000 wholesale dealers. "This concern has a system of interchange of information peculiar to itself," a Chicago journalist wrote in 1896, "which is so thorough and comprehensive that a retail lumberman out in a Dakota village cannot stand the milkman off for half a dollar's worth of tickets without every wholesale lumberman in the country being apprised of the fact before night."[27]

Business historians have long acknowledged the role commercial credit reporting agencies played in supporting the growth of long-distance trade and an integrated national economy. Yet to focus on their contribution to business-to-business communication is to miss their larger significance. Tappan's agency and those of his competitors constituted an elaborate system of mass surveillance. Unlike other private-sector bureaucracies of the mid-nineteenth century, notably those associated with the railroad and industrialization, the records kept by credit reporting firms were not primarily for internal administration.[28] Rather, these companies were bureaucratic enterprises wholly devoted to collecting, organizing, and selling information about specific people. These pioneering firms, as Scott Sandage aptly notes, were "identity brokers."[29] They turned unique human personalities into a market-friendly commodity. But the scale of their operations and the richness of their reports also made them more than a novel business intermediary. With detailed information about tens of thousands of Americans by 1850—and hundreds of thousands by the 1860s—they were a surveillance apparatus of unparalleled proportions. No government agency in the United States had anything like the intelligence-gathering reach of the mercantile agencies at that time.[30]

The history of the credit reporting industry, beginning with Tappan's agency, thus reveals the leading role the private sector played in the development of modern American surveillance. Long before government departments or law enforcement began to identify and track large segments of the population, credit reporting agencies already managed enormous archives of personal data. It was not the welfare or protection of the state that spawned the first mass surveillance systems in the United States; it was the security of capitalism. Risk-taking merchants established their own "documentary regimes of verification" ahead of state-building bureaucrats.[31] Many nineteenth-century Americans were legible economic actors before they were fully legible citizens.

TEXTUALIZING CREDITWORTHINESS

Unlike modern business rating agencies, which rely on financial statements and annual reports to evaluate a firm's creditworthiness, Tappan's nineteenth-century correspondents had no such documents to analyze. When composing their reports, they turned to their friends and associates for information. Opinion, hearsay, and anecdotes culled from local newspapers and conversation formed the basis of their reports. To contemporary observers these sources appear perilously subjective. But as Tappan indicated in the prospectus quoted earlier, his system was "not one of espionage, but the same as merchants usually employ—only on an extended plan." Based as it was upon personal knowledge and community opinion, the system was merely an attempt to formalize and elaborate these time-honored ways of knowing. "Particularly in the early years," as one historian has noted, "correspondents relied on their general, personal knowledge of business conditions in the town or area of their responsibility. Public records and financial statements were not a major component of these reports until the 1860s. Most of reports simply stated the subject's general reputation in the community."[32] Typical of such reports is the following excerpt:

> Oliver Hutchins [New York City] Shoes
>
> Apr 28/52 Has been in bus[iness] 10 yrs. Is a hard scrubbing, Indus[trious], money m[a]k[in]g man; prud[ent] & econom[ical]. [I]s s[ai]d to have made money & to be w[orth] eno[ugh] to m[a]ke him g[oo]d for all he wants. He owns R[eal] E[state] & is out of debt.[33]

At a basic level these reports served just two purposes, both of which were predictive: estimating the individual's chance of success in business, and gauging the likelihood of securing repayment, particularly in the event of failure. Toward this end, the key information was encapsulated in what would later be formalized as the "three Cs" of credit reporting: character, capacity, and capital. Each category had its own implicit indicators.

For character: the individual's work habits (hard working? conscientious?), local reputation (well liked? trusted?), and personal life (married? alcoholic? gambler? philanderer?). For capacity: age, experience in business, past employment, and known history of successes or failures. For capital: assets, liabilities, and property owned by the individual, as well as assets potentially available through well-to-do family or business connections who might rescue an individual in default.[34] When information in one category was not available, which was often the case, additional details in another might serve to compensate. Thus, for example, where little information was known of the subject's debts or property, a few extra words might be said about his or her habits or family connections.

Correspondent reports were transcribed in the agency's ledgers as they arrived. "Upwards of thirty men are constantly occupied in the details of this office alone, condensing, copying, and giving out reports, carrying on the correspondence, &c., &c.," a visitor to Tappan's New York office observed in 1851. "Their records are contained in more than 100 books, of the size of the largest leger [sic], extending to 600 and 700 pages each."[35] Within the ledgers, individual entries began with the proprietor's name, line of business, and in some cases a street address. The body of the entry appeared as a single running paragraph, punctuated by the date of each accretion, and rendered in a small hand and telegraphic prose to conserve space. Key pieces of information, particularly the sum of a subject's known assets, were sometimes glossed with brackets to accent hard data or what might be viewed as the true bottom line of an individual's financial status. As the volumes filled, a complex system of indexing and cross-referencing was implemented to locate individuals as they bought and sold businesses, worked under different names or with partners, or moved to new locations. In some cases, pointing fingers, drawn in the margins of the entries, guided clerks on their trail within and across the mountains of ledgers.

Each entry was also accompanied by codes to identify the source of the reports. The codes were not simply a matter of expedience. They protected the names of the local correspondents who, if discovered, might be stigmatized by their communities. Though local reputation served as a widely trusted indicator of creditworthiness, its formalization in written reports was often resisted as a breach of propriety. This sentiment was reflected by Edward Payson Bradstreet, a friend and distant relative of John Bradstreet who declined an offer to work for Bradstreet's fledgling agency because he "did not like the plan of constantly nosing into other people's business."[36] Indeed, one anxious agency correspondent went so far as to request preprinted return envelopes in which to mail his reports, explaining, "I fear my handwriting will be recognized at the post-office, and thus my utility will be cut off."[37]

The mercantile agency established by Tappan opened its first branch office in Boston in 1843, followed by Philadelphia in 1845 and Baltimore in 1846. By 1870 the agency had almost thirty branch offices, including several in Canada and one in London.[38] Though correspondence between reporters, branches, and the main office in New York was conducted by mail, news of "serious embarrassments, assignments, and failures" was immediately telegraphed.[39] The telegraph, despite its obvious advantages, was generally reserved for emergencies due to its cost. Seeking a competitive edge, however, at least one major wholesaling firm strung its own direct telegraph line to one of the mercantile agencies, establishing a system of real-time credit authorization. Thus "while one partner is showing off the silks and shoddy-mixed broadcloths" to a prospective customer, an 1857 account explained, another "clicks a few strokes, and learns—'owns farm worth $8000 clear, failed once five years ago, good—,' and returns to assist in bowing and assuring the stranger that he can have the goods on any terms he chooses."[40]

In 1875 R. G. Dun placed an order for one hundred Remington typewriters, making the company an early adopter of this new office technology. Branches were instructed to duplicate typed reports on tissue paper and transmit them among the sixty-five offices then in operation.[41] Typed reports soon replaced the handwritten ledger as the core of the agency's information storage and retrieval system. Commenting on the "Spenserian" beauty of the agency's early handwritten ledgers, one company historian noted that the copyists "looked upon the introduction of the typewriter as an offense against the chirographic art."[42] Yet even the copyists, whose exemplary penmanship signaled physical presence and the aura of personality, were subsumed in the disembodying machinery of the credit reporting industry.

By the early 1870s these credit reporting organizations were operating on a massive scale. "A stranger going into one of these agencies during business hours is struck by the stupendous machinery at work before him," a contemporary observer marveled. "Rows of desks, private rooms, particular departments, scores of busy clerks, hundreds of interested searchers, are around and on all sides of him. A constant stream of busy men, young and old, is flowing in and out all day, and every manuscript volume, of which there are hundreds, seems to be the subject of eager examination."[43] A visitor to the office of Dun's archrival, Bradstreet, was similarly impressed by the size of the firm's workforce, but even more so by its composition. "There are, indeed, many establishments in the country—factories, machine shops and the like—where more individuals find work, but how many private corporations are there which require the services of a thousand brain workers?"[44] This corps of brain workers was the vanguard of a new information industry.

CRISIS OF CONTROL: NARRATIVITY AND DISSEMINATION

The emergence of the mercantile agency during the 1840s reflected anxiety over the changing conduct and scale of commercial affairs. But the crisis of control that it sought to solve—the problem of rationalized credit assessment—spawned new crises directly related to the system of textualization itself. These centered around two problems: how to transmute qualitative data into quantitative fact, and how to control the release of such information to subscribers. While the idea of codifying the local reputations of merchants seemed straightforward, the use of narrative credit reporting to achieve this end was not.

Early mercantile agency reports illustrate the difficulty with which correspondents struggled to convert their local knowledge into meaningful risk assessments. Their reports were, for better or worse, highly subjective and often vague, deliberately so in cases where information was lacking and accurate statements of creditworthiness could not be ventured. Isolating relevant information proved a complex process, in part because local opinion was embedded in rich social contexts that when stripped away left individuals looking rather pallid and one-dimensional at one extreme, or hopelessly complex and contradictory at the other. In the case of Philadelphia paper dealer Charles Dull, for instance, the correspondent's report indicated that he was a sound credit risk but an unlikable fellow.

Mar 20/50 Have known him personally 10 yrs. there is a g[oo]d prej[udi]ce as among the trade—enjoys generally a poor reputation as a man, but is gen[erall]y sup[pose]d to have money—owns a g[oo]d Prop[erty] in an adjoining vil[lage] where he lives—if he gives his note he will no doubt pay it.[45]

What was a prospective creditor in a distant city to make of this? When deployed to qualify or contextualize a complicated life or personality, the narrative mode inevitably opened rather than closed the range of potential meanings and interpretations. In this regard, the legible subject was still quite blurry.

As a form of predictive data, early credit reporting often missed the mark. While it was fairly easy to identify the extremes of the business community—the up-and-up and the ne'er-do-well—it was the vast middle range that proved troublesome. Entrepreneurial activity was by its nature precarious, and even the most promising individuals might defy expectation. Consider Alfred Herrenschmidt, the son of a wealthy French leather dealer who arrived in New York City in 1852 and received a glowing credit report:

When he came here he had ab[ou]t $15⁰⁰⁰ mostly in G[oo]ds & has facilities to do an est[eeme]d bus[iness]; his fa[ther] is s[ai]d to be w[orth] $150⁰⁰⁰. There is no reason why he sh[oul]d not succeed. He is of g[oo]d char[acter] & hab[it]s & det[ermine]d[.] w[orth]y of a reason[a]ble cr[edit].

Alas, two years later Herrenschmidt was out of business and reported to have fled to Strasbourg.[46] Likewise, a more middling prospect, the industrious Oliver Hutchins cited earlier, subsequently failed several times—and continued to receive generally sympathetic credit assessments because he made an effort to repay his creditors—before finally going out of business in 1860.

To the nineteenth-century mind, the inadequacies of credit reporting were not to be found in polysemous texts, but in the fallible instruments of transcription: the correspondents. Since most of the agency's reporters were unpaid attorneys, critics argued that this work could attract only the inexperienced, inept, or predatory. "Fit tools for this kind of work," one observer wrote, "are usually found in the briefless young lawyer" who in his eagerness to gain favor with the mercantile agency and drum up business was prone to exaggeration.[47] According to Thomas Meagher, a mercantile agency defector who published what was the most thoroughgoing damnation of the system, "The substantial men in a community never sink to this work. It can only be performed . . . by the ill-at-ease, struggling, acrid spirits of the place—the meddlesome, mischief-making busy bodies, whose moving springs are envy, greed, uncharitableness, or disappointed ambition."[48] The perceived utility of the mercantile agency, implicit in its success, would seem to contradict such claims of widespread incompetence, but clearly some correspondents were better than others. Indeed, the ranks of such correspondents included several future American presidents, not least of whom was Abraham Lincoln.[49]

Even so, as bellwethers of local opinion, hardly a stable or monolithic entity itself, correspondents wielded enormous unchecked power. The possibility that private grudges might color reports, however subtly, was a legitimate concern. As late as 1890 the use of unpaid attorneys was still cited as a source of unreliability.[50] In rural communities, where divisions along political or religious lines skewed impressions, accusations of prejudice were common. "I find that in most country places there are two factions in the business community," one reporter observed in 1883. "And when the local commercial reporter belongs to one faction the other fellows will swear that he doesn't give them a fair send-off."[51]

These flaws and others were remedied to some extent by the introduction of full-time credit reporters during the 1860s and an increasing reliance on quantitative data, instead of personal opinion, as the basis of reports. During the 1870s, company balance sheets were requested as evidence, and business owners were provided with preprinted financial statement forms to submit to reporters.[52] Additionally, full-time reporters in larger cities began to specialize in a particular trade or area of commerce, thus improving their ability to gauge the prospects of those involved in such activities. Full-time reporters were also employed to corroborate the accounts of local correspondents in cases of glaring inconsistencies, an important step toward quality control. This system, one advocate concluded, "must certainly approach as near perfection as is practicable under any circumstance."[53]

Efforts to compel business owners to submit signed financial statements were resisted or ignored well into the 1890s, however, and without them agencies could only pretend to objectivity. At the turn of the century, the deficiencies of the reports came under the scrutiny of the National Association of Credit Men (NACM), an organization formed in 1896 to represent the interests of newly professionalized credit managers. Though careful not to antagonize the agencies it viewed as allies, the association immediately organized a committee for the "improvement of mercantile agency service" and registered its deep dissatisfaction with the accuracy, speed, and lack of reliable financial data in the reports.[54] As one member argued in 1897, "I should suggest stripping the reports of all unnecessary verbiage along the line of guessing and estimates, and confine the information as strictly as possible to facts."[55] Rebuffed by representatives of both R. G. Dun and Bradstreet, the association began to compile its own statistics to make its case. In 1900 the NACM conducted a survey that reflected poorly on the agencies. Among its findings, the study revealed that information in nearly 60 percent of reports received from R. G. Dun and Bradstreet either did not include a financial statement or was over a year old.[56]

While credit reporting firms were under pressure to improve the quality of their reports, the problem of controlling the information they contained remained an ongoing struggle. This difficulty involved three separate issues: unauthorized sharing between subscribers and nonsubscribers, outright theft by competitors, and the threat of libel suits. Tappan's mercantile agency had fewer than 50 subscribers in its first year of operation, but by 1851 this number had grown to nearly 2,000.[57] As already noted, this information was available only at the agency, and only in verbal format. When new information was received by the agency, a subscriber whose particular interests were affected might receive a "call slip" inviting him to visit the office. There the material would be read to him from carefully positioned ledgers behind a screened counter.

From the start, nineteenth-century credit reporting was a secretive endeavor. When filing reports for Baring Brothers in the 1830s, Thomas Wren Ward entered his comments in a "Private Remarks Book" and disguised the names and credit status of individual firms in numerical codes to protect against the "prying eyes" of "inquisitive sea captains carrying the mail" to London.[58] Tappan's subscribers were not only forbidden to disclose information from the proprietary reports; they were also encouraged to conceal their identity as subscribers to the service. "Tappan soon discovered that despite all his efforts, subscribers could not keep the information to themselves."[59] While the leaking of information to nonsubscribers reduced the agency's subscriptions, a greater problem involved libel suits brought against the agency by scandalized credit seekers whose businesses were damaged by negative reports. The issue in question was whether such credit reports should be legally protected as privileged communication between the agency and its subscribers.

The first major libel suit was entered in 1851 by John and Horace Beardsley of Norwalk, Ohio. The Beardsleys claimed that they had been barred from purchasing goods in New York because a local correspondent had informed the agency that John Beardsley's wife was about to file for divorce and alimony. The correspondent's report anticipated that this development would reduce Beardsley's real estate assets and put the partners out of business.[60] During the first trial, Tappan's successor, Benjamin Douglass, steadfastly refused to disclose the identity of any agency correspondents in Norwalk, an act of defiance that landed him in jail for twenty days. A second libel suit was brought against the agency in 1854 by Waterman L. Ormsby, a New York engraver who charged that he had been slandered. Specifically, he objected to a report that labeled him a counterfeiter and claimed that he left his wife for a prostitute. This case was decided in favor of the mercantile agency on the grounds that the report, though unfavorable to Ormsby, was without deliberate malice and had been furnished to a subscriber on terms of strict confidentiality.[61]

The Beardsley case was initially settled in favor of the plaintiff, but in 1870 the U.S. Supreme Court reversed the decision on a technicality. Though these and other suits were ultimately decided in favor of the agencies, the legal basis of commercial credit reporting in privileged communication remained contentious.[62] For the agencies, such protracted litigation under-scored the importance of secrecy and control in the dissemination of their proprietary information.

FROM NARRATIVE TO NUMBER: THE CREDIT RATING REFERENCE BOOK

The principle of privileged communication used in defending these suits was predicated, at least in part, upon the argument that subscribers received their reports orally and within the private confines of the agency office. As a result, subscribers were faced with the continual inconvenience of visiting the agency. Growing market demand and competition between the major agencies eventually led to the publication of reference books with abbreviated credit *ratings*. The first of these, *Bradstreet's Improved Commercial Agency Reports*, was published in 1857. It contained the names of some 17,000 individuals and firms in nine cities.[63] Bradstreet had begun experimenting with the publication of coded update sheets several years earlier. These consisted of abstracts from his full reports with a separate numerical key indicating words and phrases to be inserted into the text by the subscriber. For example, "1 6 8 11 14 17 21 25 following the dealer's name stood for 'making money,' 'economical,' 'business not too much extended,' 'does not pay large interest,' 'good moral character,' 'credits prudently,' and 'not sued.'"[64] Bradstreet's reference book further reduced the report to a numerical summary indicating the overall credit standing of the individual or firm.

R. G. Dun initially resisted the idea of publishing a reference book, as the owners were loath to open themselves to new libel suits or risk losing control of their valuable information by putting it directly into the hands of subscribers. However, the great popularity of Bradstreet's book encroached upon Dun's business and compelled the company to respond with its own reference book in 1859. This 519-page volume included more than 20,000 names and employed a four-part rating system that provided separate numerical ratings for three different types of creditors and a final column summarizing the subject's overall credit standing. The top ranking was A No. 1 ("credit unlimited"), followed by 1 ("unquestioned"), 1½ ("strong"), 2 ("good"), 2½ ("very fair"), 3 ("fair"), and two lower grades, 3½ and 4, so poor as to be beneath description. The ratings were further qualified through the use of pluses and minuses.[65] According to the book's preface, ratings were "based upon the historical facts upon our records, often running back eighteen years, regarding the business training, the moral and business fitness, the capital, the nature, extent, and hazards of business,

Figure 1.2 The Mercantile Agency's first credit rating reference book, published in 1859, was equipped with a fore-edge lock—detached in this example—to secure its confidential information. (Vose, *Seventy-Five Years of the Mercantile Agency*)

&c."[66] Subsequent editions were published, each bound in heavy leather and equipped with a lock to prevent unauthorized usage (figure 1.2).

The 1864 edition of R. G. Dun's reference book included a redesigned rating system whose major innovation was the ranking of "pecuniary strength"; its top category (A1+) identified individuals or firms with capital estimated at $1 million or more.[67] This marked an important break from previous rating systems: for the first time, capital was disconnected from character and capacity, and articulated in its own explicit terms. A second column, "general credit," implicitly captured character and capacity in a parallel ranking from A1 ("unlimited") to 3½ ("fair"). As the historian James D. Norris has observed, "Dun's innovation in the 1864 *Reference Book*—the inclusion of capital worth as well as general credit ratings—transformed credit-reporting to general credit ratings and allowed subscribers to make comparisons between firms and to adopt uniform rules and regulations on granting credit."[68] Though in theory an individual or firm might receive a low "general credit" rating despite having enormous capital, in practice there was a strong correlation between credit ratings and assets. This was deliberate. In a note to the New York City office, Robert Dun instructed, "There should be a constant effort to keep the credit marking in close relation to the capital marking."[69] Except for some minor modifications, the credit rating system established in 1864 remained virtually unchanged into the twentieth century.

In addition to simplifying the practice of credit rating and making ratings readily available to subscribers, reference books also solved, at least to outward appearances, the difficulty of interpreting narrative reports. Though subscribers were encouraged to call at the office for full reports (a service denied to those who only purchased the book), the reference books quickly attained an independent authority of their own. The early annual editions suffered from rapid obsolescence, but by the early 1870s they were published quarterly and supplemented with regular news sheets and pocket-sized editions for individual cities so that the apparent locus of credit authority shifted from the hidden ledgers to the published volumes. In reducing individuals to numerical values (weighted in favor of capital), the textualization of credit risk became increasingly abstract and, in contrast to earlier modes of credit assessment, disembodied and impersonal.

Despite the veneer of objectivity provided by the credit rating system—particularly as affected by the separation of capital from personality—ambiguities abounded. The "vagueness" and "looseness" of the credit rating keys were fodder for Meagher, who lambasted the logic of the capital estimates ("the millionaire and the $20,000,000 millionaire are 'all one' to the agency") and the meaningless terms employed to designate creditworthiness. (What is the difference, he asked, between "very good" and "high"?)[70] For all of Meagher's bluster in exposing the incompetence of the mercantile agency, his opposition hinged on a more profound observation: "Anything approaching a basis for a credit formula is plainly out of the question in commercial transactions," he concluded. "No system can be devised . . . to overcome, or accurately anticipate, conditions and circumstances so complex and variable."[71]

In short, Meagher saw the mercantile agency's effort to textualize and control the individual as a gross charade. The alphanumeric credit ratings, in his view, merely obscured the inherent deficiencies of a system based upon gossip and pseudo-science. His vitriol reflected a deep-seated skepticism not only toward the quantification of credit risk, but also toward the legitimacy of credit rating itself. Worse still, seen as a totalizing system of surveillance, those involved in commerce and trade were increasingly beholden to its judgments. In 1868 R. G. Dun's reference book included credit ratings for 350,000 individuals and firms. This number surpassed 500,000 in 1872 and continued to climb each year, reaching one million in 1886.[72]

FINANCIAL IDENTITY AND DISCIPLINARY SURVEILLANCE

By the mid-1850s the mercantile agency system had evolved into a sophisticated network of mass surveillance that tracked business owners throughout the nation. "A thousand folios include a page or two or more about you and your affairs," an anonymous "Merchant of Boston" warned in 1853. "Go where you may to purchase goods, a character has preceded you, either for your benefit or your destruction."[73] That business reputation was disconnected from local relationships was viewed positively by advocates of the system, who contended that such remote centralization actually freed the credit-seeker from carrying letters of recommendation or conducting business in person. "[The businessman] is known to the whole list of the agency's subscribers," one such advocate argued. "He has the range of the entire market in all the cities where these offices are established; the communication between them being such, that what is known to one is known to all. He need not even leave home to make his purchases. His order is as good as his presence, and will always be promptly met, to the extent of what his intelligent neighbors regard as safe and prudent."[74]

The textualized individual in the ledgers and reference books became the prototype of modern financial identity—disembodied data that stands in for one's economic status and reputation. Such textualized identities may have expedited commercial transactions and facilitated trust, but they were imperfect reductions of total lives and social contexts. Capital was reified as a marker of creditworthiness and, despite the agency's best efforts, character—a much more perplexing quality—was always prone to rumormongering and prejudice.

More than simply identifying and tracking individuals, the information inscribed in the mercantile agency's "thousand folios" also represented a system of disciplinary surveillance. Under the agency's omnipresent gaze, borrowers were continually monitored and judged. "In business or out, have your reputation spotless, your character clean," a business magazine reminded its readers. "Commercial agencies record every movement made from the time one enters business. If not fair and upright in all your dealings, you will be greatly hampered; if honest and trustworthy, your credit may in time be unlimited. Creditors will have nothing to do with a person tricky and unscrupulous; merchants and bankers extend credit according to their confidence in one, therefore, pay bills promptly; the delay of a day may weaken your credit."[75] Commenting on credit reporting in the South, one historian observed that "no-change" reports were as important as those detailing dramatic shifts because it "would demonstrate to eastern merchants that all storekeepers were constantly under observation."[76]

For advocates of the mercantile agency system, continual surveillance fortified the trustworthy and deterred the malignant. "It is no discredit, even to an honest man, to say that he is safe under the wholesome restraints, and jealous vigilance of society," one supporter assured. "Prudence, like the other virtues, is all the better for being watched."[77] As another reflected at the end of the nineteenth century, "The mercantile agency might well be termed a bureau for the promotion of honesty."[78] Despite the halo of beneficence donned by the agencies, it is clear that the subjects of their surveillance felt otherwise. "These institutions," an 1856 newspaper account observed, "are regarded by country merchants with something like the affection bestowed by slave-owners on conductors of the underground railroad."[79] Though welcomed by many in the business community, the mercantile agency elicited strong resistance from those who abhorred the remote, seemingly inescapable system of monitoring it entailed. During the mid-1850s one journalist described credit reporting as "an organized system of espionage, which, centered in New York, extends its ramifications to every city, village, and school district in the Union. Spies are regularly employed by this institution to travel throughout the country, and secretly obtain precise information on the property, the associations, the business, the family, and the habits of every man engaged in trade."[80]

While this persistent hostility tends to be underplayed by historians of the mercantile agency, it is important to note. Certainly wholesalers in major trading centers believed they had much to gain by patronizing the agencies, but smaller merchants and jobbers often did not. The latter's surveillance might have allayed the fears of distant creditors, but it demanded that those under their gaze surrender their privacy. As one journalist explained, "Most men see their commercial hobbies with lover's eyes, and the very possibility of having them subjected to hostile scrutiny is revolting."[81] Though the reporting agencies would eventually win broad acceptance, recent scholarship suggests that the path to legitimacy was much rockier than assumed. During the closing decades of the nineteenth century, R. G. Dun continued to fend off would-be litigants and to fret about its own unsettled legal footing. High-profile cases were just the tip of a legal iceberg. Many other libel claims were settled out of court or scuttled by legal maneuvering and intimidation.[82]

For some detractors, opposition to the agencies was not a matter of privacy but of business principle. The distrust implied by national networks of credit reporting bred hostility and resentment rather than confidence and goodwill, the cornerstones of healthy commerce. Another recurring criticism of the system was the threat implied by nonparticipation, as those who refused to subscribe believed they would receive poor ratings in retribution. "What they desire," a Brooklyn reporter observed, heaping scorn on the agencies, "is to drive the man within their own inclosure [*sic*], and force him to become a subscriber to their institution."[83] In other words, the system, once insinuated into the community, was viewed as a self-justifying cash cow that bullied merchants into participation.

From a producerist perspective, one that held the manufacture of physical things as the soul of commerce, the agencies were condemned as nothing more than parasitic middlemen. They seemed to produce nothing new themselves—no raw materials, no merchandise, no factories, no technical improvements. Instead, they merely compiled and resold a community's collective knowledge. This "scheme," as one contemporary account explained, "consisted only of getting something from the business-men for nothing and retailing it back to them again for money."[84] The idea that information could beget information, a phenomenon not unlike that of money lent at interest, was distasteful. The idea of an information economy—one in which knowledge might be packaged and sold as a commodity—was apparently inconceivable. Yet, by the end of the nineteenth century, the concept of financial identity, implicit in the prodigious ledgers of the major mercantile agencies, was firmly established in the commercial sphere and would serve as a model for new efforts to control the proliferation of "consumptive" credit.

The mercantile agency system of the 1840s introduced an entirely new way of identifying, classifying, and valuing individuals as economic subjects. What Tappan and his successors invented was not just a highly coordinated system of disciplinary surveillance, but the very idea of financial identity itself. This new technology of identification became a key infrastructural component of the modern credit economy and, in turn, produced its own category of social reality. Within the mercantile agency's integrated network of recordkeeping, financial identity served as the primary unit of analysis. Such disembodied textual representations fostered a new epistemology of risk, one that converted the means and reputation of individuals into quasi-empirical facts.[85] The purported facticity of financial identity not only imposed parameters of normative behavior, but also offered the tantalizing possibility of rational calculation.

Here the development of American credit reporting can be viewed in the broader context of nineteenth-century quantification, particularly the new sciences of statistics and accounting.[86] "The age of mystery as related to business affairs is happily passing away," one advocate of credit reporting observed at century's end.[87] The same ideals of objectivity and transparency that stimulated the quantification of populations, social phenomena, and commercial transactions were also manifest in the development of financial identity as a site of individual accountability.[88] More significantly, this national credit reporting apparatus facilitated the penetration of market values and commercial morality into the everyday lives of nineteenth-century Americans. When the norms of business transparency were transferred to consumer credit during the late nineteenth century, the cocoon of privacy surrounding personal finance was similarly punctured. The history of commercial credit reporting is thus ground zero for understanding how Americans learned to bare their financial souls, and how the language and logic of capitalism were embedded in contemporary notions of identity.

2

Coming to Terms with Credit

THE NINETEENTH-CENTURY ORIGINS OF
CONSUMER CREDIT SURVEILLANCE

American credit reporting first emerged in the commercial sphere to discipline "productive" credit, but the nation's sprawling credit system was hardly limited to the world of business loans. Contrary to the popular mythology of Yankee thrift and Victorian financial conservatism, consumer credit was ubiquitous in nineteenth-century America.[1] During the panic of 1837 one observer complained that the credit system had not only "swallow[ed] up the whole business of society, in all of its departments," but had also "gradually extended to all the minor concerns of life, so as even to include the daily consumption of personal necessities."[2] Nineteenth-century moralists, like their Puritan forebears, continued to warn their fellow citizens against the wiles of debt, but for many it simply could not be avoided. Cash, the coveted medium of instant debt cancellation, was perpetually scarce due to shortages of circulating currency and long delays between income-producing harvests. American households thus incurred small debts with local shopkeepers that were settled when hard money was available, often six to twelve months later, and sometimes longer.

The spread of installment after the Civil War, conventionally viewed as the takeoff point of modern consumer credit, merely expanded the scope and impersonality of practices already in place. The deferred payments used to buy new sewing machines and cheap mass-produced furniture had long been essential to purchase just about everything else. The key difference, of course, was the contractual formality of installment selling. These cold legal documents stood in stark contrast to the informality of credit relationships between countless local retailers and their "trusted" customers.

Even as the morality of debt was contested, the debate did not pit abstinence against devil-may-care laxity. In fact, some religious leaders regarded debt with a more permissive attitude than might be assumed. Praising the practical advantages of credit—and reassuring his audience that his remarks were "not intended to forbid men from entering into pecuniary responsibilities, or using their credit in the way of lawful business"—one prominent New York Presbyterian zeroed in on the real evil of credit: late payments. The pastor, Nathan S. S. Beman, was a trustee at Middlebury College and later vice president of Rensselaer Polytechnic Institute. Slow pay, as he and others argued, was immoral because it robbed creditors and the community of precious time in the collection of innumerable small debts. Thus the lesson of the sermon was not to eschew credit but to recognize the broad social consequences of financial bad faith. Credit properly used was not the bane of society but a force for the improvement of social relationships. "The punctual payment of debts *promotes confidence between man and man*. Mutual confidence is the strong ligament which binds together the social compact." Such confidence and the self-discipline that it entailed, as Beman explained, had "a most happy effect upon society."[3]

When retail credit was denounced by others, it was often for an even more prosaic reason: price inflation. Goods purchased on credit were more expensive, it was repeatedly argued, because sellers tacked on a premium to cover the losses inevitably incurred by delinquents. Thus "the good paymasters must suffer for the bad, as they do wherever Credit is given," a New York newspaper explained in 1845. The "customers of retail Stores" who ran up personal accounts were just as guilty for the credit system as any big city merchant.[4] A midcentury newspaper related how a well-meaning but ignorant "young mechanic" was taught this lesson by his wife, who received his jar of credit-bought peach preserves with something less than gratitude. "I know something about this credit business, and it is not a fair thing," she reproved. "Do you not know that all traders can afford to sell cheaper for cash than credit?"[5] Along these lines, an editorialist reasoned that dealers sold their goods at prices 10 to 20 percent above their real market value "merely because he knows that one in five, or, at best, one in ten, of his customers are vagabonds, who do no labor, and have no visible means of living, and will never pay him."[6] In this way credit was viewed as a collective harm rather than evidence of individual folly or vice. Indeed, one of the arguments for the implementation of consumer credit reporting would be that it promised to purge dishonest debtors from the pool of eligible buyers, thus keeping prices stable and equitable. Store credit, after all, was capital that shopkeepers loaned out to consumers, whether in the form of "personal necessities" or peach preserves.

Nineteenth-century retailers were wise to the fact that people often spent more liberally if granted credit terms. Instead of walking away from an eye-catching item that could not be purchased with cash in hand, a credit customer was granted the privilege—or curse—of instant gratification. "The temptations to expenditure are great," a Connecticut consumer noted in 1874, "when money is not required, and the sum is simply smilingly put down to the 'little' account; and it is surprising how such accounts swell into the incredible and astounding sum total."[7] While on the surface such arrangements were mutually beneficial—retailers sold more merchandise to eager consumers and simultaneously kept them away from competitors—it also made the line between harmless indulgence and profligacy difficult to perceive. When was too much really too much? Many retailers and consumers proved themselves poor judges of spending capacity. This question was complicated by the fact that credit by its very nature is a gamble on the future. The most promising debtor with the best of intentions was always subject to unforeseen disaster through injury, illness, or unemployment. Thus, for some, the temptation wrought by retail credit was its most damning quality. As one detractor reasoned, "In the Lord's Prayer we say, 'Lead us not into temptation, but deliver us from evil.' What greater temptation can be offered a poor, weak mortal than to be escorted through a magnificent establishment, invited to feast his eager eyes upon artistic wares, and to purchase the same without regard to his ability to pay?"[8]

NINETEENTH-CENTURY CREDIT AND THE CRISIS OF TRUST

The risks associated with retail credit, like those for commercial credit, remained manageable while embedded in local networks of interpersonal trust. In 1840 the most populous American city was New York, with just over 300,000 inhabitants. The next three largest cities—Baltimore, New Orleans, and Philadelphia—each had less than a third of New York's population. Chicago, which by 1890 was the second-largest city behind New York, had fewer than 5,000 inhabitants in 1840.[9] Bustling seaboard metropolises might have been dizzying to the country bumpkin, but they were not so large as to preclude functional credit relationships between neighborhood retailers and their local customers. Unlike urban wholesalers and manufacturers whose trade relationships were attenuated by expanding geography during the 1830s and 1840s, retailers in cities and towns remained in close contact with their customers. They did not serve an onslaught of out-of-town strangers, a situation faced by urban wholesalers during the buying seasons, and the sums owed to them, though perhaps exasperating to collect, were comparatively small in most cases.

The necessities of everyday life, even in large cities, were provided by neighborhood shopkeepers—grocers, butchers, bakers, and druggists—who in turn drew upon their familiarity with local people and conditions to gauge the creditworthiness of their customers. This was an imperfect system, to be sure, one that could reinforce undeserved reputations and prejudices for better or worse. Yet this age-old way of knowing through direct interaction and local opinion was the basis of retail credit assessment for most of the nineteenth century. As long as retail credit was conducted on a local basis, retailers had little incentive to develop systems of credit reporting information.

An 1869 guide to storekeeping illustrates both the unremarkable practice of retail credit selling and its limitations just after the Civil War. The author, Pennsylvania native Samuel H. Terry, went to New York in 1842 to work as a dry goods jobber. After running his own business for more than a decade, he retired to rural New Jersey to set his experiences down for the benefit of other retailers.[10] Commenting on the absence of any existing guides, Terry observed that "in all our libraries, whether public or private, we look in vain for any hand book or text book wherein one may learn something about the occupation of a retail dealer," something he found curious considering that "probably one-tenth of the community are more or less engaged in the business."[11] His popular manual, republished in numerous editions during the 1880s, includes an entire chapter devoted to retail credit selling.

While acknowledging the simplicity and safety of running a cash-only business—notably its tendency to offer customers lower prices and retailers peace of mind, "there being fewer circumstances to create difficulties between the dealer and his customers, such as refusals of credit, dunning, sueing, and the like"—Terry indicates its rarity in practice.[12] "As the retail business is conducted, it is almost impossible to do an exclusive cash business, and as every dealer doing business is desirous of selling as many goods for cash as he can, it follows that practically all retailing is more or less a combination of both cash and credit sales."[13] The desire to drive up sales through credit selling came with obvious risks, not least of which was the problem of judging the creditworthiness of one's customers. Emphasizing the importance of communal knowledge, Terry noted, "A dealer who has for a year had daily opportunities for hearing of and seeing the transactions of any particular individual in the community ought to be able to decide at once whether he is sufficiently responsible to be credited with goods, and to what amount."[14] Such confidence in the sufficiency of direct appraisal would be shaken in the next two decades.

By the early 1870s the risks associated with credit became glaringly apparent to retailers in urban centers, just as they had to credit-granting wholesalers during the 1830s. While for wholesalers the initial source of the problem was the increasing distances between commercial centers and inland traders, for retailers it was the increasing density and mobility of populations in their own home community, which made strangers out of neighbors. As Terry was quick to note, credit risk grew as one moved down the chain of dependencies, not only because the number of environmental and financial contingencies multiplied, but also because more potentially dishonest people were added to the equation. Selling on credit to a farmer, for example, necessitated only the honesty of the farmer. Selling to a mechanic who relied upon the farmer for money required the honesty of both. Credit sales to a third link in the chain would further elevate the risk, "as it would now require that all three should be honest," and so forth on down the line.[15]

At the same time, many small-time retailers, particularly grocers and butchers, were under growing competitive pressures in their own communities. This, coupled with the travesty of gauging the trustworthiness of strangers on sight, placed them in a precarious position. Loath to jeopardize a sale with prying questions about a customer's income or employment, such retailers often threw caution to the wind, relying wholly upon their instincts and impressions. "One of the greatest evils with which the retail merchant has to contend is the credit system," a Chicago writer howled in 1874, "and, until there is a radical change in society, credit-customers will be the merchant's bane."[16]

The growing number and increasing transience of Americans in established seaboard centers, as well as in flourishing interior cities such as Cincinnati, Chicago, and St. Louis—all among the ten largest American cities by 1870—stretched the interpersonal basis of retail credit to the breaking point. Within these cauldrons of urban defamiliarization and competition a desire for organized consumer credit reporting was stirred. By the end of the 1880s organizations devoted to the surveillance of retail customers existed in major urban centers throughout the nation, from New York to New Orleans and as far west as California. Writing in 1886, a Chicago journalist noted that "retail commercial agencies, such as the wholesale trade has enjoyed for years, have been established in many of the principal trade centers, modeled after the Bradstreet and Dun agencies, only differing in the fact that they report private individuals and families instead of merchants engaged in active business."[17]

The proliferation of consumer credit during the late nineteenth century was almost entirely relegated to the world of goods. Cash loans backed by collateral (whether merchandise, real estate, or equipment) were widely available for commercial use, but loans for personal consumption were denied to the vast majority of Americans until the 1910s and 1920s. Restrictive usury laws made personal loans unprofitable and unappealing for bankers, except as a quiet and generally short-term privilege of the wealthy. Under such circumstances Americans of modest or little means were forced to turn to pawnbrokers or illegal loan sharks when pressed for cash, neither of which participated in the development of credit reporting.[18] While banks employed the services of commercial credit reporting agencies, they had no interest in the organization of nineteenth-century consumer reporting.

FROM BLACKLISTS TO THE AFFIRMATIVE-NEGATIVE SYSTEM

Nineteenth-century consumer credit reporting took two basic forms: the blacklist and the affirmative-negative system. The blacklist was simply a catalog of names belonging to individuals with overdue bills. Such lists, the

Figure 2.1 An eighteenth-century blacklist, as imagined by a twentieth-century illustrator. (Walter de Maris, "Posted," *American Bankers Association Journal*, November 1933)

archetypal credit report, had long been compiled by merchants to identify slow- or nonpaying individuals in their community (figure 2.1). As a rudimentary and wholly negative system of financial identification, its sole purpose was to quarantine delinquent individuals and the worst credit risks from the pool of potential customers. Privately compiled and consulted by shopkeepers, blacklists remained a system of informal recordkeeping rather than a source of shared credit information until the late nineteenth century. This lack of cooperative communication among retailers can be attributed in large part to their resistance to disclosing the details of their own financial strength, which might be inferred by the quantity of bad debts on their books. It was not the privacy of credit customers that needed protection, but that of the merchants themselves, who sought to shield themselves from the scrutiny of their colleagues and competitors. A long list of delinquent customers reflected poorly on both the merchant's judgment in giving and his backbone in collecting.

Nineteenth-century Americans took it for granted that retailers kept their own blacklists. These "little lists of names" were tolerated as long as they remained hidden "under their counters," as a *New York Times* writer explained.[19] When confidentiality was breached, however, public outcry was sure to follow. This was the case in Corsicana, Texas, a small town south of Dallas, where in 1885 the community became "exercised" upon learning that a blacklist had been published. Noting that "the names of some of the most prompt and best paying citizens" were erroneously included on the list, a Dallas reporter dismissed the ill-advised enterprise as folly. "These lists have been tried in many places for years past, but were soon abandoned."[20]

Though retailers kept their blacklists private, American newspapers did not. During the 1830s and 1840s printers advertised the names of those with unpaid debts in their pages. As the publisher of a New York newspaper explained in 1834, "There is, we presume, no description of men in business, who suffer more from the 'credit system,' or who have poorer facilities for availing themselves of the benefit of what is justly due them, than the publishers of newspapers."[21] Such subscription-based publications, which included many religious newspapers, strongly defended their right to embarrass the egregiously negligent with "gentle personal hints" and "printer's duns." Under the headline "Is a Black List Proper?," the editor of Boston's *Trumpet and Universalist Magazine* answered, "Yes; what would the printer do without it?" In 1830 the Albany *Microscope* was reported to have produced an especially gruesome blacklist, confined to a dark, "Bastille looking" corner of the page and illustrated with the image of a disgraced man in stocks.[22] Yet for all of the satisfaction gained by exacting such humiliation, the blacklist was hardly a thoroughgoing mechanism of credit control. As chronicles of the damned, they were reactionary and punitive rather than preemptive and predictive.

The affirmative-negative system, by contrast, operated on an entirely different principle. Instead of singling out and excluding known deadbeats, it sought to identify and track the financial habits of all individuals within the geography of cities, counties, states, and ultimately the nation. This was the system pioneered by Lewis Tappan in the 1840s and ascendant in the commercial sphere. The advantage of such totalizing, continually updated surveillance was that it permitted creditors to make much finer distinctions between classes of borrowers. Instead of noting only derogatory items such as financial distress, disreputable dealings, or vices such as gambling, philandering, or drinking, the affirmative-negative system also recorded evidence of an individual's honesty, financial assets, and history of prompt payment. Blacklists failed to register the difference between the slow payer who, though perhaps aggravating, eventually settled his or her obligations and the professional deadbeat who never had any intention of making good. While the true deadbeat represented only a small fraction of all credit customers, slow payers represented a significant element of the retail credit business. Thus, to summarily damn slow payers was to unnecessarily drain the pool of potential customers.

The affirmative-negative system monitored all information pertaining to an individual's payment habits and credit standing, both positive and negative, in an effort to gauge the *limit* of the person's creditworthiness. By calculating this limit—the maximum amount of credit that an individual could reasonably be expected to repay—those selling on credit hedged against the future in the hope of maximizing sales and profits. Each consumer was treated as a unique case, one that could be isolated, classified, and analyzed separately. This was the future of credit surveillance: not blacklisting or the putative exclusion of the few, but continual monitoring and sliding scales of preference and penalties for all.

When during the late nineteenth century the affirmative-negative system was adopted by consumer credit reporting organizations, the concept of financial identity, previously relegated to business owners and the self-employed, began to extend into the general population. Laborers, journeymen, mechanics, clerks, and a whole host of wage-earning employees—all formerly invisible to the commercial credit reporting regime—suddenly acquired a second self in the form of financial identity. The affirmative-negative system was also capable of exerting a powerful disciplinary force, as it had in the commercial sphere. While blacklists could perform a similar function—the mere suggestion that merchants were compiling a blacklist would frighten at least some delinquents into settling their bills—they tended to be irregularly compiled and updated, therefore diminishing their effect. The affirmative-negative system, on the other hand, kept all consumers under perpetual surveillance, thus encouraging them to pay their debts with regularity and promptness in order to maintain their local credit privileges.

PRIVATE AGENCIES AND TRADE ASSOCIATIONS BEFORE 1900

Unlike the history of commercial credit reporting, which is well preserved in institutional archives, the early development of its consumer counterpart is far more difficult to reconstruct. The first consumer credit reporting operations were either too short-lived or too insignificant to save their records. With such a faint paper trail, the order and pattern of their diffusion is difficult to track. A pamphlet published by McKillop and Sprague, a New York commercial credit reporting agency, described the disorganization of retail credit reporting with mocking derision in 1874: "Two or three unsuccessful attempts have been made to carry the system down to the retail trade, and one or two to improve the system, but these have been so feeble as to render further allusion to them unnecessary."[23]

By the mid-1880s this was no longer the case. Retail credit reporting organizations were established in a number of major American cities.[24] These embryonic consumer data brokers sprang up in a striking variety of forms. Some were private agencies modeled directly on the mercantile agencies, some were nonprofit associations organized along trade lines, and still others were dubious offshoots of collection and detective agencies. All of these varied considerably in their methods of reporting as well, from the compilation of simple blacklists to comprehensive reference books based upon the affirmative-negative system.

The earliest private agencies most likely emerged in and around New York, where the leading commercial reporting agencies—notably, R. G. Dun and Bradstreet—were also headquartered. According to trade industry lore, the first credit reporting organization devoted to consumers was established in Brooklyn in 1869 by brothers Herman and Conrad Selss.[25] That the first retail credit reporting organization would emerge in Brooklyn is unsurprising. One of the fastest-growing and most populous American cities during the late nineteenth century, Brooklyn jumped from the seventh-largest American city in 1850 to the third-largest in 1860 (behind New York and Philadelphia), a ranking it retained until its incorporation as a borough of New York in 1898. A Brooklyn directory confirms that Conrad Selss operated a mercantile agency in 1878, and four years later a local newspaper reported that "Mr. C.E. Selss, of the Mercantile Agency," was elected president of the Brooklyn Board of Trade.[26] Beyond this, no records of the Selss enterprise exist. A credit rating book in the New York Public Library offers an additional clue. Published by the Retail Mercantile Agency for the years 1874 and 1875 (and placed in Brooklyn by an early pencil notation), this slim volume contains the names of more than 4,000 individuals and may have been the work of the Selsses.

If the Selss brothers were first, they were not alone for long. A second firm devoted to retail reporting, the Dealers' Mutual Protective Agency, was established in Brooklyn during the same year. This for-profit enterprise offered a range of business services, including credit reporting, bill collection, accounting, and detective work. The agency's "preventative department," according to an advertisement, existed

> for the purpose of protecting the trade against a certain class of customers who are continually requesting credit but never intend to pay. This class is composed of a genteel appearing set of swindlers, male

and female, who, with their oily tongues, insinuating manners and great show of bogus wealth, always succeed in victimizing the trade. They move from locality to locality, remaining long enough in each to run up bills with the grocer, butcher, baker, and all others willing to trust.

The agency boasted that retailers—as well as hotels, boardinghouses, and landlords—could "save hundreds, yes, thousands of dollars each year" through its services. In addition to investigating retail customers and prospective tenants, the agency's detective department also doubled as an employee screening program.[27]

By its second year the Dealers' Mutual Protective Agency had compiled a list of some 8,430 "contumacious debtors" in Brooklyn alone. These "dead beats" consisted of many with the means to pay, including "the gentry who live in brown stone houses," but who evaded their financial obligations through legal loopholes or by placing their property in another's name.[28] The difficulty of exacting payment from such crafty debtors prompted the agency to hold an open meeting in March 1870, during which the organization's general superintendent, C. H. Baxter, oversaw the drafting of a proposal to submit to the state legislature in Albany.[29] The meeting, it seems, was sparsely attended, and nothing came of it. However, one of Baxter's proposals, a call for wage liens against retail debtors, drew harsh criticism in the local press.[30]

The next year the Dealers' Mutual Protective Agency folded. During a summer lull in 1872 a reporter for the *Brooklyn Eagle* sought to do a story on the agency and learned from an informant that it had made "a splendid run" but ultimately failed to make good on its promise to collect difficult bills.[31] It is not clear whether this agency published a reference book or how credit information was ascertained. The emphasis on delinquents suggests that the agency's credit reporting endeavors consisted of little more than compiling blacklists from their subscribers' collection requests.

Just as this Brooklyn agency quietly closed its doors, another firm, the Retail Dealers' Protective Association (RDPA), opened across the East River in New York City. In addition to being one of the earliest consumer credit reporting organizations in the United States, the RDPA was among the longest lasting; it remained in continuous operation until 1931.[32] The RDPA was a "family affair" headed by Jesse Platt, who previously worked in the wholesale department of A. T. Stewart's dry goods emporium. Platt's uncle ran a collection service with his son, but was "not much of a business man," according to a correspondent for R. G. Dun, who noted that the uncle's drug business in upstate New York had failed. The RDPA was incorporated as a joint-stock company in 1871, and the first edition of its annual *Commercial Register* included ratings for 50,000 individuals living or working in New York and Brooklyn. When a Dun representative visited the firm in 1892, he reported that Platt, by then an "elderly man," still received a "respectable living" from his reporting business.[33]

Following the RDPA, at least ten new agencies were established between 1882 and 1890—from St. Paul, Minnesota, to New Orleans and from Lincoln, Nebraska, to Richmond, Virginia. By 1900 another fifty agencies existed "principally in the larger cities," according to an early industry historian. This estimate is probably conservative.[34] Though most early agencies were content to concentrate their business in a single city or town, a small number sought broader horizons. The American Mercantile Union, founded in 1876, boasted branch offices "in every city of note throughout the United States," including San Francisco.[35] Another, the Commercial Publishing Company of Syracuse, New York, claimed to have established a multicity network in upstate New York during the mid-1890s.[36] The difficulty of running a single office, for reasons to be explained, made efforts to organize multicity or multistate franchises the exception rather than the rule.

At the same time that profit-seeking ventures began to proliferate, a second form of consumer reporting emerged among retailers' protective associations.[37] These fraternal associations, usually established along trade lines and limited to a specific town or city, generally served to stave off price wars, regulate business practices, and defend against competitors. But many also took the policing of credit relationships as their chief objective. In 1871, for example, at least three new trade organizations, representing milk dealers, tailors, and retail coal dealers, respectively, were formed in Philadelphia. In the case of the milk and coal dealers, members agreed to provide the association with a list of their delinquent customers for the purpose of keeping a blacklist. The tailors' organization promised to protect its members through "the diffusion of information in regard to delinquent and doubtful customers."[38] In Chicago, the national financial crisis of 1873 spurred at least a hundred of the city's retail grocers to meet for the purpose of forming a protective association. The organization, dubbed the Grocers', Butchers', and Marketmen's Exchange, was centered upon the compilation of a shared blacklist.[39] Though such associations usually reflected a guildlike homogeneity, in some cases they brought together a motley assortment of interests, as was the case in St. Louis, where grocers, real estate agents specializing in boardinghouses, and physicians organized in 1878 for the purpose of devising a cooperative blacklist.[40]

Among these various trade groups, retail grocers were the most active. As providers of basic provisions, they dealt with the greatest number and variety of customers. And positioned on the front line of the swelling consumer credit economy, they suffered more than others from delinquent customers. During the late nineteenth century medium to large cities were served by thousands of local grocers. In the early 1880s, for example, a New York newspaper placed the number of grocers in New York and Brooklyn at 10,000, an estimate that may have been imprecise but is not improbable.[41] These neighborhood retailers often performed an unwanted social service role. Where no family help or charitable safety net existed, distressed local people depended upon trusting retailers for the necessities of life.

> Men who are out of work; men who do work, but are unable to collect their pay,—must live. Having no money, they go to the store, and ask for credit until they can obtain their wages. The merchant lets them have what they want, thinking that he will some time get his pay, and trusting to the men's honesty and ability to collect what is due them for work.[42]

At the inaugural meeting of the Chicago Grocers', Butchers', and Marketmen's Exchange, a fracas erupted when one grocer read a rambling diatribe against the credit system and proposed its immediate abolition. Another merchant rejected this "foolish proposition," noting that he served many "honest people" and "could not do such a cruel thing to them on such short notice." Citing the hardships wrought by the current financial panic, he added, "In this time of financial stringency, when people of ordinary means had not the currency wherewith to pay their running expenses, it would be an act of meanness to shut down credit."[43]

By the mid-1880s grocers' associations were established in many eastern cities and as far west as California.[44] When the retail grocers of Aberdeen, South Dakota (a newly incorporated town with fewer than 5,000 people), organized in 1888, they promptly compiled a "list of delinquents" to prevent their members from unwittingly offering credit to "Mr. Bad Pay."[45] One of the largest groups, the New England Retail Grocers' Association, was formed in 1882 and included some 1,100 members by its second year of existence.[46] Around the same time associations were formed in Chicago, New York, Brooklyn, St. Louis, Richmond, Syracuse, Rochester, Buffalo, and Philadelphia.[47] Though grocers' associations were the most visible and numerous, allied trade groups developed similar protective societies. In Charlotte, North Carolina, for example, the butchers banded together in 1889—three years ahead of the city's grocers—to compile a blacklist for their protection against "trusting parties who will not pay their bills."[48]

Physicians were another occupational group that bore a disproportionate burden in the credit system. Even more than grocers who incurred losses by feeding the destitute, the doctor's moral obligation to provide care often left him vulnerable to patients who took his ministrations for granted. Complaining of the penury into which American physicians were sunk as a result of uncollected bills, a Boston editorialist noted in 1840 that "the medical practitioner goes everywhere, at every hour, night or day, without knowing even the character of his patient, and much less anything about his ability to pay for medical services."[49] Nineteenth-century physicians were resigned to the fact that some under their care might be too poor to ever pay them, but they resented those who took advantage of their charity, particularly those who put them off with endless excuses while attending to other financial obligations and even "family superfluities."[50]

The dilemma physicians faced, as one editorialist noted in 1872, was differentiating between the "real delinquents," those who were truly indigent, and the "doctor-swindlers."[51] "The butcher, the grocer, or the baker may, without incurring ill will, refuse to give credit to persons who ask an accommodation. In like manner all other business men may refuse to adopt the credit system," the *Brooklyn Eagle* observed in 1873. "But the doctor, Ah! the doctor! What a 'cruel, heartless man,' he would be, if he asks for his pay as soon as his services are rendered." The "dishonest class," as the paper's correspondent noted, consisted not of those in dire financial straits but rather former patients who frequented the opera and frittered away their money on luxuries instead of settling with their doctor.[52] In 1869 the long-suffering physicians of Millville, New Jersey, hired a collection agent and compiled a blacklist of delinquent patients, vowing that names on the list would not be removed unless their bills were settled or they were exempted by "an order from an overseer of the poor."[53] Some early credit reporting ventures appealed directly to the health care niche. In 1873 the Manhattan Collecting Company, a private New York firm, published a credit reference book for the use of "Physicians, Dentists & Retail Dealers."[54]

In contrast to private firms such as the RDPA, which published annual affirmative-negative rating books, most early trade and merchants' associations seem to have compiled blacklists for the exclusive use of their members. Such lists took the form of printed handouts that were distributed directly to members or a single master ledger maintained by the association. The latter system was used by the Protective Association of Grocers in Long Island City, New York, which kept "a fair-sized account-book, with a mourning-border, containing the list of names" belonging to delinquent customers.[55]

CREDIT RATING BOOKS AND LEDGER EXPERIENCE

Among early reporting organizations, the credit rating book—typically an annual publication updated with supplemental sheets—was the state-of-the-art medium for disseminating information. Like those published by commercial reporting firms such as R. G. Dun and Bradstreet, consumer rating books contained highly confidential information, and their distribution was closely regulated to prevent both nonsubscribers and gossipmongers from gaining access.[56] Their size and format varied among organizations, from a few dozen pages to several hundred, but all shared a common function as comprehensive lists of adult individuals living within the organization's purview—usually a city or town.

Arranged alphabetically by surname, like city directories, rating books included both men and women, often with the marital status (and presumed dependency) of the latter indicated by Mrs., Miss, wife, or widow. Men who were retired, and thus relying upon questionable resources, also received special identification. Each individual's address and occupation, if known, were listed after their name. The absence of either, though not necessarily damning, might signal transience or sloth in the eyes of a skeptical merchant. In addition to these variables, another, race, appears in some rating books. Where "colored" was used as a descriptor, it is conspicuous, clearly signaling the otherness of African Americans in a world of normative whiteness. Unfortunately, with so few examples, it is difficult to make generalizations about African American participation in the white credit economy.[57] The larger point, however, is that credit rating books contained more than just ratings. The personal information that accompanied one's

```
Allen Geo. S., Roofer, 44 Court...........................BA
Allen James, Carpenter, Troy ave., near Pacific............K
Anderson George, Furniture, Atlantic, near Troy ave........K
Allshouse S. J., Confectioner, 63 Fourth, E. D.... ........A
Anderson Mrs., 29 Strong pl.................................A
Altgeld, Liquor, 1044 Atlantic ............................&
Althaus, Drugs, 191 Fulton...............................BA
Aikman S. M., Lanterns, 133 Macon..........................C
Andrus Alfred W., Clerk, 343 Navy..........................A
Anglum Michael, Feed, 233 Hamilton ave ....................B
Anderson Wm. A., Insurance, 31 Monroe......................B
Andrews Benjamin, M. D., 431 State st......................B
━━S. E. (Mrs.) widow, 430 Clermont ave...................A
Alzea, W. Carpenter, 64 Schermerhorn.......................A
Anderson R. G., Baker, Cor. Fulton & Clinton...............C
Alyea N. S. V. R., Builder, 64 Schermerhorn................A
American District Telegraph Co., Montague..................B
Bennett Wm., Plumber, 167 Bridge.........................BA
Bottger John H., Grocer, 946 Atlantic....................AB
Boade Charles T., Upholsterer, 202 Flatbush ave..........BB
Bieber Bros., Dry Goods, 249 Myrtle ave ...................B
Blaney John, Shoes, 383 Warren...........................BA
Beeching W. H., Butcher, 1619 Fulton.....................AB
```

Figure 2.2 Consumer credit ratings, as they appeared in an early rating book. The credit status of each individual listed can be deciphered using the key provided for the Retail Mercantile Agency. The "A" rating for Mrs. S. E. Allen, whose name is hand corrected, indicates that she paid promptly. (Retail Mercantile Agency, Brooklyn, N.Y., 1874)

name—from gender and marital status to address, occupation, and race—provided important circumstantial evidence bearing on nineteenth-century notions of creditworthiness.

Biographical details might offer clues, but it was the credit rating that punctuated each entry in the volume. Like the rating books of commercial reporting firms, those produced by early consumer reporting organizations employed alphanumeric codes to signify relative creditworthiness.[58] And each organization used its own system and rating key. For example, the Brooklyn-based Retail Mercantile Agency (figure 2.2) used the following key in its 1874–1875 volume:

> "B" denotes a person who pays cash; "A"—one who pays promptly; "C"—one, who, through carelessness, allows his or her account to remain unpaid when due, though perfectly responsible; "K"—one who is unfortunate and cannot pay when accounts become due, or who seems indifferent about them, but responsible; "&"—will not be rated; inquiry must be made at the office; we do this in justice to all concerned.[59]

The RDPA, which operated simultaneously across the East River, used another key:

1. Undoubtedly responsible.
2. Pays punctually.
C. Reported as habitually paying cash, and deemed responsible.
3. Regarded as responsible, but does not always pay punctually.

Individuals who received contradictory reports or whose credit was so poor as to be ranked below 3 were marked with an asterisk by the RDPA, indicating that the subscriber should make a special inquiry at the agency office for more information. This use of the asterisk or ampersand was common in credit rating books as a means to avoid publishing highly damaging—and potentially libelous—information that opened the organization to legal sanction.[60] The simplicity and stability of the RDPA's rating key was viewed as a selling point. Except for the elimination of the "C" rating in 1887, it remained essentially the same for more than a half century.

Rating keys with four or five different categories were common, but some were less parsimonious. The Union Credit Company of Cleveland, Ohio, for example, used a key consisting of twenty letter codes to indicate creditworthiness—from A1 ("Good and Prompt") to S ("Owes an Old Account")—and another thirteen numerical codes to convey financial standing.[61] The Merchants' Protective Union in Norwich, Connecticut, employed an even more baroque scheme. In addition to eleven uppercase alphabetical ratings, from A ("considered honest but unable to pay") to K ("is paying on bills formerly reported"), another eighteen lowercase letters were used to indicate the type of retailer to whom the debts were owed, from bakers and butchers to furniture dealers and undertakers.[62]

While borrowing the practice of rating credit from commercial credit reporting agencies, early consumer reporting organizations introduced an important innovation: the use of direct ledger experience. Ledger experience—a retailer's own record of his or her customers' payment history—represented a running transcript of each individual's financial behavior. When pooled with the records of other retailers, it offered a medium through which an individual's pattern of promptness, struggle, or indifference in meeting credit obligations might be discerned. The individual ratings in the RDPA's second edition, for example, were based on reports submitted by as many as twenty different retailers.[63] By the 1890s some organizations claimed to be compiling ratings from the ledger experience of more than 1,000 local merchants.[64] "As a customer has paid others he will pay you," the preface of one rating book noted, summarizing the logic of ledger experience.[65]

The use of ledger experience signaled a major development in the history of American credit reporting, one that initially set consumer reporting organizations apart from those monitoring credit in the commercial sphere. Compared to the use of distant correspondents and in-house investigators, both of which were employed by nineteenth-century commercial reporting firms, the firsthand information recorded in customer records was considered far superior.[66] In its annual reports, the RDPA went to great lengths to impress upon retailers the merits of its ratings and its impartiality as an institution. Distinguishing itself from the mercantile agency system, the RDPA asserted, "This Association does not interview for information, and does not accept statements or opinions as a basis for credit, but gives you the experience of the dealers who previously sold [to] the party, with such other facts as are necessary to enable you to form a correct judgment."[67]

Retailers had long recognized that knowledge accrued through their own interactions with customers was far more valuable than any information culled by secondhand investigators, but the problem had always been to get retailers to share such information with each other. Members of local reporting organizations were required to submit the names of their customers and information regarding their record of payment to the central office. Since many merchants feared sharing their customer information with competitors, organizations often assigned codes to each merchant to veil their identity at the main office.[68] The RDPA encouraged wary retailers by offering a 50 percent discount to subscribers who provided "full co-operation." Such cooperation involved providing the agency with "a full list of their customers with their addresses and business, as far as known, and rating them as per instructions on the blanks furnished by the association," and providing revisions and corrections as requested.[69]

Though no internal records or written reports pertaining to individual consumers survive, the use of ledger experience is apparent in the rating books themselves. Many list multiple ratings for each individual, thus indicating a range of ledger experience among local merchants. For example, the RDPA's rating books included three columns in which individuals' highest, lowest, and average credit rating could be listed beside their name (though in many cases individuals received only a single rating). More commonly, however, when an individual received more than one category of rating—for example, "Prompt pay" (P), "Medium pay" (M), "Slow pay" (S), "Limited credit" (L), and "Require cash" (R)—a string of ratings was listed, with numbers inserted to indicate their proportion. Thus "2PM7S-L-2R," which accompanied the name of B. B. Adams, a barber listed in a St. Joseph, Missouri, rating book, represents thirteen ratings, translated as follows: two merchants reported Adams as "Prompt pay," one as "Medium pay," seven as "Slow pay," one as "Limited credit," and two as "Require cash."[70] By providing a range of ledger experience to consider—which could be ambiguous or contradictory, as illustrated by the preceding example—interpretation was left to subscribers.

In this way ledger experience had the happy effect of inoculating credit reporting agencies against charges of bias or injustice in their ratings. As a prefatory letter in the RDPA's first edition explained, "The ratings are not mere opinions, but the recorded experience of business men who have had dealings with the persons reported, and fairly express their knowledge of them."[71] As mere compilers of information submitted by the community of retailers, they argued, the agency did not manufacture facts but distilled their essence for the use of its membership. Responding to those who angrily protested their rating, the RDPA countered, "To all such as these we have but one reply: *We do not rate anyone.*"[72] Moreover, the blame for incomplete or erroneous ratings was placed squarely on the retailers themselves, who were said to have introduced error by failing to report new information or by refusing to participate altogether. But in holding the retailers responsible, no one in particular was accountable, thus giving the ratings an aura of objectivity and truth that emanated from outside of the reporting agency. The agency thus presented itself to the public as a neutral medium of communication—a "view from nowhere"—that received and transmitted the collective wisdom of unnamed retailers in a given locality.[73] Ratings, in other words, were merely a neutral transcription of an individual's own financial behavior, for which he or she alone was responsible. Since reports were provided to the agency in strict confidence, a disgruntled customer could only guess at the source of his or her poor rating.

BUREAUCRATIC NIGHTMARES AND CASH-ONLY DREAMS

By 1900 organizations devoted to monitoring consumer credit were common, but few endured for long. This was the case for several reasons. First, their success hinged upon an organizer's ability to convince enough local merchants to subscribe to the service and, more important, to contribute confidential information about their customers for their collective benefit. In the absence of broad support, the organization was doomed to fail. Retailers remained deeply mistrustful of one another. Even facing throngs of unknown customers, many preferred to suffer their debtors quietly and alone rather than share information with their competitors.

Such hard-headed isolationism gave way over time, but retailers instinctively bristled at the notion of cooperation, an idea that must have seemed especially counterintuitive in an environment of tightening competition. Additionally, some retailers apparently resisted the idea of credit reporting out of fear of alienating their customers. "Some retail dealers object to this mode of self-protection, because, forsooth, their customers may become offended if their habits of non-paying their debts are made so public." This logic, a Nashville, Tennessee, reporting agency argued in 1885, was invalidated by the fact that many trusting retailers had "brought themselves to bankruptcy, and their wives and their children from a comparative state of affluence to abject poverty," as a result of their heedless goodwill.[74]

Second, at a strictly administrative level, credit reporting organizations were extremely time- and labor-intensive enterprises. The task of collecting, compiling, and regularly updating and distributing credit information was no mean feat. To give a sense of the stupendous effort involved, the preparation of a single reference book published by the RDPA in 1880 involved the deletion of 20,000 names, the addition of 20,000 new names, and changes to 45,000 existing ratings and addresses. "The 70,000 names contained in the register," the RDPA reported, "must be carefully copied and compared with all the latest directories, household and business addresses corrected, errors in spelling and alphabetical arrangement of names made right, old ratings erased or changed, and new ones inserted, all to be done in a very limited time."[75] Even in a city a third the size of New York, the effort needed to operate an effective affirmative-negative reporting system was daunting. And even when a critical mass of membership was achieved, many of these early organizations simply crumbled beneath the weight of administrative responsibilities and soon lost credibility as a result. When a Dun informant visited the RDPA in 1880, he was surprised by their success. Noting that the firm's clients were happy with the service, he wondered "how any money can be made by such an operation," owing to the limited base of subscribers and the high cost of gathering information.[76]

Subscription-based private agencies were undermined by additional factors. For one, they constantly struggled to limit access to their hard-earned proprietary information. Like earlier commercial reporting firms such as R. G. Dun, consumer reporting firms could hardly control the dissemination of their published ratings once placed in the hands of subscribers. In 1886 the RDPA was reduced to scolding its members for sharing information with nonsubscribers, a "growing evil" that stymied the enlargement of the association's membership. "It is a matter of every-day occurrence when canvassing to be told by a dealer that he does not need to subscribe because he gets the information from a friend who does without charge."[77] And unlike voluntary merchants' associations that originated from within the trade, successful for-profit ventures like the RDPA attracted unscrupulous imitators. In 1881 a pair of swindlers plagiarized the RDPA's rating book in Philadelphia. After being run out of town by duped subscribers, they established another agency under the RDPA's name in Chicago and absconded with the subscription fees.[78] Such shenanigans damaged the legitimacy of well-intentioned private agencies and even prompted the RDPA to warn its members against "irresponsible parties" that set up cut-rate operations under similar-sounding names.[79]

All of these organizational obstacles were further compounded by the laxity with which many merchants administered their business records. "No man can know too much about his business, and the majority of men don't know enough," a representative of the Sioux City Bureau of Credits complained in 1898.[80] Small retailers earned special repute for their managerial ineptitude, a problem that became evident, ironically, as commercial credit reporting firms moved to require business owners to submit signed financial statements attesting to their capital and assets. Many retailers kept only skeletal records of their transactions and understandably resisted such efforts, as these statements were legally binding documents that could be used against them if they failed. Noting the "astonishingly universal" ignorance of double-entry bookkeeping among American businessmen, Samuel Terry pleaded that any form of coherent recordkeeping— "whether it be notched sticks, chalk scores, pencil memorandums, or 'single entry' books"—was far better than nothing.[81] Sales records were easily forgotten when busy clerks allowed familiar customers to walk off with "a hoe, or a scythe, or a shovel, or some such article" with only verbal instructions to charge the item to their account.[82] Such informality bred omission and loss.

Many small retailers were unable or unwilling to commit themselves to careful bookkeeping, and some had not taken stock of their merchandise for years, as horrified commercial creditors came to realize. In 1897 New York banker James G. Cannon delivered an influential speech on the subject of "individual credits" in which he summed up the state of retail credit procedures. "I believe that very few retail merchants, if called upon for an opinion as to the basis of their credits, could give a specific or intelligent answer," Cannon scoffed. "He will often 'size up' a man on the spot and sell him a bill of goods without even knowing the party's full name, or, relying, perhaps on his supposed ability to judge something of his means or affairs because he is an acquaintance, he will trust him without any investigation as to his financial worth."[83]

At a deeper level, and perhaps more significantly, many small retailers harbored a lingering desire to impose a strict cash-only policy, one that would banish troublesome credit for good. While offering the public a welcome degree of convenience and in some cases a lifeline, credit sales were the source of much hardship for local merchants with razor-thin profit margins. As a defender of such retailers noted, the workingman might "imagine that the grocer, the dry-goods merchant, the dealer in meats and poultry, are making such large profits," but in reality they often scraped along and struggled to make ends meet.[84] In particular, they found themselves at the whim of fickle debtors and, unhappily, in a perpetual battle to collect small sums spread throughout the neighborhood. Some complained that the credit system forced them into becoming "public slaves," as they were too desperate to deny credit and perpetually abused by delinquent customers. "We may ask," a Chicago grocer wrote in 1873, "Why in the world do we trust? There is no reason why, only our own anxiety to do business and grasp at trade."[85]

Worse still, the grocer's generosity was not always appreciated. Open book accounts encouraged liberal spending, and grocers (as well as other retailers) were accused of preying upon the vanity of their customers in offering to trust them. "An open, running, unsettled account with some merchant, is about the worst calamity that can possibly happen to a farmer, laboring man, or mechanic, in moderate circumstances," one writer declaimed. "You feel quite flattered when the merchant tells you smilingly: 'No matter about the money, take the goods along; we'll make that all right sometime.' You feel like hugging the generous man for his kindness as you carry away the bundle of goods which you have purchased on credit, and which he would have sold 25 per cent. cheaper for cash."[86] Others viewed the extension of credit as a quiet conspiracy hatched by lazy and unscrupulous retailers. "Grocers, butchers, and other storekeepers who supply families with the daily necessities of life, encourage and sometime[s] literally compel their regular customers to let their accounts stand for a month or more at a time," a Brooklyn editorialist complained. The preference among storekeepers for monthly and quarterly payments, according to the writer, allowed them to bury phantom charges in lengthy invoices and to abet dishonest housekeepers who slipped items in for themselves.[87] And, as usual, retailers were blamed for driving up prices thanks to their tolerance, if not outright promotion, of credit sales.

Such complaints, whether launched by disgruntled merchants or customers, typically concluded with a radical call for the imposition of a cash-only policy. Experience could not have given them much hope. Merchants who put their foot down and insisted on running a cash business found it a Sisyphean task. "The day always comes," a Chicago journalist explained, when the established cash customer

> either left their money at home or change for a $20 bill cannot be made, resulting in a charge being made upon the books, and then— well, it is always the same story: the charges commence to accumulate, and—as he dresses well, is a clever talker, and has always paid cash in the past—the retailer thinks he is making a solid customer by his chivalry, and when the account becomes due and is presented the debtor says: "All right, I'll send this in tomorrow or the next day."[88]

Even after advocating a strict cash-only policy to free the shopkeeper from the tyranny of slow credits, a frustrated Chicago grocer admitted, "I must say that I have not got the nerve to do it. I cannot stand by and see my good customers walk over to my neighbor just for the reason that I will not accommodate them with a little credit, and he will."[89] Credit was not just a courtesy; it was a competitive advantage among local retailers.

In this way many merchants, especially small, independent retailers, felt compelled to offer credit terms though they were ill equipped to handle the administrative responsibilities that such transactions required. One of the great drawbacks of credit selling was the additional labor, both physical and mental, that it entailed. Credit sales burdened the retailer's mind with "the agitation and exciting questions of the responsibility of customers" and the problem of collections, all of which distracted him from the more important business of buying and selling goods. Citing the anxiety and emotional "wear and tear" wrought by credit, one retailer reflected, "Would I not be happier and in better condition financially, as well as physically, if I should cut off the credit part of my business entirely?"[90]

In 1876 a group of retail grocers in Atlanta conspired to ban credit sales for an entire year in reaction to legislation that prohibited them from garnishing the wages of laborers, mechanics, and journeymen.[91] Another attempt to curtail credit was reported in Boston, where that city's grocers were said to have defied naysayers and cultivated a cash-only policy of "enormous" proportions in the mid-1880s.[92] Apocryphal stories of credit resistance also circulated in local papers throughout the nation. One described a barber's technique of intimidating credit seekers. When asked by a "suspicious-looking transient customer" if he offered credit, the Nevada barber explained that deadbeats had induced him to adopt a "new system" of bookkeeping. "Whenever I shaved one of these standbys I put a little nick in his nose with my razor and kept tally that way. They got so they didn't want to run bills."[93] Here the problem of accounting and financial identity was solved in one fell swoop, to the delight of resentful merchants.

The erratic development of consumer credit reporting thus reflected not only significant administrative hurdles and deeply ingrained distrust among retailers, but also conflicting attitudes toward the legitimacy of consumer credit itself. Ultimately, cash-only policies proved untenable over any period of time in either commercial or retail business. "While it is true that on a strictly cash basis a business can be run at lower prices and quicker profits," a banker conceded in 1897, "it is also true that the class of customer who can pay cash for everything they need either for domestic and personal use or for business purposes, is a comparatively small one."[94] The emotional appeal of cash seems to have prevented at least some retailers from fully embracing *any* system of credit reporting, for to do so would have signaled surrender to the credit system and the permanent dashing of their cash-only dreams. The underlying popular longing for a cash-only utopia invariably came to the surface during the many financial crises of the nineteenth century.

But if many small retailers could not afford or countenance the institutionalization of credit, another constituency could: credit-friendly mass retailers. During the late nineteenth century, department stores, installment houses, and large specialty dealers established their own in-house credit departments and began to participate in local reporting organizations.[95] By the late 1890s the professionalization of credit management was under way, and a growing number of retailers and bureau operators began to embrace efforts to systematize its allocation and categories of consumer creditworthiness. Significantly, two of the three leading contemporary consumer credit bureaus were founded in the closing years of the century. The Chilton Company, established in Dallas by J. E. R. Chilton in 1897, would become a leader in the computerization of consumer reporting during the 1960s and was later absorbed by Experian. The Retail Credit Company, established in Atlanta by Cator Woolford in 1899, became one of the nation's largest insurance and credit reporting firms and is now Equifax. "The word credit in the retail business is a sign to a dangerous road that has led many a merchant to disaster, but a road which must be traveled," Chilton remarked in 1904, pointing to the inevitability of consumer credit and the necessity of organized credit surveillance.[96] Out of the failures and intransigence of nineteenth-century consumer reporting, an American business institution was born.

3

Credit Workers Unite

PROFESSIONALIZATION AND THE RISE OF A NATIONAL CREDIT INFRASTRUCTURE

By the late 1890s systems for evaluating the credit risk of individual consumers existed in metropolitan centers throughout the United States. "The method of doing business by retailers has changed considerably during the last decade," a Chicago journalist observed in 1886. "Organizations have been perfected by which every grocer is in honor bound to furnish a list of all delinquents or dead-beats who seek to swindle him out of his just dues, and in every locality where there are a sufficient number of retailers to form an association for mutual protection against dishonest credit customers these organizations are springing into existence."[1] With few exceptions, including several attempts to build multistate franchises, these organizations were private commercial agencies and merchant-run protective associations that worked independently and precariously in their respective home cities. Though far from "perfected," they signaled the birth of new surveillance institutions and surveillance routines in everyday life

While credit reporting organizations became increasingly influential arbiters of creditworthiness, actual lending decisions were made elsewhere. Credit reporting organizations merely provided information about local consumers. It was up to credit-granting merchants to interpret that information and to come to their own conclusions. Until the late nineteenth century, the task of evaluating individual credit risk fell to business owners and their associates. When a customer asked to put a dozen eggs on his tab, for instance, it was the grocer who sized up the customer and made mental calculations as to his trustworthiness. The growing availability of systematic credit information was a welcome aid for many merchants. But, ultimately, the value of this information—whether presented in black lists, narrative reports, or credit ratings—depended upon the judgement of its interpreter. Credit reports and credit ratings, then just as now, were imperfect summations of risk. Experienced business owners understood this, and they drew upon a wide array of sources—from local gossip to distant newspapers—for insight into the creditworthiness of their customers.

While small merchants and neighborhood businesses struggled with the continual burden of credit evaluation, some bigger firms began to hire specialists to do this work. During the last decade of the nineteenth century a new business expert, the "credit man," began to appear in the back offices of large retail establishments. As gatekeepers to the world of credit, these new professionals were responsible for personally interviewing credit customers and keeping perpetual watch over the store's existing credit accounts. This was a monumental task, one that required superior organizational skills and an ability to keep abreast of rapidly changing circumstances at the individual level and in the larger world of commerce. The professionalization of credit management was initiated by commercial credit men—that is, credit experts who judged the creditworthiness of business borrowers, not consumers—but retail credit men soon followed. By the 1920s credit departments were common in department stores and installment houses, where many Americans first encountered new bureaucratic systems of credit surveillance.

The professionalization of credit management would have an enormous impact on the institutionalization of the consumer credit surveillance. In addition to codifying the principles of credit evaluation and standardizing protocols for supervising customer accounts, retail credit managers began to organize a national network of consumer credit bureaus. During the 1910s and 1920s, the leading retail credit men's association spurred hundreds of local credit bureaus into existence and worked to coordinate their operations. Though this emergent network was a jumble of credit reporting organizations—from credit men's associations to private agencies—and the quality of each affiliate's services varied, it was the beginning of a national credit surveillance infrastructure. By the mid-1920s, the network's collective intelligence already included credit files for tens of millions of Americans.

THE CREDIT MAN AND THE SCIENCE OF CREDITS

Credit men, and the credit departments they would inhabit, grew out of the increasing volume and complexity of credit relationships within the commercial sphere, particularly in larger wholesaling and manufacturing firms where one of the owners or a trusted clerk began to specialize in the handling of credit management. Though this division of labor had long existed informally—Lewis Tappan, for example, played the untitled role of credit manager in his brother's firm before founding the Mercantile Agency in 1841—during the 1880s credit experts began to receive formal recognition and an official job designation. By then the profitability of many commercial houses depended heavily upon credit sales, making the work of a skilled credit man indispensable. These "ten-talent men," as one contemporary described them, were experts in the nascent "science" of credits, a specialization that encompassed the entire range of credit management—from risk assessment to bookkeeping, law, and collections.[2] Credit managers at some of the largest firms handled tens of thousands of individual credit accounts and commanded impressive salaries—as much as $5,000 to $10,000 a year. In 1883 a Chicago reporter inquired about these new business experts. "They're pretty sharp fellows, ain't they?" he ventured. "Sharp! Well I should say so," a man familiar with their work replied. "Why, he has the whole responsibility of selling millions of dollars worth of goods out all over the empire on credit!"[3]

As judge and jury in lending decisions, the credit man wielded enormous power over the lives and fortunes of individuals. From his desk in a firm's back offices he single-handedly determined the creditworthiness of all customers and continually tracked their accounts. While seeking to please his employer and the company's commissioned salesmen with large receipts, he was simultaneously constrained by the specter of defaulted bills and financial loss, all of which fell directly at his feet. A competent credit man was generally expected to keep losses at or below 1 percent of the firm's annual credit sales. Thus he was forced to steer an anxious course between reckless generosity and stultifying conservatism. Neither extreme was profitable; either too many good customers were turned away or too many bad risks accepted. The credit man's dilemma was summarized in a Shakespearean parody that made the rounds in the trade press during the 1890s:

To sell or not to sell;
That is the question.
Whether 'tis better to sell the goods
And take the risk of doubtful payment,
Or, make sure of what is in possession,
And, by declining, hold them.
To sell; to ship; perchance to lose—
Aye, there's the rub;
For when the goods are gone,
What charm can win them back
From slippery debtors.[4]

By the late nineteenth century the subject of credit was treated in a voluminous body of writing by business leaders, scholars, politicians, and social critics. Yet amid this cacophony of condemnation, approval, and equivocation, the merchant could find little practical instruction. Credit ethics and the importance of character figured prominently in many popular compilations of maxims for aspiring men of business, a genre of mercantile pedagogy pioneered in America by Benjamin Franklin, but none treated credit and its day-to-day regulation as a topic unto itself.[5]

In 1890 this gap was filled by Peter R. Earling, a credit manager for the Chicago household goods manufacturer L. Gould and Company. Earling's 300-page treatise, *Whom to Trust*, was the first comprehensive guide to credit management. Citing "the total absence of literature and lack of information on a topic of such vital importance," Earling promised to share the fruits of his special knowledge with a broad audience, one that included wholesale merchants and manufacturers as well as bookkeepers, accountants, cashiers, bankers, lawyers, and traveling salesmen. While he noted the obvious significance of his book for those working in a formal "Credit Department"—which, he added, are "found only in the larger houses"—the omission of "credit men" from Earling's long list of prospective readers, and its rarity as a descriptive term in the text itself, suggests the ill-defined nature of the occupation at the time of his writing. Like other early advocates of systematic credit analysis, Earling argued that most commercial losses were the result of poor management and imprudence, and thus preventable through the application of sound principles of analysis. "It is not expected that this volume will be all-sufficient in itself," Earling conceded, "but it will at least furnish the fundamental principles, and the processes of reasoning employed in determining questions of credit."[6]

Earling's book seems to have galvanized interest in the development of rational credit management, and in 1892 a new periodical, *The Lawyer and the Credit Man*, was launched to address their specific interests. The link between credit professionals and attorneys was a natural one, as the obverse of credit was collections, an activity that often involved legal intervention—or its threat. Indeed, the movement to professionalize credit management followed on the heels of three closely aligned occupations: banking (1875; American Bankers Association), law (1878; American Bar Association), and accounting (1887; America Institute of Public Accountants). Shortly after the publication of *Whom to Trust*, Earling helped organize the first formal meeting of bankers and businessmen devoted to the subject of credits. The Congress of Mercantile Credits held at the 1893 World's Fair in Chicago proved to be a momentous event. The onset of a severe national financial crisis a month prior to the congress only reinforced its urgency and significance. If the panic of 1837 prompted the development of systematic credit reporting, the financial crisis of 1893 provided the impetus for professionalized credit management. Reflecting on the depression of the 1890s, one reporter noted, "The average credit man felt as if the weight of the world was upon his shoulders, and, so far as his employers were concerned, it often was."[7] Even the president of the Chicago exposition, Harlow N. Higinbotham, a respected credit manager at Marshall Field department store, attended.

The congress's three sessions included papers bearing on various aspects of credit management, but one theme dominated: the need for mutual cooperation among creditors. Though one afternoon's proceedings coincided with a much-anticipated high-stakes horse race, a burning commitment to credit reform prevailed. "Considering the Derby's attractions the mercantile men had cause for elation in the considerable audience attending yesterday's session." The addresses, which "were among the best yet heard," according to a contemporary report, "were nearly all on the question of cooperation among business-men to secure a better credit system and to diminish the causes of failures."[8] At the conclusion of the evening session, resolutions for the formation of an official organization of mercantile credit professionals were adopted, and a committee was appointed to begin drafting its constitution and bylaws. "In this congress," a credit professional later reflected, "there was a germ of a great movement and we look upon it as the seed which later eventuated into an organization of great importance to the country's economic welfare." This organization was the National Association of Credit Men.

Founded in 1896, the NACM quickly became the driving force behind the professionalization of credit management. At the inaugural meeting, held in Toledo, Ohio, some 150 businessmen convened to espouse the principles of cooperation and mutual trust. They hailed from fourteen states, predominantly in the Northeast and the Midwest, and included delegates from at least nine local credit men's associations already established in cities such as New York, Minneapolis, St. Louis, and New Orleans. Amid much fanfare, the mayor of Toledo welcomed the delegates, and the editor of *Business* magazine presented the assembly with an honorary gavel engraved with the scales of justice holding "character" and "capital" in its level pans.[9]

Looking back on the financial spasms of the nineteenth century, the newly associated credit men took it as their mission to modernize, and presumably stabilize, the American credit system through the application of rational administration. System, method, organization, cooperation—these were the watchwords of the movement's progressive aspirations. The "practical realization of intelligent theories," an NACM official promised a gathering of hardware dealers in 1897, would replace the "miasmic swamp of irregularity and deceit" that had long characterized credit relationships.[10]

Though formed to serve the interests of commercial credit grantors—wholesalers, manufacturers, and bankers—the NACM's early membership included retailers and credit managers whose firms worked in both commercial and retail sales.

While these new professionals championed the principles of systematic management, few issues preoccupied them as much as their own qualifications. The first self-proclaimed credit men emerged from the accounting and cashier's departments of their respective firms, where they became proficient bookkeepers and developed a broad knowledge of business finance. "When in 1875 I obtained my first position in commercial life," one credit manager quipped, recalling his unwitting entrance into the profession, "I was expected to be everything from a Bookkeeper to a Porter, and incidentally also a Credit Man."[11] Guided by practical experience, and working in isolation from each other until the mid-1890s, these pioneering autodidacts turned their focus from the narrow confines of the ledger book to the full-time problem of estimating individual creditworthiness. As graduated clerks, the new credit experts were well attuned to their firm's daily operations and, more significantly, intimately acquainted with the payment habits and behaviors of its various customers. It was typically in the crucible of the counting room that the credit man learned the fundamental principles of credit.

The credit manager's work was so varied and all-encompassing that some found it impossible to summarize. As one explained in 1900, "We have no catechism, doctrine or ordination; no code of administration or practice—no license or charter. . . . Whoever hires us, tells us his rules, and we are *prima facie* credit men." The same speaker confided that he had once been mistakenly apprehended by a group of plainclothes patrolmen. When interrogated as to his occupation, he could only hand the skeptical deputies his business card and suggest that they stop by his office to see him in action. "I could not tell them what I did, and couldn't now," he conceded.[12] The credit man's work was difficult to explain not only because it was relatively new and unfamiliar to the general public—ironically, the patrolmen mistook the credit man for a confidence man—but also because it brought together so many disparate domains of knowledge, from accounting and law to agriculture, retailing, manufacturing, and banking.

In short, the credit man was expected to have a grasp of all spheres of activity with even the slightest bearing on the future financial condition of his customers, from local weather conditions to national monetary policy. News of a poor growing season might prompt a credit manager to tighten credit limits for the firm's rural customers, while knowledge of retailing might sharpen his assessment of a shopkeeper's aptitude, and thus his ability to make good on a debt. Such broad practical training, Higinbotham opined, was best gained through "a boyhood on a farm, a few years in the typical 'general store' of the average village, a period of service in the country bank and a thorough drill in the cashier's department of a wholesale house."[13] To speak of the early credit man as a specialist in this regard is misleading. He was actually a preeminent generalist. In his limitless search for clues to guide him, the credit man was an "inveterate fact hunter" with a voracious appetite for information.[14]

While the apostles of systematic credit management touted the superiority of standardization and efficiency, the ideal credit man was no "lightning calculator" or "mathematical prodigy."[15] More than anything, he stood out for his unique personality. He was uniformly described as judicious, temperate, naturally inquisitive, thorough, decisive, and polite. And with so much information coming from conversations—with customers as well as sales representatives, who in their interactions with customers often gleaned useful personal details—he was eminently tactful. "The credit man has often to ask and do many things which are unpleasant and embarrassing both to himself and to the debtor," one writer explained. "If he can do these things in such a way as to keep the customer's good will and even make himself the latter's confidant and advisor, so that the customer will voluntarily keep him informed of his condition—that is tact."[16]

Though a pleasing personality could be cultivated by anyone, the best credit men, as often noted, were possessed of innate qualities of mind and intuition that defied imitation. One of these gifts was a prodigious memory. As an information professional who managed thousands of individual accounts and sought significance in the most trifling details of everyday life, the credit man with a capacious memory was at a distinct advantage. Even while advocating for systematic recordkeeping, James G. Cannon, one of the leading figures of the NACM, remarked that "a trained and accurate memory" was the credit man's "main qualification."[17] The credit man's legendary feats of recall provided many amusing anecdotes, including one involving an Irish merchant from Kansas who forsook his usual suppliers in Chicago and St. Louis to purchase stock in New York. After introducing himself to the credit man of a New York house, the Irishman, who presumed himself a stranger, was instantly judged creditworthy.

> "All right," said the credit-man, "get what you want. I know you well enough." "But d'ye you [*sic*] know anything good about me," asked the Irishman. "O, yes; you're all right. You pay your bills promptly, and you've got considerable property." And, seeing that his man could bear a little humor, he added: "You take your regular sour-mash, and can draw it pretty fine in a bargain, but you pull for business, and get there." "Begad," said the Irishman to me afterward, "he soized me up like a book, but domme if I wouldn't like to know how he caught on."

The credit man, it turns out, had once read a credit report on the Irishman and "remembered it."[18]

Above all, the ideal credit man was a keen judge of human nature. Even as credit analysis moved in the direction of textual abstraction and quantification, the information that the credit man trusted most was that acquired through direct consultations with his customers. "His main task," one writer noted, "is to recognize artificial and superficial and false appearances when he meets them—and the average credit man meets plenty of them!"[19] Well into the twentieth century the personal interview remained the preferred mode of credit investigation. This was particularly true among retailers, who, unlike commercial creditors, did not have recourse to financial statements in making credit decisions about individual consumers. During these face-to-face encounters, the credit man relied upon his interpersonal skills to lay bare the credit customer's true character. "The ideal credit man," one expert noted, "deals largely with character, and should therefore be preeminently a safe and sane judge of human nature."[20]

What is especially striking about the development of rational credit management is its tension between science and subjectivity. This was nowhere more apparent than in the seemingly contradictory qualifications of the credit professional himself. It was in the specialized work of the credit man that the underlying tensions of credit management—textual versus interpersonal knowledge, system versus discretion, reason versus intuition—were dramatized most tellingly. The successful credit manager did not simply rubber-stamp orders that checked out with official sources; he abided by his instincts even in cases where, contrary to trusted endorsements or favorable credit reports, he had "a feeling—perhaps rather vague and indefinable—that the man is not what he claims and that his request for credit should be denied."[21] This was the crucial moment when the credit man was forced to choose between facts and impressions.

THE RETAIL CREDIT MAN

During the late 1880s and early 1890s credit specialists began to emerge in retail establishments, particularly in large dry goods stores, installment and mail order houses, and, most important, department stores. Grocers and butchers might have been the earliest to combine for retail credit protection, but it was in the large new department stores that consumer credit assessment first achieved systemization on a mass scale. Indeed, the development of retail credit management is intimately connected to the rise of the department store at the turn of the twentieth century.[22] Since the success of these spectacular emporia hinged upon the rapid turnover of large volumes of merchandise, liberal credit policies were often offered to attract customers and promote sales. When Louis Stern, proprietor of one of the most prosperous department stores in New York, was asked by a local reporter in 1889 if his firm offered credit, he was quizzical. "'Certainly, we give credit,' he said. 'And we are only too glad to have the custom. Every big house has to do it.' "[23]

Such universality was not really true. Major New York dealers such as A. T. Stewart and R. H. Macy famously maintained cash-only policies, as did retail chain stores such as F. W. Woolworth, S. S. Kresge (the future Kmart), and J. C. Penney that proliferated at the turn of the twentieth century.[24] But despite these important exceptions, credit sales were increasingly commonplace in the closing decades of the nineteenth century.

At Chicago's Marshall Field, for instance, annual retail credit sales exceeded cash sales for the first time in 1880, and by a margin that grew ever wider over the next decade.[25]

While local grocers and butchers were overwhelmed by unknown buyers in their cramped storefronts, sprawling multistoried department stores such as Stern Brothers and Marshall Field literally invited crowds of strangers into their establishments. During the 1890s department stores began to develop formal credit departments and systems for approving and tracking the charge accounts of their customers. In 1889 a New York reporter found that "the credit system practiced by the big houses" was "nearly a perfect science." This system of "lightning inquiries" relied upon the work of an unidentified "uptown retail commercial agency" (possibly the RDPA), which listed and rated "the names of thousands of persons in this city and the suburbs" in its annual reference books. Thus, when the unknown "Mrs. Moneypenny" asked to have her goods charged, the store's superintendent took down her name and references. "While a new customer is telling the superintendent or head of the firm about herself or her references, the house will have obtained her whole pedigree from a business standpoint without her knowledge, and before she leaves the store." If her name did not appear in the agency's rating book, then a quiet investigation was rapidly set into motion. "While she is talking a swift footed messenger, or perhaps the telephone, is put into play, and within a few minutes after Mrs. Moneypenny has announced herself an employe of the agency is hustling around all the dry goods stores to find out if Mrs. Moneypenny is known in any of them."[26] Other department stores employed their own investigators, or "runners," to check up on the background and reputation of their credit applicants. Recalling his start as a credit man for the New York department store H. O'Neill in 1885, a longtime credit manager at Bamberger's remarked that the runners worked together on friendly terms, in contrast to the bitter rivalries of the store owners.[27]

It was also in large department stores that many consumers first became aware of their new status as economic subjects during the late nineteenth century. The experience of encountering such financial investigation for the first time is recorded in the following anecdote. Upon moving from Chicago to New York, a woman sought to open a credit account at a local dry goods dealer. The dealer, after politely asking the woman her name and address and reviewing her references, asked her to wait a moment while he investigated her references:

> The woman was not at all satisfied, and was inclined to be indignant. "It seems to me," she said, "that there is a lot of fuss and red tape about this. I never had any such trouble in Chicago. Here are my bank book and check book. They ought to be sufficient to prove my trustworthiness." "My dear madam," said the superintendent, "I have not the slightest doubt that you are entirely trustworthy, and that we shall be very glad to give you credit. At the same time you must realize that we have to go about this business in a systematic way, and even while we are morally assured that a customer is entirely satisfactory we cannot omit the usual precautions. If we did we would slip up, and we could not afford to sell our goods as cheaply as we do."[28]

At the same time, liberal credit policies were typical among installment houses, where costly durable goods such as furniture, household appliances, and musical instruments were moved into the eager hands of cash-poor buyers. "Gradually," an installment dealer recalled in 1887, "a different class of purchasers appeared," one very unlike the "shady characters" and risky boardinghouse tenants who sought to purchase goods on time. "They were honest young mechanics, clerks, and bookkeepers who wanted to marry and have homes of their own, but who could not raise the required cash to furnish a house."[29] Deferred payment plans were not altogether new—land and housing were sold on such terms throughout the nineteenth century—but the practice became increasingly common during the 1860s after a national campaign initiated by the Singer Sewing Machine Company demonstrated its efficacy.[30] Technically speaking, installment sales differed from open book or charge accounts in that a modest down payment was required under the terms of a chattel mortgage or hire purchase. The goods taken home by the customer were legally owned by the installment dealer until the final payment was received. Armed with ironclad contracts and the right of repossession, installment dealers were in a better position than many retailers who sold on credit.

Unfortunately, these contracts were also the source of abuse. Predatory furniture dealers and "sewing-machine dens" lured the poor into impossible obligations and happily repossessed their merchandise when, inevitably, they missed a payment. Such schemes incited public outrage and colored installment selling with a tinge of disrepute during the late nineteenth century.[31] But for legitimate dealers who hoped to win the goodwill of their customers, confiscation hardly inspired community favor. These installment dealers, like other retailers, formed their own protective associations in cities such as Boston and New York and began to employ credit specialists to manage their accounts.[32]

The principles of sound credit management might have been universal, as representatives of the NACM often suggested, but retail credit specialists—those who sold to *consumers*—faced challenges that those in the commercial sphere did not. Commenting on the lack of coordinated credit information among retailers, one business writer noted, "How much more difficult must be the task of the retail credit-man and financial manager, who, to a certain extent, must rely upon the general reputation of the applicant for credit, his appearance, his action, and his dress."[33] Indeed, in 1898 a Los Angeles retailer noted the difference between commercial and retail creditors: "Wholesale merchants can get such information from proper agencies, and it saves many a good sum to be able to get such information. Why not do the same with the retail trade?"[34]

NATIONAL CONSUMER CREDIT REPORTING INFRASTRUCTURE: 1900–1940

During the first two decades of the twentieth century both retail credit reporting (outside agencies that recorded and compiled credit information) and retail credit managers (in-house professionals who oversaw the allocation of credit to the store's customers) formed national associations to represent their interests. Though the credit managers would ultimately exert a far more important influence, the first stirrings toward a national *consumer* credit infrastructure came from the proprietors of privately run retail credit reporting firms. In February 1906, a decade after the founding of the NACM, a handful of agency owners gathered in a New York City hotel to discuss the formation of a national association through which to exchange ideas and promote their collective interests.

Six months later the inaugural meeting the National Association of Retail Credit Agencies was held in New York, and its twelve attendees elected William H. Burr, an attorney and head of the Commercial Record Company in Rochester, New York, as its first president. In his address Burr cited individual honesty as the fundamental basis of retail credit, making a point of differentiating the work of the retail credit reporting agency from its counterpart in the commercial sphere. Whereas firms such as Dun and Bradstreet sought to peg "the net worth of this or that concern," Burr observed, the retail credit reporting firm asked "what is his reputation and record and does he pay his bills promptly or slowly or does he not pay them at all."[35] In short, retail credit reporting was almost entirely based upon an assessment of the borrower's character and financial behavior. The next year the organization's name was changed to the National Association of Mercantile Agencies (NAMA) to eliminate confusion with other credit men's associations.[36]

The main difficulty that early retail credit reporting agencies faced, as already noted, was soliciting enough membership to reach a critical mass. The success of such agencies, whether privately owned or run by merchants, depended upon the organizer's ability to convince enough local merchants to subscribe to the service and, more crucially, to contribute confidential information about their own customers for the agency's collective benefit. In the absence of broad support, the organization was doomed to fail. This, in fact, was the fate of many credit reporting enterprises during the late nineteenth and early twentieth centuries. "The rocks are strewn with the wrecks of retail mercantile agencies," Burr noted ominously. In addition to fostering interagency cooperation, ferreting out "fake" agencies, and working to standardize retail credit reports, NAMA devoted much attention to the problem of currying favor in the business community and, relatedly, managing agency expenses so that their reports were generally affordable. This was a constant struggle; it was difficult to economize on the overhead and labor-intensive work of collecting and compiling such information. "Let me set it down as axiomatic," one writer declaimed, "that *cheap reports are impossible*, they cannot be thorough and reliable."[37] Shoddy reports merely drove away subscribers and eroded an agency's chance at success still further.

Though originally devoted to the problems of retail credit reporting, many of NAMA's members (never numbering more than 200) dabbled in commercial credit reporting to supplement their incomes. Prosperous commercial reporting firms such as R. G. Dun and Bradstreet were kept aloft by the subscriptions of large wholesalers and manufacturers, but retail reporting service was out of reach for many small-time storekeepers. In 1909 a NAMA leader who operated an agency in Richmond, Virginia, noted that his retail business was only a fraction of his commercial reporting activities, and a third less profitable. Retail credit reporting, he summarized, was "Skimmed Milk" compared to the "Double Cream" of commercial reporting.[38] This created something of an identity crisis for the organization, and it foundered during its fifteen-year existence. But while NAMA failed to win broad support among retailers—the cooperative spirit evinced by profit-motivated agencies seems to have rung hollow—it spawned an organization that did: the Retail Credit Men's National Association (RCMNA).

Figure 3.1 Sherman L. Gilfillan, Minneapolis credit manager and first president of the Retail Credit Men's National Association, established in 1912. (*Credit World*, November 1939)

At the 1912 NAMA convention in Spokane, Washington, a splinter group of retail credit managers formed the RCMNA to represent their own professional interests. Its founding father and first president was Sherman L. Gilfillan, credit manager of the Minneapolis department store L. S. Donaldson. Born in the village of West Salem, Wisconsin, in 1870, Gilfillan grew up near the busy lumber mills of La Crosse, Wisconsin, on the Mississippi River. At age nineteen he set off for Minneapolis, where he followed the typical trajectory of the first credit professionals, beginning work as a bookkeeper. After gaining experience with rubber and fuel companies, he was hired by L. S. Donaldson.[39] "Thinking I would brush up on my newly chosen profession," he later recalled, "I called at the library for literature bearing on it, but to no avail. In fact, there was practically nothing published on Retail Credits in those days."[40] A retail credit association was formed in Minneapolis in 1904, and Gilfillan became an active member (figure 3.1).[41]

Striking upon the idea of a national association for *retail* creditors after attending the 1911 NACM convention in Minneapolis, Gilfillan arrived in Spokane the next year to realize his vision with fellow delegates from Minneapolis and St. Paul, Rochester, New York, and Boston.[42] The RCMNA's primary objectives, as laid down in its original constitution, were to support the organization of local retail credit men's associations, to promote cooperation between retail credit managers and credit reporting agencies, and to facilitate the interchange of ideas and knowledge among retail credit professionals.[43] Annual membership was set at three dollars and included a subscription to its official journal, *Credit World*, which began publication immediately. Over the next several years the RCMNA and NAMA held joint annual conventions, but the former soon eclipsed the latter. Citing the NACM rather than NAMA as its model, Gilfillan proclaimed, "Let us be to the retail world what the wholesale creditmen are to the wholesale world."[44] In 1919 the RCMNA established a permanent headquarters in St. Louis.

Like all prior ventures to form cooperative credit information networks, the RCMNA faced the daunting task of coaxing retailers out of isolation. Beginning with fewer than 40 members at its inaugural meeting in 1912, the association grew to nearly 1,000 members in 1916 and

more than 10,000 by 1921.[45] Its success is a testament to the indefatigable
boosting of its early leadership. During its formative years one official
wrote some 800 letters to rally support, and another embarked on a
19,000-mile cross-country odyssey at the height of the 1918 influenza epi-
demic, visiting cities in eighteen states to rally the formation of local affiliates.[46] Members were urged to wear association lapel buttons and to hang
framed certificates in their stores, advertising their solidarity to their
peers while communicating to their customers that they were conducting
business under the watchful eye of the credit managers' fraternity. "Now,
brother creditmen, get together," a Los Angeles representative implored.
"Call on your brother creditmen, form an association. Meet once a month
or oftener. Make friends with one another. . . . You will soon be able to
call your brother creditman and say 'Bill, what do you know about Mrs. B.,
she wants credit here.'"[47] By 1918 the RCMNA had members in forty
states and 230 cities throughout the nation.[48] Though many worked for
large retail firms, the association sought to bring together creditors from
all walks of the retail trade. "This is not a department store or a dry goods
organization," a *Credit World* advertisement insisted; "it is for *every man*
in the country who extends retail credit."[49]

The RCMNA played a key role in the professionalization of retail credit
management during the early decades of the twentieth century, but, more
important, it laid the groundwork for a national consumer credit reporting
network in the United States. As already noted, retail credit reporting operations at the turn of the twentieth century were disorganized and varied
in their methods, with very few succeeding over any period. While entrepreneurial private agencies typically failed to win the cooperation and support
of paying subscribers, voluntary merchant-run protective associations, such
as those initiated by grocers during the 1870s and 1880s, usually petered out
as dedication waned and suspicion resurfaced. Local merchant associations,
a private agency upstart scoffed in 1891, "were organized with a hurrah!" but
could never sustain enough interest or funding to survive.[50] There was ample
evidence to justify this view. Yet a dismal record among both private agencies
and merchants' associations did not deter new efforts.

Dozens of reporting organizations were formed nationwide between 1890
and 1900, primarily in urban centers.[51] Though retail credit reporting was

born in metropolitan New York, it seems to have flourished in the Midwest before 1900, particularly in states such as Ohio, Michigan, Wisconsin, Minnesota, Iowa, and Missouri. The diffusion of late nineteenth-century retail credit reporting is not only difficult to track, but also difficult to explain. For example, Philadelphia, the third most populous American city in the 1890s, with over a million people, did not have a well-established retail credit reporting infrastructure at the turn of the twentieth century, while Lincoln, Nebraska, a city a fraction of the size, apparently did.[52] As a California bureau manager recalled, retail reporting during the early 1910s was still a "nightmare of confusion, distrust, lack of cohesion, understanding, or cooperation in all but a few of the most progressive and highly systematized communities."[53]

The national credit reporting infrastructure established by the RCMNA hinged on its ability to organize and bring together hundreds of local associations. During the first decade of the twentieth century merchant associations began to emerge independently and in significant numbers. "Necessity is a force that makes strange bedfellows," the author of a 1904 credit textbook remarked, "and retailers are gradually realizing that it is the worst sort of folly to keep their losses to themselves and to permit the bad credit risk to prey on the trade generally."[54]

A national directory of "retail credit rating agencies and associations" issued in 1912 offers a rare glimpse into existing conditions just as the RCMNA was formed. Of the more than 700 organizations listed, over half are identified as merchants, retailers, or businessmen's associations. Private agencies dominated in populous eastern states such as New York and Massachusetts, but the extent to which local associations proliferated in the West is striking, especially in Texas, California, Oklahoma, and Colorado. In Texas, more than 90 percent of the state's 121 credit reporting organizations were local associations.[55] The organization of Texas owed much to J. E. R. Chilton, an influential NAMA leader and founder of the Dallas retail credit association that would later become part of Experian. But in many places, the credit bureau consisted of little more than a box of index cards kept at the local chamber of commerce. "Mercantile Agencies, Credit Companies, Credit Bureaus, Credit Associations, Merchants' Protective Associations, and many others, are all working for the same end, though using many different systems," one writer observed in 1914.[56]

Despite such examples, the desire to form local associations and bureaus was often wanting in less-populated regions. "Merchants in small towns have little conception of the benefits of a modern credit bureau," a credit manager in northern Colorado complained.[57] Though geographic isolation had once offered some protection, the proliferation of automobiles during the 1920s greatly expanded the radius of consumer activity. In arguing the merits of a national association, RCMNA representatives often warned that those slow to organize were a magnet for deadbeats. A city without an active association was not only "a dumping ground for undesirables"; it was also "an illuminated invitation for the undesirables to come and settle down, but never settle up."[58] By painting such unaffiliated cities as outposts of degeneracy, the organization underscored the progressive and, indeed, civilizing effect of credit organization.

During the RCMNA's first five years, new local associations in St. Louis and Los Angeles were brought into its fold, along with others in Duluth, Nashville, Denver, Memphis, Milwaukee, Pittsburgh, and New York. "The sufferings of the retail credit men of this city—and throughout the country, for that matter—at the hands of Mrs. S. Low Paye and Mrs. D. Ed Beete are about to end," the *New York Times* announced in 1917 when an RCMNA affiliate was formed in that city.[59] By 1920 the RCMNA included ninety-four local associations in cities throughout the United States.[60] Regional associations were soon formed to coordinate the activities of growing local associations in the Northwest, Midwest, and New England, and in 1920 the retail credit managers of California organized the first state conference, a milestone important enough to feature a celebrity appearance by Will Rogers.[61]

By the mid-1920s the RCMNA had 15,000 members, including a growing number of "credit women." Despite the association's sexist name, women had long worked for credit departments and credit bureaus, not only as clerks and secretaries, but also as managers. In 1913 Miss E. M. Fleming, a retail credit manager in Kewanee, Illinois, became the first female member of the RCMNA and, the next year, the first woman to attend the national convention.[62] Five years later a *Women's Wear* columnist was struck by the "unusual number of women" at the national convention.[63] A shortage of male labor brought many women into credit work

Figure 3.2 Hundreds of credit women gathered at a breakfast club meeting in Spokane, Washington, to celebrate the national association's twenty-fifth anniversary. The first credit women's breakfast club was formed in Portland, Oregon, in 1930. (*Credit World*, August 1937)

during World War I, but the vast expansion of consumer credit during the 1920s opened even more doors. As a representative of the local association in Davenport, Iowa, reported, "We have more credit women in Davenport than credit men. They are employed in all our largest department stores and in all our ladies' ready-to-wear stores and one men's ready-to-wear store and shops of various kinds."[64] During the 1920s job-seeking women advertised themselves beside job-seeking men in the classified section of *Credit World*. One "Southern woman" touted more than a decade of experience and her qualifications to "take entire charge of [a] small office."[65]

During the 1930s women continued to gain recognition and status within the profession. Their visibility was enhanced by the growth of credit women's breakfast clubs. These locally organized social networks brought women together from cities and towns across the United States. The movement was inspired by Edith Shaw, a credit bureau worker in Portland, Oregon, who watched with envy as her male colleagues bonded at credit association meetings. "It irked her just a bit to realize what little opportunity the girls had for forming such friendships," a fellow club member recalled.[66] Shaw's idea quickly spread far beyond the Pacific Northwest. In 1937 the Credit Women's Breakfast Clubs of North America included some sixty chapters and more than 3,000 members (figure 3.2). By then the organization was also recognized as an official division of the national association.[67] This was a welcome gesture of inclusion from the profession's male establishment, but credit women had already won a more momentous affirmation a decade earlier. In 1927 the national association voted unanimously to drop "men" from its name. As the editor of *Credit World* explained, "The masculine note in our name is resented, and justly so, by many capable women credit managers."[68] Thenceforward, the organization became the National Retail Credit Association.[69]

During the 1920s and 1930s, a true national credit reporting infrastructure began to take shape. In communities without a credit bureau, newly formed local associations often established their own. Conflicts arose, however, when existing private agencies failed to cooperate with the merchants' association or when, more often, the private agencies were incompetent. For good reason the proprietors of private agencies were concerned that retailers' bureaus would drive them out of business. As the owner of a Memphis mercantile agency admitted, "When the Retail Credit Men's Association was first formed, I was, frankly speaking, afraid of it; I thought perhaps my bread and butter might be at stake, and I did not favor the growth of the movement."[70] The fact that private reporting agencies—the very institutions that initially supported and gave impetus to the development of retailers' associations—were either "obliterated or absorbed by the Merchant-owned Bureau" was, as the manager of the San Francisco association remarked, "a strange paradox."[71]

In 1918 a truce was arranged with NAMA to arbitrate disputes and to prevent the incursion of retailers' bureaus where existing private agencies were satisfactory. Yet difficulties persisted; the concept of free interchange was problematic for profit-seeking agencies, and too many simply offered inferior service. As one experienced credit manager quipped, "To err is human, to forgive, divine. Mercantile agencies are human. They must be forgiven a whole lot."[72] In 1921 NAMA was finally absorbed by the retail credit association, surrendering its own name and reorganized as the Credit Service Exchange Division of the latter organization. By 1926 the service division included 800 bureaus, which together made nine million reports per year with its collective fifty million credit records.[73] "We are building for America a Retail Credit structure," the national association's leader proclaimed.[74]

As a national network began to emerge, the interchange of information between bureaus in distant cities remained a problem. In addition to variations in quality, pricing discrepancies led to disputes, especially when "foreign" reports were requested between bureaus in different cities or regions. The development of coupon systems, whereby associated bureaus used prepurchased tickets to pay for services, helped to standardize fee structures and smooth exchanges.[75] But even as interbureau reporting became more efficient, some merchants circumvented the bureau altogether, particularly when seeking information concerning credit applicants who were out-of-town visitors or newly relocated, and thus did not have established credit records in the community. Direct inquiries might have been expedient for individual credit managers, but they burdened other merchants with multiple requests for the same credit information. Department stores and large specialty houses often accommodated such requests, particularly among themselves, but came to resent them when they suspected smaller retailers of pillaging the information in their expensive credit departments.[76]

During the 1930s the national association sought to consolidate its network of bureaus, which by then numbered more than 1,000. Though credit associations first emerged to serve local merchants, a national market for credit reports was growing, particularly among automobile, finance, petroleum, and direct sales companies selling to consumers throughout the country. To secure this business, the National Consumer Credit Reporting Corporation (NCCRC) was established as a subsidiary of the national association in 1932. This new entity, which assigned the bureaus to exclusive territories and implemented standardized reports and pricing, immediately attracted attention from the Department of Justice. In 1933 the U.S. District Court in St. Louis filed a petition against the national association for violating federal antitrust regulations.

The monopolistic design of credit reporting presented an interesting problem. After all, competition among multiple bureaus in a single location was entirely counterproductive; it duplicated the effort of each retailer to make reports and, even worse, divided retailers against themselves where loyalties were split among two or more reporting organizations. During the 1920s credit reporting associations devoted to a specific business— lumber, coal, hardware, or furniture dealers, for example—operated along- side retail credit associations and were denounced by the national associa- tion. "Because of the very needs and conditions it must serve," one credit manager argued, "a credit bureau is a natural monopoly; more than one credit bureau in a city is of as much nuisance as more than one telephone system, and a greater financial menace, because of the incompleteness of reports each must render."[77]

The federal antitrust charge denied this public utility argument. However, its rationale was remarkable for treating credit reports—mere information—as a commodity. Since the early days of the mercantile agency, the primary legal challenge facing credit reporting organizations was slander and libel. In effect, the antitrust case acknowledged formally what credit reporting had done since the 1840s: commodify personal identity. Observing that the association's "1,200-odd affiliated bureaus sell nothing but credit reports," a service rather than a good or process, *Business Week* remarked on the unprecedented nature of the case.[78] Though agreeing to a consent decree, which prohibited the designation of exclusive territories and denial of service to nonmembers, the national association was charged with violating its terms and fined in 1935. Two years later the interbureau reporting services of the NCCRC were turned over to a new organization, the Associated Credit Bureaus of America, which would lead the industry through World War II and the postwar decades.[79]

Despite these setbacks and the hardships of the Great Depression, a na- tional credit reporting network was well established by 1940. It was not a perfect surveillance system, to be sure. Indeed, many retailers continued to grant credit on the basis of an honest face or a personal reference, something that vexed advocates of rational credit management. Additionally, many re- tail creditors did not have their own credit departments or full-time credit managers. In 1938 *Barron's* reported that only 10 percent of small business owners employed a credit manager, though 91 percent offered credit terms to their customers.[80]

Yet the growing influence of consumer credit bureaus was undeniable. In 1930 the U.S. Department of Commerce sponsored a National Retail Credit Survey, which queried 12,000 retailers about their credit-granting practices. According to the results, more than 70 percent of American retail businesses relied upon credit bureaus for information (figure 3.3). Though a smaller percentage depended entirely upon credit bureau information—among department stores, for example, 32.7 percent relied on credit bureau information alone, while 52.9 percent used credit bureau information to supplement their own investigations—the study highlighted the credit bureau's vital role.[81] "Think for a moment of the depressing condition of business generally, if there were no reporting agencies in this country," the chairman of the national association's Credit Service Exchange Division remarked in 1928. "The undesirable credit risk would run

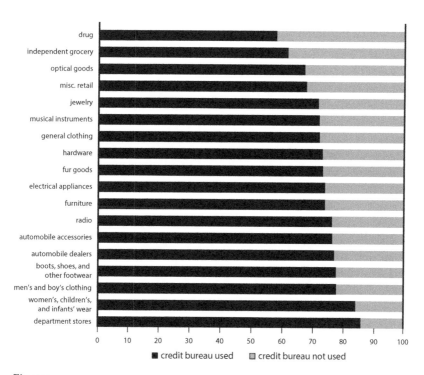

Figure 3.3
Source: U.S. Department of Commerce, *National Retail Credit Survey*, Part 1, Washington, D.C.: GPO, 1930.

rampant through the country. The credit system would deteriorate and gradually collapse."[82]

When Sherman Gilfillan, the national association's beloved founding father, died in 1939, his passing marked the end of the consumer reporting industry's infancy. "We owe practically our very existence to Mr. Gilfillan," a *Credit World* tribute acknowledged.[83] In less than three decades, the association he founded with a handful of colleagues had grown into a national surveillance infrastructure supported by thousands of professional credit managers, trade journals and textbooks devoted to the subject, and standard protocols for communicating credit information from coast to coast. This new business edifice had weathered the Depression and was poised to oversee a massive expansion of postwar consumer credit spending. On the eve of World War II, the national association's affiliated bureaus had "individual master cards" for sixty million people. Together, these records provided a window into the domestic and financial affairs of twenty million households, or about three out of four American families.[84]

4

Running the Credit Gantlet

EXTRACTING, ORDERING, AND COMMUNICATING CONSUMER INFORMATION

During the early twentieth century millions of Americans came under the watchful gaze of newly formed credit bureaus. But these bureaus were only one arm of the emergent consumer credit apparatus. Their counterpart was the credit department of individual stores, where credit managers interviewed, documented, and tracked customers for their own benefit and that of the local bureau. "The obscure credit department, just a stripling yesterday, is a big one today—a recognized unit and one of the organized thirty-five thousand strong throughout the country," a credit manager for L. S. Ayres, Indianapolis's leading department store, observed.[1] Credit departments and credit bureaus operated separately and with fundamental differences— namely, credit departments actually made credit-granting decisions, while credit bureaus merely compiled information for consultation. Together, they formed complementary systems of risk management. "The bureau is in reality but a branch of the credit department and the workers therein his colleagues," a Massachusetts credit manager explained.[2] Though specialized credit departments were the province of larger retail establishments, particularly department stores, specialty shops, and installment houses, small-time merchants were encouraged to adopt the same administrative principles and protocols to manage their credit customers. Within this interlocking system, the concept of financial identity was the primary unit of analysis.

The pursuit of efficient records management was central to the development of credit reporting and authorizations systems during the early twentieth century. "It is not long ago," the credit manager of Manhattan's Franklin Simon department store remarked in 1920, "when not much attention was given to the systematic filing of records, but not so now."[3] The sheer volume and anonymity of credit customers worked against embodied and interpersonal knowledge, encouraging credit managers to rely more heavily on filing systems to recall individual cases and make decisions. Increasingly, personal identities were converted into paper identities, and face-to-face work vied with new forms of paperwork.[4] As the credit manager of San Francisco's Emporium department store observed, "Mass supervision of credits and collections has developed a machinery which is impersonal in its mechanism but is so devised and maintained as to have all the appearance to the customer of intimate personal contact."[5] Thus credit examination was to be converted into a neutral instrumentality while retaining the appearance of the personal touch. A fine-grained account of this process reveals the difficulty with which credit professionals reconciled embodied and textual ways of knowing.

THE CREDIT INTERVIEW

While credit bureaus served as repositories of a community's collective credit data, it was in a store's credit department that consumers opened accounts and divulged the intimate details of their financial circumstances. There, the individual was subjected to the scrutiny of prying credit managers who evaluated and recorded their financial performance, producing the raw material for their financial identity in the local credit bureau. Individual credit accounts were typically opened in one of two ways. Either the customer applied directly for a credit account or, upon checkout, he or she requested that the items be charged. In both cases the sales clerk referred the customer to the credit manager (or, in stores without credit departments, the office manager or proprietor) for consideration. Here, the social nature of credit reached a moment of high drama. Credit, after all, is a measure of social trust. To have one's creditworthiness subjected to judgment is no small matter; it is a referendum on one's morality and social standing. To be refused implies that one is undeserving, deficient, suspect. " 'Touch the question of credit with one of your customers and you have drilled into the most sensitive nerve in his body' is the summing up of the credit situation in the department house," a Chicago journalist reported in 1908.[6] The stakes of a direct request were great for all involved. Both parties stood toe to toe with much to lose depending on the content and delicacy of the answer.

Though credit reporting had done much to disembody and depersonalize financial reputation, personal character was widely regarded as the most useful predictor of credit risk. This view was nearly axiomatic among all creditors, commercial and consumer, well into the twentieth century.[7] The financier John Pierpont Morgan affirmed this in his widely reported (and quoted) congressional testimony during a 1912 money trust investigation. Asked whether credit was "based primarily upon money or property," Morgan corrected, "No, sir; the first thing is character."[8] The questions that early twentieth-century retailers asked in determining a customer's creditworthiness were the same as those posed in the 1880s: "Does the buyer live within his income and pay his bills promptly; or will he incur obligations without the means to meet them? Is he honest? Is his family extravagant? Did he leave a good record behind him when he moved? If unfortunate enough to lose his present position will he pay up old scores when he can?"[9] Where credit was liberal and the recovery of debts difficult, it was the borrower's perceived honesty and morality that mattered most. Character, a prominent retail credit expert declared in 1927, was "the greatest of all assets."[10]

Even the staunchest advocates of rational credit management cited character as the sine qua non of creditworthiness. When James G. Cannon, a New York banker and one of the most respected proponents of credit reform, spoke before an audience of young men and women at Packard's Business College in 1898, he presented an orthodox explication of character that emphasized its uniqueness and authenticity as a marker of identity. "You can not jump into a character as you would into a suit of clothes, unless it be an assumed character. The man with an assumed character is a hypocrite, whom we all despise."[11] But to the untrained eye, character was a nebulous and easily concealed quality, one that required new technologies—or a skilled credit manager—to decipher. Instead of abandoning character as a hopelessly elusive trait, retail credit managers looked for it in the speech and body language of their customers. As Cannon instructed the Packard students, "Turn the X-rays on your characters to-day and see what they reveal."[12]

To penetrate the mysteries of the financial self, the modern credit manager relied upon a wide array of textual sources, from personal correspondence and credit reports to newspapers, local and national business forecasts, references, and information provided by applicants. Yet textual sources did not supplant one-on-one meetings with prospective customers. The personal interview remained a privileged investigatory technique long into the twentieth century. For all of their insistence on textual protocols, few credit managers trusted credit reports over their own powers of direct observation. The credit interview was not only an administrative ritual during which customers offered up their basic personal and financial information; it was also an opportunity for the credit manager to take in the general appearance and disposition of the applicant. In looking for physical markers of deceit, credit managers, like poker players, looked for their adversary's tell. To be creditable was to be credible. An astonished writer for *American Magazine* recounted how a credit manager quickly appraised the trustworthiness of a "well-dressed young man" as he filled out an application card. "After looking at the man and the card, the credit man can guess that the man doesn't own a home, is living somewhat beyond his means, is selfish, therefore not well-balanced—inclined to please himself at the expense of somebody else—and should not be trusted too far."[13]

Describing the work of the credit manager in almost erotic terms, one professional explained, "The credit man comes into more intimate contact with the customers of a house than any other man, his relations are most delicate, he touches a man where he is most sensitive—on the question of his character and his ability. He must be pre-eminently a man who can handle people, who can reach their real selves."[14] It was only through direct interaction that the credit man could probe beneath the surface of mere facts and figures to discern the true character of the individual. "In versatility they rank with the diplomat," one writer boasted of credit managers, "and their keen perception in judging human nature excites admiration and makes Conan Doyle's Sherlock Holmes look like a miserable four-flusher."[15]

Yet judging by appearances cut both ways. The early trade literature is dotted with cautionary tales to prove this point. "A customer may reside in an elegant mansion in which he has not a single dollar of equity," one writer warned, and he "may be the loudest-voiced individual in church service, and yet be wearing the livery of the Lord only to serve the devil."[16] For precisely this reason some credit experts discouraged interviews. As critics noted, interviews ran counter to the depersonalized objectivity of rational credit assessment and gave silver-tongued rogues the opportunity to bamboozle the credit manager. Commenting on the relative merits of interviews and credit reports, Earling came down on the side of the latter in his foundational 1890 text. "When we have cold-blooded facts to deal with," he reasoned, "at least we accept them as facts and our cool reasoning faculties and judgment alone are exercised, and our sympathies are in no wise appealed to or endangered."[17]

If the written credit report compressed social reputations into text, the credit interview was designed to compress a lifetime of social interactions into a brief, unnatural encounter with a single individual. The credit manager's office was often described as the "sweat box," suggesting the panic these dreaded ordeals induced among applicants. "I have seen worthy applicants for credit trembling with fear on being introduced to an austere, sour-faced credit man who acts as though he were conducting a trial by jury," a San Francisco credit manager remarked.[18] Financial modesty was deeply ingrained, and many customers, particularly those who had never been subjected to commercial credit reporting, did not understand the new norms of credit assessment. "Women especially have such a terror of these interviews," one writer noted, so much so that some refused to open accounts. "They think that all their private history and personal secrets will be brutally exposed to the examination of a cold-blooded person who will delight in prying into their personal affairs."[19] In one case a woman who sought to purchase a Chinese rug complained to her husband, "Why, a young man in the credit office asked me the most personal questions, all about you, our children, and positively insulted me," resulting in her boycott of the store.[20] Not surprisingly, credit managers inspired fear and resentment among customers of both sexes. "The credit man," a Denver attorney remarked with wry humor, "is described, by some people, to be a cold-blooded heartless creature, possessing some of the characteristics of the porcupine and the pole-cat—hard to skin, very offensive when thoroughly aroused; usually found secured in huge cages in down-town department stores."[21]

Indeed, the location of early credit departments in dingy basements and attics hardly inspired confidence. One writer was "astonished beyond measure to see some of the dens and caves of the early days in which credit men are housed, which carry the misnomer—credit office, and to which the public are invited."[22] One indication that credit managers had gained professional legitimacy was their relocation to more spacious and well-lit offices with private rooms in which to meet customers. "Interviewing customers at a railcounter or window has long ago been eliminated by the most modern Retailers," one expert attested in 1929.[23] Still, closed-door interviews were not standard for all applicants. In some stores customers were assigned to consultation rooms with varying degrees of privacy, from open to secluded, depending upon their desirability. Those making large purchases at one Denver furniture company, for example, were escorted into an "overstuffed living-room suite" to rest and recover before beginning to "discuss the credit angle of the transaction."[24] Noting that applicants "at ease physically" were "more at ease mentally," the credit manager of Cleveland's May Company instructed interviewers to be sure that the customer "does not stand up, but is comfortably seated."[25] The décor of the room was also taken into consideration. "The walls are a restful color scheme," the authors of one textbook recommended, "and the decorations, while interesting, arouse confidence—photographs of the family, a fishing scene, a college diploma."[26]

It was imperative that credit managers pacify their customers, not out of empathy but to lower their defenses in the interest of extracting as much information as possible. In taking an application from a prospective customer, the credit manager discussed personal matters that many found disconcerting. Those who spoke intimately with fawning sales clerks often clammed up when set before the credit manager. While questions about a husband's occupation embarrassed women of middling or lesser means, they insulted "the dowager or society matron" who considered the source of her spouse's income beneath discussion.[27] When a new account was opened by a married woman, as was often the case, many retailers sent a letter of confirmation to both the home residence and the husband's office, a practice that, a St. Louis credit manager attested, saved the store the "grief" of dealing with a sneaky wife or a controlling husband.[28] Ascertaining an applicant's wages was complicated not only by the resentment it might stir in the applicant, but also by the unwillingness of employers to divulge the sums they paid their employees. Even the seemingly innocuous matter of recording the applicant's full name risked effrontery.

Tact and a winning personality were the most effective tools in the credit manager's repertoire. In dealing with a broad range of social and professional groups, the successful credit manager was a dynamic personality who mixed easily with people from all walks of life. Unlike commercial credit reporting, which was relegated to business owners, consumer credit reporting tracked anyone who sought retail credit, from the millionaire industrialist to the earnest young shop clerk. Though in principle each credit application was a mere transcription of facts, in practice the credit interview was tailored to meet the social expectations of different clienteles. As one credit manager explained, "It is asinine to use the same procedure in conversing with, say[,] a lady of social standing, whose husband is an executive in a well known firm, and a problematic stenographer, who resides in the apartment house district."[29]

Ironically, to access the inner character of their customers, credit managers relied upon the same superficial charms deployed by the worst swindlers. While taking the application, the credit manager sought to engage his customers in self-revelatory dialogue. Disarming conversation, rather than "point blank questions," was by all accounts the most productive way to obtain information from the applicant. "Anyone can get information of a certain kind by asking direct questions in a direct way and putting them down in a cold, unfeeling manner, with an 'I know-you're-dishonest-anyway' attitude—working the customer up to such a murderous frame of mind that the least he can do is to refuse to buy if he does get credit," one writer attested. "But the man who can talk to a customer pleasantly and interestedly about his affairs and circumstances, getting a fact here and an admission there, until he has all the information he wants, without a direct question, will secure more complete and reliable facts than those obtained by a brutal, straightforward examination, and will add a friend and perhaps a customer to the house."[30]

Through casual talk, credit managers were able to ascertain valuable details bearing on the applicant's financial obligations, such as the number of children or adult dependents in the family and whether they owned (or were paying off) an automobile. Equally important, though a more delicate matter, the credit manager might learn the names of the applicant's relatives and friends, who could be harried if the customer left town without settling his or her bills. Credit experts repeatedly stressed the importance of getting this information at the time of the application. Easy to obtain while the customer was sitting in a position of supplication, it would not be forthcoming once the goods were out the door. Some credit managers also recorded a physical description—"such as build, height, complexion"—and comments about the applicant's personality, which were kept "for use in identification at some later date."[31]

As women entered credit department work in growing numbers during the 1910s, they began to conduct interviews as well. Female credit managers were thought to be especially adept in dealing with certain constituencies, particularly "young unmarried girls employed in offices and shops down town, who have decided tendencies to live beyond their means." The problematic "working girl," one writer suggested, could be turned into a responsible and profitable credit customer through the "grandmotherly" counsel of a credit woman.[32] Pandering to the prejudices of the male credit establishment, some women suggested that their natural sociability and weakness for gossip gave them a distinct advantage in such work.[33] While female credit managers had gained legitimacy in the eyes of their male colleagues, their authority was challenged at times by chauvinistic customers who demanded to speak with a male superior. In one such case, a derisive male customer erupted, "What kind of a d—d High School business is this, etc.?," when a credit woman attempted to question him.[34] Credit women, even more than their newly professionalized male colleagues, relied on their (male) employers to back up their authority. Such paternalistic support was motivated less by egalitarianism than an interest in protecting less costly female labor.

If tact was essential to cajole applicants to lay bare their financial circumstances, it was even more important when credit privileges were denied. Rejecting an applicant was a minor art in itself. Those who were turned away for credit were still desired as cash customers, and no retailer wanted to send an angry applicant into the community to spread tales of injustice and ill will. Not infrequently credit managers found themselves embroiled in marital battles that tested their powers of diplomacy. When vindictive husbands shut down charge accounts to embarrass their wives or when profligate women ran up accounts to spite their husbands, it fell to the credit manager to deliver the unhappy news to the abused party.

In refusing a credit account, the credit manager's greatest difficulty was providing a satisfactory explanation. Customers who were declined due to a poor payment history in that particular store could simply be shown their ledger card as evidence, but when decisions were based on reports made through the credit bureau this became problematic. The retailer often did not know the source of the unfavorable information (credit bureaus used codes to protect the identity of retailers), and if he or she did, was unable to tell the declined customer without implicating another merchant who assumed his or her reports to be confidential. Under such circumstances, a declined customer could only be referred to the credit bureau to resolve the matter. One of the conveniences of credit bureaus was that they kept the credit manager's inquiries secret, preserving the illusion that his or her approval was a matter of kindness and personal trust. The alternative, by which individual merchants called in a "reporter" to investigate a credit applicant, immediately alerted the customer to the credit manager's skepticism and threatened to embitter the customer. Yet declines, even properly handled, could place retailers in an uncomfortable position. As a San Francisco bureau manager noted, "An indignant customer, particularly if it be a woman, will visit each store in an effort to determine which one made the derogatory report, creating commotion and embarrassment."[35]

By the late 1920s credit managers were urged to dispense with the artifice of treating credit applicants as if they were the beneficiaries of a royal privilege. "The time was," a Philadelphia publisher recalled, "when to say: 'I have a charge account at Wanamaker's, or at Strawbridge and Clothiers, or McCreery's,' might have been a mark of distinction," but with so many thousands in possession of "a collection of coins or means of identification by which they can walk into one store or another and charge merchandise," this privilege had lost its aura of exclusivity.[36] In this new environment of virtual entitlement, the retail credit manager was a service professional, and an unfriendly or heavy-handed credit interview was simply insulting. Though the American public remained largely unaware of the complex information infrastructure that facilitated their credit purchases, the credit man was its most conspicuous, and in many cases the only, visible instrument of its operation.

CREDIT FILES AND THE NEW VISIBILITY

While personal encounters remained an essential mode of credit evaluation during much of the twentieth century, the information recorded during these interactions—along with ledger reports, public records, and newspaper clippings compiled by credit bureaus—all served to textualize (and thereby depersonalize) credit relationships. "We once could watch our credit as it browsed about in Tom, Dick & Harry, or on the backs of those individuals, much as a good shepherd watches his sheep," a Dallas credit manager recalled in 1921. "But today the pasture is too big. . . . There are a great many more sheep to the square inch than once there were."[37] It was a rare credit manager who would turn down the opportunity to size up an applicant in person, but textual records became increasingly important to track the identities, personal circumstances, and financial behavior of consumers in dense urban centers and porous outlying towns alike.

Where the storied credit man of old relied upon his superior powers of memory and intuition, the new credit professional turned unabashedly to his files. "A good credit man cannot remember each name on his ledgers, when they contain thirty-five to forty thousand in number," a St. Louis credit manager acknowledged in 1915, "hence he relies more or less upon his records, and feels very secure in knowing that they have not been kept in a hap-hazzard [sic] manner."[38] The transcript of an individual's personal and financial information, housed in the files of credit departments and credit bureaus, came to replace the living person as an embodied index of trustworthiness. Touting the objectivity of the national association's sixty million shared credit files in 1930, one writer marveled, "Their faces are not there—only their records."[39]

During the early twentieth century, credit departments and credit bureaus adopted state-of-the-art filing and recordkeeping technologies to reconstitute and control the disappearing consumer body. The development of office filing equipment underwent dramatic changes at the turn of the twentieth century. Until this time business records were preserved in ledger books, pigeonholes, spike files, and assorted boxes, all of which were limited in their capacity to compile, combine, and retrieve information. Records contained in ledger books, for example, were entered chronologically as the volume filled, thus requiring supplementary indices to locate information scattered throughout multiple volumes. Likewise, documents housed in pigeonholes or bundled in boxes required time-consuming unpacking and rifling whenever information was needed. The introduction of card file systems during the late 1870s (pioneered by the librarian Melvil Dewey) and vertical filing during the 1890s permitted more flexible and efficient recordkeeping, with far-reaching implications. The resulting "filing revolution," as the business historian JoAnne Yates has explained, not only accommodated the growing demands of business correspondence and corporate management, but also opened up vast reservoirs of underutilized or forgotten information within organizations.[40] These new filing systems, as Yates suggests, revolutionized the idea of information as something easily stored, handled, located, and useful in contexts previously too cumbersome or expensive to exploit.

One of these contexts was consumer credit surveillance. Advances in filing technology permitted retailers and credit bureaus to document the identities and activities of large populations with greater ease and precision. By the 1910s card file systems were standard in both credit departments and credit bureaus. Within such systems, individual consumers were represented by a single master card on which their full personal and financial information was transcribed. Though the format of such cards varied considerably among credit departments and credit bureaus, all contained fields for the subject's name, address, occupation, and income. Additional information, such as the individual's marital status, age, length of time at his or her current residence and occupation, status as a renter or homeowner, names and addresses of references, bank accounts, lists of credit accounts and balances with other merchants, and notes regarding the individual's character or appearance, was also recorded. Credit bureau files, unlike those of credit departments, also included codes to indicate the individual's overall credit rating and payment habits at various stores. The greater flexibility of card files, coupled with the widespread use of the telephone at the turn of the twentieth century, pushed the credit rating book toward obsolescence. "The method using the rating book is the oldest," one writer noted in 1915, but was "fast becoming the most unpopular method."[41] By the 1920s rating books had fallen out of fashion.[42]

At the same time, card filing systems were perfectly suited for the use of credit limits in store credit departments. Merchants had always imposed mental limits beyond which they would not extend credit to an individual. But the concept of formalized systems for ascribing exact parameters was new at the turn of the twentieth century. By assigning each customer a maximum allowance for credit purchases, a sum based upon information gathered in the credit application and noted on the master card, store credit could be rapidly approved as long as customers remained below their limit.[43] Each credit purchase was authorized by clerks in the credit department who simply referred to the credit limit as indicated on the individual's file card. "Now, when the account reaches the limit placed upon it by the credit man," a New York credit manager explained, "some sort of code or signal is used to call attention to the fact that the account has reached the danger mark."[44] Acting as an automatic silent alarm, credit limits freed credit managers from the burden of personally approving all credit purchases, while allowing them to approve new accounts quickly and with little risk by assigning nominal credit limits.

More important, credit limits provided retailers with a new technique for differentiating among their customers and tailoring individual service. Limits were assigned without the customer's knowledge and could be strategically adjusted over time to accommodate the prompt-paying, to discipline the negligent, or to choke off the dishonest. As safeguards against overextension, credit limits could function as blunt instruments or elaborate systems of fine-grained distinction. At Wanamaker's in Philadelphia, for example, more than forty different codes were used to identify various credit limits, exclusions, and exceptions among the store's thousands of customers. These included limits for specific departments and a "U" code to indicate that the customer and the store had arrived at an "understanding."[45] In cases where a customer sought to exceed his or her proscribed limit, the credit manager was called in to reevaluate the account, which usually involved a request for additional information concerning the customer's employment, income, and ability to pay.[46]

In addition to master card files, credit departments and credit bureaus often maintained separate "watchdog" cabinets. These miscellanies housed snatches of derogatory information—divorces, bankruptcies, lawsuits, accounts of irresponsible or immoral behavior—gleaned from newspapers, court records, and public notices. In some places the watchdog cabinet was built directly into the primary filing system. This was the case in Grand Rapids, Michigan, where the local bureau's 250,000 master cards included a concealed compartment in which news of legal trouble or immorality (for example, "moonshine activities") was kept.[47] Such "pick up" material, as a University of Kansas business researcher referred to it, included "building permits, marriages, births, deaths, suicides, divorces, and 'personals'" clipped from newspapers by "alert" bureau secretaries.[48] This information might not have an immediate impact on an individual's credit standing, but it was held as evidence for future use, reflecting the obsessive, all-encompassing nature of such work. The proprietor of one credit bureau admitted to developing a "pet hobby" for newspaper clippings, which he filed in specially made envelopes. Over time he collected so much negative information that individuals described in the files could be evaluated without further consultation.[49] By the late 1930s the accumulated newspaper clippings of some credit bureaus were touted as a valuable resource in their own right.[50] "Every possible source of information is used to keep this great reference library of personalities alive," the author of a 1938 article in *Reader's Digest* explained. "The newspapers in your town are scanned. So are trade journals. *Variety*, magazine of theatrical people, is a gold mine of data for New York and Los Angeles. Every clipping, favorable or unfavorable, that might affect an individual's ability to pay is cut out and pasted on a card."[51]

As the credit manager's gaze shifted away from the corporeal customer and into the filing cabinet, "visualization" became the mantra of rational credit management. The new principle of visibility was linked to the introduction of "visible" card file technologies during the first two decades of the twentieth century (figure 4.1). Developed and marketed by the Rand Company (which merged with Kardex in 1925 and with Remington in 1927), visible filing systems were designed to display file cards in columns, held upright on rotary panels or laid flat in pull-out trays.[52] Each card overlapped the next in the column, and the names of customers or account numbers appeared on the exposed margins. To access the full information on a given card, the column of overlapping cards above it was simply flipped up. Compared to "blind" card systems that required users to thumb through, extract, and replace cards, visible systems allowed their users to quickly scan

Figure 4.1 Kardex visible filing systems were used in the credit department of Stix, Baer & Fuller, a St. Louis department store. Authorizations were communicated to floor staff through pneumatic tubes, which can be seen on the back wall. (Kardex brochure, 1920s. Courtesy of the Hagley Museum and Library)

the margins for the desired card and to view its contents without removing (and possibly misfiling) anything.

Visible systems also accommodated color-coding schemes to quickly distinguish among classes of customers. As was common, a Massachusetts department store indicated individual credit limits with colored discs attached to each file: red for no credit, black for $25, blue for $50, green for $100, and gold for $150 or more.[53] During the 1920s Rand visible file systems were marketed with their own transparent celluloid tabs in various colors for this purpose. The color coding of cards or ink could also be used to mark poor performers. In one system all customer files were initially recorded on white cards but changed to blue if the subject became problematic and to red if turned over to collections. Significantly, files converted to blue or red were permanently tainted, never being returned to white.[54] By linking credit authorization with internal accounting systems, notably those that tracked the diminishing returns of unpaid bills as they "aged," accounting itself became a technology of disciplinary surveillance in many department stores.[55] Such systems allowed creditors to identify gradations of unprofitable customers and to dun them accordingly.

The impetus toward standardization also extended to the development of uniform credit forms. Early trade publications and textbooks offered many examples for emulation. In 1920 the national association established a Credit Literature Department, which compiled albums of sample application blanks and reference sheets for the use of its membership.[56] While serving as a guide to the collection of customer information, standardized forms were found to have unanticipated advantages. Interestingly, credit managers reported that individuals who balked at disclosing their financial condition verbally gave the same information willingly when presented with a blank application form.[57] While consumers blanched at personal interrogation, they bowed before bureaucracy.

Standard forms bearing the local association's official seal were also thought to exert a disciplinary effect on the applicant by giving the impression of perfect efficiency and cooperation among a town's merchants. By using forms of identical color and format, one writer claimed, customers beheld the credit manager as "a wide awake progressive one, in touch with the other Credit Men in his city and therefore in a position to get immediate verification"—in other words, not one to provoke with pointless bluffs or false statements.[58] While credit managers continued to scrutinize their customers in personal interviews, these embodied interactions were increasingly structured by the requirements of the forms themselves. For those who continued to regard credit assessment primarily as an art, standard forms were an affront. "The mediocre credit man can hide behind his form, and will soon lapse into a deadly formalism," thus hampering his ability to coax information from his applicants, one writer argued.[59] In cases where an applicant seemed to be a good risk but was especially reticent, the credit manager might make a show of tossing aside the application and taking an off-the-cuff approach, especially when the same information could be obtained elsewhere, through public records, for instance.

Though many credit experts contended that credit analysis was too complex to ever be reduced to a science, the orderly accumulation of information in visible and other new filing technologies suggested otherwise. Indeed, the standardization of personal identity and financial performance on uniform blanks and file cards, with their gridlike fields, multicolor signals, and coded credit limits and credit ratings, gave the impression of mechanical precision. "It is only within late years that the granting of credit has been placed upon what may properly be called a scientific basis," a textbook noted in 1915, "and though it may not yet have assumed the dignity of a full-fledged science, it will be admitted that the work of a well-managed credit department is now conducted with a thoroughness of method and a certainty of results which characterize scientific processes in other lines of activity."[60] As the information used by credit professionals migrated from embodied memory to vast textual repositories, the entire enterprise of credit analysis seemed to take on a new air of facticity. "Intuition, that mythical sixth sense, has wrecked many a good business," one prominent writer noted, but "facts properly applied never have."[61] Visibility—clearly documented and systematized information—was touted as the antidote to foggy ideas and vague hunches. "A science of credit control is being developed," a writer for a company magazine published by Rand, manufacturer of visible filing equipment, asserted. "In short, executives are demanding and getting a complete picture of activities as they occur."[62]

While the space limitations of card files encouraged the use of code numbers and abbreviations, the narrative mode died hard. Most credit bureau cards included a "remarks" section where information that escaped the proscribed fields could be added. These notes were often derogatory, but in some cases they contextualized an otherwise unsympathetic picture. "The remark column serves in many valuable ways," one writer noted, "but most especially to explain extenuating circumstances, such as 'been sick,' or 'lost crop in floods,' or 'spendthrift,' or 'chronic returner of goods,' etc., which things help to explain the ratings."[63] Amid the drive to systematize and quantify credit information, some found these open-ended narrative spaces confounding. Complaining that most reports were filled with the cross-reference "see remarks," one member carped, "Why not put the entire narrative in remarks?" Here the ongoing tension between codification and qualification, science and art, was again dramatized. Defending the remarks section—and humanity itself—against standardization, one longtime credit manager responded, "When the histories of men and movements, can be made interchangeable by the mere insertion of a few figures or dates, then will 'personality' be dropped from the dictionary and the names will all be 'robot.' "[64]

COMMUNICATION TECHNOLOGIES

Whatever form the information stored in the master files took—narrative, code, or clipping—it was only as useful as it was quickly accessible. To meet the time-sensitive needs of their members, early twentieth-century credit bureaus evolved into sophisticated communication command centers. By the 1910s the telephone was the bureau's primary technology. Describing the mechanics of a "model credit bureau," one writer explained, "The important matter of accessibility to the credit bureau means to a great degree the telephone."[65] By the late 1920s many credit bureaus answered 90 percent or more of their report requests via telephone.[66] In addition to answering incoming credit inquiries, credit information was collected and verified through direct calls to employers, landlords, neighbors, local merchants, and utility companies. During the 1920s many bureaus made significant investments in telecommunication upgrades. The local bureau of

Omaha, Nebraska, for example, was equipped with ten inbound telephone lines and twenty direct lines to credit departments throughout the city, while a Washington, D.C., bureau installed fifty telephones to answer the 16,000 inquiries per month it was receiving in 1926.[67]

By the mid-1920s city credit bureaus operated multiline telephone stations with direct lines to the credit departments of the city's major retailers. Similar systems were common in credit bureaus throughout the nation.[68] The local bureau of Pittsburgh, Pennsylvania, became one of the most advanced in 1928 when after six months of study by Bell Telephone engineers it was specially equipped with 160 telephone lines, expandable to 300.[69] The credit bureau in Fort Worth, Texas, answered more than 58,000 reports in 1925 at any average cost of 34.5 cents per request. With a staff of sixteen, including eleven women, requests were usually answered within five minutes. Those for individuals with an updated record on file could be answered almost instantly, while new arrivals or out-of-town visitors might take up to half an hour.[70]

Technological innovation, however, did not remove the human element from credit work. At the center of the credit bureau's filing and communi-

Figure 4.2 Operators answer calls for credit information at the Merchants Credit Bureau of Detroit. (*Credit World*, December 1927)

cation systems were live operators who answered telephones, pulled master cards, and conveyed information to the local merchants and credit departments (figure 4.2). This work was largely performed by women whose hands and voices bridged the mechanical gulf between the paper files and open lines. Women served not only as "switches," as the historian Kenneth Lipartito has noted in reference to the early telephone industry, but also as the motherboards of early data processing systems.[71] In a San Francisco bureau, for example, two sets of files were positioned on either side of the operator so that, with "many thousands of credit records" at her fingertips, "she seldom need[ed] to rise from her chair."[72] Either standing or sitting (sometimes in wheeled chairs), operators in many large bureaus wore headsets with long cords tethered to switchboards, allowing them to move among the file cabinets to locate individual records as inquiries were received. Operators were typically assigned to a limited range of the alphabet (surnames beginning with A through D, for example), which distributed the work among many sets of hands and permitted each to develop a degree of familiarity within their domains. The following scenario—a response to an incoming call from a local department store—illustrates the operator's work in a Milwaukee credit bureau:

> "Hold the line a moment, please," responds the Credit Bureau girl, whereupon she goes to the steel files, pulls out one of the many drawers, extracts the desired card from a multiplicity of records, and returns to the telephone. She answers, "XX-23," meaning that I. Shure Skinem is absolutely unworthy of credit and that others are anxious to learn his whereabouts. "Thank you," says the girl of the Wide Awake Department Store as she hangs up the receiver, smiling, no doubt, because she has saved the boss from a poor credit customer.[73]

Just as credit departments sought to foster goodwill among their credit customers, credit bureaus worked to impress their local members with the convenience and utility of their reports, which presumably justified the time and expense of participation. Stressing the importance of courtesy when providing telephone reports, the manager of the Harrisburg, Pennsylvania, credit bureau asserted that the "credit reporters" working the phones "should be girls whose voices give off smiles."[74]

The introduction of telautograph and teletype machines during the late 1910s offered a new channel of rapid communication between credit bureaus and their members. The former, patented by Elisha Gray in 1888 and a forerunner of the modern facsimile machine, transmitted handwritten messages; the latter, developed during the early twentieth century and adopted by the Associated Press in 1914, transmitted typewritten messages. Both sped service by allowing operators to read incoming inquiries rather than wait to have the names and addresses spelled out. Messages could also be sent and received asynchronously so that time was not wasted waiting on the telephone or by interruptions from incoming calls.[75] Additionally, the machines permitted bureau operators to send reports or special bulletins simultaneously to a number of different retailers instead of requiring separate telephone calls.[76] A single teletype report took one minute to send, compared to five on the telephone. Allaying concerns about new technology's effect on its female operators, the manager of the Grand Rapids credit bureau reassured his colleagues, "We don't believe the girl is more tired working on the telautograph than she might be on the telephone."[77] Both systems also allowed store credit managers to silently submit inquiries to the local bureau without offending the customer, who might be standing nearby.

Store credit departments, like credit bureaus, also relied upon specialized communication technologies to send and receive credit information. In addition to outgoing lines that connected to the local credit bureau, many large retail establishments maintained their own elaborate internal communication systems between the store's credit department and its cashiers and managers on the selling floor. Two different systems, the electrical and the pneumatic, vied for supremacy during the early twentieth century.

The electrical system, produced by National Cash Register Company, was essentially an in-house telephone system through which sales associates or "inspectors" called operators in the credit department to authorize a waiting customer's credit purchase. Authorizers in the credit department had ready access to the store's credit files and, after quickly consulting a customer's record, either approved or declined the request. By 1920 one

Minneapolis department store had 120 telephone stations throughout the building. When a credit sale was requested, an inspector pressed a button that produced a flashing signal in the credit department. If approved, the credit operator pressed an "O.K. button" that automatically stamped the charge slip. According to the credit manager of the Minneapolis store, 95 percent of credit authorizations could be answered immediately and the remaining 5 percent that required closer scrutiny were referred to the credit manager, taking on average about two minutes to produce a decision. The electric system had speed in its favor, but it was also riskier because information conveyed orally was vulnerable to misunderstanding and error, particularly with similar-sounding names and addresses. According to an "error form" kept in one store, telephone operators were hindered by the ineptitude of sales clerks and inspectors who spoke too quickly, overly loud, "indistinctly," or even "unnecessarily."[78] Stressing the importance of employing only experienced operators as authorizers in the credit department, the Minneapolis credit manager boasted that the "girls" in his store "can get the name and address and amount more accurately over the 'phone than they could if they were looking at the ticket."[79]

By contrast, the pneumatic system, produced by the Lamson Company, allowed credit requests to be physically sent to the credit department in carriers via pressurized tubes.[80] Though slower than the electrical system, the pneumatic system offered greater accuracy because authorizers were able to review the original charge slip. Touting the virtue of direct inspection, an advertisement for Lamson's "belt type pneumatic tube desk" announced, "No sale is authorized unless the slip is legible in every particular and agrees with the central credit record."[81] Arguing for the superiority of the pneumatic system, a St. Louis credit manager explained, "The whole thing sums itself up in two words—Visible Authorization—you see the check you are approving and keep it in your office."[82] Unable to compete with the lightning speed of electricity, the efficiency of pneumatic systems was improved by the introduction of "mechanical separators" that enabled credit requests to be routed directly to the credit department instead of through multiple intervening stations. By installing baskets to receive the carriers consecutively, the pneumatic system permitted authorizers to answer requests in the order in which they were received, which, as proponents argued, stood in contrast to the electric system's randomly blinking switchboards.

If the pneumatic system surrendered speed to accuracy, the waiting customer's time was compensated with a modicum of privacy. Unlike the electric system, which required that a sales clerk or inspector announce the customer's name, address, and charge amount into the telephone receiver, the tube system was entirely discreet. Illustrating the desirability of privacy—and the violation caused by the electric system—a credit manager recalled, "One day one of the wealthiest ladies in the city came to me and said: 'Mr. Jackson, I have been trading here for a great many years and I don't see why it is necessary to call my name out in the presence of everyone every time I make a purchase.'"[83] As another advertisement proclaimed, "Customers Like the Quiet Dignity of LAMSON Authorizing."[84] Additionally, as some credit managers noted, the electric system was open to a rudimentary form of identity theft, as an unscrupulous person within earshot of the sales clerk speaking into the telephone might hear the cus-

Figure 4.3 The credit bureau and its filing cabinets were at the center of local consumer surveillance networks. (*Credit World*, July 1933)

tomer's name and go to another department to make fraudulent purchases under that account.

During the first half of the twentieth century the consumer credit gantlet involved an array of human and mechanical techniques to extract and manage credit information. Together these diverse points of contact—personal interviews, filing systems, standardized forms, telephones, and vacuum tubes—brought individuals into networks of communication over which they had little control or knowledge (figure 4.3). Those who bought on credit were automatically entered into the credit reporting system; it was not optional. "No matter whether you know it or not, whether you approve or disapprove," the manager of the Milwaukee retail credit bureau explained in 1922, all those credit customers received a rating of " 'prompt,' 'slow' or 'never pay' " in the bureau's 400,000 records. "Just which category you belong to, is dependent upon the manner in which you discharge your obligations."[85]

Despite the millions of coded records documenting the personal and financial lives of Americans in every part of the nation, the idea that credit assessment could be fully textualized and automated was doubted by practitioners. The development of consumer credit reporting was characterized, above all, by fundamental tensions between vying forms of knowledge: embodied versus textual, intuition versus science, singularity versus standardization, subjectivity versus system. Recalling a lifetime of retail credit work, a Massachusetts credit manager marveled at the rapid progression from cumbersome ledger books to rapid telephone communication that he had witnessed since his start in 1886. "But the inventive genius of man has not yet produced a robot which can judge between a desirable and undesirable applicant for credit," he concluded in 1935.[86] The fantasy of the robot credit manager stirred mixed feelings: it signaled the perfection of the science of credits and the obsolescence of the credit professional. Twenty-five years later, the introduction of computerized credit scoring would turn this fantasy into reality and challenge fundamental understandings of creditworthiness.

5

"You Are Judged by Your Credit"

TEACHING AND TARGETING THE CONSUMER

During the first half of the twentieth century professional credit managers established a national credit reporting infrastructure that operated with impressive efficiency. But the institutionalization of credit reporting was more than the sum of its affiliated bureaus and information-processing technologies. It was not enough for credit bureaus and credit departments to merely identify, track, and quarantine slow payers and deadbeats. "We must go further," the president of the national association argued in 1918. "Let us preach the doctrine that credit is character, and that a person who willfully abuses his credit and refuses to heed the warning must become an outcast in the business and social world."[1] While working to solve organizational and technical difficulties, credit managers evinced a more profound role in American life as agents of moral instruction. As Herbert Marcus, cofounder of the upscale Dallas department store Neiman-Marcus, remarked, "It is the credit man who pricks the conscience of the public not to the realization that they are false to others, but that they are not true to themselves."[2]

From the beginning, credit reporting organizations recognized the disciplinary effects of their surveillance. Commercial reporting firms such as R. G. Dun and Bradstreet were hailed (and reviled) for their ability to coerce merchants into abiding by business norms and practices that suited the interests of wholesalers and jobbers. The disciplinary power of commercial credit reporting continued to guide the personal behavior of business people well into the twentieth century. When the sociologists Robert and Helen Lynd investigated the everyday life of small-town America during the mid-1920s, they were struck by the degree to which such surveillance shaped the lives of its inhabitants. The "sensitive institution of credit," they observed in their landmark *Middletown* study, "serve[d] as a repressive agent tending to standardize widening sectors of the habits of the business class— to vote the Republican ticket, to adopt golf as their recreation, and to refrain from 'queer,' i.e., atypical behavior."[3] Credit relationships, they realized, imposed normative standards that regulated the conduct of individuals even in seemingly noneconomic domains of life.

The disciplinary power of credit surveillance was equally seductive when turned on consumers. "From a moral standpoint," the national association's educational director observed, "I know of no single thing, save the churches, which has so splendid a moral influence in the community as does a properly organized and effectively operated credit bureau."[4] Indeed, the mere suggestion that a bureau was operating could exert marvelous power, as illustrated in 1920 when the retailers of a "fair-sized city not far from New York" cashed in with a well-executed ruse. By advertising the formation of a local credit bureau—though none actually existed—they received "a small flood" of payments from dilatory customers.[5] Such disciplinary effects were nullified as long as the bureau's existence remained shrouded in mystery. Unlike the highly secretive world of twenty-first-century credit reporting, early credit bureaus and associations went to great lengths to publicize their work. In 1926 even the local association of desolate Mesa County, Colorado, was "keeping their name constantly before the public" with one hundred eye-catching metal signs affixed to telegraph poles.[6]

At the same time, credit professionals actively worked to educate the American public on the moral foundation of credit. "The people understand issues such as disarmament, child welfare, sanitation, biologic living, eugenics," the president of a California credit association complained in 1928, "but it does not know that *credit is a moral issue*, at least it does not conceive of it as such."[7] Ironically, as credit relationships became institutionalized and impersonal, merchants found it necessary to remind their customers of credit's basis in individual trust and confidence—in other words, its social embeddedness. The message of credit morality, delivered via mass media and in countless private consultations throughout the country, equated credit and character in explicit terms. Abandoning the notion that one's moral disposition was inborn, credit professionals turned from nature to nurture to produce profitable customers. "By the proper use of credit machinery there is no doubt that stores can train customers into new and better ways of buying, thus cultivating and maintaining their confidence and good-will," the credit manager of Gimbel's department store asserted in an influential credit text. "This should be the great object whenever credit is granted."[8]

While seeking to direct consumer behavior through education, credit department managers also explored new methods of statistical analysis to systematize credit evaluation and to channel new business. Beginning with crude generalizations based on occupation, retailers developed increasingly sophisticated techniques for analyzing the financial behavior of entire classes of customers. By the 1920s credit managers were no longer simply tracking customers and making authorizations; they were also mining their rich repositories of customer information for the purpose of targeted sales promotions. In this way systematic credit management began to develop into an instrument of social classification and control with broader implications.

THE DEMOCRATIZATION OF CREDIT AND
THE DISCOVERY OF HONESTY

Amid an explosion of credit spending during the 1910s and 1920s, credit professionals sought to prove their expertise and to silence critics who questioned the safety of spiraling consumer debt. Total outstanding U.S. consumer credit debt reached nearly $8 billion in 1929 and, after bottoming out below $4 billion in 1933, soared to more than $10 billion in 1941.[9] As both champions and disciplinarians of debt, credit professionals found themselves in a precarious position. Like modern beer companies whose advertising celebrates immaturity while preaching responsibility in lame disclaimers, credit managers authorized an orgy of consumer spending while espousing the virtue of self-control. This dubious stance was maintained through a double discourse that extolled the honesty of the American people as a whole, while asserting the moral imperative of credit at the individual level. At the center of this discourse was the idea that credit had been "democratized."

The proliferation of installment plans and charge accounts, as well as personal loan and finance companies that emerged during the 1910s, liberalized credit and granted millions of Americans unprecedented access to goods and services, all heralding a rising quality of life. The democratization of credit was explained by its proponents as a world-historical transformation. "With the gradual progress of civilization," a 1917 credit textbook explained, "men learned to trust each other; and out of this increasing confidence of man in his fellow-man the use of credit was gradually developed."[10] Where credit was once the preserve of wealth and hereditary privilege, according to this narrative, the average American had emerged from the "creditless masses" to assume his or her birthright as a fully enfranchised citizen-consumer.[11] As Morris R. Neifeld, a finance company statistician and tireless booster of consumer credit, pronounced, "John Smith, individual, is here; and just as his journey from nonentity to entity has been through the democratization of rights and liberties, so his progress has more recently called for the democratization of credit."[12]

If retailers found efficiency in trusting one another, they found prosperity in trusting their customers. The democratization of credit rested largely upon the newly "discovered" honesty of the American people. "The old adage, 'To Trust is to Bust,' is now forgotten," a New Orleans credit association official remarked in 1930. "A new mode of living is offered and enjoyed by everyone."[13] Noting that Americans were "not only honest, but scrupulously so," a journalist observed at the turn of the twentieth century, "The people as a whole are trusted as they never have been trusted before in all the world's history."[14] By the 1920s the near-universal honesty of Americans was touted in popular magazines and trade publications. Trustworthy citizens, estimated at 98 or 99 percent of the buying public—but never lower than 95 percent—were hailed as the engine of national prosperity.[15] In 1927 the chairman of General Motors' finance committee effused, "How little opponents of consumers' credit appreciate the fact that inherent honesty and character of our wage earners constitute the great foundation upon which consumers' credit rests!"[16]

As an ideological position, the democratization of credit ran parallel to the development of systematic credit evaluation. In principle, standardized checking procedures obviated personal relationships in questions of credit granting. Like the one-price system, which replaced haggling and democratized mass retailing during the 1870s, universal credit verification policies were democratic in that they eliminated preferential treatment among different classes of customers. The individual citizen-consumer thus assumed equal rights under the law of objective credit reporting. Whether a customer was rich or poor was far less important than whether he or she honored financial obligations and made timely payments. As a Kansas City credit manager instructed, "All applicants for credit should be treated just as nearly alike as possible," leaving no room for personal favoritism.[17] Of course the blind justice of large, impersonal stores could also produce absurdity, as illustrated by John D. Rockefeller's credit check in 1913. Still, the concept of democratization was a powerful narrative. It would be invoked by later advocates of statistical credit scoring, who saw new computational technologies as a tool for expanding credit markets and for eliminating unfair biases.

CREDIT PROPAGANDA AND CONSUMER EDUCATION

The flourishing of retail credit management coincided with World War I, providing an opportunity for credit managers to join their message of credit responsibility with that of national allegiance. During the war the U.S. government asked retailers to curtail credit sales to free up capital flows, and at the 1918 convention the national association pledged its support.[18] While the message of thrift and conservation was no boon to business, credit managers turned the patriotic call to their advantage, using the opportunity to assert the civic duty of prompt payment from their credit customers. Retailers in Boston and other parts of the country sent letters to their charge customers urging them to contribute to the war effort by paying promptly. In New York the retail credit men spoke directly to the public through the newspaper.[19] Commenting on the credit manager's increased responsibilities during the war, Edward A. Filene, head of the Filene's department store in Boston, told a gathering of his peers that in "back of all the guns, back of all the military preparations, the winning of the war depends upon the morale of men, and credit men understand men and know how to influence them."[20]

At the same time retailers also worked together to impose community credit policies, including regular billing cycles that required customers to settle balances in now-familiar thirty-day intervals. Many credit customers accustomed to running open-ended accounts had to be informed of these new expectations. "In the majority of cases the merchant is dealing with customers having little or no knowledge of business principles," a Cleveland retailer reminded his colleagues in 1918.[21] Some customers apparently left balances because they assumed, erroneously, that by settling in full their account would be closed. "The war gave retailers the long-sought for opportunity to stir up their delinquent accounts and to give a new sense of responsibility to charge customers who disregarded the terms upon which the accommodation was extended to them," an Indianapolis chamber of commerce journal noted.[22]

As World War I drew to a close, local credit associations launched a new propaganda war on the home front. "Prompt pay" or "pay up" campaigns were run in cities and towns throughout the nation to alert the public to the credit policies of local merchants and the policing role of credit bureaus.[23] More important, prompt pay campaigns impressed on the public the moral obligations of credit and reminded them that individual credit ratings were entirely self-made. One's credit rating was not assigned by local merchants or the credit bureau, they asserted, but represented a purely factual transcription of one's own financial behavior. To possess a favorable credit rating, as repeatedly explained, was entirely up to the individual consumer. "Being trusted is a wonderful feeling," an advertisement published by a Nebraska reporting organization read. "If you don't believe it, have some merchant refuse you credit, on account of your credit rating, which you have made for yourself."[24]

While some exalted the freedom and pleasures of credit, others portrayed the frightful costs of irresponsibility. "A person with bad credit is terribly handicapped all through life," a Minneapolis advertisement warned. "Day after day he and his family are shamed by the refusal of merchants to give him credit. Goods are delivered to his house C.O.D., for the neighbors to whisper about."[25] Though many campaigns consisted of little more than a series of newspaper advertisements and didactic editorials, others were multimedia extravaganzas. A 1919 "Pay-Up Time" campaign in Oklahoma City, for example, included a 40,000-piece mass mailing, 900 "two-color cards" placed in local store windows, "colored slides" presented to movie theater audiences, posters affixed to the dashes of the city's streetcars, and fifteen billboards, including six that were "painted and electrically lighted."[26]

Prompt pay campaigns quickly spread throughout the country, and in 1920 the first of several national "Pay Your Bills Promptly" campaigns was organized.[27] These campaigns addressed the following concerns, summarized by an Oklahoma credit manager: "How are we, as credit men, going to impress on the minds of our customers the high dignity of a charge privilege; the importance of this trust to them and the consequent detriment to their credit standing if they should fail to carry out their trust and permit their accounts to become delinquent?"[28] During 1927, hundreds of cities participated in a weeklong national campaign involving some 2.6 million leaflets and tens of thousands of store displays, which together delivered the message of credit responsibility to an estimated forty million people.[29] Ironically, during these campaigns dedicated to thrift and restraint some stores ran sales promotions.[30]

Over the next decade the message shifted from the narrow issue of prompt payment to the more expansive concept of "credit consciousness." In 1930 the national association launched a $7 million media blitz to cultivate a "national consumer credit conscience."[31] Retailers and credit bureaus also turned increasingly to radio to broadcast their message. Regular programs such as *Creditime* in Philadelphia and *Character Builders* in Houston were aired for mass audiences, and in 1939 the popular comedy duo

Lum 'n' Abner were enlisted to take up the subject of credit in a series of nationally syndicated episodes sponsored by General Foods.[32] According to a 1930 survey of some 400 credit bureaus, 38 percent were running prompt payment campaigns, while 30 percent of those that did not were interested in starting one.[33] During the same year the credit bureau of Boston entered a float in the city's tricentennial parade that displayed the equipment of the "modern credit bureau," including steel filing cabinets, a switchboard, and a desk. But the coup de grâce was a massive replica rating book placed atop a fifteen-foot-tall pedestal, on which it was announced in gold letters, "Our files contain bill paying habits of over 1,250,000 charge customers."[34] Surely some of the event's two million spectators took note.

Some local credit bureaus advertised their importance by moving into more-impressive office buildings. Such aesthetic improvements, like those intended to elevate the work of store credit departments, were intended to impress both retailers and consumers with their scale and displays of technological prowess. During the late 1920s the Cleveland bureau, for example, moved into a 7,000-square-foot space with a palatial Spanish archway, broad halls, glass-enclosed offices, and a well-appointed reception room. "Many an irate debtor coming to the Bureau in search of a battle has lost most of his belligerence at this impressive, friendly entry," the bureau secretary noted. "The impressive view gives visiting debtors a new respect for credit, and brings them into this or that Bureau executive prepared to respect and trust whatever that executive has to tell them."[35]

While appealing to the public through broad-based campaigns, credit managers were also urged to turn their personal interactions with customers into teachable moments. The credit interview in particular was regarded as a key opportunity to press home the morality of financial behavior. During the application process, the credit manager laid out the terms of the account and discussed the consequences of neglected payments. The importance of "doing some credit education in the interview," a 1941 guidebook explained, was due to the fact that "the great mass of consumers are so abysmally ignorant of what constitutes a good credit rating."[36] Even those who paid in cash were taken aside for counseling. In former times, they were told, it might have been admirable to abstain from debt, but it was now an outmoded and ill-advised habit. Charge accounts, after all, were not simply a convenience; they were necessary to establish a record of creditworthiness with local merchants. Those without "a scratch of a pen in any credit department, or in the credit bureau," would not be able to prove their reliability on some future day when an accommodation was requested.[37] Noting the exclusion that cash payers faced, one writer taunted, "It seems, you see, that the 'boob' who pays cash isn't known."[38]

The message of credit morality was a peculiar form of counterpropaganda set amid a sea of advertising designed to incite consumer desire. "Advertising on a gigantic scale has made this a nation of automobile users, toothbrush followers, and orange, lemon, and prune consumers," the authors of a 1928 credit text noted. Thus, it followed, "Advertising can make the United States a nation where good credit habits are a characteristic of the population mass."[39] Not surprisingly, in communicating their message, credit professionals adopted the same strategies as those pushing consumption—notably, scare tactics that appealed to the social anxieties of aspirational Americans. In 1930 a national association leader proposed advertising that would "awaken and accentuate feelings of inadequacy and insecurity" among those inclined to let their bills pile up, presenting prompt payers in contrast as "superior people."[40] Fear rather than reason would be necessary to teach credit responsibility. "The delinquent must become infra dig, socially disapproved, tabooed."[41]

By then the pedagogical force of shame was well recognized. Citing the example of Listerine antiseptic mouthwash, whose advertisements so effectively dramatized halitosis-induced social death, credit professionals recommended similar tactics to change consumer attitudes toward credit: "If Listerine produced a social consciousness that changed the breath of a whole nation you can produce a credit consciousness that will change the buying habits of your people, teach them to pay promptly, happily, and systematically."[42] The danger of social stigma, long a staple of collection letters and dunning notices, had by the 1930s developed into a veritable literary genre.[43] It was also thoroughly exploited in prompt payment campaigns and in "credit-education inserts," enclosed in customer statements with titles such as "You Are Judged by Your Credit" and "Your Credit Record Follows You!"[44] Another campaign introduced the concept of "Q.C.," or questionable credit, as a source of humiliating gossip. A 1937 advertisement pictured a small group of women huddled in conversation with the warning, "Friends Talk About 'Q.C.' Too!"[45]

In the end, consumer credit education was hegemonic in the terms attributed to the Italian communist Antonio Gramsci.[46] Credit professionals sought to win consent through ideological inculcation rather than through compulsion. "The positive credit man realizes that the best results in business can only be obtained by 'consent,'" one admitted. "In this world we cannot 'compel' people to do very much."[47] Where the force of law exerted only a superficial influence over individual behavior, credit education functioned as an ideological discourse of self-government, as theorized by Michel Foucault. "No Nation can successfully legislate morality," a manager at Boston's R. H. White department store argued in 1921. "There must be a training of the mind and a development of the soul if the result is to be permanent."[48] During the same year the national association established a Credit Education Department whose sole purpose was to foster public awareness of credit behavior. In less than a century the great chain of credit and its deeply personal relationships had become

Figure 5.1 Public awareness campaigns asserted the credit bureau's importance and the morality of creditworthiness. "Character," considered the cornerstone of creditworthiness, was at the center of the national association's official seal. (*Credit World*, August 1932)

unfamiliar to many Americans. The nineteenth-century interdependencies of Squire Jones, butcher Muggs, and shoemaker Cripps had lost their valence in a twentieth-century world of strangers. Consumers had to be reminded of credit's moral nature and taught to feel shame at neglecting the faceless institutional lenders that "trusted" them (figure 5.1).

One of the most striking aspects of early consumer credit reporting, particularly from the perspective of our privacy-obsessed age, is that it generated so little public reaction. While many credit applicants feared and resented the credit manager's interrogation, and some were annoyed by administrative delays caused by authorizations, there is nothing to suggest that Americans were particularly concerned about their privacy or the circulation of their personal information among credit bureaus and credit departments. This is conspicuous in light of the vitriol hurled at the nineteenth-century mercantile agency system. Why investigations into the business reputations of Americans incited more outrage than those aimed at consumers cannot be readily answered. Perhaps a half century of mercantile credit reporting, coupled with the American consumer's eagerness for instant gratification, mitigated this.

Though credit bureaus and local associations went to great lengths to advertise their role in the community, much of the American public seems to have remained ignorant or indifferent. Analyzing popular press coverage of consumer credit reporting between 1910 and 1930, one scholar has suggested that opposition was neutralized, or at least kept at bay, by its portrayal as a "necessary, proper, non-threatening" check.[49] In this way, credit surveillance was presented as a socially redeeming technology that merely affirmed the goodness of honest Americans while exposing the professional crooks and the arrogant rich. A rare expression of discontent appeared in a San Diego newspaper in 1930. "No reasonably honest citizen objects to it," the writer observed. Such blind acceptance was "picturesque proof of the docility with which we submit, for the sake of business, to a spy system which we would indignantly resent if it were set up on behalf of government."[50] Underwriting the credit bureau's disciplinary surveillance was an ideology of financial morality that privileged the economic welfare of the nation over that of the individual.

CREDIT AS A BUSINESS BUILDER

Systematic credit management originated as a progressive movement to quarantine poor credit risks. "By cutting off the unworthy from credit," Earling observed with satisfaction in 1904, "we are in a position to extend it to the worthy more than we ever could before."[51] Retailers had of course long understood that all debtors are not equal. In his 1869 manual Samuel Terry identified eight "classes" of consumers that could be trusted very little, if at all. Along with the usual suspects—the lazy, extravagant, and immoral—these included the gravely ill, minors and married women who were not legally responsible for their debts, single men without any family attachments to keep them from fleeing, transient strangers, and the middle aged ("say fifty years of age") who had no savings and had not made arrangements for retirement.[52] For Terry, writing just after the Civil War, the safest risks were agricultural producers with harvests in hand. But by the turn of the twentieth century things had changed. Retailers looked to the growing ranks of office workers, managers, and civil servants with steady incomes and a taste for modern amenities and respectability. By the 1920s the safest credit prospect was no longer the farmer but the salaried professional man and his wife, with an established credit history and good references.

The formalization of credit reporting encouraged merchants to classify their customers with new specificity. By adopting affirmative-negative systems in which *all* customers—the good, the bad, and middling—were rated, merchants were forced to parse degrees of creditworthiness between the clear-cut extremes. This proved enormously difficult. Credit rating cards filled with positive ratings inspired a "grand and glorious feeling" among retailers, as one admitted, but it was the "mixed card" that screwed up "the bland countenance of even the cheerful credit man."[53] Yet the "mixed card" was not the exception; it was the rule. The vast middle ground between the best and worst risks required constant decision making. It was inhabited by "slow payers" and "honest debtors" who neglected to settle their accounts out of either thoughtlessness or privation, or perhaps both. The difference was important; those who dragged their feet for no good reason were a constant source of woe for retailers, while those who were punctual but temporarily strapped might be counted on in the long run. As James G. Cannon asserted, "It is the man who pretends to be good and is not, who must be refused and avoided."[54]

Since wealth ensured nothing and character was a variable impossible to isolate or measure systematically, credit professionals turned to other metrics to predict trustworthiness. Occupation, with its connection to income both in terms of amount and regularity, attracted special interest. In 1925 a Bloomingdale's executive offered the following hierarchy of credit customers in descending order of desirability: "the salaried class; the wage-earning class with permanent positions; journeymen laborers whose occupation is seasonal and whose employment changes frequently, such as painters, carpenters, etc.; and last, the day laborer engaged in unskilled work that is seasonal and where the employer changes frequently."[55]

While such impressionistic, commonsense distinctions had long been made by experienced merchants, the relationship between occupation and risk began to receive systematic analysis. In 1929, for example, a southern department store classified its losses by occupational categories and was surprised to report that office workers and merchants, two classes typically considered safe, were responsible for the largest percentage of annual losses.[56] The next year the Bureau of Business Research at the University of Texas sponsored a detailed analysis of credit risk according to occupational categories. Using data gathered at twenty-three department stores in that state, the report found, perhaps not surprisingly, that "business executives" received the highest average sums of credit, while "railroad employees" received the lowest and took longer than average to pay off the balance.[57] Though suggesting that the findings might be useful in establishing credit limits, the author cautioned that occupation was an unreliable variable in isolation.[58]

In 1931 Paul D. Converse, a University of Illinois business professor and marketing scholar, headed the first of two studies that investigated the relationship between occupation and credit ratings. Rather than examining correlations based upon actual ledger data, however, he tested the *perception* of such correlations among credit managers and credit bureau operators. Converse's first study polled 250 credit bureaus and a number of department stores in the Midwest. While noting that the stability of an individual's income—even more than the sum—was the most important factor in determining credit ratings, the survey revealed that credit managers used occupation to make inferences about individuals. Police and firemen often had steady incomes, for example, but received "fair" credit ratings because in the eyes of credit managers "they feel that the public is under obligation to them and hence they take all the time they want to pay their debts."[59] Likewise, credit managers approved individuals employed in lines of work that they regarded favorably. One such profession was schoolteachers, whose salaries, albeit modest, were known and could be counted on. "Teachers['] accounts have proven to be the best type of account to solicit," one credit expert attested, citing the value of teachers' directories for locating new customers.[60] When referring to city directories for business, the same writer instructed, the occupation listed for each individual could be used to "eliminate the classes you do not wish to solicit."[61]

That many merchants used occupation as a guide for making credit decisions is illustrated by a comprehensive list of "high skip risk" occupations published in a 1934 text coauthored by the president of the national association. This catalog of the damned is essentially an inventory of transient, marginal, and morally suspect work:

Actors, acrobats, amusement park employees, aviators, barbers, bootleggers, carpenters, constables, collectors, contractors, circus performers, concessionaries, detectives, deputies, farm laborers, grain buyers, grain elevator employees, fruit and vegetable peddlers, healthseekers, jockeys and other race track workers, coal miners, hotel employees, insurance salesmen, instalment house outside men (collectors and canvassers), labor union workers, loan company officers and employees, club and lodge organizers, marines, musicians, painters and paper hangers, persons "in business for self," post office employees, pool room owners, road construction laborers, pawnbrokers, petty business men in restaurant, cleaning and pressing, automotive and other traders requiring little capital, powder employees, telegraph operators, civic employees, prize fighters, sailors, boardinghouse keepers, nurses (both sexes), colored ministers, professional baseball players, salesmen on commission, section hands, soldiers, structural steel workers, truck drivers, brokerage house employees, taxicab drivers, second-hand merchants, waitresses.[62]

Converse repeated his study a decade later with a larger national sample and the cooperation of the Associated Credit Bureaus of America. Again confirming the primacy of steady income in determining risk, he reported much anecdotal evidence to illustrate the use of occupation in making moral inferences. "In some instances occupation does indicate something of the character and sense of responsibility of workers," he conceded. "For example, teachers, retail salespeople, nurses, doctors, and ministers usually have a considerable sense of responsibility. On the other hand, this sense seems to be developed to a relatively lower degree among workers in some occupations—for example unskilled laborers, waiters, miners, barbers, janitors, and painters."[63]

While Converse was quick to add that exceptions always disproved the rule, many credit managers, particularly those faced with thousands of accounts to review, found such generalizations useful. At a retailers' convention in 1930 the question arose as to whether all new credit accounts should be investigated through the local credit bureau. According to one participant, occupational classifications were used to screen applicants in his store without the use of credit reports. While schoolteachers "as a class" were immediately approved—"Some of them are slow but none of them are bad"—painters and laboring men were summarily refused "nine times out of ten" without even calling the credit bureau.[64] "A man's occupation, profession or business, or his color, should neither bar him from credit nor render him eligible," a 1928 credit text instructed, but such information, the authors concluded, was also not to be ignored.[65]

Another mechanism for screening applicants was geography. Individuals from affluent neighborhoods received special consideration despite the trouble that the well to do so often caused. "Some houses take note of where purchases are sent," a dry goods dealer admitted in the late 1880s, "and whenever a fashionable address appears on their shipping books write the lady at that address offering to put her name on the credit list."[66] A primitive method of target marketing, this practice was old and commonplace. The same principle, however, also worked in reverse. The residents of entire buildings or streets were denied credit privileges by some retailers. "Houses have bad credit reputations as well as people," a Chicago reporter explained. "On a block with a dozen apartment houses some will stand well in the neighborhood, some badly. They may all look the same outwardly, and the rents may be the same, yet there will be a marked difference." Unfortunately, those who bought or rented in "a 'wrong house'" soon discovered that they could not find a local merchant willing to sell to them on credit.[67] One credit text indicated that the "veteran credit man" should "possess a complete and accurate mental map of his community" to recall "blacklisted neighborhoods and sections."[68] In this way individuals remained embedded in distinct social geographies and might be punished for the collective sin (real or imagined) of their neighbors.

Here it is essential to note that the development of retail credit reporting was largely devoted to the world of white Americans and European immigrants. This is not to suggest that African Americans were excluded from all white credit networks, but to underscore the normative assumption of whiteness among early credit professionals. African Americans did have access to retail credit during the early twentieth century, though, as the historian Martha Olney has shown, they turned in greater numbers than whites to installment purchases with their heavy down payments and looming threats of repossession.[69] The limited participation of African Americans in the white credit economy can be inferred from the pages of early credit rating books. There, as already noted, the names of African Americans—never many in any volume—are identified by racial designations, thus suggesting their exceptional status.[70] In at least one case, an African American credit-reporting service was proposed to counteract such invisibility. The plan, advertised in 1914, was to publish a credit rating guide specifically for the African American community in Chicago. "We as a race are generally discredited when applying for favor, and in the loop district are turned down without consideration," an advocate of the plan explained in the *Chicago Defender*. "Why? Because the credit man cannot satisfy his house, having no way to distinguish between the honest man and the crook."[71] The service does not seem to have come to fruition, but it highlights the racial segregation of American credit relationships.[72]

During the first half of the twentieth century, racial and ethnic prejudice was not only unproblematic for white credit managers; it was also
codified as standard operating procedure. "Negroes, East Indians, [and]
foreigners" were at the bottom of the hierarchy of credit risks, above only
"men and women of questionable character" and "gamblers," according to a
1922 guidebook prepared by the Associated Retail Credit Men's Association
of New York City.[73] Another guide, published several years later, noted that
"Negroes, Mexicans, [and] East Indians" were considered "substandard
risks." Though the authors insisted that skin color was not destiny when it
came to creditworthiness, they stopped short of disavowing the utility of
such "presumptions."[74] Given the widely accepted moral conception of
creditworthiness, the classification of non-whites as substandard risks was
more than just an acknowledgment of economic inequality. Risk hierarchies
doubled as moral hierarchies, converting racist assumptions about the honesty, thrift, and work ethic of non-whites into bureaucratic facts. Instructional texts such as these legitimized established racial prejudice in the
world of consumer credit. So, too, did boilerplate office forms with prompts
to document the credit applicant's racial identity.

Along with race, many retailers considered nationality—a proxy for non-
native ethnic prejudice—to be a useful marker of trustworthiness. In the
mid-1920s, for instance, an installment jeweler analyzed 3,000 accounts on
his books and reported that English, Canadian, and German customers
were the most reliable (ahead of bona fide "Americans"), and that Greeks,
Russians, and Italians were the least trustworthy, even less than "colored"
Americans.[75] Inferences based upon national origin were not simply the
hobbyhorse of an eccentric merchant. A 1922 U.S. Chamber of Commerce
guide to credit bureaus cited nationality as a piece of circumstantial evidence to consider in determining an individual's "responsibility."[76] One reason the customer's full name was requested on credit applications, according to New York City's retail credit men, was "because the first name often
reveals the nationality of a person, and this is an important item of information to the credit grantor."[77] The precise use of such information must have
been obvious to contemporaries, because it is not specified.

As credit professionals cast about for reliable metrics, some even considered intelligence. Citing the results of intelligence tests administered by

the French psychologist Alfred Binet, a *Credit World* contributor alerted his colleagues to the horrifying implications. A full third of the general public were "in the lower registers—feeble-minded, borderline and dull." The dimwitted could never be considered safe credit risks because, as the writer explained, they could hardly manage their own affairs.[78] In a subsequent article the same writer reported the result of intelligence tests administered to U.S. troops during World War I that distributed mental ability by occupation. Not surprisingly, the army tests confirmed existing prejudices among credit professionals. Doctors and engineers appeared at the top of the scale, while laborers, union workers, and tradesmen were at the bottom.[79] If intelligence was any guide, these tests suggested that individuals engaged in low-skill and transient work were less capable credit customers.

Merchants also paid attention to the buying patterns of individuals. "Close buying" customers who were attentive to prices and insistent upon receiving the full weight of their meats and dry goods were viewed favorably as credit risks, even if they were irritating to deal with. On the other hand, waste and mismanagement were viewed with a jaundiced eye. "Thus," a journalist explained, "the woman who uses a 5 cent telephone call to order a 5 cent article, or who sends in two telephone calls in rapid succession, the second asking 'please hurry that butter,' for instance, is apt to begin to get in that store's bad graces."[80] Sudden changes in spending behavior were also noted. If a man who purchased only necessities "suddenly begins to buy 'jimcracks,'" then it was thought likely that he had fallen into a foolish courtship or had taken to abusing his credit privilege. In general, early efforts to classify credit customers and to monitor spending behavior were punitive insofar as their primary purpose was to identify and exclude the worst risks. During the 1920s, however, as retailers sought to expand and intensify their sales, credit managers turned to customer behavior not only for warning signs but also for sales opportunities.

CUSTOMER CONTROL

Nineteenth-century mass retailers were wise to the fact that credit customers spent more in their stores than cash customers. Cash customers, it was often pointed out, flitted from store to store and were nobody's customer. Though some merchants continued to resist credit, clinging to visions of a cash-only utopia, others embraced the intimacy of the creditor-debtor relationship. The latter viewed charge accounts as a means to insinuate themselves into the households of their customers, a position that if handled adroitly fostered goodwill and bonds of loyalty, if not actual fealty, to the store. While interviewing a New York retailer in 1889, an out-of-town journalist was shocked not only by the lengths to which the proprietor went to accommodate his fickle credit customers, but also by his seemingly masochistic desire "to swell their number." When the incredulous visitor could not grasp the point of such solitude, the retailer revealed his motive:

> Mercy! what a greeny you are. . . . A lady who has a bill at our store spends all the way from fifty per cent. to five hundred per cent. more than if she hadn't. Not only does she buy every thing she wants at this store where she has a bill, passing all the rest every day, but she buys things she does not always want and can not always afford. You need not laugh; men do the same thing. We are glad to get men to run bills here as well as women.[81]

Working for such retailers and installment houses, the credit manager—and the credit reporting associations that many participated in forming—initially performed a security function, interrogating applicants and scanning the information environment for evidence of deceit. As early credit professionals continuously lamented, they were viewed rather resentfully by their employers as a necessary evil, a costly and unproductive expense that was merely tolerated as a preventative check.[82]

Seeking to gain the respect of their employers, credit managers began to assert their contributions as "business builders." This new identity, which crystallized after World War I, reflected their increasingly service-oriented role, taking credit applications and promoting the advantages of their establishment to new customers. A sharp economic downturn in 1920–1921 was an additional spur. Faced with contracting profits, credit managers were urged to "get the sales point of view" and to adopt "constructive credit" policies that placed customer service at the forefront.[83] In daily customer interactions, which so often touched upon delicate personal matters, the credit manager was in a unique position to cultivate grateful and loyal patronage. While such intimacy also lay at the heart of the Pauline injunction to "owe no man anything"—debt, after all, placed borrowers in a compromised and weakened position—credit managers sought to turn this vice into a virtue. "The Credit Department," a national association figure proclaimed, was "the tie that binds the customer to the store."[84]

As an agent of salesmanship, the credit manager's first responsibility was to solicit new customers. Newspaper advertising and mass mailings were common, but a more judicious approach involved direct mailing campaigns aimed at only the best prospects. No stones were left unturned in compiling lists of potential customers. Credit managers scoured city directories and telephone books (both of which could be used to target individuals in desirable neighborhoods) as well as birth and marriage records, tax lists, building permits, automobile registrations, hunting licenses, and bank and college directories. The local newspaper was also a cheap and handy source of business leads. "Watch the newspapers for live items such as: 'Mrs. Jones is going to Europe'; 'John Smith elected to head Elks,' or 'Miss Evelyn Blank is home from Vassar.'"[85] Engagements, weddings, birth announcements, real estate transactions, and news concerning the social, political, business, or church activities of prominent community members were all eyed for angles to drum up new business. No publication was too marginal or sacrosanct. Credit managers looking to solicit new business even pored over the *Congressional Record*.

Among these myriad sources, one was particularly cherished: credit rating books. The widespread adoption of telephones by credit bureaus diminished the prevalence of rating books by the 1920s (inquiries and reports were conveyed orally), but where they existed merchants eagerly mined them. Credit managers compiled lists of individuals with good credit ratings in the books and, like the "preapproved" credit offers that flooded the credit card market in the 1970s, sent each a personally addressed letter indicating that the store had opened a charge account in his or her name. "Rating books issued by retail commercial agencies, if available, are especially valuable in that the names of the desired class of customer may be segregated," a Washington, D.C., retailer explained.[86] Merchants recognized the sales potential of credit rating books as soon as they appeared in the late 1850s. Indeed, this "misuse" of the books had been one argument against their publication by pioneering commercial reporting firms such as R. G. Dun and Bradstreet.

The transformation of credit information from an instrument of prevention to one of promotion signaled a major development in the history of American business practice. Alert retailers had always scanned their ledgers for useful information about their existing customers. "Merchants are prone to regard their customers only in the mass; it is better to think of them as units, each of which is a little center of influence that may help to make or mar your future," an unnamed "Tradesman" observed in 1889. He recommended that merchants use a "moderate-sized blank book" to record each customer's name and address, his visits and sums spent, discounts, and "personal peculiarities."[87] Early efforts to record such transactional data were laborious and required an iron will to maintain. Yet their potential value inspired continuous effort. At Wanamaker's in Philadelphia, for example, managers tracked the activity of the store's credit customers by referring to the ledgers at regular intervals. This "plan," in place by 1902, was designed to identify credit customers who had drifted away and who might be lured back to the store with a personalized appeal for their missed business.[88] During the early 1920s, a business consultant urged credit managers to make their "ledgers talk" by analyzing the buying habits of the store's customers and designing targeted promotions.[89]

Mass credit policies, with their generous customer service and elaborate authorization, billing, and collection procedures, were expensive to maintain. But as this consultant anticipated and credit managers soon discovered, the systematic recordkeeping necessitated by mass credit was its own reward. Not only did credit customers spend more than cash customers; they also produced vast reservoirs of valuable information in the process. For unlike cash customers, who came and went anonymously, credit customers submitted their entire personal and financial history to the credit manager in exchange for their trust. New bookkeeping devices developed during the early 1920s also allowed credit managers to track the financial behavior of individual customers with greater specificity. The Elliott-Fisher bookkeeping machine, for example, enabled the "100% informed credit manager" to itemize all of the store's transactions in detailed daily reports. "You not only can tell when purchases are made," according to an advertisement for the system, "but the character of the goods bought, and how and when paid for—*all without* extra work."[90] "I think there is no place in a department store where there is so much record of information that is of value as in the Credit Department of the store," a Detroit sales executive noted in 1926. "It is sometimes difficult to get that information out, but once you have analyzed it and once you have been able to get that information, it is illuminating."[91] The task of extracting such information took on new urgency after the economic crash of 1929.

By early 1930 many credit managers began to turn to their accumulated files to study the buying behavior of customers already on their books. This new practice of systematic analysis became known as "customer control."[92] The basic premise underlying customer control was that a store's established credit customers were its most valuable customers. Previously, credit promotions focused on attracting new customers. But as many merchants came to realize, it was far more difficult and expensive to secure new customers than to simply reclaim those it already had. Mailing lists of the store's existing charge customers, the credit manager of Neiman-Marcus remarked, were "almost invaluable," as they represented the "most fertile channels" for direct advertising.[93] Credit managers thus searched their files for inactive accounts and sent these customers letters urging them to return to the store. In some cases a special promotion was used as a pretense for the correspondence, but more frequently, retailers addressed the recipients as valuable customers who were missed. A San Francisco men's clothing store sent its inactive customers the following letter, which appealed simultaneously to the moral distinction and social leveling of American credit:

Not all of us have our names in the Social Register—
All of us, whether of high or low estate, are catalogued in the
    records of the merchants with whom we trade.
The merchant's faith in his customers is the life of his business. . . .
You who have justified that faith have built for yourself a credit
    record of more value than the Social Register can ever convey.
May we see you again—real soon?[94]

Letters of this kind could be remarkably effective. In 1929, for example, a Minneapolis store drummed up $10,000 in business over four months by simply sending letters to inactive charge customers, a handsome 38 percent return on the cost on the mailing.[95]

One of the first firms to demonstrate the efficacy of customer control was Chicago clothier Capper and Capper. In 1929 the store's addressograph machine was modified to classify the buying habits its existing credit customers. A printed card was attached to a nameplate for each customer, with the position of movable tabs on the frame used to indicate in which departments (suits, coats, hats, men's furnishings, and sports apparel) the customer had made purchases and whether or not a purchase had been made during the previous season. Additional colored tabs indicated whether the customer lived within store's delivery range, bought expensive items, made purchases at any of the store's seven branch locations, or purchased during sales. Female customers were classified separately by marital status and the departments (men's or women's) in which they made purchases.[96] Since women often shopped for the entire family, a pattern of buying exclusively in the men's departments suggested that she might be persuaded to buy for herself as well in the women's department. Conversely, if only buying for herself, she might be persuaded to make purchases for her husband. Using this system to mail personalized letters to different classes of customers, Capper and Capper revived some 3,500 inactive accounts and more than doubled the number of its customers making purchases in more than one of the store's departments during the first year it was used.[97]

As the Depression curtailed consumer buying power, retailers looked to customer control as a way to extract greater sales volume from their tried and trusted customers. As a Bloomingdale's executive remarked in 1931, the credit manager was moved into a "promotional rather than a critical capacity."[98] In 1932 business publisher Dartnell conducted a survey of 415 retailers and found that "the vast majority" had either already implemented a customer control system or were making plans to do so.[99] According to the report, credit-granting stores were at the forefront of the movement. A variety of customer control systems were put into use during the 1930s. Some were manual, such as visible index or loose-leaf systems in which

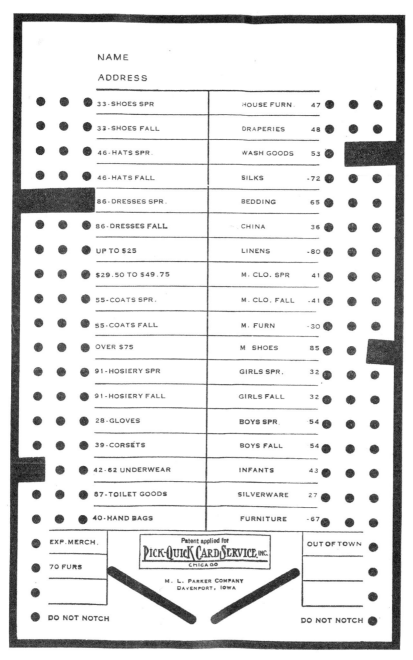

Figure 5.2 A customer control punch card. This system allowed retailers to track the buying patterns of individual store customers, including the seasonal spending, sales totals, and purchase categories of each. (Special report, Dartnell Corporation, 1932)

each customer's sales activity was coded with check marks in small boxes on individual cards or sheets. Each box represented a different field, typically one of the store's departments or the month or season of the year. When a mailing campaign was planned, clerks reviewed the coded cards or sheets and compiled a list of customers meeting the selected criteria. Other systems, however, were mechanical. In addition to the addressograph system used by Capper and Capper and others, sophisticated punch card systems were developed. Punch cards not only permitted more detailed and elaborate classification schemes, but the retrieval process was generally faster and more accurate than that of manual systems, as the punched holes transferred sales and customer information directly from the store's ledgers (figure 5.2). The manufacturer of one such system, Selectric, claimed that "an average office girl" could maintain cards for 20,000 customers and produce an entire customer list in several hours.[100]

Though customer control was initially embraced as a means to revive inactive accounts, its broader applications were immediately apparent. While tracking the purchasing patterns of their customers, retailers were surprised to learn that most buyers concentrated their purchases in one or two of a store's departments, ignoring the others altogether. Customer control was thus turned to the problem of getting customers to spend both more heavily and more expansively. "The ideal system is to have every charge customer trading in all of the major departments of the store," the credit manager of Denver's Cottrell Clothing Company noted, "and the customer's control system is an excellent guide to the purchasing habits of the customers."[101] Customer control allowed retailers to identify departments that individual customers neglected and to design personalized letters encouraging them to visit these "forgotten" departments. In this way, customers who regularly purchased hosiery from the store but never bought shoes might be sent promotional materials directing them to the advantages of the latter department.

In one case, an unnamed Chicago department store sent promotional letters to charge customers who had purchased in the women's ready-to-wear departments but had never bought a coat. "While apparently you have never purchased coats from us, we would like to tell you about 'Shagmoor' coats. These coats are ideal for spring wear—they are dust-proof, rain-proof, and wrinkle-proof, making them particularly good for motoring." Following the mailing, 300 customers from a list of more than 16,000 bought coats for the first time, amounting to sales in excess of $21,000.[102] Information collected by customer control systems was used to produce increasingly personalized entreaties. "We notice from our records that you have made several purchases in our Clothing Department but have not visited our Furnishings Department," a letter used by Cottrell Clothing Company read, adding, "We are now showing some new numbers in Stetson hat [sic] which I am sure will look well with that suit you bought from us recently."[103] By encouraging their active customers to buy in all of the store's departments, they hoped to wrestle money out of the hands of competitors for the same customers.

Likewise, customer control systems allowed retailers to direct promotional mailings to the primary buyer of the account, thus reaching more deeply into an entire family of customers. As already noted, many women did the majority of their family's shopping, buying goods for themselves as well as their children and spouses. However, direct mailing campaigns were typically addressed to the account holder, usually the woman's husband. This presented a missed opportunity on two counts; the man to whom the mailing was addressed was not an active buyer, while the actual user of the account was ignored completely. Using customer control to classify each account by gender and marital status, promotional campaigns could be designed to reach husbands and wives, as well as a family's children through appeals to their mothers.[104]

As customer control became more sophisticated, retailers attempted to further differentiate their credit customers by price line, taste, and average expenditures. Customers with the means to buy expensive items were identified and addressed separately. "Obviously there is little use in inducing a customer to buy a $3,000 mink coat if an analysis of her credit purchases reveals that the top price of previous coat purchases averaged $50.00," a retail trade publication noted, attesting to the utility of customer control.[105] One store demonstrated the usefulness of income segmentation while seeking to boost sales of fur coats. Among the store's 40,000 charge customers, 10,000 female customers who had never purchased a coat but had the resources to do so were mailed invitations to an exclusive one-day private sale. The event produced $25,000 in sales and was a smashing success.[106] Additionally, price buyers (those who waited for sales) and quality buyers were classified separately, permitting retailers to tailor different promotions for bargain hunters and full-price customers. Moreover, customer control allowed merchants to appeal to upper-income customers exclusively, in a way that did not leave them feeling that they were "being lumped with laborers, clerks, women and children and besought to buy, buy, buy."[107] At the same time, individuals in lower income brackets were tracked for promotional efforts. Customers who had recently completed installment purchases or budget plans, for instance, were regarded as good prospects. "This class of people," the credit manager of a Davenport, Iowa, department store noted, "have respect for the credit obligations which they have assumed and are the type which will make the most desirable charge customers."[108]

Customer control sought to reclaim, albeit by mechanical artifice, the personal equation that was lost in the development of impersonal mass retailing. Where once the neighborhood storekeeper had known all of his or her customers and could make recommendations to suit individual tastes, the modern department store was a selling machine that processed thousands of transactions each day. "The individual customer disappeared in the great crowds that thronged the stores," one proponent of customer control observed. "Little attempt has been made to analyze these crowds, to reduce them to the individual customer and know for certain whether or not profits came in equal proportion with numbers. The time for that is coming."[109] Customer control offered a way to personalize mass retailing by appealing directly to the special interests and habits of individual customers. "Never before has it been so necessary that the credit department 'know your customer,'" one customer control advocate asserted. It was necessary, he added, "to know them well enough to promote new business through the contact their account affords to the credit department."[110]

Underlying the development of customer control was a more profound realization: not all customers are equally valuable. In 1930 Robert B. Gile, manufacturer of the Selectric system, conducted a nationwide survey of more than one hundred department, specialty, and men's clothing stores and reported that 40 percent of the average store's customers purchased

77 percent of its merchandise.[111] Several years later another study indicated that 16 percent of charge customers buy 49 percent of a store's merchandise.[112] These stunning findings not only reinforced the importance of courting one's existing customers, but also suggested that whole segments of the buying public were not worth the expense of engaging at all. Indeed, according to Gile, a full 60 percent of a store's patrons produced little or no profit. What Gile and his contemporaries intuited would come to be known as the Pareto principle, or the 80/20 rule, famously codified by management consultant Joseph M. Juran a decade later. Applied to retailing, Juran's concept of "the vital few and trivial many" would suggest that 20 percent of a store's customers produced 80 percent of its sales. By this logic, a retailer was wise to direct its promotional effort to the small but profitable segment of regular customers rather than the "trivial many." Invoking a Dust Bowl metaphor, Gile claimed that so much wasted effort on useless land was akin to "dry farming."[113]

Used to identify the most profitable segments of a store's patronage, customer control facilitated a more sweeping form of market discrimination with important ties to credit rating. The most valuable credit customers, after all, were those who demonstrated their ability and willingness to pay. In one case, a clothing company sought to revive a list of some 2,000 inactive customers by appealing directly to their superior credit status. "When we say you are a preferred credit risk, we mean just that," the promotional letter explained. "A customer to whom we can point with pride, your record here entitles you to a splendid credit rating."[114] In contrast, trouble accounts or individuals with poor credit ratings, for whatever reason, were by definition excluded. The exclusionary effects of customer control were illustrated by a Chicago men's clothing store whose promotional campaigns addressed only its "very best paying customers," roughly a third of its 20,000, with all those deemed "poor credit risk[s]" eliminated.[115]

Customer control developed in credit departments, rather than sales or advertising departments, precisely because it was there that the financial viability of each customer was known, and from which inferences could be made. Within such systems, the credit and purchasing histories of individuals appeared together, one informing the other. As the author of a 1933 business thesis explained, "Credit ratings, credit limit, overdue amounts, dates and amounts of installment payments, chronic conditions in connection with adjustments and returned goods, and similar information" enhanced the value of customer control records as sales tools.[116] As the privilege of credit was diluted through ubiquity, customer control introduced a new and intensified form of target marketing and customer relationship management that fostered bonds of loyalty by rewarding the profitable few.

Yet customer control was complex and required a level of organization and investment well beyond the means of most retailers. Dismissing customer control as "well nigh impossible for any but a group of true geniuses," a St. Louis direct mail expert acknowledged, "It is unquestionably a wonderful thing to be able to write to a large portion of your 100,000 customers each month and say, 'Mrs. Smith, six weeks ago you purchased half a dozen pairs of silk stockings from us, size 8½, and we trust that they have been entirely satisfactory and that we may have the pleasure of selling you some more during the next week when we have a special on two of our leading hosiery lines."[117] By the late 1930s customer control was touted as a powerful marketing tool. "A new technique is now being developed by certain progressive stores which makes a customer of theirs virtually a guinea-pig subject to the most elaborate and ramified classification of customer data the modern punch card equipment permits."[118]

While credit departments were increasingly involved in sales work, credit bureaus were not. Credit departments provided local bureaus with confidential customer information, but the bureaus themselves maintained their function as neutral compilers and repositories. Or, as one journalist put it, "It is like the taking of an X-ray picture; the credit bureau takes the picture and the credit store manager diagnoses it."[119] Early credit bureaus had nothing to do with the promotional strategies of individual stores. Their primary concern was to maintain the support and active participation of local subscribers and to improve the efficiency (thereby reducing the cost) of credit bureau management. It was not until the late twentieth century that computerized credit bureaus began to parlay their valuable databases of consumer information into marketable commodities.

While the specter of mass society loomed in the minds of early twentieth-century politicians and cultural critics, credit managers were already beginning to deconstruct it. In an age of mass consumption and mass advertising, customer control was far ahead of its time. The forces of target marketing that broke up the American mass market during the late twentieth century began with the dissection of local retail buyers a half century earlier. Ironically, the seeds of segmentation were sown in efforts to produce a stable, predictable American mass market—a shape-shifting entity whose close examination highlighted differences rather than similarities among its various constituent parts. The democratization of American mass consumption during the first quarter of the twentieth century thus contained a now-familiar countermovement toward tribalization as consumers were sorted into income, demographic, and lifestyle enclaves. During the 1920s and 1930s credit managers not only demonstrated how personal and financial information could be used to identify and segregate individuals, but also embedded such classificatory schemes within the moral order of credit standing and financial identity.

6

"File Clerk's Paradise"

POSTWAR CREDIT REPORTING ON
THE EVE OF AUTOMATION

"You've heard the term 'credit rating,' but do not think that you have one," *Life* magazine teased its readers in 1953. "Your own financial affairs, you feel, are too trifling." The feature story, published in late December as many Americans piled up holiday debts, illuminated the inner workings of the consumer credit bureau. As millions of Americans took advantage of flush credit to finance homes and automobiles and to furnish postwar suburbia, a vast surveillance network shadowed them. Comparing local bureaus to "branches of the FBI"—and citing the then 1,700 affiliates of the Associated Credit Bureaus of America (ACB of A) as proof of their reach—the *Life* author quipped that this national surveillance regime would "make even the head of the Soviet secret police gnash his teeth in envy."[1] Not only did most citizens have a file in the local bureau, the writer added, but these files contained "the intimate stuff." To drive the point home, the article included an excerpted credit report for a fifty-year-old Cleveland man. The typewritten original, said to have run two single-spaced pages, recounted the subject's involvement in a bar fight during his early thirties (the case was dismissed) and that during his late twenties "excessive drinking, some social gambling and running expensive parties" had compromised his financial and professional standing.

Though American citizens remained largely ignorant of the credit bureau's function and magnitude during the 1950s—a fact that perplexed credit industry professionals—its importance was obvious to the larger business community, including banks and oil companies that had begun launching aggressive credit card programs. Noting that credit bureaus were taking on a "bigger role" in the American economy, *Business Week* reported the impressive scale of their operations. In 1958 the Credit Bureau of Greater New York—the largest bureau in the nation—had 1,500 members, including "most of the city's big retail establishments," and a staff of several hundred employees who used the bureau's 6.5 million individual credit files to answer between 7,000 and 8,000 inquiries each day.[2] Indeed, the postwar credit bureau was a "file clerk's paradise," *Business Week* observed. Hailed as the apotheosis of modern bureaucratic recordkeeping—rivaling even that of Cold War intelligence agencies, as *Life* ominously suggested— the credit bureau had quietly become an indispensable institution in the twentieth-century American economy.

This was a paper paradise, however, one that required an army of office workers to pick through and organize millions of cards, slips, documents, and clippings. Except for the addition of portable microfilm machines (used to duplicate merchant ledgers and courthouse records), answering machines (which gave the bureau the semblance of twenty-four-hour service), and new photocopying devices (to duplicate reports for mailing or for simultaneous in-house use), the technology of postwar reporting remained remarkably similar to that of the 1920s and earlier (figure 6.1). A 1959 government guide to entering the business listed among the necessary equipment only typewriters, a duplicating machine, desks, chairs, steel files, and "a good telephone system."[3] In all cases, credit inquiries required a bureau clerk to physically retrieve individual files and to convey information orally or in writing to waiting subscribers. "Like circling bees extracting and feeding pollen, they would dip into the files, pluck out the appropriate card, and then read the information over a nearby phone," one writer recalled after visiting the Credit Bureau of Greater New York. "The pollen they gathered actually consisted of the private and personal histories of people who planned to charge such items as a pair of shoes, a washing machine or a wedding dress."[4] Inquiries were answered more rapidly with the

Figure 6.1 The Credit Bureau of Greater New York, the largest credit bureau in the United States. (*Credit World*, June 1952)

introduction of conveyer belt systems such as Remington Rand's Kard-Veyer, which literally transported files between bureau clerks and telephone operators, but these systems did not change the fact that credit bureau work was fundamentally about pushing paper.[5]

All of this changed during the mid-1960s when the reporting industry moved to convert its paper paradises into computer databases. The automation of credit reporting was neither simple nor straightforward; it was an enormously complicated and disjointed process that occurred over decades. Still, computerization represented a radical break in the history of consumer credit surveillance, one that affected much more than the speed of reporting. It also affected the categories and moral language of creditworthiness itself. To understand the full impact of computerization and, in turn, the transformation of late twentieth-century financial identity, it is essential to detail the content and circulation of midcentury consumer reports. These standardized reports, and the teeming archives of personal information from which they were assembled, typically contained a broad array of nonfinancial information. The details of one's personal life and domestic arrangements, health, employment, legal affairs, and misdemeanors— all considered essential in judging creditworthiness—sat comfortably beside records of one's past payment history, income, and assets. This information, moreover, was obtained from a wide variety of sources, ranging from merchant ledger data and court records to newspaper clippings and investigative interviews. As the credit bureau's bulging paper files and open-ended narrative reports were converted into machine-readable code, credit information became increasingly reductive and quantitative. Computerization, in other words, converted financial identity into a new form of technological fact.

An examination of midcentury reporting is also essential to grasp the broader role that credit bureaus played in the development of contemporary surveillance. As industry professionals quickly learned, the bureau's rich congeries of consumer data placed them in a unique position as information brokers. Their records were valuable not only to creditors, but also to a wide array of business and government organizations with an interest in risk management and social control. To capitalize on these opportunities, many bureaus systematically repackaged and resold their information to third parties—insurance companies, employers, landlords, and law enforcement—none of whose investigations were directly related to creditworthiness. Even more, during the 1960s some credit bureaus began branching into new promotional services, including prescreening programs and the sale of customer lists, a departure from their established role as neutral compilers of local ledger data. While postwar credit bureaus codified and automated financial identity, as purveyors of consumer data they also emerged as a major player in the new information economy.

THE CONTENT AND THE FORM: CONSUMER
CREDIT REPORTS, 1930–1970

Contrary to the *Life* feature, the main business of the postwar credit bureau was not credit rating but credit *reporting*. Though many early consumer credit reporting organizations did initially publish rating books, most bureaus abandoned these during the early twentieth century. Instead, telephones were used to offer more timely and affordable oral reports to subscribers. (Exceptions did exist, notably Chilton's Red Book in Dallas and the Yellow Book in Minneapolis, both of which were published into the 1960s.)[6] It must be emphasized that consumer financial identity did not circulate primarily in the form of individual credit ratings or scores but as formulaic reports that bureaus conveyed to subscribers verbally and in writing upon request. Such reports were based on a variety of sources, including local ledger data, court records, newspaper clippings, and narrative summaries written by bureau investigators. It was out of these promiscuous textual accretions, in which the personal, financial, and legal intermingled, that the raw material of financial identity was produced.

By the early twentieth century two basic types of credit reports dominated: the trade clearance and the antecedent report. *Trade clearances* were the least expensive and most time-sensitive reports. Sometimes referred to as "in-file" clearances, they were thumbnail summaries of an individual's credit standing based on existing information in the bureau's files. In most cases the information in these reports was conveyed verbally by telephone operators when subscribers called (and often as the customer waited). Some larger firms—department stores, banks, and finance companies—received trade clearances directly via telautograph or teletype machines.[7] Trade clearances included only basic identifying information—name, spouse's name, and current address—and ledger data expressed as a list of open credit accounts with maximum balances and the customer's history of repaying each. Subscribers could purchase updated trade clearances for an additional fee. Updates required a bureau worker to contact the subject's creditors for up-to-the-minute ledger data and, in some cases, to confirm his or her employment, residence, or credit references.

Antecedent reports, by contrast, were comprehensive accounts of an individual's personal, financial, and employment history. Along with the information included in trade clearances, antecedent reports typically recorded the subject's age, race, marital status, number of dependents, current and former employers and positions held, salary and other sources of income, bank account information, whether the subject owned or rented, and any records of bankruptcy or legal action involving the subject. They often included a "remarks" section as well, where supplementary comment on the subject's home life, personality, reputation, employment, or income was provided in terse narrative. Because of the additional effort required to prepare these longer investigative reports, they were more expensive than trade clearances.

Despite family resemblances, the content and style of trade clearances and antecedent reports varied considerably among bureaus before World War II. Even the nomenclature of reports differed from bureau to bureau and city to city, making it difficult to compare local information or to order out-of-town ("foreign") reports. The antecedent report, for instance, was variously referred to as a special report, a complete report, or a standard report. To remedy this confusion the ACB of A and its only serious national competitor, the Retail Credit Company, initiated separate programs to standardize their respective credit reporting forms. Such standardization did far more than merely streamline internal operations and communication between bureaus and subscribers. In effect, the standardization of reports codified the categories of knowledge that determined creditworthiness. The most influential sites of such codification were the standard forms of the ACB of A and the RCC, the leading purveyors of postwar consumer reports.

The Factbilt Standard Consumer Report

During the early 1940s the ACB of A launched a new series of "Factbilt" standard forms. The series, whose very name suggested foundational truth, consisted of forms for more than twenty different types of reports, including trade clearances and antecedent reports as well as personnel reports to be used by prospective employers, tenant reports for landlords, "character reports" for G.I. and Veterans Administration (VA) loans, and reports for credit card–issuing petroleum companies.[8] The gold standard of the series was the Factbilt antecedent report, designated form No. 1 and given the definitive title Standard Consumer Report. Factbilt standard reports included all of the information found in a typical antecedent report, noted above, as well as a separate rubric with questions bearing on the subject's personal character:

Is applicant well regarded as to character, habits and morals?
　Is applicant favorably regarded by employer?
　Any suspicion of illegal practice past or present?

Additionally, the remarks section at the foot of the report instructed the bureau clerk to "give a brief word picture of the subject's history."[9] Such literary nonfiction offered bureau investigators an opportunity to elaborate upon the subject's "marital or other domestic difficulties" or employment problems related to "frequent absenteeism."[10] Though no actual reports from the period are available to analyze, samples in numerous instructional texts offer a glimpse of their content and evolution. Except for minor changes in format and phrasing, the Factbilt standard report of the early 1940s remained largely unchanged for two decades. The subject's race was included in reports well into the 1960s, with "White, Black, Red, Yellow" presented as options in some iterations. In other examples nationality was also indicated, as in "white, American."[11] Responses to questions regarding the subject's morality and reputation varied from perfunctory answers (yes, no, none, and good) to brief comments.

Though the Factbilt series was designed to standardize reporting within the national association, some member bureaus modified the forms to suit their own needs. For instance, the standard report used by a Dallas credit bureau (presumably Chilton's) included space for the subject's credit rating, and the Philadelphia Credit Bureau provided "complete" reports with rubrics for member codes, the name of the subject's landlord, and a remarks section instructing the investigator to provide a "picture of customer's reputation[,] type of neighborhood, etc."[12] The extent to which Factbilt reports were adapted or ignored by the association's members is impossible to know from so few examples. But evidence of deviations at the Dallas and Philadelphia bureaus, both headed by prominent leaders in the national association, suggests that local variation might have been common.

Retail Credit Company's Character Credit Report

Though the ACB of A and its member bureaus were the clear leaders of the consumer reporting industry—they collectively maintained fifty million credit records in 1952—the RCC was an influential rival.[13] Founded in 1899, the RCC was initially organized as a local ledger exchange bureau for Atlanta retailers. After shifting its focus to more lucrative insurance reporting and allowing its credit reporting service to wither during the 1910s and 1920s, the company reentered the field during the 1930s.[14] In 1934 the RCC purchased the Retail Commercial Agency in New York, a firm reputed to have descended from the original Brooklyn-based Selss agency through several changes of hand. The RCC also acquired local bureaus in Georgia and South Carolina, and a Canadian foothold in Montreal.[15] Unlike the ACB of A, which was a network of independent local affiliates, the RCC worked to establish itself as a national reporting agency, though primarily in the insurance business. The firm was incorporated in 1913 and two years later had fifteen branch offices throughout the continental United States.[16] The RCC never matched the annual volume of credit reports produced by the ACB of A's membership, but it was a formidable national competitor and a leader in the postwar reporting industry. Renamed Equifax in 1976, it remains one of the three dominant credit bureaus in the United States today.

Like the ACB of A, the RCC also sought to standardize service through the use of specialized forms for each of its various reports. In the early 1930s it developed what it called the Character Credit Report, which remained the firm's standard consumer report into the 1970s.[17] The RCC Character Credit Report resembled the Factbilt Standard Consumer Report, including a "character" rubric with similar prompts:

Is reputation as to honesty and fair dealing good?

Do you learn of any illegal activities, or domestic troubles? (If so, explain)

Any illness (physical or mental) affecting ability to pay? (If so, explain)

In addition to columns for documenting the subject's credit accounts and payment history, a section for narrative remarks also instructed RCC employees to comment on the individual's neighborhood reputation and to "amplify any unusual information pertaining to domestic troubles, illness learned or other features that would affect earnings or paying ability."[18]

DIRECT INVESTIGATION AND DEROGATORY INFORMATION

Though the standardized reports of the ACB of A and the RCC bore many similarities, their information came from very different sources. Because of its primary focus on insurance reporting, the RCC developed a fundamentally different approach to consumer reporting, one based on direct investigation rather than shared ledger data. Insurance reports traditionally required detailed information regarding an applicant's health, family life, and personality, all of which was used to estimate his or her risk of injury, disease, or premature death.[19] This information was best acquired through direct interviews with the insurance applicant and his or her acquaintances rather than local merchants.

To this end, the RCC employed large numbers of local investigators, or "inspectors," to compile insurance reports, thus creating an information-gathering network that resembled the correspondent system of nineteenth-century commercial credit reporting firms such as R. G. Dun and Bradstreet. By 1968 the RCC had more than 300 branch offices throughout North America and employed 6,300 inspectors.[20] This same infrastructure was also used to compile its credit reports. When the RCC received a request for a credit report, inspectors were sent to interview the credit applicant, his or her family members, and "other logical sources" such as "employers, former employers, references, fellow club members, neighbors and former neighbors, financial and professional people."[21] Unlike ACB of A reports, which relied upon customer account information and payment histories submitted to the bureau by local creditors, RCC reports were compiled by inspectors on a case-by-case basis. Ledger data did not become a significant element of RCC consumer reports until the late 1960s, after the firm acquired nearly sixty local credit bureaus concentrated in the South and the Northeast.[22]

While the main focus of ACB of A reports was the ledger experience of the group's local members, ACB of A bureaus were hardly passive clearing-houses. Factbilt reports, as an advertisement boasted, included "all the facts from anywhere and everywhere."[23] Like the RCC, ACB of A affiliates also conducted their own direct investigations. This was usually the case when fleshing out new or old files. If a report was requested for an individual who did not have a current file, bureau officials hit the phones. The subject's employer, bank, and landlord were all contacted for informa-tion.[24] Landlords were especially prized because they often offered com-ment on the subject's "personal habits" and "manners" as well as his or her record of rent payment, number of dependents, and history at the ad-dress.[25] If the subject's landlord and employer were unknown, bureau in-vestigators called neighbors. And if neighbors were unhelpful, the bureau called a grocer or drugstore "around the corner" to develop leads. "The im-portance of having a thorough knowledge on 'the art' of 'calling around the corner' in order to develop information on the subject, cannot be over-emphasized too greatly," a 1961 manual instructed.[26]

Since direct investigations were largely conducted by telephone, bureau workers honed special techniques to win the confidence and cooperation of informants. "The key to getting information lies in the way you project yourself, either by 'phone or in person," the same manual explained. "By 'phone, your voice must be flexible with exaggerated inflection. You must be extremely polite and considerate, and always businesslike."[27] Investiga-tors were firmly warned against using subterfuge (except when locating "skips") and instructed to identify themselves as representatives of the local bureau. However, they were given latitude in explaining the reason for their call. The recommended half-truth was that the investigator was sim-ply updating or revising the bureau's files, in which the subject's name nat-urally appeared. The subject of the investigation was called only as a last resort, and only if the business with whom the applicant sought credit gave the bureau permission to do so.[28]

Personal visits to the subject's neighborhood were not considered nec-essary for credit reports unless the subject and his or her neighbors could not be reached by telephone, which was sometimes the case in poorer communities where telephones were scarce.[29] The Credit Bureau of Greater New York had "six outside men who travel[ed] in automobiles" to conduct investigations that could not be handled over the phone.[30] Bureau investigators were advised to cultivate trusted informants, to meet privately to ensure confidentiality, and to conceal notebooks or pre-preprinted forms that might "arouse suspicion" as to the inquisitorial purpose of the discussion.[31]

Direct investigations may have been expedient, but they introduced an air of espionage that would come under harsh criticism during the late 1960s. So did the use of "derogatory" reports. Though consumer credit surveillance had long operated on the principle of affirmative-negative reporting—that is, compiling both favorable *and* unfavorable information bearing on creditworthiness—derogatory reports, as their name suggests, singled out only the damning. Such information typically involved news of legal action, default, or criminal charges. This "bias to negative information," as James B. Rule observed in his groundbreaking sociological study of credit surveillance, was common among bureaus and reflected their impulse to quickly identify and quarantine the community's most dangerous risks.[32] "In a way we are like the F.B.I. which keeps a record of people who commit crimes," explained Rudolph Severa, the manager of New York's bureau and one of the most vocal champions of derogatory reporting. "Here we are concerned with people who are poor risks and who might commit crimes against business."[33] To communicate this time-sensitive information, especially suspicious new accounts or sudden heavy buying, many bureaus offered "watch" services to warn local merchants. In 1960, Severa's New York bureau issued between 600 and 800 derogatory alerts each day.[34]

Derogatory information usually entered the files through one of three channels: press clippings, public records, or member feedback. News items regarding marriages, births, divorces, deaths, business sales and promotions, accidents and calamities, and arrests were clipped from local newspapers and added to the master files. Even reports of stillborn or premature births were recorded as adverse information, following the logic that such personal tragedies were often accompanied by a handful of new debts to doctors, hospitals, and morticians.[35] To obtain public record information, bureau clerks regularly descended upon local courthouses and municipal offices. There they meticulously copied all items pertaining to real estate transactions, civil and criminal lawsuits, tax assessments and liens, bankruptcies, indictments, and arrests. This information, like that clipped from newspapers and other periodicals, was also added to the master files. Some bureaus even published a daily bulletin of public record items for their members.[36]

Along with these published and public sources, postwar bureaus increasingly sought out derogatory information from their members. The nation's credit surveillance infrastructure was severely tested by the enormous growth of consumer credit during the 1950s, which placed new pressures on bureaus and retailers to develop more-rapid systems for evaluating individual credit risk. "With the tremendous volume of credit you have now," one credit professional remarked, "it is pure idiocy to go on the old-time principle of getting a complete report."[37] Though credit scoring would emerge as a partial solution a decade later, derogatory reporting underwent a revival as an inexpensive stopgap. " 'All we want to know is if you have any derogatory information' " was the refrain of credit managers in Philadelphia, a local bureau representative explained. "The credit bureaus of the future," he predicted, "will consist of files of derogatory information which will be available immediately by telephone. That is what we are going to do—not give the person's life history."[38] This never came to pass, but derogatory information remained a key factor in the development of automated credit card and bank authorization systems during the 1960s, many of which were designed to scan for adverse information—an overdue bill, over-limit account, or bad check—before approving by default.

Though derogatory information was mainly concerned with bankruptcies and legal actions for nonpayment—in other words, categories of financial knowledge—it was not limited to such topics. Derogatory reports, or "garbage," as they were called in the business, captured "anything that might serve as an indicator of an individual's character."[39] Thus criminal charges, evictions, and tidbits regarding a person's "drinking habits, family trouble, and irregularities of employment" were also entered into the files. Such information might not be circulated in derogatory alerts or bulletins, but it became embedded in one's record and could appear in later reports. Over time these clippings and odd scraps tended to clutter bureau files. Even a small bureau in Georgia claimed to add 35,000 public record items to its files each year, including a special "liquor file" in which "liquor violations" were recorded for use by "automobile dealers and motor finance companies," presumably a hedge against car-wrecking drunk drivers.[40] In Minneapolis, the bureau's main files were paired with secondary "confidential" files—"often necessitating two envelopes for each name"—in which sensitive information was housed.[41]

The trouble taken to acquire such delicate information also made it hard to part with. Old court and police records that might not be available later were retained indefinitely.[42] The sample report published by *Life* in 1953, for instance, noted the subject's involvement in a twenty-year-old bar fight, a piece of old information that may well have been expunged from local police records but persisted in the credit bureau's files. Some derogatory items were so damaging—and the risk of a defamation suit so great—that they could not be conveyed to subscribers by telephone or in writing. Instead, members were called into the bureau to receive an "office report" directly from the manager. Such derogatory information was compared to a "loaded shotgun," so hazardous that, as one manual recommended, files in which it appeared should be physically separated from the others and securely locked.[43]

REPURPOSED INFORMATION AND DATA MARKETING

Because creditworthiness was never simply a matter of economic calculation, credit files always contained a wide range of personal information bearing on one's work, home, and private life. Credit surveillance, as its handlers quickly grasped, produced enormous surplus capital that could be put to work. Like retail credit departments, which discovered that their credit records were valuable for much more than simply opening and managing credit accounts, credit bureaus also found new ways to repackage and monetize their "priceless by-product of data."[44] In addition to credit reports, many postwar bureaus sold specialized reports for employers, insurance companies, automobile dealers, government loan programs, and landlords.[45] Tenant reports, for instance, detailed the "playing habits" rather than the "paying habits" of prospective renters. "Credit bureau files have turned up such fascinating characters as the man who kept a live alligator in his bathtub [and] another who decorated apartment walls with risqué murals," as well as noisy musicians, "chronic jitter-bugs" who caused chaos with their late-night "rug-cutting," and "fire-bugs."[46] Both the ACB of A and the RCC had their own standardized forms to provide such secondary services. "Job applicants tell you what they want you to know," a 1962 advertisement for the ACB of A's Factbilt personnel report warned. "Finding out what they may *not* want you to know is up to you."[47] This multiservice approach dated to the first consumer reporting organizations, some of which mingled credit surveillance with employee screening and detective work.

The most common noncredit reports involved insurance and employment. The RCC became a leader in both of these fields during the early twentieth century. As the firm quickly realized, the same qualities that made an individual a poor insurance risk—illness, drug or alcohol abuse, erratic or unconventional behavior—also made one a poor credit risk in the eyes of many creditors. Information gathered for insurance reports could thus be repurposed for sale as consumer credit or personnel reports. In this way noncredit information acquired in more probing (and profitable) insurance reports could be leveraged for its consumer reporting services. By pooling its data for a variety of reports, the RCC maximized the value of its information and achieved profitable economies of scale. While ACB of A reports were based primarily upon shared ledger data from local merchants, RCC reports were produced by inspectors on a case-by-case basis. Where the ACB of A achieved efficiencies by sharing information both locally and nationally among its affiliated members, the RCC developed its own national reservoir of personal information, which was collected via direct investigations by its inspectors and often in contexts completely unrelated to credit evaluation—namely, in the form of insurance and personnel reports.

Though ACB of A bureaus never challenged the dominance of the RCC in the specialized field of insurance reporting, its members did offer a suite of secondary services including personnel, tenant, and Federal Housing Administration (FHA) reports. Since the ACB of A's local bureaus had geographic limits beyond which it was difficult to grow new credit reporting business, such ancillary reports were seen as a way to drum up additional revenue (figure 6.2). As an ACB of A manual observed, "More and more employers are asking credit bureaus for information about the character, credit record and employment history of individuals seeking employment or advancement. By adding to its master file information designed

Who am I?

I may be a credit applicant in your store . . . I may be seeking a job with a new firm . . . a patient applying for credit in a dentist's office.

I may be married, single, divorced, widowed; I may have children or be supporting my parents. I may be a housewife, a working girl, or a combination of the two.

No matter what problems my application presents to you, you can find the answers in a *Factbilt* credit report from your local ACBofA credit bureau. Call them today - - they'll tell you who I really am.

Figure 6.2 An advertisement for Factbilt credit reports. (*Credit World*, September 1952)

for personnel reports, the credit bureau is able to render a new and increasingly important service both to employers and to applicants for employment in the community."[48] Not only were personnel reports easily produced using information already in the bureau's files, they could also be sold for more than three times the price of a credit report.[49] "How important a small clipping, showing an arrest or conviction, becomes when we are later asked to prepare a special personnel report for a prospective employer, whether it be in the employing of a clerk, salesman or cashier for the business, or a servant, maid or child's nurse for the home," a credit professional observed in the late 1930s. "Our ceaseless recordings are proving far more valuable than our fondest expectations."[50]

Practically speaking, personnel reports were "an expanded credit report" with "additional facts" concerning the subject's "health, morals, loyalty, cooperation with fellow employees and management, ability and work experience" mixed in.[51] Encouraging its members to consider this lucrative sideline, an ACB of A manual illustrated how a request for a personnel report should be answered. If, for example, "Jim," an officer of a local fraternal organization, asked the bureau to investigate an unknown applicant—"We don't want to be calling him 'Brother' if he isn't the right type"—a report verifying the subject's identity, education, employment, "character and reputation," and credit history could be generated. For this fictitious applicant, unfortunately, the report was not flattering. "All the informants I've talked to [about Jim] do not speak very highly of him as to stability and general habits. They seem to feel, however, his early home life has probably contributed to this condition and may in part account for his actions. He is known to the police and has been brought in on several occasions for questioning."[52] "Jim" also had unpaid rent, clothing, and grocery bills and had lost a job for "drinking on company premises." Noting the ease with which such reports could be prepared, the manual concluded, "Probably there is not a bureau affiliated with the ACB of A that could not answer such a request in the above manner."[53]

It is impossible to guess the number or percentage of total business that such reports represented among ACB of A members. Official instructional texts such as this strongly suggest that at least some of its affiliates engaged in personnel and other forms of "investigative" reporting. Major operations such as Chilton's Dallas bureau and the Credit Bureau of Greater New York had entire departments devoted to personnel reporting and related services. The latter had an "investigative staff" of sixty to meet demand for "F.H.A., theatrical, business, and other types of special reports."[54] Even the Credit Bureau of Hawaii offered "comprehensive personnel reports" in addition to FHA, VA, and oil company reports.[55] Yet many other bureaus, perhaps even most, only dabbled in such work. The association's president later testified that more than 98 percent of ACB of A bureaus sold only credit reports. "A few do personnel reporting," he added. "Very, very few, if any, do insurance reporting."[56] By contrast, only a fifth of the RCC's total business involved consumer reports (accounting for 10 percent) or personnel reporting (another 10 percent); its main work was insurance reporting (80 percent).[57]

Our understanding of the postwar reporting industry would obviously be enhanced if data regarding the volume of noncredit reports were available. But in some ways this is beside the point. The fact that the attributes of creditworthiness, health, and employability all overlapped is telling. What this overlap reflected was an implicit understanding that creditworthiness—one's trustworthiness as a financial subject—was conceptually linked to moral qualities involving one's lifestyle, reputation, physical fitness, and social conformity. This overlap, moreover, was entirely unproblematic in postwar American society. Nineteenth-century credit professionals had codified creditworthiness in the three Cs—character, capital, and capacity—but the notion that the first of these, character, was germane to creditworthiness persisted well into the twentieth century.

Credit reporting bled into insurance and personnel reporting because all three shared common denominators: personal honesty, consistency, agreeability, and clean living. The credit bureau, a 1950 manual explained, "translates thrift, sobriety, prompt payment of obligations and right living into very real and concrete terms for each individual."[58] When the industry was dragged before federal lawmakers and lambasted in the press during the late 1960s, it was not because the fundamental qualities of creditworthiness were in dispute. Rather, it was because there were few rules for collecting, sharing, and, most important, *correcting* this information. Privacy concerns led to new laws and limitations, but the underlying idea that one's credit record was relevant to insurance and employment risk did not change.

Following the lead of retail credit departments, which reimagined their role as one of sales promotion rather than just loss prevention during the 1920s, postwar credit bureaus began to reposition themselves as business builders. "Credit bureaus were started as a deterrent to putting bad credit on the books," the ACB of A's president noted. "Now credit and credit bureau functions are sales tools."[59] During the 1950s and 1960s a number of credit bureaus moved into the business of selling promotional lists and customer screening services. This was an important break with tradition. The sale of customer lists, especially lists containing the names of top-shelf local prospects, had long been anathema to credit bureaus. To burnish their reputation for impartiality and to mollify subscribers who were reluctant to share their confidential customer information, early consumer bureaus took the position that "lists of names are sacred and never shall a name be suggested to one credit bureau customer unless it is available to all."[60]

Consumer reporting organizations had long shielded themselves from criticism by insisting that they did not "rate" anyone's creditworthiness; rather, the bureau merely collected the experiences of local merchants and shared this ledger information with subscribers. By eschewing blacklists and lists of "good" or "preferred" risks, bureaus were able to steer clear of defamation suits that aggrieved consumers might bring against them.[61] One's creditworthiness was thus decided elsewhere—by retailers, merchants, banks, finance companies, and other service providers who independently evaluated the bureau's reports and came to their own conclusions. "The credit bureau itself does not rate you 'A' or 'BB,'" an early personal finance magazine, *Changing Times* (now *Kiplinger's*) informed its readers in 1950, clarifying the distinction between consumer bureaus and business rating firms like Dun & Bradstreet. After reviewing a credit report and other sources of information, "the credit manager or loan officer must use his own judgment."[62]

Many postwar bureaus dipped their toes into promotional business by offering "newcomer" services. These programs were directly modeled on the Welcome Wagon, a popular national syndicate established in 1928 by Memphis native Thomas W. Briggs. In essence, Welcome Wagon was a business promotion vehicle thinly disguised as a charitable civic association. When a new family moved into town, they were greeted by a cheery female representative of the local Welcome Wagon chapter who offered helpful information about neighborhood schools, shopping, churches, and other community amenities. At the same time, she also presented gifts and coupons from local merchants. This was her real purpose: to introduce new customers to Welcome Wagon subscribers, who hoped to win their business and loyalty through gestures of goodwill. Welcome Wagon hostesses often arrived in shiny new cars provided by local automobile dealers, on which the dealer's name was prominently affixed. By the early 1950s more than 1,000 American communities had a local chapter to connect with new arrivals. Praising the founder's ingenuity, the *Saturday Evening Post* noted that Briggs had found a way to convert the natural sociability of "nice, matronly, middle-aged, gossipy" women into a multimillion dollar business.[63]

During the 1950s credit bureaus began to found similar-sounding organizations to smuggle credit promotion and surveillance into the homes of new arrivals. Along with gifts and coupons from local merchants, however, their specially trained hostesses provided new residents with a credit application. After the visit, the hostess returned to the bureau with either a completed application or, at minimum, the family's previous address so that a credit report could be requested from the bureau in their former hometown. The new arrival's credit information was thus on hand before he or she even attempted to make a purchase or open an account in the community. If the advance report was favorable, local merchants could then make a grand show of welcoming the new customer with a complimentary charge account in his or her name.

In St. Paul, Minnesota, where the local credit bureau ran a Downtown Welcome Association, its hostess greeted more than 4,100 new arrivals over a two-year period (figure 6.3). During these visits, she presented new residents with brochures and took credit applications "in an 'off the cuff' manner" to put them at ease.[64] New arrivals were said to appreciate the privacy of completing a credit application in their home, rather than in the downtown office of an inquisitorial credit manager. In 1956 the Dallas Chilton bureau began its own Welcome Newcomer service, a program so

Figure 6.3 A representative of the Downtown Welcome Association in St. Paul, Minnesota, greeted new community members at their homes and solicited credit applications for the local credit bureau. (*Credit World*, July 1957)

successful that it was soon duplicated in forty other cities.[65] Even bureaus without Welcome Wagon–style operations prepared lists of new arrivals for their subscribers and mailed welcome letters to newcomers, alerting them to the local bureau's existence and the importance of forwarding their credit information to the bureau. With their ears constantly to ground, bureaus learned of new arrivals from public utilities, real estate companies, newspapers, public records, and milk-delivering dairies.[66]

By offering such screening and listing services, credit bureaus were entering new territory. In some places newcomer programs were integrated into local credit card programs, notably Charga-Plate. Introduced in the late 1920s by the Boston-based Farrington Manufacturing Company, Charga-Plate superficially resembled a modern credit card in that customers were issued a small metal plate embossed with their name, address, and account number, which they presented in lieu of cash to make purchases. Unlike later universal credit cards such as Visa or MasterCard, however, Charga-Plate was organized locally and typically accepted by only larger retailers, especially department stores.[67] In St. Paul, Charga-Plates were automatically issued to newcomers whose applications, collected by the bureau's welcome hostess, met established qualifications.[68] In other cities, such as Dallas, Cincinnati, Pittsburgh, and Seattle, the local bureau actually ran the local Charga-Plate organization.[69]

Where bureaus did not operate the local Charga-Plate association, some provided screening services that essentially enabled credit departments to outsource their credit approval process. The New York bureau, for instance, offered a "Selective Screening Service," by which subscribers submitted new credit applications directly to the bureau. There "specially trained 'Screeners'" reviewed the application against the bureau's in-file information and determined how much credit, if any, could be safely offered to the applicant.[70] A similar service was offered by a Washington, D.C., credit bureau after local merchants, overwhelmed by credit applications, asked the bureau to investigate and "make the decision without bothering [them]."[71] Credit managers remained the ultimate arbiter of their store accounts—ambiguous applications were returned to them for their expert judgment—but this small concession of authority was a harbinger of major change as new credit-screening technologies began to erode the credit manager's function during the 1960s.

Among postwar credit reporting organizations, the Dallas Chilton bureau was unique in its aggressive effort to marry credit surveillance with credit promotion. In addition to establishing its own credit card, the Golden Charg-It Card, in 1958, it sold prescreened lists of top-rated credit customers to local merchants. (The Chilton bureau, as already noted, was one of the few major postwar bureaus to publish a credit rating guide for its members.) Even more, Chilton's prescreened lists could be sorted by mailing zones, and each zone could be further "broken down into income, age, profession, renter or home owner groups."[72] This type of target marketing and consumer analytics—now a core service offered by all three national credit bureaus—was far ahead of its time. Throughout the 1960s the Chiltons pursued a strategy of rapid expansion and diversification, acquiring more than forty bureaus and developing a variety of new information services, from check verification systems to computer consulting.[73] Chilton's zealous business extensions even encompassed forays into polygraph testing and a babysitting service.[74] "The philosophy of the credit bureau business is changing," J. E R. Chilton III, heir to Dallas bureau, noted in 1962. "Although one of our primary functions is to protect merchants from credit losses, we are rapidly becoming more of a promotion-type business."[75] In 1969, a new umbrella entity, the Chilton Corporation, was formed, and the firm built a powerful computerized credit reporting network and list marketing business during the next decade. The company was sold to Borg-Warner Corporation, a Chicago-based manufacturing firm, in 1985 and acquired three years later by TRW (now Experian).

CONFIDENTIALITY AND THE PUBLIC GOOD

From the beginning, credit reporting organizations had a powerful incentive to keep their information on a very short leash. In addition to the risk of having their valuable ledger data poached by competitors or shared with free-riding nonsubscribers, local bureaus sought to avoid costly defamation suits by restricting access to their reports. In general, the principle of privileged communication, established for commercial credit reporting during the late nineteenth century, shielded consumer credit bureaus from prosecution. This legal bulwark gave bureaus room to operate, but an angry or overcurious consumer could cause much trouble. To protect themselves, credit professionals—both credit managers and bureau operators— followed two cardinal rules: never tell a credit applicant what specific information led to their rejection, and never let an individual see his or her own credit record.

The first of these rules was essential for credit managers when turning down credit applicants. Despite their natural inclination to save face when delivering this unhappy news, credit managers were prohibited from divulging the source of black marks on the customer's credit report. To do so, in many cases, would be to identify another merchant (and possibly one's competitor) as the "reason" for the applicant's rejection. This sowed ill will and often placed one bureau member in the path of another's irate clients when the rejected applicant marched from the credit office of one to confront the unsuspecting manager of another. Even worse, divulging derogatory items in a report—especially criminal charges that might have been dismissed or references to character flaws or domestic turmoil—exposed the bureau to lawsuits. Credit bureau contracts typically forbade their subscribers from divulging report information to their subjects. Instead, declined applicants were given the bland explanation that the information in their credit report was incomplete or, the ambiguous term of choice, "insufficient."[76] If applicants protested, they were referred to the credit bureau.

The second cardinal rule applied primarily to bureau operators, whose responsibility it was to handle rejected and disgruntled applicants. "The policy in most credit bureaus is to give *careful attention* to any individual who shows a personal interest in his own credit report," an ACB of A manual instructed. However, it emphasized, "avoid *letting anyone see his own credit report*."[77] Instead bureau officials politely listened to the individual's grievance and collected a fresh credit application or written statement. These meetings, referred to as credit bureau "interviews," were part public relations exercise and part opportunistic investigation. To avoid violating the conditions of privileged communication, bureau officials maintained a Sphinxlike silence on the actual content of the individual's file. And under no circumstance was the consumer to receive direct access to his or her credit report. After the individual left, information acquired during the interview was verified and cross-checked against the bureau's existing file for errors or omissions.

The credit reporting industry's primary loyalty was to the business community, which it defended against fraudulent and unprofitable consumers. At the same time, however, bureau operators were acutely aware of their public obligation to protect the sensitive personal information in their charge. The virtue of confidentiality was not only asserted in instructional texts and official publications, but enshrined in the national association's original code of ethics as "a matter of professional honor."[78] "One of the first things that new employees should be taught," a guide to entering the business explained, "is that the credit bureau is entrusted with more information about persons and firms than any other organization in the community."[79] Loose lips and gossip tarnished the bureau's integrity. Worse still, they undermined the confidence of local subscribers and put the entire enterprise in legal jeopardy. "Often you may see files on your relatives and on persons you know," an ACB of A manual warned. "You may work on reports or bulletins which contain items your friends might consider 'juicy.' You are doing a great service to everyone when you keep this information where it belongs—in the file or on a report."[80] The imperatives of confidentiality even extended to the demeanor of bureau employees. Clerks were instructed to maintain an air of impassivity when providing telephone reports and to resist the entreaties of frazzled credit managers to speak bluntly or subjectively about an individual's creditworthiness. "If a member asks, 'What do you think?' or 'How do you rate him? it is necessary that you answer, 'I am sorry we are unable to give an opinion.' "[81] Likewise, expressions of "surprise" or "personal interest" were discouraged, as they betrayed an unbusinesslike curiosity about the human subjects of the bureau's surveillance.

While there is no reason to doubt the reporting industry's commitment to confidentiality, whether motivated by honor or fear of litigation, it was not absolute. In their perpetual quest to vanquish deadbeats and to safeguard the nation's credit economy, bureau operators viewed themselves as something more than purveyors of a mundane business service; they were patriotic agents of social order. Seeing little difference between their own protective function and that of law enforcement, credit bureaus opened their strongholds of personal data to government officials in the spirit of public service. Significantly, World War I commenced just as the professionalization of consumer credit management was gaining steam. Eager to demonstrate their loyalty to the state and its cause, members of the National Association of Mercantile Agencies—an early trade organization that represented consumer credit bureaus—gave the U.S. government unfettered access to its files.[82] This cooperative arrangement was further cemented in 1937 when the U.S. Department of Justice contracted with the National Consumer Credit Reporting Corporation (the reporting arm of the national association during the 1930s) to purchase reports from its affiliates for use by FBI agents.[83] Credit bureaus had previously provided this information gratis.

The intersection of credit reporting and police work—like the overlapping criteria of creditworthiness, insurance risk, and employability—was unproblematic among credit professionals. Commenting on the importance of collaboration with local authorities, a California credit manager advised, "If the 'desk sergeant' calls, ask no questions. Give him—get for him—all you have or can get and he will tell you what about and why, later, if and when it is proper."[84] This collegial relationship between credit bureaus and government agencies continued after World War II. In the early

1960s, the Credit Bureau of Greater New York "set aside a table for F.B.I. agents, Treasury men and the New York Police Department" who came each day to fill gaps in their own dossiers.[85] And in Houston, the city's leading bureau had a contract not only with the FBI, but also with the Internal Revenue Service (IRS), to which it sold discounted reports for the purpose of hunting down delinquent taxpayers. As a Houston official explained, summarizing the reporting industry's civic duty, "Credit bureaus consider it a responsibility in the interest of good government to assist government investigations with information that may be helpful."[86] In their work to prevent "crimes against business," credit professionals believed that they were self-evidently on the right side.

Though later revelations would cast these arrangements in a sinister light, this was only the most objectionable link between commercial and government surveillance. In reality, private and public agencies had long maintained a symbiotic relationship. Private-sector credit bureaus depended upon access to public records in local courthouses and municipal offices, while public loan programs, such as those run through the FHA and the VA, relied on private credit bureaus to supply detailed investigative reports. This interpenetration of public and private surveillance systems, institutionalized before World War II, suggests a much more complicated history of contemporary American surveillance, one that does not assume a clean separation between commercial and government interests. Even after legislation was enacted in 1970 to prohibit credit bureaus from selling information to non–credit-granting government agencies, it did not prevent agencies such as the FBI or the IRS from gaining access to their files. It simply required that they obtain a court order to do so. This was an important new constitutional safeguard, to be sure, but it misses a larger point. The same bureaus that would make "the head of the Soviet secret police gnash his teeth in envy," as *Life* magazine joked in 1953, were—and still are—at the service of the U.S. government. Contemporary privacy debates that focus exclusively on government surveillance ignore the hidden power of private-sector databases, whose digital collections of our "intimate stuff" are always just a subpoena away. This troubling reality has become apparent in the wake of massive post-9/11 government data sweeps, but it has much deeper roots.

One link in particular would prove crucial in unifying public and private surveillance: the Social Security number. First issued in 1936, a year after the passage of the Social Security Act, these nine-digit numbers were never intended to serve as a national identification system. Public aversion to compulsory government identification ran deep in the United States. Days before the 1936 presidential election, Franklin D. Roosevelt was even accused of ordering metal identification tags, each stamped with a Social Security number, to be issued to American workers.[87] The claim was false and the smear campaign failed to derail Roosevelt's reelection, but popular fears of modern "regimentation" were not unfounded.[88] For the administration of mass society, the efficiency of such a number proved irresistible. In 1943 President Roosevelt issued an executive order to expand the Social Security number's use for identification among federal agencies, and in 1962 the IRS officially adopted the number to identify the nation's taxpayers.[89] By the early 1960s Social Security numbers were also an increasingly common form of customer identification in the private sector, including credit bureaus and credit departments. As computer-generated credit reports and statistical credit scoring systems converted financial identity into an impersonal, quantitative fact, it was this government-issued number that became the code to unlock it.

7

Encoding the Consumer

THE COMPUTERIZATION OF CREDIT
REPORTING AND CREDIT SCORING

As computers moved out of defense and into business after World War II, they were quickly put to work in a wide range of industries. These "giant brains," nurtured by government-sponsored military research during the war, introduced fantastic new possibilities for automating complex calculations, routine tasks, and mechanical operations. The defining feature of this modern industrial revolution would not be nature's domination by heavy machinery, as postwar technologist John Diebold predicted in the *Harvard Business Review*. The most "spectacular and far-reaching" effects would be felt in the "information handling functions of business."[1] Paper, not steam, would be converted into an intangible but no less earthshaking commodity: information. During the late twentieth century computerized credit reporting would become a key element of this new information economy and push the commodification of personal identity to new limits.

The race to automate consumer reporting began in 1965, when the first computerized bureau went online in Southern California. "This centralized credit computer is not a far-fetched Buck Rogers–type idea," an IBM executive explained in 1967; it already existed and was being put into action.[2] Though the conversion process was complicated and uneven—

fully automated bureaus did not dominate the industry until the late 1970s—computerization ushered in a period of rapid consolidation as a handful of large computerized bureaus extended their reach, buying out or absorbing smaller locally owned bureaus throughout the country. Automation, as one banking journal observed, augured "a radical transformation of the credit reporting industry."[3]

This transformation went beyond merely speeding and centralizing credit information. Computer coding influenced the very structure and content of credit reports. Narrative remarks and subjective interpretations did not easily fit into the flattened, formulaic language of data processing, especially as developed by outside engineers and programmers. The imperatives of universal, reductive coding were reinforced as many bureau subscribers automated their own accounting systems, from which ledger data could be easily transferred. Shortly before congressional investigations exposed damning moralistic statements in credit reports during the late 1960s, computerization was already pushing the reporting industry toward cryptic summarization and quantification.

While the automation of credit reporting was a seismic event in the development of modern consumer credit surveillance, computers played an equally important role in a second dimension of this emergent system: statistical credit scoring. During the late 1950s business consultants and researchers began using computers to create sophisticated scoring systems for major banks and retailers. Computer-assisted credit scoring precipitated a fundamental shift in the concept and language of creditworthiness, even more so than computerized reporting. In addition to reducing or eliminating human contact between creditors and borrowers, scoring systems redefined creditworthiness as a function of abstract statistical risk.

CREDIT SURVEILLANCE ENTERS
THE COMPUTER AGE: 1960–1970

During the mid-1950s many major American corporations, from General Electric to Bank of America, were eager to harness new commercially available computers.[4] In addition to streamlining production and mechanical processes, computers were ideal for automating tedious clerical functions such as accounting, billing, and inventory control. Indeed, when Vannevar Bush sketched out his mind-bending vision of postwar computing in "As We May Think" (1945), commercial recordkeeping was one of the innovations he highlighted. In addition to presaging the concepts of hypertext and the World Wide Web, Bush's seminal essay predicted that computers might offer a less exalted but no less miraculous solution to "the prosaic problem of the great department store"—specifically, the problem of processing credit and billing information for thousands of individual charge customers.[5]

The automation of banking and accounting during the late 1950s suggested that instant, friction-free transactions were on the horizon. Electronic data would usher in not only the fabled paperless office, but also a checkless and cashless society.[6] In this near-future world, many predicted that checks and cash would be replaced by a single identification card that linked all of one's bank, credit, and personal information.[7] This was a utopian system straight out of Edward Bellamy's *Looking Backward* (1888). In Bellamy's best-selling novel, a Boston aristocrat awakens in the year 2000, Rip Van Winkle–like, to discover that the injustices of industrial capitalism have been vanquished. Among the many technological innovations effecting social harmony in this new America, "pasteboard" cards, similar to modern credit and debit cards, have replaced cash as the medium of exchange. Of course Bellamy's financial science fiction now seems prescient. Along with checkbooks and cash, twenty-first-century Americans carry an array of universal payment cards to perform precisely this function, albeit with fees and interest rates that are often dystopian.

Yet electronic payment was only one part of this emergent system. In reality, authorization systems were also essential to confirm that a cardholder had funds or credit available and, just as important, to confirm that the person presenting the card was who he or she claimed to be. Though the checkless society was technically feasible during the 1960s, it was stymied by "the relatively simple problem of determining who is eligible for credit and how much"—in other words, the problem of personal identification. To solve this human stumbling block—"the difficulty of fitting people into the new technology," as the *New York Times* put it—the use of fingerprints or voice spectrographs was proposed as a fail-safe technological bridge between shape-shifting bodies and their data.[8] As people and money dematerialized in postwar mass society, mistaken identity and fraud became a serious issue. The fast-approaching checkless-cashless society required much more than complex systems of integrated computers and electronic registers. It also required a new high-speed surveillance infrastructure to identify and monitor the nation's population.

The computerization of credit reporting and credit scoring was part of a more general movement toward the automation of consumer surveillance, from charge card authorizations to personal check verification, during the mid-1960s. "The next major market for commercial electronic systems may well be 'the anti-deadbeat market,'" an electronics industry writer noted, describing a credit authorization system under development in Southern California with Sears and the May Company.[9] By the late 1960s the "largely untapped field" of credit security—separate from the consumer credit reporting industry—was already getting crowded. In 1966, for example, Macy's adopted Validator, an in-store service that allowed sales clerks to authorize credit purchases by entering a customer's account number into an electronic desktop device. The same year in Chicago, Carson, Pirie, Scott installed Telecredit, yet another verification service that was a "combination touch-tone telephone and audio response unit connected to a computer."[10] Even the Dallas-based Chilton credit bureau established its own automated check verification service prior to computerizing its credit records. The system, called Veri-Check, compiled a database of "names, physical descriptions, and up-to-date check cashing histories" for local individuals.[11]

THE COMPUTERIZATION OF CONSUMER CREDIT REPORTING

Against this backdrop of electronic payment and authorization systems, the computerization of credit information was soon imagined. With postwar consumer debt soaring and new credit instruments proliferating, from revolving store charge cards to new universal credit cards, rapid access to accurate, up-to-date credit information took on growing appeal. "Some nationwide system of computerized credit information is doubtless in the offing, but what form it will take is still undetermined," a banking journal observed. "A computer at a bank or a department store or a finance company could, conceivably, interchange information with another similar computer on the other side of town or the other side of the United States."[12]

The idea, however, did not come from the credit reporting industry, but from a manufacturer of radios and televisions. In 1961 Robert W. Galvin, president of Motorola, made news with his "speculative" plan to establish a central repository for consumer credit data. The hypothetical system, dubbed FACTS (Fully Automated Credit Transaction System), would require consumers to carry a "market card," similar to a credit card, which could be inserted into an "electric register" at the point of purchase, giving the merchant instant access to the individual's complete credit record.[13] Motorola had no intention to develop the system, Galvin admitted, but the plan suggested that the dream of perfect credit information—and perfect credit evaluation—was within reach.

Credit Data Corporation

The first mover in the computerization of consumer reporting was Credit Data Corporation (CDC), a privately owned firm based in California. During the mid-1960s its founder, Harry C. Jordan, launched an ambitious campaign to form a national reporting network. Though CDC appeared as an insurgent outsider to existing West Coast bureaus, Jordan was no newcomer to credit reporting. His father owned the Michigan Merchants Credit Association, a Detroit-based credit bureau that the elder Jordan had established in 1930. Upon his father's death in 1956, Jordan, a graduate student in biophysics at the University of Rochester, returned to run the family business. Remarkably, he continued his studies and earned a doctorate in 1959 while also working on a cancer research project at the University of Michigan. If Jordan's intellectual accomplishments were unusual for a bureau operator, his plan to single-handedly forge a national computer reporting system was even more so.[14]

Rather than working to gain the cooperation of local bureaus in every city and town throughout the nation, Jordan sought to establish regional centers in three "vast economic amalgams": the Los Angeles to San Francisco region, the Boston to Washington corridor, and a swath between

Chicago and Buffalo. Noting that 43 percent of the U.S. population lived in one of these three sprawling "super cities," Jordan's vision was to consolidate coverage in each of these areas and to link them together.[15] In this way CDC's national coverage was never designed to be exhaustive; instead, it addressed what Jordan believed was at the root of flawed credit information: the mobility of American consumers. Explaining the selection of Los Angeles for the CDC's first computerized bureau, he noted, "Its nine million persons are a population on wheels, who live, work, and spend their income within an area of approximately 3,000 square miles."[16] It was the mobility of Southern Californians, a CDC rival later suggested, that was the "trigger in the credit industry revolution."[17]

CDC's Los Angeles bureau cost $3 million to install and went online in 1965. Using IBM 1401 computers leased at a cost of $20,000 per month, the bureau provided reports in ninety seconds at a price of sixty-three cents per inquiry (thirty-three cents if no record could be produced for an individual).[18] The next year the price of inquiries dropped to twenty-two cents.[19] With five million credit histories stored in its Los Angeles system, CDC moved quickly to expand and consolidate coverage in California. Subscribers in San Diego, Ventura, and Santa Barbara were added in 1966, and its Los Angeles office was linked to San Francisco, where Jordan purchased a bureau in 1962 and had its 3.5 million records computerized.[20] A year after opening in Los Angeles, CDC boasted statewide coverage with combined credit records exceeding eleven million.[21] Praising CDC's automated system, an oil industry journalist noted, "This will be a far cry from the present tedious, time-consuming, fragmented system in which often handwritten credit reports are prepared in thousands of credit bureaus scattered across the country. And it all comes for less than half the price."[22]

While establishing a West Coast regional center, CDC immediately turned to the East. In 1966 Jordan's Detroit bureau was computerized at a cost of $3 million, becoming the nucleus of CDC's Midwest stronghold between Buffalo and Chicago. The Detroit bureau had three million files and answered nearly 80 percent of that city's credit inquiries.[23] The same year, a New York office was opened and credit information for six million individuals was quickly amassed.[24] By connecting its regional bureaus in the East, West, and Midwest via "telephone computer communications,"

CDC aimed not only to consolidate credit surveillance within the modern megalopolis, but also to permit "rapid access to credit information from any point in the United States."[25] The first step toward this goal was achieved in 1969, when CDC's New York office could remotely access credit data in its Los Angeles headquarters.[26]

On the surface, the sudden ascent of CDC during the mid-1960s contradicted assumptions about how and under whose leadership computerized credit information would emerge. As American banks, retailers, and credit card companies moved to automate their accounting and record-keeping, it was not obvious that credit bureaus would play *any* role in the future of credit information. Instead, it was widely assumed that credit automation would be led by the banking industry, which was far ahead of all other major stakeholders in the market for consumer credit information and had already revolutionized check clearing with the development of ERMA (Electronic Recording Machine Accounting) and MICR (Magnetic Ink Character Recognition) technologies.[27] Retailers gradually joined bankers as heavy computer users, but they were not at the forefront of the diffusion of this technology.[28] This was a future in which bankers, not retailers or credit bureaus, would be at the technological vanguard of the emergent consumer information economy.

Though the consumer reporting industry was a fixture of the postwar commercial landscape, it was excluded from future visions of centralized reporting for two main reasons. First, most bureaus were simply too small to marshal the necessary capital to computerize, which eliminated them from serious consideration. A local population of at least four million was necessary to support a computerized bureau, according to CDC's founder, and the number of U.S. cities fitting this description "could be counted on one's fingers."[29] Second, and more significantly, the consumer reporting industry was so fragmented and the quality of information and service among bureaus so variable that it was hard to imagine a unified system emerging from these organizations. Such inconsistencies were most glaring between urban and rural bureaus.

Unlike big-city bureaus that were supported by department stores and other large subscribers, small-town bureaus were often severely undercapitalized and ill equipped to provide thorough or reliable information. Even in urban centers competition and fragmentation caused much confusion; in many cases multiple bureaus vied with one another for the same subscribers or, alternatively, served a specific trade or industry in isolation from one another. In 1963 the *Wall Street Journal* noted that twenty-seven different bureaus served San Francisco alone.[30] Speaking before an audience of credit professionals in 1962, *American Banker*'s consumer finance editor observed with alarm that credit reporting was a "patch quilt design of reporting agencies." Various constituencies—banks, finance companies, retailers—each had their own sources of information. Consequently, he complained, "there is no *one* source to which a credit granter can turn to get the complete picture of Donohue, first name Edward, wife Madeline."[31] "The weak link in the total system of credit information," another banking journalist noted, shifting the blame away from banks themselves, was "the lack of sufficient current reports at local and national credit bureaus."[32]

But while the banking industry was better positioned, financially and technologically, to lead the computerization of credit data, it did not. The explanation for why it failed to do so falls in large part to the industry's attitude toward personal information. Bankers were conservative professionals with a long history of strict client confidentiality; they were loath to divulge any information about their account holders. Retailers and local consumer service providers, by contrast, had no such ethical qualms. In fact, when they initially balked at sharing ledger data with local credit reporting organizations, it was out of concern for their *own* privacy. (If their best customers were discovered, they feared, these customers might be poached by competitors.) Banks, on the other hand, regarded their clients' personal and financial information as sacrosanct; many even refused to divulge information without the account holder's written consent.[33] In this regard, the banking industry's defense of consumer privacy was quite forward looking.

For this reason the relationship between banks and consumer credit bureaus had never been one of complete harmony. From the beginning many banks declined to participate in local reporting ventures, whether private or merchant associations, and when they did, they often shared little more than basic identifying information and grudging ballpark figures. Instead, banks relied on their own in-house records and intrabank relationships for customer information.[34] "There is a sort of freemasonry among modern banks," a business writer noted earlier in the century, commenting on the free flow of confidential information between banks. "So if you are turned down by the Tenth National Bank because you are slow in paying for your automobile or for frequenting the ball park daily, you may be tolerably sure that the Eighth or Ninth National Bank will not be ignorant of your failings."[35] Credit inquiries from nonbankers, including federal loan agencies and pushy credit managers, on the other hand, were resented by many bankers.

By the mid-1960s, however, the volume of postwar consumer credit—as well as increasingly blurry distinctions among credit instruments such as charge accounts and credit cards—led some bankers to conclude that greater information interchange with nonbanking institutions was inevitable. "If you take any one consumer at random and consider the number of charge accounts, credit cards, etc., he carries," one observed, "the gathering of up-to-date financial information can be quite difficult."[36] While credit bureaus were certainly part of this problem, as this writer pointed out, so were the banking fraternity's reticence and self-insulation. In 1965, ACB of A member bureaus received less than 10 percent of their income from banks. Most of their business came from retailers (40 percent) and finance companies (18 percent).[37]

In this light, the mysterious ascent of CDC is easily explained by its main subscribers: banks. Where consumer bureaus had long failed to win the support of the banking industry, CDC was virtually its surrogate. When CDC's Los Angeles bureau opened in 1965, its original 225 subscribers included nearly all of the city's installment credit banks and large credit card–issuing oil companies.[38] More important, they also included national credit card issuers such as American Express and Bank of America, the latter of which submitted "8 million data items" to help establish CDC's initial files. By 1967 CDC also handled all authorizations for Master Charge.[39] "Credit Data has approached banking houses and has obtained their participation in its program, both as suppliers of information and as users of the service," a banking journal observed. "Credit bureaus have also requested access to bank credit files but so far reportedly have met with little encouragement from the commercial bankers."[40] When CDC opened its New York office in 1967, its subscribers included Chase Manhattan, First National Bank, Bank of New York, and more than one hundred other banks in the New York metropolitan region, Connecticut, and New Jersey, as well as major finance companies such as General Motors Acceptance Corporation and General Electric Credit Corporation.[41] By 1969 CDC was processing five million charge authorization inquiries per month, each in less than three minutes.[42]

Why did banks flock to CDC? The behind-the-scenes negotiations are unknown, but one reason is certain: CDC's information-gathering protocols conformed to the banking industry's protective attitude toward customer privacy. From the start, Jordan insisted that CDC files would contain only basic identifying information and financial data—an individual's payment history and the types, amounts, and limits of his or her unpaid loans and open credit accounts. Importantly, CDC files did not include any information about an individual's race, religion, psychological profile or personality, medical records, or gossip culled from neighbors, newspapers, or employers.[43] Such minimalism stood in stark contrast to the information maximalism of most postwar bureaus.

Historically, credit bureaus were omnivorous in their quest for information that shed light on ingrained understandings of creditworthiness—namely, the concept of personal character. Moreover, many bureaus mixed credit reporting with personnel reporting, investigative mortgage reporting, and insurance reporting. Among such bureaus, a wide variety of personal information—from news of marital discord to the fastidiousness of one's home—could be fodder for an individual's file and stored for future use (and reuse) in multiple reporting contexts. CDC dispensed with this entirely. Jordan acknowledged that while it was technically feasible to include such information, his firm and his subscribers had agreed that it overstepped the rights of the individual.[44] CDC's example might have influenced the future of consumer privacy, but it did not. Instead its campaign to computerize consumer reporting merely touched off a race to bring American consumers under an increasingly totalizing system of private-sector surveillance.

Industry Response to CDC

CDC was both a spur and an existential threat to the consumer reporting industry. Local bureaus in California, for instance, suddenly found themselves at risk of being circumvented altogether. In 1966 a new consortium, Computer Reporting Systems, Inc. (CRS), was formed in Los Angeles to help Southern California bureaus compete with CDC. CRS provided its subscribers with full credit information in ninety seconds—a speed matching that of CDC—when they called a toll-free number and spoke with an operator at a central terminal. In 1967 CRS had four million "complete" files in its system—these included employment and banking information as well as payment histories—and received ten million accounts receivable records on magnetic tape from its subscribers. The same year, CRS was also working to computerize and link more than forty bureaus in Arizona, Nevada, and Southern California.[45] By 1967 a second organization, Credit Bureaus, Inc. (CBI), was working to computerize West Coast reporting in the north. Based in Salem, Oregon, CBI converted the manual records of forty bureaus in Oregon, California, Washington, and Idaho—four million files combined—to magnetic tape.[46] In late 1965 even the Credit Bureau of Hawaii was reported to have ordered an IBM 360 to automate information in its 500,000 individual files.[47]

CRS and CBI represented an immediate local response to CDC's encroachment on the West Coast, but the latter's most significant competitor was the ACB of A. As the nation's largest and most influential organization of consumer bureaus, the ACB of A included more than 2,000 member bureaus throughout the country and had a major stake in the future of the industry. Unlike CDC, however, the ACB of A represented a motley range of bureaus, from large urban bureaus supported by downtown department stores to suburban satellite bureaus that catered to local merchants and small rural bureaus. In both urban and suburban locations, several ACB of A member bureaus often provided overlapping and competing coverage. Indeed, the proliferation of postwar suburban "bedroom" bureaus was viewed by metropolitan bureaus as an especially pernicious development, one that further scattered information.[48]

In representing such diverse interests, the ACB of A faced a special challenge on the eve of computerization. The underlying issue was not computerization itself, but centralization. The efficiency of computerized credit reporting was not simply its speed, but also the consolidation of information at a single source. For those who followed this logic, it was obvious that computerization would put most bureaus out of business as one or several large bureaus devoured the rest. That many of its members would be "engulfed by the 'push button monster' in the big city" was an uncomfortable reality.[49] Yet the ACB of A understood that if they did not lead the industry's computerization, someone else would, as CDC had already shown and others threatened. In 1966 another firm, Hooper-Holmes, announced plans to link its 155 branch offices and six million files through a computerized national network with regional offices. Though the New Jersey–based firm specialized in insurance and personnel reporting rather than credit reporting, its clients included credit card and oil companies as well as retailers.[50]

In 1965 the ACB of A launched Project CB-360, a computerization initiative in Texas that involved the privately owned Chilton bureau in Dallas, the merchant-run Credit Bureau of Houston, and IBM. The project, whose name referenced the application of IBM System 360 computers, originated as a feasibility study two years ahead of CDC's arrival.[51] The real leader behind the effort was the Chilton Dallas bureau. During the early 1960s the Chiltons expanded their reach beyond Dallas and, in 1963, formed Credit Bureau Management, an umbrella company for some forty bureaus that they owned or advised in Texas, Arizona, and Arkansas.[52] In 1964 Chilton's Dallas bureau and Credit Bureau Management moved into a spacious new $1.5 million office with an eye to installing a computer system and diversifying their business in credit card promotions.[53] That year Chilton also entered into a contract with IBM to install its 360 computer, which took more than two years to fully set up and program. Noting the dramatic increase in Dallas credit accounts, bureau president Bob Chilton explained, "We are moving into an entirely credit-oriented world. We are trying to keep up with this constant and completely economic picture."[54]

When the new Dallas bureau was officially opened at the start of 1966, its principals participated in a ceremonial "key punching" instead of a ribbon cutting. The punched keys produced a credit report via computer for "John Doe" of Los Angeles. The inaugural report, retrieved in less than a second, indicated that Doe (the pseudonym for a real case) was "solvent," though he and his wife were in the process of divorcing.[55] By the late 1960s Chilton was repositioning itself as a diversified communications firm and consultant for bureau automation programs. Rather than purchasing new bureaus and expanding its national reach, Chilton developed electronic data processing packages that it sold to other bureaus through the ACB of A. One of its most important clients was the Credit Bureau of Cook County, Illinois, which contracted with Chilton to computerize its Chicago files in 1968.[56]

Automation and Data Reduction

The main advantage of computerized reporting was of course its speed. Accuracy was crucial, but even perfect credit information was only as useful as it was quickly available. "The consumer takes months to decide to buy a color television, but the day he decides, he wants it delivered immediately," a credit bureau official explained.[57] This same urgency drove department stores to install pneumatic tube and internal telephone systems during the early twentieth century, through which customer identities and credit limits were rapidly communicated between credit departments and personnel on the selling floor. Before computerization, the *Los Angeles Times* noted, "a cautious credit manager may have had to make as many as 10 calls" to obtain updated information regarding a credit applicant. "The process could easily take a half day, sometimes two days. Written reports could take up to 10 days."[58] Computerized credit reports cut this time from hours and minutes to seconds. Speed was also achieved through the malleability of electronic records. Where paper files could be used by only one operator at a time, computerization allowed several operators to access the same record simultaneously, thus averting "out of file" delays, a perennial bureau problem.

Additionally, automation sped the laborious process of updating and weeding existing credit files. Since the 1870s, when consumer reporting organizations first emerged, the revision of credit information had always been a daunting ordeal. Each file—literally tens of thousands of them— had to be periodically reviewed and brought up to date. In the Houston credit bureau, for example, twenty-five employees were required to simply audit the bureau's 1.2 million files.[59] As computer systems became more sophisticated, credit data could be revised by operators in real time as new information was received during telephone queries. By 1968 Chilton's system permitted operators to override old information with revised data, which was inputted on the spot and automatically date stamped.[60]

The process of updating credit information was further streamlined and accelerated as the credit bureau's subscribers also began to computerize their own accounting and billing departments during the mid-1960s. Local credit bureaus had always struggled to compel their members to submit updated ledger information on a regular basis. As a clearinghouse of credit information, the bureau was only as timely and accurate as the ledger data it received from its members, from downtown department stores to corner grocers. At least some of a bureau's members failed to submit ledger information in prescribed intervals or, in some cases, at all. That some merchants would balk at or ignore this basic obligation is not surprising. The manual compilation of ledger information, like the revision and weeding of credit bureau files, was a burdensome chore, one that was easily neglected during busy periods or staffing shortages. As major retailers and other consumer credit grantors turned to automation, the compilation of ledger information was no longer a separate activity; it was easily produced by new electronic data processing systems. Ledger data, the manager of the Credit Bureau of Greater Boston explained in 1968, was now generated "as a by-product of their internal bookkeeping," offering its members little excuse not to contribute more frequent and complete information.[61] When submitted on magnetic tape or transmitted electronically, ledger data was quickly merged into the credit bureau's own computer files. "Our system," the ACB of A's director of automation noted, "*will* make major use of automated tapes and cards from the billing applications of credit granters."[62]

Though speed was the primary appeal of computerization, storage was a close second. Paper-based credit reports were housed in filing cabinets that required significant office space, especially in large urban bureaus. "Many bureaus have no formal program for purging or weeding files," one expert observed. "Whenever their files fill up they simply buy more file cabinets."[63] Computer files miniaturized such space requirements. When the

Dallas bureau computerized its paper files in 1966, all of the bureau's one million records, previously stored in filing cabinets requiring over 3,000 square feet of office space, were transferred to a "'data cell' about the size of an office waste basket."[64] Computerization also permitted the cheap and easy duplication of credit files. This was no small appeal in an industry whose stock in trade is information. A bureau's rows of cabinets, each containing thousands of painstakingly cultivated paper master files, were vulnerable to irretrievable loss in the event of fire or other environmental catastrophes. Backing up credit records on magnetic tape and storing them at a remote location greatly reduced this possibility.

More significantly, computerization influenced how creditworthiness was described and evaluated. To conform to the technical constraints of computers—specifically, their demand for categorical clarity and data reduction—the content of credit reports became more spare and quantitative. In 1965, the same year the ACB of A launched its computerization initiative, the association also unveiled a new alphanumeric "common language" to communicate ledger data in its credit reports.[65] The idea of business-specific computing languages was already in the air. The most important of these, COBOL (Common Business Oriented Language), was introduced in 1960 and soon became an industry standard. To accommodate the demands of competing hardware and nonscientist users, COBOL employed a reduced character set and naturalistic English-language commands.[66]

The ACB of A's new language was a simplistic imitation of such high-level systems. It consisted of intuitive letter codes to differentiate between classes of creditors (for example, "A" for automobile dealers, "B" for banks, and "D" for department and variety stores) and letter codes to distinguish different types of credit ("O" for open account, "R" for revolving account, and "I" for installment account). Importantly, the new coding scheme used numbers to clearly express how a customer paid his or her bills. Credit bureaus and their subscribers had long complained about the use of ambiguous terms such as "fair," "slow but good," and "paid as agreed" to describe an individual's credit standing. What exactly was "slow"? A department store would probably consider payment in sixty days slow, but a jeweler or the corner grocer might think it fair.

Such language was often meaningless across commercial contexts, and especially so as bureaus began to cater to national credit card–issuing banks and oil companies. "At earlier stages of consumer credit industry progress, a system of standard terminology was merely desirable," an ACB of A official noted in 1964. "Within a short time, it will become imperative."[67] Numbers thus replaced verbiage: "1" indicated that the customer paid within thirty days; "2," within thirty to sixty days; "3," within sixty to ninety days; and so forth. Credit professionals were urged to "forget localisms and establish a common language acceptable to all bureaus and credit grantors"—a language, moreover, that was "compatible with a computer and with transmission by automatic means."[68] Such coding was no doubt useful, but its bias toward the strict thirty-day cycle of major retailers and finance companies left less room for informal, personalized credit relationships. In this way, the standardization of credit language pushed the concept of credit risk further toward impersonality and abstraction.

Shortly before going online, the ACB of A also introduced Factbilt form No. 100. This new, streamlined report was designed to answer a variety of credit inquiries, including trade clearances and antecedent reports. Significantly, rubrics regarding character and reputation were omitted. Instructions to create a narrative "word picture" of the subject were also eliminated, though space was still provided to insert public record items and miscellaneous "trade information."[69] As with all credit reports from this era, it is impossible to determine the extent of the adoption and actual use of such forms among ACB of A bureaus. Differences probably existed between large urban bureaus with an eye to computerization and smaller suburban and rural outfits for which older methods sufficed. However, the association's leadership clearly saw data reduction in the industry's future. Pointing to "possibilities for new, abbreviated reports and the use of codes," the head of the Houston bureau during its computerization suggested that "many credit grantors could effectively extend credit with less detailed information" from the local bureau.[70] Though the ACB of A moved cautiously toward data reduction during the 1960s, CDC reports were devoid of narrative and subjective information from the start (figure 7.1). As its founder explained, "We try to keep our information quantitative."[71]

				680 WILSHIRE PLACE — LOS ANGELES		

cdc CREDIT DATA CORPORATION

30-200	ROBERTSON WILLIAM J MARY	3-30-66
	01212 WILSHIRE LA DOUGLAS	386-32-1362

PREVIOUS ADDRESS CHECKS   FILE EMPLOYMENT — DOUGLAS
CURRENT ADDRESS CHECKS   SOCIAL SECURITY NUMBER CHECKS

INDUSTRY	CODE	FILE DATE	TYPE	AMOUNT	MO'S	RATING OR COMMENT	DATE RATED
BANK	15-310	02-62	AUTO	$1500 TO $2000	24	EARLY PAY	03-63
RETAIL	41-053	06-64	CHG ACCT	$250 TO $500	10	OPEN ACCT	06-64
RETAIL	43-011	04-65	SECURED	UNDER $250	06	PD UNSAT	12-65
FINANCE	22-910	09-65	PERSONAL	$250 TO $500	18	DELINQ 60	01-66
OIL	30-900	01-66	CHG ACCT		01	INQUIRY	01-66

Figure 7.1 A sample Credit Data Corporation credit report. CDC's computerized reports exemplified the movement toward quantitative clarity, including the use of social security numbers as personal identifiers. (*Robert Morris Associates Bulletin*, August 1966)

Despite such differences, early computerized credit bureaus all faced one common problem: how to identify an individual. As retailers and credit grantors across the nation automated their recordkeeping, each adopted its own unique system of customer identification, typically an alphanumeric code.[72] Such numbers were nothing new, but the growth in the numbers and mobility of postwar Americans made traditional systems of identification—name and address—increasingly impractical and unreliable. Some "universal numbering system" was "sorely needed," CDC's founder lamented. "For the purposes of personal identification, a worse system than name and address would be difficult to devise."[73] In a nation with "1.9 million Smiths and 1.5 million Johnsons," mistaken identity had become a serious liability. After all, "Mrs. William H. Smith will be unhappy if the dress she ordered gets delivered to Mrs. W. Henry Smith, and Mrs. Will H. Smith will be even more unhappy if she receives the bill."[74] This small recordkeeping matter became a major problem when the computerized ledger data of each subscriber was merged with the bureau's master files. "You can't just store in a computer all of the different types of J. C. Penney's account numbers, Sears, Sanger's, Neiman's and on down the pike. Somehow, you have got to come up with one number."[75]

In the call for a universal identification number, the obvious candidate was the Social Security number. Its use among federal agencies was already expanding during the early 1960s, and no rules prohibited its use outside of government. The ACB of A's form No. 100 included space for the subject's Social Security number (as well as that of his or her spouse), and CDC recorded Social Security numbers as "secondary identifiers." The legitimacy of the Social Security number in the commercial sphere was all but certified in 1968 when the American Bankers Association recommended its use as "a nationwide personal identification system" among its members.[76] Months later, a banking journal noted that credit bureaus were requesting Social Security numbers from credit applicants, as this was "the best universal identifier currently available."[77]

By the early 1970s, the head of Chilton's computerized Dallas bureau envisioned the Social Security number as the magic key to financial identity: "Imagine if all our customers had computer terminals. . . . A person walks in and says, 'Here is my social security number. I would like an account with you.' They pick up the telephone and punch in the social security number and back comes the code."[78] Financial identity thus acquired its magic key, and American consumers were literally reduced to numbers.

CREDIT SCORING AND THE QUANTIFICATION OF CREDITWORTHINESS

While computers accelerated the process of updating and communicating credit bureau information, the main recipients of credit reports, credit managers, still grappled with their interpretation. An applicant's credit history was frequently ambiguous or incomplete, leaving credit managers to rely on instinct when deciding how much credit, if any, an individual could be trusted to repay. Credit managers had long dreamt of a magic formula to alleviate the stress and uncertainty of their work, some foolproof system to identify deadbeats before the goods and money were out the door. But creditworthiness, as many believed, was simply too complex and too idiosyncratic to be reduced to ironclad rules and measures.

During the 1960s, character was still considered the foundation of consumer creditworthiness, and the ability to judge this elusive personal quality was still at the top of the credit manager's skill set. Though credit reports could provide insight into an applicant's character, especially information pertaining to occupation, domestic arrangements, and records of past debt payments, many credit managers insisted on the importance of credit interviews. "Personal impressions are fallible," a business professor and leading expert conceded in a 1967 credit textbook, "but from visual contact with applicants, creditors make useful observations of character, integrity toward debt, attitudes toward credit service, and the economic competence of the customer."[79] So important was the interview that during the 1950s some credit managers resisted the new practice of offering blank credit applications to store customers. These "silent interviewers," as they were referred to disparagingly, allowed customers to complete their own applications privately and without the intervention of credit managers. By bypassing the interview, the credit manager was thus deprived of the chance to meet and evaluate the applicant in his or her totality. "Interviewing the credit applicant is one of the fine arts of retailing and should be so regarded," a leading credit professional asserted, commenting on the inferiority of customer-supplied applications. "It is certainly not the assignment for an automaton or a novice."[80]

Yet by the early 1960s something like an automatic system—one, moreover, that could be operated by novices—was in fact being developed. "A prospective borrower is still asked the familiar questions about his age, marital status, whether he owns or rents a home, how long he has been on the present job," the New York Times reported. But there was a key difference in this new regime of credit evaluation. "By applying a scientifically determined series of weights to each factor and adding up a total score, the credit manager in thirty seconds is able to reject those applications almost certain to result in charge-offs."[81] This new system was statistical credit scoring.

The Development of Statistical Scoring

Statistical credit scoring was not widely adopted until the 1960s, but efforts to quantify creditworthiness began decades earlier. One of the most ambitious programs was initiated by the Chicago mail order giant Spiegel, which established a "pointing" system in 1934 to screen credit applications.

Spiegel's initial system consisted of just five variables: the amount of the order and the occupation, marital status, race, and geographical location of the applicant.[82] For mail order firms like Spiegel, which did not meet its far-flung national customers in person, the tedious work of processing applications was performed by young women with little or no credit experience. During the holiday season, a Spiegel representative later recalled, "pointing clerks" were recruited off the street "by the carload" and quickly trained.[83]

By the late 1930s consumer lenders also began to experiment with internal scoring systems. In 1938 a Phoenix bank touted the success of a five-variable formula it designed to safely "'mine' a pretty steady volume of good ore" from salaried and wage-earning installment borrowers.[84] And in San Francisco, a finance company credit manager reported his scheme to convert the three Cs—character, capital, and capacity—into a "standard valuation table."[85] Scoring systems were not limited to the private sector. Indeed, the most expansive was implemented by the FHA, whose official *Underwriting Manual*, published in 1935, included rubrics for scoring the risk of loans. In addition to evaluating the condition and location of the property, these "underwriting grids" also rated individual borrowers. And, not surprisingly, the variable at the top of the grid and most heavily weighted—ahead of the applicant's "ability to pay" and "prospects for future"—was the borrower's "character."[86] Despite the (presumed) efficacy of these early systems, none were grounded in statistical theory. "True, it was merely a trial and error method," the creator of the San Francisco finance company's system confessed, "but the main thing is that it worked."[87]

When credit managers dreamed of formulas for predicting credit risk, they typically looked to the insurance industry for inspiration. If actuarial methods could be successfully applied to mortality, some wondered, why not to creditworthiness as well? One problem of course was that, unlike death, the end point of all insurance policies, the repayment of debt was never inevitable. In fact, debts could live forever. Even more perplexing, creditworthiness was believed to be rooted in interior qualities that could not be directly quantified. But while character itself could not be isolated and measured, it might be inferred through related variables that could. Spiegel's pointing system, for instance, sought to infer the character of its credit applicants by scoring the individual's occupation, marital status, race, and home location—all variables believed to be indicative of moral qualities.

In the late 1930s the National Bureau of Economic Research (NBER) turned its attention to consumer credit and published a series of studies on the subject. Noting that consumer financing had survived the shocks of the Depression with only minor losses, the eighth installment of the series, published in 1941, looked specifically at how such lenders evaluated consumer creditworthiness. The author, David Durand, was interested in testing not only the validity of established methods, but also the possibility of devising "purely objective credit formulae by statistical methods."[88] As Durand noted, reprising a familiar refrain, "The actuarial analysis of risk along the lines used in insurance is the goal toward which credit research should strive."[89] With the records of more than 7,000 loans at his disposal, data handed over to the NBER by several dozen banks and finance companies, his experiment showed how it could be done.

Durand turned to discriminant analysis, an advanced statistical method only recently developed by the English statistician and eugenicist Ronald A. Fisher. This new technique enabled researchers to estimate the significance of multiple variables associated with two mutually exclusive categories or outcomes. Fisher had pioneered this method to study natural selection, but it could also be applied to credit risk. A statistician, for instance, could select a random sample of "good" loans (paid in full) and "bad" loans (defaulted)—two distinct outcomes—and analyze the relative significance of variables such as the borrower's age, occupation, or income in predicting these outcomes. Discriminant analysis, in other words, allowed researchers to develop scoring systems in which the information from a credit application was reduced to a litany of discrete variables, each with its own value and weight to reflect statistical associations with payment or default. The sum (usually) of a person's numeric values on these variables, multiplied by their relative weight in predicting the likelihood of making timely repayments, resulted in a credit "score."

Durand's conclusions, for all of their future import, were remarkable for their ambivalence. He was able to show that applicants with a stable job, a stable residence, and a bank account were positively associated with good credit risk. And to the surprise of sexist creditors, he also found that women were much better risks than men. Other variables, such as an applicant's age, marital status, income, assets, and number of dependents, were found to be of little or no predictive value. Despite the rigor and creativity of his study, Durand believed that his findings offered little of interest "to practical credit executives." His sample was skewed and his analysis was intelligible only to "trained mathematicians." But more damningly, his data set did not include information about the past payment history or personal character and reputation of borrowers. Thus, he conceded, he was unable to study the moral characteristics of borrowers, the one variable that credit managers considered paramount in determining creditworthiness.[90]

Durand's report, which doubled as a doctoral dissertation at Columbia University, inspired no immediate action. Published on the eve of U.S. involvement in World War II and before the development of commercially available computers, few firms were in a position to act on its findings. But even fewer credit managers believed mathematical approaches offered much of value. When the subject of credit formulas was raised at a meeting of retail credit experts in 1946, it was dismissed by representatives of the nation's leading department stores. "I don't think there is any such thing as scientific evaluation of a credit risk," a May Company manager remarked. "The credit man just has to know." A Neiman-Marcus representative agreed, adding that "the ability to pick character" was the "No. 1 prerequisite" in credit evaluation, scientific or not.[91]

The Rise of Postwar Credit Scoring

During the late 1950s statistical scoring received renewed interest, largely through intellectual contributions that emerged out of West Coast research centers such as the Stanford Research Institute (SRI). Working with Bank of America, SRI had already revolutionized the banking industry with the development of automated check-clearing technologies. Related lines of inquiry also came out of human factors and operations research, two interdisciplinary fields devoted to the study of organizational efficiency and technological mediation. However, it was a San

Rafael–based consulting firm, Fair, Isaac, and Company, that succeeded in bringing credit scoring into mainstream commercial practice.[92]

Founded in 1956, Fair Isaac was the business venture of two former SRI analysts, William R. Fair, an electrical engineer, and Earl J. Isaac, a mathematician.[93] After a discouraging start they received a major break. In 1958 the American Investment Company (AIC), one of the nation's leading consumer finance companies—and, according to Fair Isaac lore, the only lender to respond to its original prospectus—hired the upstart firm to analyze its credit files. Reasoning that "insurance companies, given information such as a man's age and his occupation, can predict fairly accurately how good an insurance risk the man's life is," AIC embraced the opportunity to apply scientific principles to credit risk.[94] To develop a scoring system for AIC, Fair Isaac used the same statistical techniques as Durand. Noting that discriminant analysis itself was not new, earlier writers on credit scoring typically reduced its sudden appeal to a single cause: computers. As the director of research at AIC explained, "To find these relative values in the days before electronic computers, a mathematician would have to try every possible combination of weights for each characteristic. This would involve literally millions of calculations."[95] Isaac illustrated this mind-boggling complexity with a striking image. If a grain of sand was used to represent each possible set of weights for a scoring system based on eighteen variables, the sand would

Figure 7.2 Fair Isaac researchers, including cofounder Earl Isaac (second from left), at work on a credit scoring system. (*Burroughs Clearing House*, April 1972. Courtesy of Unisys Corporation)

form a ball the size of our entire solar system. "We have a truly tremendous task if we want to find that particular grain of sand which best separates the good from the bad credit risks."[96] With computers, however, such calculations could be completed in a day (figure 7.2).

During the early 1960s a number of major firms, including AIC and General Electric Credit Corporation (GECC), began to adopt credit scoring systems. AIC used its scoring system to screen 65,000 loan applications per month, and by 1965 GECC had already invested $125 million in the development of scoring systems; both firms employed computers to perform this work.[97] In 1968, a questionnaire sent to 200 of the nation's largest banks revealed that more than a third were using a scoring system and another third were considering one.[98] At the same time, large and medium-sized retailers began to develop in-house point scoring systems in conjunction with the transition to automated systems. In 1962, for example, the computerization of Grand Auto Stores, an eighteen-store chain based in California, incorporated a point scoring system developed by psychologists. "Due to these electronic capabilities," its credit manager boasted, "we have been able to produce a truly electronic credit department."[99]

For all of the promise of credit scoring, early adopters were quick to note its difficulties. For one, the authors of early scoring systems were at pains to identify which variables even predicted creditworthiness. Since personal honesty and responsibility could not be quantified directly, early scoring systems attempted to infer these "intangible qualities" obliquely. During the 1960s, a wide range of variables were tested, from the applicant's occupation and family size to whether the individual had bank accounts (but not how much they contained) or a telephone in his or her home. A single variable in isolation might not be important in predicting the repayment of a debt, but discriminant analysis allowed its practitioners to test correlations between multiple variables. Thus, for instance, "the 'number of rooms' in the home of a credit seeker may be meaningless if taken alone," Spiegel's director of research explained. "However, 2 rooms in combination with 5 or more children in the family may indicate undesirable socioeconomic conditions" and high risk of delinquency.[100]

The information used in early credit scoring systems was typically acquired from the firm's own credit applications. Since the determinants of creditworthiness, at least those that could be measured statistically, were not entirely clear, the credit application itself became a vessel for fishing expeditions. Each item on the application, in some cases as many as forty, was converted into a numerical value and tested for good measure. "Theoretically, an unlimited number of questions could be asked of the credit applicant and then tested for their significance," Spiegel's research director noted. "However, the size of the questionnaire and mounting sales resistance limit in practice the number of questions to 10 to 15."[101] As early practitioners learned, there were no universally predictive variables or systems of weights. "We don't have the foggiest idea what makes people creditworthy," Fair Isaac's vice president later told *Money* magazine. "Statistics tell the analysts that certain questions work and others don't," the *Money* journalist explained, "but they don't know why."[102]

Importantly, the variables with the greatest predictive power often had little to do with how much money one earned. As a 1964 Wharton study revealed, an applicant's monthly income and payment to income ratio—pieces of financial information with seemingly obvious relevance—were far less useful in predicting default than whether borrowers had a telephone, owned their home, or had a bank account (but, again, without knowing how much was in it).[103] These results were not anomalous. They were typical. Study after study listed these variables and others, such as length of time at one's current job and address, as the most predictive of good and bad loans. The leading determinants of creditworthiness, in other words, were only indirectly or loosely financial. Simply having a telephone in one's home, a mortgage, and a checking or savings account—evidence of community and institutional connectedness—were among the best predictors of "good" borrowers. If personal character could not be measured, social and economic "stability" took its place. With its easily coded attributes—homeownership, telephone lines, banking relationships, marriage, and long-term commitments to a single employer and address—stability became a rough proxy for character.

A second problem that early adopters faced was maintaining the validity of their scoring systems. Since each business, whether a retailer, bank, or finance company, dealt with statistically different populations, each had to develop its own battery of scoreable questions and weights. No two systems were the same because no two businesses dealt with exactly the same borrowers. For this reason, one business could not copy the scoring system of another. Each system was a custom product. Even small behavioral or socioeconomic differences skewed statistical scoring systems and risked potentially disastrous miscalculations. To accommodate geographic variations among its national customers, credit grantors like GECC used as many as fifteen to twenty different versions of its scoring system.[104] Environmental contingency was not the only problem; creditworthiness was also a moving target. Over time, small changes in a statistical pool of customers caused even the most carefully devised systems to lose their predictive power. Thus each business had to continually resample its customer files and make adjustments to its weights. No credit scoring system, once set in motion, was replicable or permanent.

Despite such difficulties, statistical credit scoring, like computerized credit reporting, increased the speed of credit evaluation. As postwar consumer lending ballooned, many credit departments were understaffed, and new hires could not learn the subtle art of credit evaluation fast enough. Credit scoring was presented as a solution to both problems. By scoring applications and establishing credit limits—above and below which an application was automatically accepted or declined—the extremes were quickly identified. This sped the overall process and reduced credit managers' workloads, freeing them to focus their precious expertise on ambiguous cases in the notorious "gray" area. "Tough decisions are segregated for personal attention. Easy decisions are segregated for procedural handling," as one business consultant put it.[105] At the same time, the cost of investigation was reduced because expensive credit bureau information was purchased only for middling or marginal cases that required close scrutiny.

Even more than saving time, credit scoring saved money in reduced labor costs. By laying bare the wisdom of seasoned credit managers, early scoring systems were touted as a useful training tool for "budding credit men."[106] As one scoring advocate explained, "One will then speak of a '19-pointer' or a '26-pointer' rather than a 'marginal' or 'fairly good' risk; the numeric designation is a more precise way of communicating, bringing into mind a category with very definite risk characteristics."[107] In practice, the cultivation of junior executives was a minor concern. Credit scoring was a simple task, "much like grading a multiple-choice examination," and could therefore be done by cheap, low-skill workers.[108] As a result, credit evaluation went from an expertly choreographed personal encounter to a rote clerical operation. Even the tedious process of preparing credit records for statistical analysis was performed by low-wage labor. During the 1960s and 1970s, Fair Isaac outsourced its manual coding to hundreds of California homemakers.[109]

While speeding and deskilling credit evaluation, statistical credit scoring had an even more profound impact on credit management. This was especially true in the area of credit policy. Prior to credit scoring, a lender responded to fluctuations in economic and business conditions by instructing its credit department to "tighten" or "loosen" credit standards. Where credit decisions were largely a matter of expert judgment, it was impossible to implement such executive directives with any precision. What exactly did tighten or loosen mean? Credit scoring gave vague terms real specificity. With creditworthiness represented by a number, credit standards could be easily adjusted by raising or lowering cut-off scores. "This approach," a banker noted, "is far more effective than writing a memo to all credit personnel asking them to 'tighten up' on check credit applications."[110]

But this was just the beginning. By converting credit decisions into uniform, quantitative rules, scoring systems also allowed managers to quickly generate reports that displayed patterns of profit or loss and to calculate the level of risk of its various portfolios. This was especially useful for large firms with multiple offices to supervise. In addition to giving management a tool for auditing the performance of credit departments and individual personnel—in effect, turning the system's surveillance function against its users—such reports helped executives anticipate and adapt to changing conditions. Scoring, in other words, provided a means for the constant monitoring and forecasting of credit business. These managerial "byproducts of credit scoring," an MIT professor observed, "come close to rivaling its main function in importance."[111] More than simply a device to grade credit applications, a *Harvard Business Review* article on the subject emphasized, credit scoring was a "comprehensive management information system."[112]

As statistical scoring matured during the late 1960s, its broader promotional applications also became apparent. Scoring systems identified not only the worst risks, but also the best. These top-rated customers could be singled out for premium services and financial products. At AIC, for instance, "credit analysis reports" allowed managers to identify undersold borrowers—customers who had high credit scores but borrowed small amounts—so that additional loans could be offered.[113] In effect, scoring systems, with their need for continuous sampling and analysis of customer records, were sophisticated internal research programs. Those at the helm of computerized scoring systems, like the managers of earlier paper-based credit departments, soon realized that their statistical data was a marketing gold mine. Beyond locating low-hanging fruit, such systems could be used to study consumers and to make even finer distinctions among them. "A major by-product of a well-designed credit scoring system," representatives of Fair Isaac noted, "is the wealth of information obtained from the sample of applicants"—information about the rejected as well as the accepted. By analyzing the "personal characteristics of people having different odds for success," they suggested, promotional campaigns could thus be targeted more precisely to the desired segment.[114] The data used to score credit applications could be handed off to the marketing department and merged with other customer information such as zip codes and loan amounts, all of which offered new possibilities for screening, sorting, and classifying consumers. "The extent to which such data can be usefully analyzed is almost endless," one writer enthused.[115]

By quantifying credit risk, credit grantors could also begin to experiment with variable interest rates. With statistical probability as a guide, lenders could offer lower rates to high-scoring customers and higher rates to those scoring at the margins or below.[116] Variable rates in the form of risk-based premiums were standard practice in the insurance business. The application of actuarial methods to credit risk opened the door to similar practices in lending. Durand grasped this application of credit scoring in his 1941 NBER report, though he doubted that it would be pursued because of "the difficulty, if not the impossibility," of compiling enough statistical data and "the unpracticality of discriminating between borrowers."[117] He was wrong. Ultimately the real power of statistical credit scoring was not to give more attractive rates to high-scoring customers. Rather, it enabled creditors to push credit risk to its furthest limit at the *bottom* margin. The true analytical edge of scoring, as Durand observed, was not identifying good and bad risks, but identifying the poor risks that were not so poor as to be unprofitable.[118] Statistical scoring systems did this and unleashed a new race to the bottom. This pursuit of credit customers at the razor's edge of profitability—and beyond—would lead to the development of "subprime" lending.

COMPUTERIZED RISK MANAGEMENT AND
THE FUTURE OF FINANCIAL IDENTITY

It would be easy to see computerized credit reporting and statistical credit scoring as business problems that technology "solved." Thanks to computers, credit reports, once scattered and inconsistent, were centralized and standardized; and individual creditworthiness, once determined subjectively by fallible credit managers, was made calculable and objective by numerical scoring. However, it is always perilous to identify technology as the root cause of any large-scale social, economic, or political change. This is to commit the sin of technological determinism: ascribing agency or inevitable outcomes to the lifeless tools of human invention. In the case of credit surveillance, such determinism would be especially misleading. It may be hard to imagine the development of manual systems for credit reporting or scoring that could match the velocity, scale, or power of electronic information processing, but the form these computerized systems took during the 1960s was not inevitable. Rather, credit professionals very consciously decided to privilege speed and volume over established systems of omnivorous information gathering and "judgmental" credit evaluation. The decision was made under duress as the rapid expansion of consumer credit strained the entire credit surveillance apparatus, but it was a human decision nonetheless, not the work of an invisible technological hand.

By the 1970s computerized credit reporting and credit scoring had begun to expand the parameters of financial identity in the United States. Together they represented a powerful system of surveillance that extended beyond the narrow problem of credit risk. Credit bureaus became important purveyors of consumer information, and credit scoring firms such as

Fair Isaac led developments in marketing and behavioral modeling. By marrying credit records, personal data, and purchasing histories with new technologies of risk management and targeted promotion, computerized credit surveillance offered novel ways to evaluate consumers. Though credit reporting had long informed insurance and personnel decisions, both conceptually linked to creditworthiness, new systems of computerized credit surveillance predicted the profitability of individuals in a range of contexts and separated Americans into different categories of value.

Looking at the development of risk scoring in the late 1970s, one expert foresaw its expansion. "The implementation of quantified systems will broaden as systems are predicted for uses other than the traditional granting of credit. We will see point tables to make decisions such as: lease / don't lease, promote / don't promote, insure / don't insure, hire / don't hire, open / don't open a checking account, and so forth."[119] In this algorithmic future world, credit scores would be just one of many metrics available for judging trustworthiness and calculating an individual's economic value.

8

Database Panic

COMPUTERIZED CREDIT SURVEILLANCE
AND ITS DISCONTENTS

Credit professionals had long marveled at the ignorance of the American public when it came to consumer credit surveillance. "I am constantly amazed at the average person's complete lack of understanding of the functions of a credit bureau," the national association's education director confessed in 1954. "There is, in my opinion, no organization that affects the daily lives of so many people that is so little understood as the credit bureau."[1] This abruptly changed in the mid-1960s, but not in the industry's favor. The public was awakened, and Americans were outraged.

In 1966 a congressional committee was convened to investigate the privacy risks of a hypothetical federal database. In the process, it uncovered a much more disturbing reality. Centralized private-sector databases, including those belonging to the credit reporting industry, were already online and tracking millions of Americans. The reporting industry's reach and sophistication shocked lawmakers. Computerized credit reporting, one congressman declaimed, was "really a national data center in private hands," but without any of the regulatory safeguards to protect the citizen-consumer from abuse.[2] Big Brother had not arrived in the guise of Orwellian technocrats, but rather as a business system for controlling consumers.

By the end of the decade the reporting industry found itself at the center of a public firestorm that left its benevolent self-image in tatters. Ignited by fear of computerization, subsequent investigations into reporting practices soon raised serious questions about the ethics and professionalism of the entire enterprise. What information should credit bureaus be permitted to collect, and what rules dictated its handling and circulation? Credit bureau operators had long understood the seriousness of their work and thought themselves to be conscientious custodians of the personal information in their charge. Yet lawmakers and consumer advocates discovered during congressional hearings that they had more than databases to fear. The credit surveillance apparatus and its vast collection of files, both paper and digital, were governed by little more than professional norms and toothless ethical codes. Errors were common, and American citizens had little control over the manufacture and sale of their reputations. "The person seeking credit often feels that his whole life history is either at the mercy of merciless computers or in the hands of people who hear only one side," President Richard Nixon's special assistant for consumer affairs observed. "Unfortunately, the credit reporting agency has become associated in the consumer's mind with ultrasecrecy, electronic eavesdropping, almost a privately run spy network."[3]

Computerized credit reporting was only the most visible manifestation of technological change in the credit industry during the 1960s. Consumer credit surveillance was undergoing a second revolution from within. Statistical credit scoring, assisted by powerful computers, was transforming the way lenders evaluated individual creditworthiness. Where credit decisions had long been made by seasoned credit managers who met in person with borrowers to take applications, many lenders began to turn to risk scoring instead. These systems were especially attractive to large national banks, retailers, and finance companies as they struggled to keep pace with the growing volume of postwar credit. "For hundreds of years, the lending of money has been an art form in the sense that judgments have had to be based on the intuitive consideration of qualitative information," a Fair Isaac representative observed in 1972. "Only in the last two decades have innovations in technology changed the money lending activity from an art form to a scientific process, which enables people to reach decisions based on quantitative data."[4]

This shift, moreover, posed a direct threat to the professional expertise of credit managers. Scoring advocates argued that statistical risk modeling made credit evaluation more consistent and fair, but others, including many credit managers, saw it as dehumanizing. Computers and their statistical creations seemed to be undermining the moral foundation of creditworthiness.

THE END OF IGNORANCE (AND INNOCENCE)

In the summer of 1966 a House subcommittee met to investigate an ominous new threat to American society: the database computer. The hearing, chaired by Representative Cornelius Gallagher of New Jersey, was called in response to a plan to develop a federal data center. The center was the brainchild of the American Economic Association and the Social Science Research Council, an independent nonprofit organization that created an exploratory committee in 1960 to study the preservation and use of federal economic data. The committee's findings, referred to as the Ruggles Report after its chairman, Yale economist Richard Ruggles, recommended that federal statistics, then scattered among numerous agencies, be centralized to give researchers more efficient access to government data sets.

The proposed center would pool machine-readable records from the Census Bureau, the Bureau of Labor Statistics, and the IRS, among others, to facilitate high-level (and anonymized) socioeconomic analysis.[5] From the perspective of data-hungry social scientists, the plan was entirely sensible and benign. In the eyes of Representative Gallagher and other lawmakers, however, a centralized government database was at best an affront to the privacy of American citizens and at worst a gateway to totalitarianism. "'The Computerized Man,'" Gallagher prophesied, "would be stripped of all his individuality and privacy. . . . His status in society would be measured by the computer, and he would lose his personal identity."[6] Amid such grandstanding, the federal data center was abandoned.

Yet the hearings revealed that Congress's concerns were entirely misplaced. Centralized databases were already operational in the private sector, including the consumer credit reporting industry. The testimony of Paul Baran, a Rand Corporation computer expert, opened eyes. Baran was a key figure in the creation of networked communication systems and would later be recognized as one of the Internet's chief architects. As he described the development and inevitable consolidation of commercial databases, including "independent credit systems," Representative Benjamin Rosenthal interrupted. "So, is the point you make that even though the Government has not put their stamp of approval on building this system it is growing on its own because various groups are independently developing its starting points." Baran's reply—"Precisely"—sent shivers.[7]

By the time credit bureaus came under congressional scrutiny during the mid-1960s, their function and operation should not have been a secret to anyone. Along with the ACB of A's own media campaigns to raise public awareness of the local bureau's role, feature stories in national publications such as *Life* magazine left little to the imagination. Even fear-baiting accounts of credit bureau espionage in several best-selling books—Hillel Black's *Buy Now, Pay Later* (1961), Myron Brenton's *The Privacy Invaders* (1964), and Vance Packard's *The Naked Society* (1964)—failed to raise concern. *Buy Now, Pay Later* included an entire chapter devoted to credit bureaus under the nefarious title "Big Brothers' Big Brother." The book's main target was consumer credit itself—its irrationality and false convenience—but the modern credit bureau figured prominently as the undergirding upon which it all rested. "If the files of the nation's credit bureaus were destroyed tomorrow," Black wrote, "it is conceivable that our entire economy would spin into a depression the likes of which would make the nineteen thirties appear as a polite economic burp."[8]

Three years later Brenton and Packard covered the same ground in separate accounts of postwar surveillance. In both, the credit bureaus' machinations were overshadowed by descriptions of more-sinister new technologies for electronic eavesdropping, lie detection, and psychological testing. By comparison, old-fashioned filing cabinets seemed quaint, and filing cabinets operated by the private sector even more so. In the context of McCarthyism and Cold War paranoia, it was the intelligence gathering of central government, not business, that frightened most Americans. Reviews of Brenton's and Packard's books include frequent references to Big Brother but few if any remarks on credit bureaus.[9] As one disdainful reviewer wrote, "Mr. Packard's lengthy report on the investigative activities of Credit Bureaus arouses my indignation not at all: if you want to keep your finances private, you can always pay cash."[10] What reviewers such as this one failed to understand was that credit bureaus did not operate in isolation. Rather, they were part of an emergent surveillance assemblage, one that included both government and commercial institutions and within which information often flowed far beyond its origins.

If American consumers and the book-reviewing intelligentsia were blind to the credit bureau's growing influence, the federal government could claim no such ignorance. The Department of Justice, for one, was well aware of the industry's reach. It had imposed an antitrust injunction against the ACB of A in 1933 (amended in 1953) to prohibit monopolistic information-sharing practices among the group's members. The content of its reports and the industry's benefit to the larger business community were unquestioned. After World War II the Department of Commerce even published educational material recommending its services. Credit bureaus, the 1948 brochure explained, gave the "whole picture" to merchants when evaluating individual creditworthiness. "Courthouse records are checked for chattel mortgages, liens, bankruptcies, deeds, etc. Police records are noted, and newspaper items containing vital facts are clipped and placed in the permanent record."[11] The value of this information was not lost on the FBI or the IRS. Both had contracts with major metropolitan bureaus to purchase reports for their own investigations. In New York alone the FBI and the State Department received some 20,000 reports each year from the city's largest bureau.[12]

The government's most significant institutional relationship with the reporting industry was through loan programs offered by the FHA and the VA. The FHA was not itself a heavy purchaser of credit reports—it bought 12,000 to 15,000 reports in 1967—but lending institutions typically submitted reports with each loan application. With some 500,000 applications received per year, the FHA was indirectly a major bureau client.[13] In fact, shortly before the reporting industry came under congressional fire, credit bureaus were already drawing heat from the FHA. In 1963 the agency complained of "horrendous omissions" in the credit reports it received. One egregious case involved an Alabama man who defaulted on his FHA mortgage after only six months. Subsequent investigation revealed that a shoddy credit report was largely to blame. Though the report suggested that the man was a "satisfactory" borrower, it neglected to point out that his gas service had been repeatedly cut off, that his furniture had been repossessed, and that he was the subject of several lawsuits. According to an FHA analysis, this was not an isolated case. After reviewing more than 1,200 defaulted mortgages, the FHA determined that nearly a third would have been rejected if not for "deficient or inaccurate" credit bureau reports, and another 12 percent would have received "downgraded" ratings. Ironically, to combat such uneven quality, the FHA compiled its own white list of trustworthy credit bureaus.[14] Since no standards governed the qualifications of a bureau operator, anyone could get into the business. Thus, the former head of the Mortgage Bankers Association of America complained, "you get some lousy credit reporting."[15]

CONGRESSIONAL HEARINGS AND THE FAIR CREDIT REPORTING ACT

Congress's 1966 discovery of private-sector databases soon led to a fresh round of hearings, this time directed specifically at the consumer reporting industry. During the 1968 and 1969 hearings, industry leaders were trotted before lawmakers and grilled about the content of credit reports and the information-handling practices of their organizations.[16] Where the existence of millions of individual paper files, dispersed among thousands of local credit bureaus, had been uncontroversial, the prospect of this detailed personal information flowing directly into a single database produced terror. "What we are really reaching," Representative Gallagher declaimed, "is a total surveillance society and a totally managed society, where all information goes into a centrally located data base."[17]

The consumer credit surveillance system in the United States was imposing before computerization, but the industry's overall fragmentation and the inefficiencies of paper files and telephone reporting seemed to afford some semblance of privacy. No single bureau knew *everything* about a particular person, and the extra effort and cost required to assemble comprehensive dossiers were enough to limit such investigations. Networked databases would eliminate such human and offline safeguards. "Now— with the advent of computer technology—we see the possibility of complete dossiers on every American citizen being available within seconds to whoever wants to buy them," Senator Philip A. Hart warned. This was especially troubling because, as he noted, the reporting industry already showed signs of concentration in three national networks—the CDC, ACB of A, and RCC.[18]

If left unchecked, lawmakers and privacy advocates feared, the credit bureau might become an information "omnibus" that spit out an individual's entire life history at the push of a button. This was exactly what the legal scholar Arthur R. Miller foresaw. "The credit network of the future," he told a Senate subcommittee in 1968, "may be used by insurance companies, bill collectors, all levels of government, employers in a variety of industries, and anyone in need of specialized mailing or solicitation lists. What today generally is a simple service for credit grantors may tomorrow emerge as a full line, all purpose information gathering and reporting network."[19]

For an industry that had long viewed itself as a patriotic defender of American business and the national credit economy, the hearings were a disaster. Unlike nineteenth-century commercial credit reporting firms such as R. G. Dun and Bradstreet, which were continually harried by resentful merchants and litigants, consumer credit bureaus operated with virtual impunity. Except for antitrust regulation during the 1930s and existing protections against defamation, the consumer reporting industry was left to its own discretion. "We have protected privacy for the past 60 years and we believe we can protect it in the future," ACB of A executive John L. Spafford told subcommittee members during the 1968 House hearing. "We believe we can do it with computers—and frankly, gentlemen, we believe we can do it with whatever comes after computers."[20] Spafford's boys' club assurance fell on deaf ears.

Congressional testimony quickly revealed systemic flaws in the confidentiality, accuracy, and use of information in bureau reports. The House hearing's first witness, the law professor Alan F. Westin, illustrated the laxity with which credit bureau information circulated. To test the difficulty of gaining access, Westin wrote to the Credit Bureau of Greater New York to request "a report on the character" of a female research assistant who worked for him at Columbia University. The woman (who was in on the ruse) was said to be under consideration for a job at Columbia. A day later the bureau manager called, read the woman's credit file to a member of Westin's staff, and agreed to mail a typed copy of the report. Amazingly, this "outrageous disclosure of personal information" was provided free of charge as a goodwill gesture to the university.[21]

While Westin's stunt exposed serious lapses in confidentiality at one the nation's largest credit bureaus (and an ACB of A member), it also showed that such bureaus dealt in much more than credit information. Some of the most incendiary testimony during the hearings centered on the reporting industry's investigative procedures and collection of moral and personal anecdote. The "previous residence report" that Westin received, for example, included information about the woman's prior employment, credit history, income, and status as homeowner, renter, or boarder as well as rubrics to indicate her "character, habits, and morals," her employer's opinion of her, evidence of "illegal" activity, and lawsuits or judgments against her. Though ACB of A leaders claimed that "extraneous" noncredit information was excluded from its credit reports and that its member bureaus did not conduct outside investigations, lawmakers cited evidence to the contrary. In addition to producing a recent ACB of A credit report in which the subject's IQ was included, the operation of ACB of A Welcome Newcomer services was held up as an example of invasive domestic surveillance. A promotional sideline offered by some fifty to seventy-five of the association's members, newcomer programs were accused of employing bureau "hostesses" to collect information about the home conditions and possessions of new residents.[22] These and other violations were seized upon by journalists and became emblematic of the entire credit reporting business.

As Westin pointed out, one did not have to represent a credit-granting organization to get a wealth of detailed personal information about an individual. If the bureaus could not protect access to their paper files—the New York bureau was not yet computerized—how could they be trusted to safeguard personal privacy in an age of databases? Even more disturbing, government itself was one of the many noncreditors that purchased bureau information. During the hearings, lawmakers learned that the RCC and ACB of A member bureaus sold information to a wide range of federal agencies, including the IRS and the FBI. When pressed to defend this practice, industry representatives responded with some of the most naïve and cringe-worthy testimony. Both RCC president W. Lee Burge and ACB of A executive Spafford claimed that their organizations' cooperation with government agencies was a service to the public. Representative Gallagher asked Spafford, "Do you perform a public service for the FBI, the IRS, or the citizen?" Spafford answered, "Does the FBI represent the citizens? Doesn't the government?" Gallagher shot back, "There are citizens who disagree from time to time with the IRS. You have thrown your lot in with the IRS which is sometimes in disagreement with the citizen. After all, the Bill of Rights was not written for the king's men."[23] If government could obtain detailed personal and financial information about its citizens without a court order, perhaps a federal database was not even needed. The information could simply be purchased or subpoenaed directly from commercial data brokers like the credit bureau. Technology had "outpaced social responsibility," Representative Rosenthal lamented. "In the old days of the nice neighborhood bank, I would go in, and they would know me, and they wouldn't spread that information out."[24]

While credit reporting looked bad, personnel and insurance reporting looked even worse. The RCC, in particular, took the brunt of congressional hammering. As the nation's largest reporting agency and a firm whose model of information gathering centered upon personal investigations (rather than merchant-supplied ledger data), the RCC relied heavily upon the opinions of informants. During the hearings, lawmakers questioned the RCC's use of information from former employers and neighbors that amounted to unsubstantiated hearsay. In one case, a woman struggled to find work after information in RCC files, furnished by her neighbor, described her as "psychotic and neurotic." The RCC's attorney defended the injurious characterization. Whether the woman was psychotic according to its medical definition was beside the point. The local people who knew the woman thought that she was crazy, and that was all that mattered to prospective employers. "So what you are doing then is reporting on her reputation in the community by using these words?" a member of the Senate subcommittee asked. "Exactly," the attorney answered.[25]

In essence, the RCC followed the model of commercial credit surveillance developed by Lewis Tappan in the 1840s. As Tappan had explained, his mercantile agency system—the origin of mass credit surveillance in the United States—was nothing more than a plan for collecting the local reputations of all American business owners and centralizing this information for the use of faraway creditors. Reproducing Tappan's nineteenth-century alibi almost verbatim, the RCC attorney argued that the firm was doing nothing wrong by simply compiling what local people already knew and thought about one another. "What is wrong with hearsay?" he challenged. "If nobody acted on hearsay you won't have any civilization. I mean we all act on hearsay every day of our lives."[26] The problem of course was that hearsay embedded in impersonal surveillance networks and broadcasted beyond local contexts was amplified, difficult to contextualize or correct, and potentially far more damaging.

The content of RCC life and automobile insurance reports raised similar concerns. The firm's life insurance report, for instance, included space for detailed remarks about an applicant's alcoholic consumption. William Proxmire, chairman of the 1969 Senate hearing and the sponsor of the Fair Credit Reporting Act (FCRA), conceded that there might be a connection between "alcoholism and mortality." However, he pointed out, one section of the report asked investigators to describe "how the applicant drinks, if social or solitary, or if because of domestic or other trouble." For Senator Proxmire, this strained credulity. "Not only do you want to know if a person drinks, you want to know why he drinks. Are your inspectors trained psychiatrists? Do you really think you can determine why a person drinks after talking to his neighbor for a few minutes?"[27] Other standard questions about the applicant's "living conditions or neighborhood" and whether he or she was an "argumentative, antagonistic type" revealed the depth and seeming caprice of the RCC's surveillance.

When asked why such questions even appeared on their forms, President Burge pointed to the RCC's clients: the RCC was merely giving insurers the information they asked for. Life insurers, he presumed, were not using neighborhood information to redline applicants who lived in ghettos, but to estimate the impact of "unhealthful, overcrowded conditions" on their longevity.[28] Automobile insurers, he speculated, believed that antagonistic personality types were at greater risk of road rage. It stood to reason that an antagonistic man "might be the kind who, when behind the wheel, is argumentative with his bumpers and with his fenders as well as with his voice."[29] All of this disparate information—personal, professional, psychological, health—intermingled in RCC files. The ACB of A at least claimed that its member bureaus segregated credit information from that used in personnel or insurance reports. The RCC did not. In the process of becoming "a data-rich society," Representative Gallagher warned, America was at risk of becoming "privacy poor."[30]

Despite such egregious violations of privacy, the interconnectedness of personal, credit, employment, and health information in reporting industry files was not overly troubling to lawmakers. The difference between credit bureau reports and "investigative" reports for employment and insurance was explained, and most accepted that clients for each had legitimate reasons for considering different types of information. An employer or insurer, for example, demanded more-probing details about an individual's personality, habits, and health—even if attempts to adduce one's motivation for drinking were absurd. As Representative Gallagher clarified, the industry's task of compiling "a complete and accurate picture of an individual's credit activity and certain general remarks about reliability and character" for their clients was understood and even praiseworthy. "This subcommittee has neither the wish nor the jurisdiction to alter this tradition."[31] As long as credit, personnel, and insurance information was segregated in the bureaus' files, and as long as the information was factually true, then congressional leaders were willing to give it a pass.

What really troubled lawmakers and many consumer advocates was that information in bureau files was not accurate and that individuals had no clear way to intervene. During the hearings, the reporting industry's unchecked power was illustrated by Kafkaesque tales in which individuals, rejected for credit or employment due to erroneous information or spiteful obstruction, were helpless to clear their name. It was in this context that databases appeared especially frightening. With their lightning speed, their ability to transfer massive quantities of data, and their totalizing memories, computer networks might compound existing errors and, even worse, enshrine such errors and all of one's past missteps in a permanent digital record. Computers represented "a radical new element in the credit bureau industry," Representative Gallagher warned, and "probably in

American life as well." "You have now put a machine into an old and tried business," he admonished CDC president Harry C. Jordan. "This is what makes it dangerous."[32]

While the ACB of A and the RCC were caught flat-footed during the hearings and pilloried in the press, the third major player in the reporting industry, CDC, came off much better. Before going online in 1965 with the nation's first computerized credit reporting system, CDC had carefully hashed out guidelines to govern the content and circulation of its centralized files. Working with an advisory committee representing its original subscribers—predominantly banks, finance companies, and national credit card issuers—CDC decided at the outset that its records would contain only an individual's basic identifying information, account and payment history, current and previous employment, and public record items such as bankruptcies, lawsuits, judgments, and liens. All personal and employment information came from the customer's credit application form. Account and payment information came directly from subscribers—transferred to CDC via computer as a by-product of automated accounting systems—and public record items were separately collected from published sources.

Importantly, CDC would not conduct any outside investigations or collect information about an individual's personality, health, or domestic life. It sold information only to bona fide credit grantors for the purpose of credit evaluation (though, as a courtesy, CDC did allow its subscribers to use reports to screen their own prospective employees). The firm steadfastly refused to traffic in promotional customer lists. "Thou shalt not sell the lists" was etched in stone, according to Jordan.[33] But CDC's most aggressive defense of privacy was its refusal to share information with non-credit-granting government agencies, such as law enforcement and the IRS, without a court order. CDC had already defied three IRS demands for information, for which it had received a summons.[34]

Compared to the RCC and ACB of A, CDC had been proactive and forward-thinking in its efforts to safeguard personal privacy. Its president also provided compelling testimony in defense of computerized surveillance itself. Jordan, after all, had a doctorate in biophysics and a sophisticated understanding of information theory and technology. While laying out CDC's clearly defined information-handling protocols, he argued that centralized databases were nothing to be feared. Networked reporting systems, designed with forethought and intelligence, could be managed to achieve socially desirable objectives. Technology, in other words, could only do what its human masters allowed. It was technically feasible to program computers to record almost any kind of information, he acknowledged, including hearsay about an individual's personality, psychological profile, and home life. His firm had purposely designed its system to exclude such information. Likewise, it was technically possible (albeit expensive then) for a computer to store one's total life history for long periods of time, perhaps even forever. But again, Jordan's system was designed to make this impossible. CDC computers were programmed to erase black marks on one's record at regular intervals; missed or slow payments disappeared after five years, bankruptcies after fifteen. "It is part of civilized tradition that all men have the right to rectify or live down past transgressions," Jordan asserted, debunking the popular misconception that "mechanical brains" never forget.[35]

Even more, Jordan argued that digital records afforded *more* privacy control than traditional paper files. Unlike the vast rows of filing cabinets in a typical manual bureau, among which dozens of employees roamed without supervision, the information in computerized reporting systems—invisible to the naked eye—was accessible to only a small number of experts and programmers. Even Westin saw the computer's opacity as an advantage. "A fifth of bourbon won't get you as far with an IBM 360 as with a junior clerk in a particular credit bureau in 'X' city. How you lubricate a computer is a little different than we do in the buddy system."[36] This perspective assumed that highly educated male computer technicians were ethically superior to low-paid, mostly female bureau operators. But even if they were not, the computer's own recordkeeping functions provided a powerful deterrent. Since special codes were required to access computer reports, the source of violations and breaches could be identified simply by reviewing automated logs. Workplace computers provided management with new modes of employee surveillance. "In short, you can build into a computer program crosschecks that will electronically smell a rat," Jordan explained.[37]

Even the quantitative language of CDC reports worked indirectly toward greater personal privacy. "As opposed to a paper file where any little girl can write down anything, the computer can only assign finite ratings. So we can't write down a little note that we heard he had a fight with his wife last night. The computer has no way to enter this data."[38] This was not reassuring to Representative Gallagher. "I worry about who that little girl is. Wouldn't you, if she is processing the profiles of 20 million Americans?"[39] Jordan brushed aside such concerns, noting that 80 percent of the data transferred into the CDC's files was communicated between computers.

Though Jordan offered a social shaping of technology perspective with regard to the content and operational details of computerized reporting, he was fatalistic when it came to its proliferation. CDC was adding 50,000 new files to its database each week, and he estimated that it would have files for all Americans in five years. Noting that his firm was not the only one in the process of automating, he predicted that all credit information would be computerized within a decade and that this information would be controlled by a handful of companies.[40] At the time of the hearings, computerized bureaus were still in the minority. The RCC had not even begun to computerize, and some major urban bureaus had no plans to do so. "Credit is primarily a local affair," the manager of the Credit Bureau of Greater Boston explained. "We simply don't have enough need for contact in another part of the country to justify the expense of a computer interconnection."[41] By 1973, however, credit bureaus in all of the nation's largest cities were computerized. The march toward automation slowed as smaller bureaus balked at the cost and trouble of converting, but the genie was out of the bottle.[42]

If computerization could not be stopped, new rules for handling credit information could be imposed. Not surprisingly, the reporting industry insisted that reform should come through voluntary self-policing rather than heavy-handed federal regulation. In January 1969, the ACB of A unveiled a fresh set of guidelines that granted consumers the right to learn the contents of their file, placed limits on government access to credit records, and instructed that adverse items be deleted after seven years (with the exception of bankruptcies). The RCC adopted the ACB of A guidelines, but CDC chose to adhere to its own, more "restrictive" code of ethics.[43] While all mouthed concern for consumer rights, industry leaders shrugged off complaints and errors as anomalous and rare given the huge volume of reports they produced. Even Jordan dismissed mistakes as inevitable and of minor concern. Credit reporting did not require the same standards of infallibility as critical infrastructure. When an air traffic control system made "a boo-boo," he noted, it was catastrophic; when a credit bureau did, the individual merely experienced "a slight inconvenience."[44] Lawmakers disagreed. Credit access had become indispensable in American life and its oversight too important to be left to voluntary, inconsistent, and unenforceable insider remedies. Indeed, credit surveillance had become a critical part of the nation's economic infrastructure.

The FCRA was passed in October 1970 and signed into law by President Nixon two weeks later. Along with the Consumer Credit Protection Act of 1968 (which included Truth-in-Lending provisions), the FCRA reflected the growing influence of the consumer protection movement in American politics. Its major provisions established the following new rules. Credit reports could be procured only for a "legitimate business need." Government agencies had to have a court order to obtain reports (though certain identifying information could be shared without one). Credit reporting organizations had to disclose the "nature and substance" of information in an individual's file, as well as the sources of the information, if requested by the subject. Adverse items were to be deleted after seven years (fourteen years for bankruptcies). Individuals who were denied credit, insurance, or employment, or whose interest rates or premiums were raised on the basis of an adverse credit report, had to be notified and provided with the credit bureau's contact information. And individuals for whom an investigative report was ordered had to be notified; in the case of employment reports, the subject had to be notified if the report included adverse public record information.[45]

The FCRA, which was to be enforced by the Federal Trade Commission (FTC), gave consumers new powers to review, correct, and monitor the circulation of their personal information. In this regard, it was an important step toward addressing the problem of inaccuracies. However, serious problems quickly emerged. For one, the law required only that credit bureaus disclose "the nature and content of all information" in an individual's file. It did not specify *how* the information was to be shared. During congressional hearings, the reporting industry vigorously opposed any rule that would require them to give consumers a copy of their credit report. They argued that consumers would be confused by the cryptic language and that, as Jordan suggested, consumers could not be trusted to protect the confidentiality of their own reports.[46] The FCRA gave consumers the right to know what was in their report, but technically it did not give them the right to inspect it directly. Thus, reverting to the secretive methods of nineteenth-century mercantile agencies, credit bureaus refused to give visiting consumers a copy of reports. Instead, bureau employees read the contents of reports to consumers, paraphrasing or omitting details as they saw fit.[47]

The FCRA did even less to protect privacy. Government agencies could still obtain basic information without a court order, and the content of bureau files was unrestricted. Since credit bureau violations were very difficult to prove, and long-standing privileged communication laws protected them from defamation, they had little fear of being sued. As a result, they had no incentive to rein in their information-collection practices.[48] Additionally, the "legitimate business need" stipulation was practically an open door. The FCRA specifically permitted the use of credit reports by creditors, insurers, and employers, but the "legitimate business need" catchall could easily be used to justify the sale of credit information to landlords, market researchers, and consumer list vendors, not to mention attorneys, collection agencies, or private investigators. This loophole would become a major point of contention as credit bureaus redefined themselves as comprehensive data providers.

Though new firms like CDC refused to sell reports to anyone but credit grantors, narrowly defined, other computerized bureaus such as Chilton's were moving to expand and diversify their services. With huge investments sunk in new technology and facilities, the temptation to monetize information in wider contexts was very real.[49] CDC had already become a pawn of corporate diversification. In 1968 it was acquired by TRW, a defense industry giant that engineered nuclear missiles and satellites, among many other things. Eager to hop into the rapidly growing information technology

market, TRW saw CDC as an opportunity to quickly acquire "a big proprietary database" and a dominant position.[50] Over the next two decades,
TRW and the largest computerized bureaus would develop a growing array
of credit screening and marketing programs. The FCRA, with its modest
requirements and loose definitions, did not even begin to address larger
forces that were shaping the future of consumer surveillance in the United
States.

More than anything, the investigations leading to passage of the FCRA
revealed the reporting industry's insatiable appetite for information. While
public debate revolved around issues of accuracy and privacy, a more profound question loomed in the background: What information was *relevant* in making a credit decision? Financial information was only a small
part of what credit bureaus collected. In addition to documenting the income, assets, and past payment histories of American consumers, bureau
files contained a wealth of "nonfinancial" detail, from gender, age, and
marital status to one's address, occupation and employment history, status
as a renter or homeowner, and legal judgments. Even more, credit reporting
was tangled up with insurance risk and employment decisions, both of
which had deep historical and conceptual links to creditworthiness.
Though the FCRA distinguished between credit bureau reports and more
invasive "investigative" reports—the kind prepared for employers and
insurers—it did little to limit their intermingling. Galling accounts of investigative insurance reporting, most involving the inquisitorial practices
of the RCC, continued to grab attention even after the FCRA went into
effect.[51] This prompted the question: What information, if any, was officially out of bounds?

Relevance was a problem for credit evaluation because it was not clear
where financial information ended and nonfinancial information began.
Was an individual's employment *history*—not his or her current job and
salary—financial information or personal information? What about gender, age, or the number of one's dependents? All of these variables might be
used to infer the future profitability of a borrower, insurance policy, or employee, but none was financial data. The problem was that financial and
personal information overlapped and informed each other. Evidence of

steady past employment, for instance, might suggest that an applicant was hardworking and reliable. Thus, at a fundamental level it was not clear where the lender's due diligence ended and prying began.

The issue was directly addressed by Kenneth V. Larkin, a Bank of America executive who spoke on behalf of the American Bankers Association during the 1969 Senate hearings. "Today the need of consumer credit lenders is for more, not less, credit information," he asserted. In particular, he objected to language in FCRA legislation that would limit credit bureau information to "essential" items only. "In the typical credit decision," he explained, "it is difficult to define any one item as 'essential' in contrast with other others which are 'unessential' or 'marginal.' In fact, a credit decision is a judgment based on the totality of available information."[52] At the center of this totality was character, the first of the three Cs of creditworthiness. The borrower's "integrity, honesty, [and] the willingness to pay" were the foundation of creditworthiness, Larkin insisted, and could not be judged simply by examining his or her past payment history.[53] Larkin's plea for information maximalism and the primacy of character was striking given that his employer, Bank of America, was a major CDC client. The limit to "essential" information was struck from the bill, and credit bureaus remained free to compile just about any information they chose to as long as they made "reasonable" efforts to ensure its accuracy and dumped adverse items after seven years.

Though the FCRA left the problem of relevant information unresolved, the debate was still very much alive. The political movement to end credit discrimination by banning gender, race, and other personal characteristics from credit decisions—in effect, making this information irrelevant— would highlight the problem during the early 1970s. Behind the scenes, credit managers also were waging a war on relevance. With the growing popularity of statistical scoring systems, the credit manager's expert judgment was being replaced by computers. Creditworthiness, refigured as credit risk, was simply a function of statistical calculation and association. Computer-aided scoring not only made the credit manager's human judgment irrelevant; it also threatened to make the entire profession irrelevant.

PROFESSIONAL PANIC: STATISTICAL SCORING
AND THE CREDIT MANAGER

By the early 1970s, more than a decade after the *New York Times* announced the stunning deadbeat detecting power of credit scoring, many credit managers still did not want these computer-powered systems. There was no denying that computing made complex statistical calculations easy and cost-effective. But for many credit managers, scoring seemed to offer little or no operational benefit. As a Fair Isaac executive later recalled, "When the idea of replacing the traditional judgmental procedure for making credit decisions with scoring was first offered to the credit establishment it was not received with any conspicuous enthusiasm. Far from it."[54] Many credit managers resisted scoring systems because, quite simply, they did not perceive credit evaluation as a problem. Large and multibranch firms like AIC, which processed thousands of applications per day, may have seen economic advantage in systematizing this routine, but many small and medium-sized businesses did not.

When early statistical systems were adopted, it was not because they were considered superior to the judgment of experienced credit managers. "Consumer credit institutions lend billions of dollars each year, much of it to people they have never seen before. Yet their losses often seem surprisingly low." This, a Wharton professor noted in 1964, was due to either the honesty of the American public or "the efficiency of the screening systems" already in place.[55] Credit managers had become quite good at evaluating individual credit risk, in many cases keeping losses below 1 percent of total credit sales. Their judgmental methods worked and posed no threat to the stability of ballooning postwar consumer debt. The problem, rather, was that there were simply not enough of these seasoned credit professionals to handle the avalanche of new applications. "A good credit manager nowadays is hard to find is heard more frequently than ever," an ACB of A official noted in 1962.[56] Credit scoring initially solved a more prosaic problem: a shortage of skilled labor. In solving this problem, however, scoring systems soon redefined credit evaluation procedures and the notion of creditworthiness itself.

Where personal interviewing was possible, it continued because credit managers believed that every application was unique and that their professional judgment was superior to the cryptic mathematical models of outsiders. "The word 'model' causes apprehension among some business people," a statistics professor admitted in describing the advantages of scoring systems. "To them it suggests a lack of reality."[57] Indeed, for many credit managers, nothing suggested eggheaded unreality more than the idea of forfeiting their professional judgment to what amounted to complex gambling odds. During the 1968 House hearing on credit reporting, Representative John Meyers of Indiana attested to the credit manager's powers of discernment. Meyers, who had worked in a bank prior to going to Washington, told his colleagues, "You can pretty well diagnose a person who walks in for a loan. If he looks wild-eyed and wants a private room, instead of standing out front, he is likely a poor risk."[58]

If credit managers initially resisted scoring systems because they seemed to be more trouble than they were worth, they soon had a more personal

Figure 8.1 The automation of credit judgment, once dismissed as fantasy, became all too real for postwar credit managers as statistical credit scoring threatened their professional expertise. (*Credit World*, June 1933)

and emotional reason to oppose them. Credit scoring threatened their jobs. Since the late nineteenth century, when credit management was professionalized, these office workers had struggled to win the approval of their employers. Early credit managers, unlike sales and merchandising personnel, were often viewed grudgingly as an expensive but necessary bulwark against fraud and loss. By the 1950s, credit management was finally a well-established executive role in many firms. The development of postwar scoring systems—and automation more generally—threated to undo these gains (figure 8.1).

New credit scoring systems effectively removed the human element from credit evaluation by eliminating the need for personal contact between credit managers and credit seekers. The reliance on interviews, during which the credit manager eyed the condition of a consumer's shoes, had its flaws, to be sure.[59] Personal prejudice, rather than professional wisdom, skewed many credit decisions along lines of class, gender, and race, not to mention more idiosyncratic biases. But while credit scoring promised to remove such prejudice—indeed, to democratize credit evaluation—it also reduced personal creditworthiness to the sum of statistical probabilities. The applicant was no longer an individual credit risk, but a faceless swimmer in larger pools of risk. Within such risk populations, individuals shared little more than superficial economic and demographic qualities. In this new world of statistical truth, the human intervention of credit managers was not simply discouraged; it was refigured as distortion and error. Scoring thus challenged long-held assumptions about the concept of creditworthiness itself. If creditworthiness was no longer a function of personal character—one's honesty, responsibility, and morality—then *what* exactly did credit scoring measure? Could financial and moral qualities really be disentangled? For many credit managers, the answer was no.[60]

By the early 1970s, the credit manager was stuck in an "uncomfortable posture," with one foot in the past and the other in the future.[61] Traditional methods were no longer economically viable, but scoring was professional suicide. At an American Bankers Association meeting in 1975, a representative of the First National Bank of Boston sounded the death knell for traditional credit managers. Amazingly, the executive reported, the bank could have prevented 25 percent of its annual losses during the previous two years if its "credit analysts" had been replaced by a scoring system. There was nothing wrong with the bank's analysts, he insisted, but they could not match the odds-making accuracy of scoring systems, whose operation required "individuals who were smart enough just to add up a column of figures."[62] Before long, even human tabulators would be replaced by machines.

DEMOCRATIZING OR DEHUMANIZING? CREDITWORTHINESS AND THE EQUAL CREDIT OPPORTUNITY ACT

As the use of computerized credit reporting and statistical credit scoring became a fact of life during the late 1960s, the evaluation of credit risk underwent a dramatic shift. Computerized bureaus reduced an individual's personal details and record of payment to a series of numbers and codes that looked more like a spreadsheet than a biography. Statistical scoring converted creditworthiness into the mathematical analysis of faceless populations, ignoring the flesh-and-blood person. In both cases, credit evaluation was migrating from the world of human interactions into the black box of machines. As Alan Westin observed, "Our world is rapidly becoming one with few face-to-face contacts left. Department stores and credit card companies and so forth are relying more and more on the credit report alone. They never see the individual or have any contact with him. He might just be a cipher to them."[63]

The introduction of computers into credit evaluation was profoundly alienating for many Americans. Creditworthiness had always been a matter of trust. It was not enough that one had the financial ability to repay a debt, but whether one would resist the selfish impulse to delay and actually send the money. Indeed, the "genius" of the American credit system, as Austrian immigrant Francis Grund observed in the 1830s, was its deeply personal nature. American creditworthiness was not determined by wealth or privilege; it was embedded in the individual's sense of moral obligation and responsibility. These were intangible personal qualities that could not be seen, let alone quantified. It followed, then, that credit evaluation could never really be reduced to mere financial calculation. Even early proponents of credit scoring saw statistical systems as an aid, not a replacement, for human credit judgment.

Yet as lending institutions, retailers, and credit card companies grew to national proportions, the human element receded. Multibranch and regional credit departments processed thousands of credit applications without ever meeting their subjects. The institutionalization of credit relationships was certainly not a new problem. It dated to the 1840s, when the first commercial credit reporting organizations began to compile information about American merchants throughout the nation. Then, as in the late 1960s, many Americans resented that their personal information was being ferried away to distant city offices, where it was used by strangers to make judgments about their reputations. Computerized systems for reporting and scoring creditworthiness further dehumanized credit evaluation in ways that nineteenth-century critics could never have imagined. With computers, ledger data and credit reports were communicated between machines, not people, and statistical scoring systems judged abstract populations rather than unique individuals.

If database surveillance raised the specter of totalitarianism among its critics, industry officials saw exactly the opposite. Computerized reporting and scoring systems did not oppress the American people. Rather, they served to expand and democratize economic opportunity. By tracking all adult citizens and analyzing statistical populations, consumer credit was cheaper, more convenient, and more widely available than ever. This had long been a key selling point of credit surveillance. By identifying the worst risks in the community, reporting organizations helped lenders extend credit to the trustworthy and profitable majority. The much-heralded "democratization" of consumer credit during the 1910s and 1920s hinged upon the rational administration of credit bureaus and credit departments. Paradoxically, the totalizing gaze of credit surveillance made credit evaluation more fair and convenient. Where everyone was subjected to credit checks, as the Rockefeller incident revealed in 1913, creditworthiness was a function of impersonal recordkeeping, not wealth or privilege or prejudice. The tradeoff for democratized credit was constant surveillance. For lenders and, indeed, many consumers, this was a reasonable bargain.

Until the late 1960s, however, most Americans had no idea how much they were giving up in the trade.

The massive growth of postwar credit was certainly a compelling argument in favor of democratization. Yet access to credit was neither equally distributed nor entirely democratic. During the late 1960s and early 1970s, many women and minorities still found it difficult to secure credit or loans. Middle-class white women had long been recognized as valuable credit customers, especially among department stores and larger retailers, but their charge accounts were often tied to a creditworthy husband or male cosigner. Many single and divorced women could not open an account or obtain a credit card in their own names, even if they produced their own income. At the same time, lower-income urban minorities were often trapped by predatory lenders in their own neighborhoods. Thanks to these "ghetto merchants," the poor not only paid more, but many were unable to establish official credit histories, which mainstream retailers and national lenders required when offering charge accounts or credit cards. As a result, many inner-city minorities were effectively frozen out of the larger world of consumer credit.[64]

By the early 1970s, these forms of credit discrimination became the target of legislative intervention. The FCRA, though forcing credit bureaus to be slightly more transparent, did nothing to prohibit such discrimination. As credit bureau operators had insisted for a century, they merely provided subscribers with information about prospective borrowers. They did not "rate" anyone. The decision to lend or not was entirely up to the credit grantor. "As a practical matter, there are no standards for credit managers," a representative for the National Small Business Association told lawmakers during a Senate hearing on credit reporting. Credit decisions, he noted, were often a matter of "judgment" and "intuition."[65] Regulating the reporting industry, in other words, had done little to change the way creditworthiness was evaluated by lenders on the ground.

The problem of relevance was finally addressed head on by the Equal Credit Opportunity Act (ECOA). Passed in 1974 on the heels of the FCRA, the ECOA made it illegal to deny credit to anyone on the basis of gender or marital status. The act was amended in 1976 to further prohibit lenders from considering a credit applicant's race, nationality, religion, age, or receipt of public assistance.[66] In effect, the ECOA made these elements of personal information *irrelevant* to creditworthiness. As a step toward the goals of social equality, the ECOA was an important political victory. By the 1970s many Americans, including many in the business community, believed that it was unethical to reduce creditworthiness to biology or skin color. Many lenders had already removed these offending categories from their applications and scoring systems. However, credit discrimination was not that simple. Consumer lenders and retailers were in business to make money. Generally speaking, they did not reject female credit applicants because of their gender, but because women typically earned less than men and often left the workforce (and their own incomes) to have and raise children. Likewise, lenders did not uniformly refuse to lend to African Americans as a class, but avoided dealing with residents of unstable, low-income inner-city neighborhoods where many African Americans lived. For individuals who experienced such discrimination, this distinction—the difference between economic calculation and outright sexism or racism—was a moot point. It *was* discriminatory. However, it was not entirely arbitrary. Credit decisions that privileged men over women and whites over African Americans were a reflection of real structural inequalities in American society.

While defining the legal parameters of relevant credit information, the ECOA raised as many new questions as it answered. Nowhere was this more apparent than in the development of statistical scoring. As a technological fix for the problem of discrimination, scoring systems seemed ideal. Their use had even been endorsed by the National Commission on Consumer Finance, a bipartisan investigatory body formed in 1968 as part of the Consumer Credit Protection Act. In its 1972 final report, the commission concluded that "statistically-based discrimination" used for credit granting was no different than that used for insurance underwriting and should be accepted.[67] Unlike "judgmental" credit managers, whose evaluations of creditworthiness were by definition subjective and idiosyncratic, scoring systems were objective and uniform. As a credit manager for Montgomery Ward testified in 1975, "The system's reliance on numerical values removes the possibility that an individual credit manager will be biased or prejudiced against any individual or segment of applicants."[68]

Better yet, discriminatory categories of information could be formally excluded from scoring systems. If gender was banned from consideration, then this information was simply taken out of the statistical calculations. The actuarial principles of credit scoring appealed to many lawmakers and the Federal Reserve Board (FRB), which was charged with the law's oversight and interpretation. The ECOA's rules, codified in Regulation B, even granted scoring systems an exception with regard to age. According to the FRB, age could be included in "statistically sound, empirically derived" systems for determining creditworthiness, so long as the calculations were to the advantage of older applicants. In other words, younger applicants could be penalized for their relative lack of work and credit experience, but elderly and retired applicants on fixed incomes could not.

In theory, statistical scoring was supremely rational, consistent, and transparent. In practice, discrimination was much harder to root out. In part, this was because statistical scoring systems did not weigh individual variables in isolation. Rather, they relied on complex calculations in which multiple variables interacted with and affected the predictive power of the others. No single variable could be eliminated without affecting all of the others. Where marital status was removed, for instance, greater weight shifted to other variables, such as occupational categories or whether one owned or rented one's home. This conundrum was highlighted by the ECOA's requirement that lenders give each declined credit applicant a specific reason for their rejection. Lenders argued that it was impossible to pinpoint which variable was the most important when an application was turned down. Even Fair Isaac vigorously contested this requirement. In a written statement to the FTC, the firm asserted that "reference to any single item, or to any group of items as the cause for rejection is a deliberate and unwarranted falsehood which can do nothing but mislead the applicant."[69] While this argument was disingenuous—variables with subpar values could be cited as the source of a depressed score—it pointed to the unease that lenders felt in reducing creditworthiness to mathematical facts—facts, moreover, that they were legally required to defend.

Most troubling of all, variables associated with statistical credit risk were so deeply embedded in socioeconomic contexts that they were virtually impossible to disentangle. Even if gender and race were excluded from scoring systems, for example, protected classes could still experience negative bias. This occurred because gender and race were closely associated with "secondary" variables that were not prohibited, such as occupational category, length of employment, or whether one rented or owned one's home. Both women and minorities were statistically more likely to have lower-paying, less-skilled jobs, which counted against them. Likewise, women who left the work force to have children were more apt to have truncated employment histories, and minorities, particularly in the inner city, were more likely to rent rather than own their homes. In short, statistical credit scoring could not end discrimination by excluding superficial personal characteristics because gender and racial inequities were woven directly into the fabric of American society. Proxy problems immediately became apparent where legal secondary variables were intertwined with prohibited primary variables.

Though lenders supported the broad philosophical aims of the ECOA, they feared the incursion of legislation into the credit decision process. Much of this fear centered on the concept of discrimination itself. Among lenders and economists, discrimination was not a dirty word. As a term used to describe rational economic choice, it accurately captured the fundamental aim of credit evaluation: to identify good and bad risks and to treat them differently. In fact, this was accomplished by the application of discriminant analysis in statistical credit scoring systems. Credit evaluation was unabashedly discriminatory; the question was whether or not it was arbitrary or irrational discrimination, as prohibited by the ECOA. A case could certainly be made that it was entirely rational, from a purely economic perspective, to use any variable that was statistically predictive in credit scoring models. During subsequent hearings on credit card redlining, William Fair, president of Fair Isaac, gave his opinion that *no* variable should be banned, including the race, religion, sex, marital status, or ethnic origin of a credit applicant, if it was statistically correlated with credit risk. As Fair argued, more information was always better. The real "villain" was "not a possibly racist or misogynist credit grantor . . . not an unfeeling designer of credit scoring systems, but the absence of knowledge and information."[70]

As Fair and others freely admitted, scoring systems merely revealed correlations among variables. They said nothing about the underlying *causes* of these interrelationships. "The scoring system models the behavior of borrowers; it does not analyze the reason for their behavior."[71] Thus a scoring system could demonstrate that homeownership, certain occupations, or one's zip code were more or less associated with credit risk, but it offered no explanation as to why. The authors of statistical scoring systems professed no interest in sociological or behavioral theory. "Since we do not know *why* one person pays some particular creditor while another does not," Fair explained, "we must seek for any relationship we can find."[72] If Fair's omnivorous approach to data and his indifference to theory were at odds with social scientific norms during the 1970s, they would not be for long. Fair's information maximalism would become the mantra of big data evangelists during the early twenty-first century.[73]

It quickly became obvious, however, that statistical analysis devoid of theory could—and did—produce absurdities. Credit models often included variables with no obvious relationship to creditworthiness, as pointed out by Noel Capon, a Columbia University business professor and one of credit scoring's fiercest critics. Some models, he noted, considered factors such as the age of one's automobile, membership in a trade union, the age difference between a husband and wife, and the first letter of one's last name.[74] If predictive correlation was the only basis for selecting variables, then any scrap of trivia was fair game. Mocking the illogic of Fair's testimony, Capon asked, why not also consider "color of hair (if any), left- or right-handedness, wear eyeglasses, height, weight, early morning drink preference (coffee, tea, milk, other)," and a litany of other spurious variables?[75] Capon also observed that most scoring models did not include the one category of information that seemed to be the most relevant: the applicant's record of past payment.

Until the late 1980s credit scoring systems typically relied upon information collected through credit applications alone. By using application data—information that customers provided at no cost—lenders were able to avoid the purchase of credit bureau reports, in which payment histories appeared. At the time, scoring advocates such as Fair also argued that credit reports were too inaccurate and inconsistent to be incorporated into scoring systems.[76] Yet, as Capon noted, past payment performance, rather than arbitrary statistical associations, was self-evidently relevant to credit-worthiness. "How many representatives of the credit industry in this hearing room today were promoted to their current positions because of their place of residence or the age of their automobiles?" Capon asked during a Senate hearing. His point was well made. The inclusion of past payment data in subsequent credit models would blunt some of Capon's critique, but not his larger argument against the dangers of "brute force empiricism."

For lenders, the ECOA was seen as a slippery slope toward increasingly restrictive prohibitions that would degrade their scoring models and cut into profits. Worst still, the ECOA's ambiguities caused some lenders to worry that they might be held accountable for structural inequalities and sued by rejected credit applicants who were bent on social justice. "Credit grantors cannot, and must not, be compelled by legislation to be the scape-goats for other social ills," a representative for the National Consumer Finance Association pleaded to lawmakers.[77] If women were denied credit at a higher rate than men, he argued, then of course they were suffering from discrimination. The cause was not lenders, but unfair labor markets in which women were relegated to low-paying jobs. Consumer lenders and retailers acknowledged the obvious: social and economic disparity was a fact of American society. But the fact that statistical differences might be real—in other words, that women and other protected classes might actually be less creditworthy than white men—was a "third-rail" political issue that none dared to address.[78] Lawmakers preferred to see statistical scoring as a technological magic wand rather than an ugly mirror.

While seeking to democratize access to credit, the ECOA had a profound effect on the future of creditworthiness. Ironically, the new law accelerated the adoption of credit scoring systems. What originated as a labor-saving technology to speed credit evaluation was by the late 1970s a tool of legal compliance. Faced with prohibited categories of personal information and rules requiring the disclosure of credit criteria, lenders turned to scoring systems as a shield against discrimination suits. At minimum, such systems enabled a lender to prove that it applied the same standards to all credit applicants and to demonstrate its formal rules for decision making. "You are dealing with a difficult and sophisticated problem in this area," *Banking* magazine warned its readers. "Credit judgments, by their very nature, are discriminatory. You must be ready to prove they are not *unfairly* discriminatory."[79] The ECOA thus accomplished overnight what consultants and industry insiders had failed to do for a decade: convince skeptical credit managers to embrace statistical scoring.

More significantly, by pushing lenders toward impersonal computer scoring, the ECOA fostered a new version of creditworthiness. This version did not reside in the personality or context of the individual, but in the obscure statistical associations among large anonymous populations. Paradoxically, by protecting specific classes of disadvantaged Americans, the ECOA legitimized an approach to credit evaluation that favored groups—demographic and behavioral populations—over the unique individual. In 1975, as the amended ECOA was being finalized behind closed doors, Senator Joseph Biden, chairman of the Subcommittee on Consumer Affairs, voiced his concern about scoring systems. If statistical analysis could show that any particular group was an inferior credit risk, what was to stop this information from being used to discriminate against that group? "I guess I just don't like the point scoring system," Biden admitted. "If you don't allow the point scoring systems," fellow committee member Senator Jake Garn replied, "[on] what basis do you expect people to be able to grant or restrict credit?" Citing the huge volume of applications that national retailers such as Sears and J. C. Penney processed, Garn added, "There is no way they can sit with each individual and go through the personal type of credit granting system. If they can't use some kind of system, what will they do?"[80] The scale and speed of late twentieth-century America had made such personal transactions impossible. In this shift, intangible personal character, long the cornerstone of creditworthiness, was replaced by an equally intangible but quantifiable metric: statistical risk.

9

From Debts to Data

CREDIT BUREAUS IN THE NEW
INFORMATION ECONOMY

In January 1976 an envelope from Bank of America arrived in the mailbox of Bruce Steinberg. The enclosed letter congratulated Steinberg's "excellent credit reputation" and invited him to apply for a BankAmericard account. Rather than tossing the unwanted solicitation into the trash, the final destination of most junk mail, its recipient became angry. Steinberg, a San Francisco photographer and designer of record album covers, had never had an account with Bank of America. How, he wondered, could this bank know anything about his financial affairs? And why was he singled out to receive this credit card offer—an offer, no less, that boasted of such intimate familiarity?

Steinberg wrote to Bank of America for an explanation. He eventually learned that in preparing its promotion the bank had rented a list of consumers from R. H. Donnelley, a national list marketing firm. The rented list was then given to a credit bureau, TRW Credit Data, which matched names in its own database with those on the Donnelley list. The cross-referenced list was then further vetted by TRW according to variables provided by Bank of America. Steinberg had received the BankAmericard offer because his name appeared in two commercial databases, and his personal profile matched the bank's secret definition of an attractive customer. In short, he had been "prescreened." Legally speaking, none of the three firms had done anything wrong. Prescreening was permitted under the Fair Credit Reporting Act, as interpreted by the FTC.[1] But Steinberg was not mollified. He sued TRW and won a $35,000 settlement.

When Steinberg's story broke in 1980, his legal battle was presented as a quixotic crusade against junk mail. As TRW testified—and the *Wall Street Journal* reported to comic effect—the BankAmericard offer was mailed to 352,484 individuals, of which 42,018 responded. Only one person, Steinberg, had complained.[2] Even Senator Paul Tsongas, chair of the consumer affairs committee before which Steinberg later testified, was perplexed by his outrage. "You receive a letter saying you are a nice fellow and you have got a good credit rating and we would like to embrace you, and you say, 'no.'" Most people would be flattered, Tsongas suggested.[3] Steinberg was unmoved. The credit bureau, he insisted, had violated his privacy by disclosing information about his personal finances to a third party without his knowledge or consent. Such promiscuous data sharing was tantamount to "a rape of our files," as he crudely put it, "because nobody even bothers to ask."[4]

Steinberg's BankAmericard letter arrived at a pivotal moment in the history of consumer surveillance. During the 1970s databases proliferated and became integral to the conduct of everyday life in the United States. By 1974 the federal government operated more than 800 databases, which together included more than a *billion* records pertaining to individual citizens.[5] Government databases were just those that were publicly accountable, and therefore countable. Many more whirred behind the scenes in the private sector. Banks, insurance companies, retailers, airlines, hotels, mail order firms, and other businesses had their own databases. "We live, inescapably, in an 'information society,'" a blue-ribbon presidential commission on privacy reported in 1977, "and few of us have the option of avoiding relationships with record-keeping organizations."[6] As recordkeeping organizations adopted databases, the information society also became, inescapably, a surveillance society.

When institutional databases first appeared during the 1960s, the overriding public concern was with government overreach and, in particular, centralization. Orwellian visions of an omniscient blinking box, housed in the bowels of a remote federal building, spurred the first congressional hearings on information privacy. Yet what lawmakers failed to understand or to anticipate was that decentralization offered scant protection when it came to privacy. Information in one database could easily be transferred to another through storage media or directly via interlinked telecommunications. Computer records, after all, were fundamentally unlike paper records. Electronic data were malleable, modular, easily searched, and even more easily reproduced. Without a legal framework to forestall such data sharing, consumer information became a gold rush commodity. By the 1970s data about Americans was not only more plentiful; it also circulated with greater frequency and velocity within and between commercial interests. This is exactly what Steinberg had discovered.

As late twentieth-century capitalism became "informational," the American economy was driven by data—its production, management, and commodification.[7] Newly computerized credit bureaus were in the vanguard of these developments. During the 1970s and 1980s the consumer reporting industry was reduced to a handful of powerful bureaus with networked databases and a national reach. Unlike the thousands of local bureaus they replaced, these consolidated bureaus were multimillion-dollar corporations with much larger ambitions. When the RCC, one of the nation's leading bureaus, changed its name to Equifax in 1976, these ambitions were made clear. "We've renamed ourselves because we're so much more than a gatherer of credit information," a full-page ad announced in the *Wall Street Journal*. "We're a network of companies available to provide whatever kind of business information you need."[8] The credit bureau of the future would no longer be primarily concerned with tracking unpaid debts, as Equifax and its close competitors were quick to grasp. It would deal more broadly with data—very big consumer data.

As credit bureaus computerized and amassed huge databases of consumer information, they were in a unique position to leverage their information capital. Though credit reporting remained their core business, the leading bureaus moved to diversify their services and to redefine their role in the new information economy. Prescreening was just the beginning. A decade after Steinberg received his BankAmericard letter, the three dominant bureaus—Equifax, TransUnion, and TRW (now Experian)—were deeply involved in an array of ancillary businesses, from risk scoring to consumer profiling and direct marketing. Together, these new businesses generated synergistic flows of information within their parent companies. Credit databases were mined for risk-scoring programs, direct mail databases were cross-pollinated with credit databases, and consumer profiling and marketing systems drew insights from all of these databases. At the end of the twentieth century, the term *credit bureau* was a misnomer. "A bureau is somewhere you put your socks," Equifax's chief executive scoffed in 1997, refusing the label for his firm.[9] By then the three major bureaus had morphed into something else. They had become consumer data brokers.

THE COMPUTERIZED GIANTS TAKE OVER

Computers not only sped credit bureau service and reduced the cost of credit reports; they also tilted the balance of power toward a handful of large bureaus with capital to invest in data processing equipment. During the 1970s and 1980s scores of smaller bureaus and their carefully curated paper records vanished in waves of mergers and acquisitions, exactly as many had feared when computers entered the business. The industry's rapid consolidation was evident in the declining membership of the leading professional organization. After reaching a peak of 2,200 affiliated bureaus in 1969, total membership of the ACB of A dropped to 1,800 within five years. Among the remaining 1,800 members, 200 were computerized bureaus.[10]

For the credit bureau's main customers—notably banks and retailers—consolidation was a welcome development. The ideal credit bureau, in their eyes, was more like a monopolistic public utility than a throng of vying intelligence agencies. Where multiple bureaus competed in the same city or town, credit information was scattered among the various bureaus. If no bureau had complete information, then diligent creditors were compelled to purchase reports from more than one bureau. From the perspective of subscribers, consolidation promised to increase efficiency and reduce the costs of their investigations. Even the federal government, which had intervened during the 1930s to quash monopolistic credit reporting networks, offered little resistance to the industry's rapid concentration during the 1970s and 1980s. Once unleashed, the forces of consolidation were relentless. By the mid-1970s the industry was dominated by a five-bureau oligopoly: TRW Credit Data (later TRW Information Systems), the Chilton Corporation, Associated Credit Services of Houston, Credit Bureau Incorporated of Georgia (a subsidiary of Equifax), and TransUnion. By 1980 approximately 70 percent of all consumer credit reports—200 million per year—were provided by one of the major computerized credit bureaus.[11]

The last of these bureaus, TransUnion, was a newcomer to credit reporting.[12] Like TRW Credit Data, which sprang into existence when its defense and aerospace parent acquired CDC, TransUnion was a product of corporate diversification. In 1968 Union Tank Car, a freight car leasing firm based in Chicago, purchased that city's largest credit bureau and oversaw its computerization. Within two years the credit reporting division of the renamed umbrella company, TransUnion, held six credit bureaus— five in the Chicago region and one in St. Louis.[13] During the 1970s Trans-Union proceeded to acquire major bureaus in the Northeast, including the nation's largest, in New York City, and installed computer systems in each. By mid-decade its credit reporting network was bolstered by contracts with dozens of independent bureaus and a "microwave communications system" that linked central computers in Chicago to the firm's metropolitan affiliates. With files for forty million Americans in 1975, TransUnion was already among the nation's leading credit reporting firms.[14]

During the late 1980s additional mergers winnowed the five major bureaus down to three. In 1988 Chilton was acquired by TRW and Associated Credit Services of Houston (purchased in 1982 by Computer Sciences Corporation) became an adjunct of Equifax through a service agreement. Thus, at the end of the decade the consumer reporting industry was effectively controlled by three national credit reporting agencies: Equifax, TRW, and TransUnion. In 1996, TRW Information Systems was spun off from its parent and sold for $1 billion to a pair of Boston-based private equity firms, Thomas H. Lee and Bain Capital. Renamed Experian, the former TRW credit bureau and its information subsidiaries were promptly resold to Great Universal Stores (GUS), a British retailing giant best known for its mail order catalogs and ownership of the Burberry designer brand.

While consolidation reshaped the organizational structure of the reporting industry, the dominant bureaus also looked for opportunities to diversify their information services. Credit bureaus had long recognized the surplus values of their credit files and were eager to find new uses for their voluminous dossiers. During the 1980s, the leading bureaus moved far beyond the reshuffled intelligence they sold as employment, insurance, and tenant reports. Instead, they dove headlong into risk modeling and database marketing. These were new information-age businesses that relied upon powerful computers and huge reservoirs of consumer data. By then the leading credit bureaus had both. While consolidating their hold on the reporting industry, they also established their role as key players in a new kind of surveillance society, one that brought together thousands of data points and sorted millions of individuals into categories of statistical risk and value. Fed by torrents of data and equipped with new predictive technologies, credit bureaus and their corporate affiliates would wield growing power over the lives and life chances of individuals.[15]

FROM PRESCREENING TO RISK SCORING

During the 1970s and 1980s the dominant credit bureaus moved aggressively into the kinds of prescreening programs that had targeted Bruce Steinberg. Though the term *prescreening* was new, the concept itself was not. Credit bureaus had been vetting downtown charge card programs and assembling promotional lists since the 1950s. The difference was that these programs were locally organized and processed manually. Computers vastly expanded the scope of such operations. Drawing upon their own databases—as well as those of their clients and specialized list brokers—credit bureaus could easily compile huge rosters of prospective customers. With so much data readily accessible, prescreening quickly moved from a lucrative sideline to a core service among the leading computerized bureaus. When Steinberg received his prescreened offer, 7 percent of TRW's annual revenue came from prescreening.[16] By the end of the 1980s, Equifax earned between 10 and 20 percent of its total revenue from prescreening.[17]

The growth of prescreening reflected demand from one of the computerized bureau's most important subscribers: credit card–issuing banks.

When major banks moved into the credit card business during the 1960s, they faced a classic chicken-and-egg dilemma. Merchants would not accept the bank's credit cards if consumers did not attempt to use them. And consumers had little interest in using their new plastic talismans if few merchants accepted them. The bank's solution was to shower the public with active credit cards, which were mass mailed directly to consumers whether they wanted them or not. This promotional strategy resulted in rampant fraud, significant losses, and more than one family dog with a credit card in his name. After an outpouring of complaints, the practice was banned in 1970. Prescreening thus emerged as an economical—and legal—middle path. Rather than blindly mailing applications to the public, credit card issuers targeted only those who were "prequalified."

At first, computerized bureaus merely ran the bank's lists through their credit databases using the bank's own criteria to assemble rosters of direct mail prospects. According to the *Wall Street Journal*, credit card–issuing banks selected individuals with affluent zip codes, outstanding loans on German luxury cars, and prestige cards like American Express.[18] Such variables, though unscientific and intuitively obvious, were top secret. Even Steinberg, an intrepid investigator himself, could not get Bank of America to reveal the "jealously guarded" criteria that earned him a spot on its prescreened list.[19] During the mid-1980s prescreening became far more sophisticated. The turning point was PreScore, a new statistical scoring model developed by Fair Isaac.

What distinguished PreScore from all previous scoring models was that it incorporated credit bureau information. Remarkably, until the mid-1980s credit bureau data was *not* a part of credit scoring models. Instead, each model was constructed using the client's data. Banks and retailers, for example, provided vendors such as Fair Isaac with their own customer information, which was used to develop custom models based on the attributes and behaviors of their unique customer populations. Since no two customer populations were identical—Bank of America customers, for instance, were not exactly the same as Chase Manhattan customers—a scoring model built for one firm was not intended to be used by another.

Fair Isaac's PreScore broke new ground on two fronts. In addition to using credit bureau information, it also introduced the concept of a "generic" model. By the 1980s the leading credit bureaus had databases with hundreds of millions of credit files and a national reach. These databases were not only useful for evaluating individual credit risk; they could also be tapped for large statistical samples. Since these samples included representatives from everyone's customer files—Bank of America customers *and* Chase Manhattan customers, for instance—risk models based on credit bureau data were generalizable. A generic model, in other words, was statistically valid and predictive for many different kinds of lenders, including small and medium-sized businesses that could not afford to build their own custom models. At the time, a bank could expect to spend between $50,000 and $100,000 to develop a scorecard using its own customer data.[20] And this initial outlay did not even include the expense of continually updating and retesting the scorecard.

Once introduced, generic models quickly took off. In 1987 another credit scoring firm, Management Decision Systems (MDS), developed generic models with each of the three leading bureaus: the Delinquency Alert System for Equifax, Delphi for TransUnion, and the Gold Report for TRW.[21] Though MDS would be an important innovator in the field of credit scoring—the Atlanta-based firm, established in 1976, produced cutting-edge models and a cohort of experts that shaped the risk-scoring business—its contributions have been overshadowed by its category-defining predecessor, Fair Isaac. In 1989 Fair Isaac unveiled a new generic credit bureau model that would become the industry standard. The model—separately branded as Beacon for Equifax, Empirica for TransUnion, and the TRW Fair Isaac Model—translated risk rankings into numbers between 300 and 900, with higher numbers representing the least risk of default. These all-important three digits would be better known as a FICO score.[22]

Though credit scoring had been used for decades, it did not burst into public consciousness until the mid-1990s. The watershed moment involved home loans. In 1995 the Federal Home Loan Mortgage Corporation (Freddie Mac) instructed its lenders to use credit scoring for all new mortgage applications. Two months later, the Federal National Mortgage Association (Fannie Mae) followed suit. With the endorsement of the nation's two largest home loan brokers, credit scoring was institutionalized almost overnight. If Americans were oblivious to the scoring models that quietly governed their credit cards, it was a different matter when scores determined where they could live. "The days when a mortgage applicant could explain away blemishes on his credit report with a single letter are long gone," the *Chicago Tribune* reported in 1998. "Thanks to a statistical modeling technique known as credit scoring, there's little a would-be borrower can do to improve his chances of obtaining a loan once he's applied."[23] Getting rejected was not the only problem. Applicants with lower scores were offered mortgages with higher interest rates and heavier monthly payments, putting homeownership out of reach for some.

Within the mortgage industry, the shift to scoring was not without controversy. Just as earlier efforts to force the adoption of statistical credit scoring in retail credit departments were met with resistance, some brokers balked at automated underwriting.[24] As one industry writer observed, transposing Winston Churchill's grudging endorsement of democracy to credit scoring, "It may not be perfect, but it's better than anything else we've got."[25] Once again, the free market was not the driving force behind the diffusion of credit scoring. Government had tipped the scales. Just as federal antidiscrimination laws spurred the use of scoring technologies in the personal finance market during the 1970s, government-sponsored home loan organizations legitimized credit scoring in the mortgage industry during the 1990s. In both cases it was public bureaucrats, not corporate credit professionals, who pushed credit scoring as a cheaper and more just measure of creditworthiness.

During the 1990s, Americans were classified, ranked, and sorted by a growing array of risk models. This was especially true in the saturated credit card market.[26] As fresh prospects became scarce and profit margins shrank, a new generation of models predicted everything from response rates to attrition. "It took 20 years to get people to understand credit scoring," an MDS executive explained in 1989, "but now everybody is doing just about the same thing and we're after the same customers." "The new thrust," he added, "will be to model *profitability* instead of just good and bad credit risks."[27] A profitable card was one that was regularly used and, more to the point, one that yielded a steady stream of interest payments and fees. Toward this end, credit bureau scoring models such as Trans-

Union's Revenue Projection Management and Equifax's Bankcard Usage Predictor helped lenders target prospects that were likely to respond to direct mail solicitations and to run up balances.[28] "Modelling just (credit) risk is passé," TRW's director of privacy and consumer policy admitted in 1995. The real risk, he explained, "might be that a customer is not profitable."[29]

While Fair Isaac's FICO score became the public face of credit scoring, in reality it was just one of many commercially available scores. At the turn of the twenty-first century, there were literally dozens of generic models that predicted risk and profitability, from the cost-benefit of mailing a solicitation to the collectability of a charged-off account.[30] And as risk models proliferated, they became increasingly specialized. When Fair Isaac updated TransUnion's generic bureau model in 1994, the new system included multiple versions for different kinds of debts. Credit cards, automobile loans, installment loans, and personal finance loans each could be scored according to specially tailored formulas.[31] Moreover, many lenders used scoring models in combination. "People had assumed"—erroneously, as an MDS executive explained—"that one model in itself was going to give them everything they need." When custom scoring models were overlaid with generic credit bureau models, for example, smaller populations were more finely segmented, and new revenue opportunities could be squeezed from the data.[32]

By the late 1990s all three major bureaus—Equifax, TransUnion, and Experian—had their own risk modeling units. Indeed, when GUS acquired Experian in 1996, it was no coincidence that the British retailing conglomerate also owned CCN Group, which had acquired MDS ten years earlier. Thus when CCN was officially merged with Experian in 1997, a risk-scoring and credit reporting juggernaut was formed. The risk-scoring market was so hot during the 1990s that Equifax rolled out a succession of new credit and marketing models just to stay competitive. "New products are the lifeline of any company," an Equifax executive explained. "And if you don't keep pumping them out, it's going to be a pretty short run."[33]

Significantly, all of these new risk models represented a departure from the scorecard's original function. By the late 1980s it was no longer enough to clear the initial hurdle of the credit application. One's financial performance was under never-ending review long after the application was accepted and the account opened. As creditors took a "lifetime value" perspective, cardholders were evaluated and reevaluated by scoring algorithms to see who was abiding by patterns of maximum profitability—paying on time and carrying an interest-generating balance without maxing out—and who was not. At the same time, delinquency alert models, offered by all three major credit bureaus, allowed lenders to continuously track the risk and performance of an individual across all of his or her accounts. Those who missed payments or maintained high balances with *other* lenders had their credit limits slashed and interest rates raised. While lenders can hardly be blamed for keeping an eye on their existing customers, new generic delinquency models expanded the context and regularity of consumer credit scoring. The entire lending relationship was "colonized" by risk calculation, as the sociologist Donncha Marron has observed.[34]

But risk's colonization did not stop at credit. During the 1990s new scoring products were developed for gas and electric companies, wireless telephone carriers, and healthcare providers. Equifax's Energy Risk Assessment Model, for instance, predicted whether a utility customer was likely to generate unpaid bills, and therefore whether he or she should be required to provide a security deposit.[35] More controversially, credit information also became the basis of specialized insurance scoring models. Fair Isaac and Choicepoint, an Equifax division that was spun off in 1996, developed risk models for automobile and property insurers. Three years later, TransUnion introduced its own insurance scoring program, also developed in collaboration with Fair Isaac.[36] Though insurance risk models drew upon credit bureau data, they did not predict payment behavior. Rather, they predicted the likelihood that a policy holder would submit an unprofitable claim, particularly a dubious or fraudulent claim.[37] The underlying reasons for such correlations were immaterial, as industry representatives argued, echoing the causal agnosticism of earlier credit scoring proponents and future big data analysts. The connection between creditworthiness and insurance loss was simply "a hard, cold fact," as an Allstate attorney noted.[38] As risk-scoring technologies spread into noncredit contexts, the individual was further reduced to a statistical artifact. And as data got exponentially bigger, more of the individual's life would be determined by correlations—behavioral "facts" devoid of theory or explanation.

DATABASE MARKETING AND TECHNOLOGIES OF TARGETING

While the leading bureaus expanded into risk scoring, they also developed complementary interests in database marketing. Until the 1970s, the credit reporting industry had steered away from marketing services. As clearing-houses of local information, credit bureaus had long asserted their impartiality by refusing to peddle lists of the community's best custom-ers. Though the growth of newcomer and prescreening services during the 1950s signaled a shifting stance on this issue, the impropriety of list marketing was ingrained in the industry. The president of the nation's first computerized credit bureau had promised that its credit files would never be used for marketing. By the early 1980s this pledge was broken.[39] The industry was reduced to a coterie of national bureaus that catered to major financial institutions and retailers, not local businesses and their petty jealousies. The bureau's new corporate clients were more than happy to take advantage of new analytical marketing services.

Consumer marketing, like consumer credit reporting, underwent its own technological upheaval during the 1970s and 1980s. In the process, another information industry, database marketing, was spawned. Database marketing represented a convergence of two separate businesses—one old, the other new. The old business was direct mail.[40] During the 1960s and 1970s, firms that specialized in compiling promotional mailing lists began to computerize their files. One of these companies was R. H. Donnelley, the list broker that sold Bruce Steinberg's name to Bank of America. Founded in the 1880s as a telephone directory publisher—its thick yellow books would be ubiquitous in American homes—Donnelley parlayed its access to millions of names and addresses into a thriving direct mail busi-ness.[41] By 1980 Donnelley could boast that it maintained the largest data-base of residential listings in the United States. With sixty-eight million names, its databases covered nearly 87 percent of all households.[42] Donnel-ley was just one of many computerized list brokers. Its chief rivals, R. L. Polk (founded in the 1870s by a former patent medicine peddler) and

Metromail, were similarly endowed with consumer data. When R. L. Polk shifted to computers in 1960, the firm already had sixty-five million names on file, gleaned from its city directory business and automobile registration lists.[43] With computers, direct mail moved from an advertising backwater to the center of an emergent consumer data economy.

Along with the old business of direct mail, database marketing was spurred by the new business of geo-demographic analysis. This niche industry emerged during the 1970s as upstart firms raced to convert newly available statistical data into valuable market intelligence. The principal source of this data was not the private sector, however. It was the U.S. Census Bureau. The raw data of the 1970 census—all of the population and housing information, with names removed for confidentiality—was put up for sale. This was the first time that the agency had made all of its data available to the public. The full set of summary files spanned 2,000 reels of magnetic tape and could be purchased for around $120,000.[44] While this was prohibitively expensive for the average citizen, it was a gold mine for enterprising technologists with a nose for marketing.

One of the most influential of these new geo-demographic data companies was Claritas Corporation. Established in 1971 by an Ivy League–educated social scientist, Claritas entered the industry at the ground floor as one of the first firms to mine the Census Bureau's tapes. In 1974 Claritas introduced an innovative program that sorted Americans into forty different "lifestyle segments," each with its own fanciful name. The segments ranged from "Blue Blood Estates" and "Money and Brains" at the top of the value hierarchy to "Hard Scrabble" and "Public Assistance" at the bottom. The key insight offered by Claritas was that people with similar income, backgrounds, and interests tend to live near each other. Or, colloquially, birds of a feather flock together. While census data served as the nucleus of its analysis, Claritas relied on another government creation—postal zip codes—to translate its segments into actionable target markets.[45] In 1978 Claritas launched PRIZM (Potential Rating Index for Zip Markets), an enhanced system that drew together even more data, including automobile registrations, consumer surveys, and television viewing reports.[46] As its name suggested, PRIZM also linked the system's lifestyle segments to the nation's 36,000 zip codes. "If you tell me your ZIP code," the company's founder boasted, "I can predict what you eat, drink, drive—even think."[47]

Claritas was not alone in its efforts to sort the buying public into data-driven categories. During the 1980s and 1990s consumer segmentation systems proliferated as the business community reacted to broad cultural and economic changes in the United States. From the perspective of advertisers and media firms, American society and the mass markets that once defined it were breaking apart. The source of such fragmentation could be traced to a wide range of causes, from the political turmoil of the 1960s to the rise of cable television.[48] As consumers retreated into individualistic lifestyle bubbles during the 1970s and 1980s, industry leaders feared that they could no longer be reached by traditional mass media campaigns. Database marketing was seen as a technological solution to the problem of social fragmentation. If mass consumers were scattering and disappearing, then list brokers and geo-demographic data firms like Donnelley and Claritas would track them down and deliver them to businesses. In particular, database marketing promised to help businesses put their promotional letters, postcards, flyers, coupons, and catalogs in the mailboxes of their best prospects. "The days of the great eight-million-piece mailing are over," one advertising executive proclaimed in 1983. "We've weeded out the people who are not in the target market."[49]

It did not take long for computerized credit bureaus to see how database marketing could augment and enrich their own core businesses. As Equifax mulled ways to "make use of [its] consumer credit data base" in 1983, it was already eyeing database marketing. "One possibility," its annual report suggested, "is to provide certain types of demographic data to support marketing research and other promotional activities."[50] By then Equifax had purchased Elrick & Lavidge, a Chicago-based market research firm. The acquisition made perfect sense, an Equifax officer noted, because it brought Equifax's "data gathering" abilities together with the smaller firm's strengths in "market research planning and interpretation."[51] Equifax officially entered the database marketing business in 1986 when it purchased an interest in National Decision Systems (NDS), a successful West Coast target marketing firm with advanced demographic modeling programs. The Equifax-NDS partnership resulted in products such as

MicroVision, a consumer segmentation program that sorted Americans into groups with Claritas-like designations such as "Upper Crust" and "Living off the Land," and MicroNames, a mailing list service that involved additional collaborations with Polk, Metromail, and Acxiom.[52] By 1987 Equifax's marketing division contributed $64 million to the company's operating revenue. Credit services, by contrast, generated $157 million.[53]

Equifax had a jump start on its rivals, but TransUnion and TRW quickly followed into database marketing. During the late 1980s Trans-Union established TransMark, a direct mail division with lists derived from its vast consumer credit database. Billed as a one-stop service, Trans-Mark lists—which were regularly updated "to assure freshness"—could be prescreened and segmented according to credit card use, shopping habits, lifestyle, and other demographic attributes.[54] In 1987 TRW created its own target marketing division and purchased Executive Services Companies, a Texas-based list broker, to seed it. Executive Services had a large roster of direct mail clients and consumer databases, culled from driver's licenses and voter registration records. Even more valuable was the firm's sophisticated profiling and targeting software, which TRW acquired in the deal.[55] "Executive Services has been able to infer all sorts of information from its two sources," an industry journalist noted. "For example, from the ages and number of people at one address, it can determine family structure."[56] These kinds of demographic insights allowed marketers to target different kinds of consumers—young singles versus young families, for example— with greater precision. Demographic segmentation was so valuable, in fact, that TRW partnered with Claritas to develop P$YCLE, a new product that embedded Claritas's segmentation codes directly into TRW's credit files.[57] According to one account, the program allowed marketers to segment eighty-seven million addresses by their head of household's "age, weight, height, ethnicity, income, net worth and financial behavior, among other things."[58]

While the leading bureaus courted the business community with new marketing services, they discovered a previously overlooked client: consumers. As Americans became increasingly concerned about the security of their financial reputations, now circulating in databases that were prey to computer hackers and clever identity thieves, one of the leading bureaus sensed an opportunity. In 1986 TRW introduced Credentials, an identity management service that promised to help consumers monitor their credit reputations. For $35 a year, subscribers received unlimited access to their own credit reports, automatic notifications when their credit records were queried, and a special service for canceling lost or stolen credit cards. The program was heavily advertised and quickly enrolled 250,000 subscribers in California alone.[59] "People want to feel that they're part of the credit loop, that they're in control," a TRW manager noted, explaining Credentials' popularity.[60]

Though presented as a savvy tool for empowered consumers, the TRW service was of questionable value. Americans could already buy a copy of their credit report for a nominal fee, as critics noted, and anyone denied credit or employment due to information in a credit report was entitled to a free copy of the report. The program seemed doubly exploitative because its necessity stemmed in part from the bureau's own inability to protect its data. With their well-known caches of personal information, credit bureau databases were an early target for computer hackers. TRW's own computers were the subject of a high-profile breach in 1984, one that compromised the privacy of ninety million people in its national database.[61] While providing peace of mind, Credentials shifted the cost and responsibility of credit monitoring to consumers. The program's success also provided a model for future direct-to-consumer credit bureau services, which would become profitable business lines in their own right.

Significantly, the strategic value of Credentials was not in its subscription fees. When registering for the TRW service, subscribers were asked to submit supplementary information about their personal incomes, employment histories, bank accounts, investments, and other assets. This volunteered information enhanced the bureau's own databases and, more important, it was also repackaged and sold to third parties. What was billed as a tool of consumer protection was really a Trojan horse for collecting more consumer data. The target audience for Credentials was "young, upwardly mobile adults" with annual household incomes over $20,000, a coveted demographic among marketers.[62] TRW's credit monitoring service did more than just show how credit bureaus could sell consumer information back to themselves. Perversely, it illustrated how businesses could extract even more information from consumers under the banner of privacy.

Though database marketing managed to avoid major controversy during the 1980s, the honeymoon ended in 1990. The source of discontent was Lotus Marketplace: Households, a marketing database created by Lotus Development Corporation, a Cambridge, Massachusetts, software company, and Equifax. Lotus Marketplace contained names, addresses, approximate incomes, and buying profiles for 120 million adults in 80 million American households nationwide. The program's information was gleaned from census and postal service data, consumer surveys, and Equifax's own credit files. Within the program, households were sorted into fifty segments, ranging from "accumulated wealth" to "mobile home families." None of this was revolutionary. What set this database apart from all the others was that it could be purchased on CD-ROM for about $700. Any business with an Apple Macintosh computer could buy the disks and begin producing its own targeted promotional lists. To industry observers, Marketplace augured a new age of economical "desktop marketing" for small businesses. "Even the corner dentist will be able to use it," a Lotus software developer boasted.[63]

When news of the program reached the public, the backlash was swift. The database could not be searched for specific people—though an individual's name and address would appear within selected segments—and personal income and credit information were not included. But aggregated data could be sorted to generate remarkably detailed group portraits. "You could ask for a list of single women over the age of 65 living in Revere, Massachusetts, and MarketPlace [sic] would obligingly produce it," as Langdon Winner, a prominent critic of technocratic society, noted.[64] The sense of violation was compounded by the fact that so much sensitive data was concentrated in a single, inexpensive disk. Confronted by an avalanche of angry letters—the "first computer privacy protest," as one expert later recalled—Lotus and Equifax scuttled the program.[65] "We knew we were treading on new ground by bringing this kind of capability to a broader audience," an Equifax executive admitted. "We take privacy very, very seriously."[66]

In the end, both companies blamed the product's failure on consumer ignorance. In a sense, they were right. Consumers were outraged that the details of their lives—millions of their lives—could be reduced to a palm-sized disk. But what consumers did not understand was that all of this information was already available elsewhere. Even if the data was not sold on CD-ROM, it would still be sold in other guises by list brokers, retailers and financial institutions, credit bureaus, and government agencies such as the Census Bureau. As a Silicon Valley forecaster observed, "Lotus Market Place [sic] may be the first product in a new category killed not because it didn't work as advertised, but because it might have worked too well."[67]

BIGGER DATA AND CONTEXT CREEP

By the early 1990s the credit reporting industry was at the center of privacy debates once again, this time for its involvement in database marketing. According to the rules of the FCRA, credit bureaus were prohibited from selling information in their files for purposes other than credit, insurance, or employment decisions. If the contents of a credit file were shared, then the subject of the file had to either consent to the inquiry or be given a "firm offer" of credit. The latter condition provided legal cover for pre-screening. As the leading bureaus moved into database marketing—serving, in effect, as list brokers and consumer analysts—the line between their credit reporting and marketing operations blurred.

Part of the ambiguity stemmed from the properties of electronic information itself. What was to stop a credit bureau from merging or matching names in its credit databases with those in its marketing databases? Where paper records might be physically segregated from each other—in separate filing cabinets, for instance—the violability of digital information was less easily supervised. The boundary between credit databases and marketing databases was porous, to say the least. During a congressional hearing in 1989, a TRW official acknowledged that its target marketing division tapped the company's credit databases to enhance its direct marketing capabilities and to develop predictive models. He insisted, however, that any improper intermingling was prevented because the marketing unit's computers were "located away from the Credit Data division."[68] To anyone who understood the mobility of computer data, this was not a convincing safeguard. TRW's competitor, Equifax, had already dispensed with such artifice. In 1989 the company moved to a new twenty-acre "technology center" where all of its credit, marketing, and insurance databases were brought together under one roof.[69]

The problem of information sharing was at the heart of database critiques during the late 1970s. The most troubling development, as David F. Linowes, chair of the federal Privacy Protection Study Commission, warned, was not that a single organization, such as the federal government, would amass all of our personal information. The danger was that numerous organizations, public and private, would amass pieces of information about our identities, our relationships, and our behaviors, and that these disparate elements could be brought together. "Anything put into the data bank of one organization can be tied together with another organization's databank," Linowes explained at a Senate hearing in 1980. "It is this linkage which has the potential for creating one of the greatest threats to the privacy of the individual and eventually our way of life."[70] Linowes was not describing some dystopian future world. When Bruce Steinberg testified at the same hearing later that day, his story illustrated the reality of the problem.

When the FCRA was drawn up in 1970, data sharing was not a major concern. Rather, it was the centripetal force of information that alarmed lawmakers and experts. Left unchecked, as the legal scholar Arthur R. Miller warned, newly automated credit bureaus might become "full service, online, completely computerized omnibus information networks."[71] While there was truth to this, centralization was only part of the problem. So too was unchecked data sharing—the linking of databases, as Linowes had warned. The rise of database marketing, after all, depended upon access to public information—Census Bureau datasets in particular, but also automobile and voter registration lists and postal service change-of-address notifications. All of this information, collected in government databases, flowed into commercial databases, where it was processed, merged with other data, and resold in consumer lists, segmentation programs, and risk models. Fears about centralization also failed to account for the changing corporate structure of the credit reporting industry. When the FCRA was drafted, there were more than 2,000 independent credit bureaus throughout the nation. By the late 1980s there were just three major bureaus, and each was a branch of larger information enterprises. The bureaus did not have to collect and house all of their own data. They could acquire it from their parent company's other holdings or through strategic alliances with other information-processing firms. And they could also get it from municipal, state, and federal databases.

As the major bureaus moved into database marketing, they pushed against the constraints of the FCRA. While the law delimited the permissible uses of credit information, it contained a significant loophole. In addition to credit, insurance, and employment contexts, the FCRA allowed credit reporting agencies to sell their information to any party with "a legitimate business need for the information in connection with a business transaction with the consumer."[72] Did direct mail and consumer profiling programs constitute a "legitimate need" for information? The leading bureaus thought so. "New micro-targeting techniques help businesses understand more precisely who their customers are," as an Equifax executive told lawmakers in 1989. "We are trying to help them with our information services to improve their effectiveness."[73] When database marketing was addressed during the 1980s, it was almost always in the myopic context of junk mail. "I don't think there's a privacy concern here," a TRW executive insisted. By sharing credit bureau data with marketers, he noted, "we think we'll be able to reduce the clutter in your mailbox."[74]

In the face of mounting criticism, the leading bureaus were at pains to defend their information-handling practices. In a show of corporate responsibility, Equifax commissioned a national consumer opinion survey to gauge public attitudes about privacy and the circulation of personal information. The survey, conducted by an outside polling firm in 1990, was headed by Alan F. Westin, the Columbia law professor who had embarrassed the credit reporting industry during earlier congressional hearings. Westin's participation lent legitimacy to the Equifax survey, but its findings were still unflattering. When it came to handling personal information, only 59 percent of Americans had a "high or moderate degree of trust" in credit bureaus. Government agencies, including the notoriously unpopular IRS, were trusted more than credit bureaus. On topics related to database marketing, the news was worse. Three-quarters of Americans said that the practice of prescreening was "not acceptable," and 69 percent said that the business of selling consumer lists—lists that included information "such as income level, residential area, and credit card use"—was a "bad thing."[75]

On the latter point, government officials agreed. In 1991 Equifax and TRW were slapped with multistate lawsuits that challenged the legality of their database marketing operations. By then Equifax had credit files for 120 million Americans, which it used to develop consumer lists for more than 200 direct marketers. Each list could be segmented according to a variety of demographic variables, including age, sex, and income. "Consumers are unaware that the credit-reporting agencies are reaping significant profits by unlawfully raiding their personal credit histories to create mailing lists for junk mailers," New York's attorney general argued in the case against Equifax.[76] Under pressure from state counselors, Equifax abandoned its mailing list services and TRW entered into a consent agreement with the FTC. The next year TransUnion was also hit with an FTC complaint and ordered to halt its marketing list business.[77] Unlike its competitors, TransUnion defied the injunction and took its case to court. After a decade of legal wrangling, however, the U.S. Supreme Court rejected TransUnion's petition for a new appeal, and the bureau's argument ground to a halt.

Though the fate of the industry's database marketing operations seemed to hinge on TransUnion's epic battle with the FTC, a key concession had already been made. In 1993 TRW's original consent agreement was quietly amended. New language was inserted to give the bureau permission to use "identifying information" in its credit databases for the purpose of list marketing. This included the names, telephone numbers, addresses, zip codes, birth years and ages, and Social Security numbers of individuals in its credit files.[78] In effect, the amended agreement broke the credit file into two parts—consumer identification information that appeared at the top of each file, and account details and payment histories that appeared "below the line." The information at the top of the file, referred to as "header" data, would be exempted from the rules of the FCRA.[79] This concession basically acknowledged what credit bureaus had been arguing all along. The identifying information at the top of a credit report was no longer privileged intelligence. It was commercially available from a wide array of list brokers and database marketers, none of which were beholden to the rules of the FCRA. By then this kind of information was even being sold to third parties by banks.

During the 1990s the same risk-scoring and consumer-targeting technologies that pushed credit bureaus into promotional services also blurred the line between lending and marketing in the financial sector. Lawmakers awoke to this reality as they prepared to pass the Financial Services Modernization Act of 1999, better known as the Gramm-Leach-Bliley Act (GLBA). The main purpose of the GLBA was to repeal the Glass-Steagall Act, a Depression-era law that separated the activities of banks and investment houses. By lifting Glass-Steagall's restrictions, the GLBA allowed banks, securities firms, and insurance companies to flock into new mergers and combinations. With such operational bulwarks removed, lawmakers suddenly realized that consumer information would cascade throughout the diverse holdings of new financial giants and leach out to third parties beyond. As the GLBA was being finalized, a Minnesota-based bank got into trouble for selling information about its customers to telemarketers, and one House committee member was scandalized by the arrival of a lingerie catalog at his Washington apartment, which he blamed on the indiscretion of his hometown credit union.[80]

More than anything, the GLBA revealed the shifting sands of consumer privacy at the turn of the twenty-first century. In an effort to limit unfettered data sharing, the new law identified the most sensitive class of consumer information—"nonpublic personal information" (NPI)—and placed restrictions around its use. NPI included information provided by consumers in their applications (name, address, income, and Social Security number) and information generated through subsequent transactions, such as account types, balances, and payment behavior. Under Title V of the GLBA, financial institutions could not share this information without providing their customers with a privacy notice and a thirty-day window of opportunity to opt out. On the surface, these rules offered a measure of transparency and agency for consumers. In practice, they were toothless. Financial institutions could still share customer information with their affiliates—that is, any bank or business in the same "corporate family"—and with third parties when engaged in "joint marketing" activities. Consumers could not opt out of these arrangements. Post-GLBA financial institutions, it turned out, were not only too big to fail; they were also too big to offer any meaningful protection against the circulation of consumer information.

Ironically, the GLBA's construction also revealed the extent to which the boundary between credit bureaus and financial institutions had collapsed. In the new world of diversified, data-rich financial behemoths, consumer information collected by one affiliate could be used by another to evaluate the creditworthiness of prospective customers. A credit card–issuing bank, for instance, could share its customers' account and payment history with another bank or mortgage company under the same corporate umbrella. If this information was used to make credit decisions, then the credit card–issuing bank was essentially playing the role of the credit bureau. This slippage had already become apparent before the GLBA was passed. In 1997 new language was added to the FCRA to clarify that credit information sharing among business affiliates would *not* be considered a credit report, and therefore would not be subject to the rules of the FCRA.[81] This distinction was crucial. Without it, the nation's financial institutions would have to follow the FCRA's much narrower rules concerning the use of consumer information.

All of these cracks in data privacy were on display in TransUnion's case for selling marketing lists. In particular, as credit bureaus moved into promotional services, they found themselves in direct competition with list brokers and database marketers. These unregulated businesses profited from the sale of consumer information that they culled from public records and directories. Yet as TransUnion's attorneys pointed out, much of this information—names, addresses, and telephone numbers—was essentially the same as the "nonfinancial" information in the credit bureau headers. If they were all selling the same information, why should credit bureaus be forced to follow rules that did not apply to their competitors? On this specific issue, TransUnion had a point.[82]

The difference, according to the FTC, was the *context* in which credit bureaus acquired this information. Credit bureau data was received under the presumption of confidentiality and for the express purpose of credit evaluation. Subsequent sharing in noncredit contexts would thus violate these initial conditions. List brokers and database marketers, by contrast, compiled their information from public sources that were by definition not confidential. The GLBA's rules concerning NPI added another layer of protection for the "contextual integrity" of consumer data.[83] Credit bureaus, like financial institutions, could not collect consumer information for one purpose (credit evaluation) and resell it for another (marketing) without providing consumers with privacy notices and an opt-out mechanism. The new rules stymied the sale of credit header information.

During the mid-1990s efforts to corral the context of consumer data collection and sharing were further undermined by yet another revolutionary technology: the Internet. New user-friendly interfaces, including web browsers and welcoming portals like America Online, quickly turned the formerly obscure Cold War defense network into a bustling mainstream destination. While many politicians, business leaders, and futurists swooned over the Internet's transformative potential, it soon became apparent that cyberspace was no utopia. In addition to the usual moral panics that accompany new media—fears that civic life will be degraded, children will be exploited, and pornography will take over—the Internet introduced a more harrowing concern: the prospect of total surveillance. The looking-glass structure of the Internet meant that all interactions— from logging on to browsing, buying, and communicating—were recordable interactions. One was under surveillance simply by *being* online.

With the Internet as the backbone of the "new economy," consumer data became its lifeblood. In 1998 an FTC survey found that an overwhelming majority of commercial websites—more than 85 percent—collected personal information about consumers, most commonly e-mail addresses, but also names, addresses, and telephone numbers.[84] Surveillance was recast as "interactivity," and consumers were encouraged to customize their online experience by sharing more information about themselves. All of this information would become fodder for marketing and data-mining programs. "There's nothing sinister about what we do," Equifax's chief executive reassured in 1995, defending his own firm's data siphoning practices. "In an interactive society, we have to realize that none of us are alone anymore."[85] Four years later the situation was summed up more bluntly by Sun Microsystems executive Scott McNealy: "You have zero privacy anyway—get over it."[86]

CREDITWORTHINESS AND THE FUTURE
OF CONSUMER SURVEILLANCE

When Bruce Steinberg testified before the Senate in 1980, his larger privacy concerns were ignored. At the time lawmakers were preoccupied with other issues, notably credit discrimination and the accuracy of credit bureau information. Both of these were—and still are—real problems that require serious attention. But Steinberg was not claiming that his credit application had been unfairly rejected or that his credit file was riddled with falsities. To outward appearances, he was a winner in the game of credit. Bank of America had decided he was "a nice fellow" and wanted to "embrace" him as a customer, as Senator Tsongas pointed out. Steinberg resented the unauthorized sharing of his personal information, but what galled him more than anything was that commercial surveillance was being normalized. "The real harm of pre-approved credit offers," as he told Tsonga's committee, was that they "conditioned" the public "to accept routine invasions of privacy."[87]

Steinberg's critique was prescient. At the turn of the twenty-first century Americans would be under continual commercial surveillance thanks to networked communication and ubiquitous computing. While lawmakers focused on procedural fixes to protect consumers from the worst kinds of credit injustice, they failed to protect them from broader forces at work in the credit reporting industry and beyond. As the leading bureaus diversified their operations into risk scoring and consumer profiling, they were no longer merely concerned with creditworthiness. They were in the more expansive business of consumer data. "We are a data base company that has gone from just storing data all the way to predicting the future of portfolios and individual customers," Equifax's president explained in 1998.[88]

Steinberg saw the writing on the wall when it came to privacy, but neither he nor lawmakers grasped the larger implications of data aggregation and credit screening programs. By the 1990s consumer data was big data, and statistical models were no longer limited to calculating just credit risk. Secret formulas like the one that landed Steinberg on Bank of America's preapproved list would become far more sophisticated and consequential. The leading credit bureaus and analytics firms would develop proprietary systems for sorting Americans into categories of preference and differential pricing, inferring sociodemographic attributes and personal interests, and predicting future behavior and spending. The real harm of prescreening, it turns out, was not just that it acclimated Americans to commercial surveillance. It also normalized the role of black-boxed algorithms in the adjudication of everyday life.

If policy makers have struggled to enforce legal boundaries around the use of credit information, it is because in the age of big data the distinction between credit and noncredit data has lost its meaning. Where credit bureaus were once a privileged site of personal information, they are now just one of many consumer data brokers that peddle names, addresses, and behavioral clues to one's income, spending, and interests. According to a 2014 FTC report, one of the most powerful data brokers, Acxiom, maintains profiles for 700 million consumers worldwide, including 3,000 data points for each American.[89] In this data-rich environment, the credit bureau's special access to consumer account information and past payment behavior is no longer essential. Creditworthiness can be inferred from other variables that have no direct connection to credit history, such as one's social media activity, where one attended college, or even one's use of capitalization in an online application (typing in all caps is a red flag). A new generation of "alternative" credit scoring firms has already emerged to mine our digital detritus for these kinds of predictive associations. The motto of one such financial technology startup summarized the total collapse of credit's protected status: "All data is credit data."[90]

After decades of hard-fought legal battles, consumers seemed to be back where they started. Laws passed in the 1970s to rein in the information maximalism of credit reporting and to end discriminatory lending were at risk of being circumvented altogether. Instead of local hearsay or prejudiced credit managers, which colored past conceptions of creditworthiness, Americans would be judged by even more inscrutable surveillance networks and algorithms.

Epilogue

Looking back at the history of American credit surveillance, it is easy to understand why systems of organized credit reporting were created in the first place. As the nation's population became more numerous and mobile, one was more likely to transact with strangers. And as impersonal market relationships—relationships based on contracts, prices, and monetary exchange—displaced traditional bonds of obligation, human interactions became more abstract. "In the complex march of modern affairs, business has become more mechanical," the author of a credit textbook remarked in 1895. "We have lost the personal equation of our customers, or get it only at second-hand. The name of the debtor or creditor on our books is only a symbol which might as well be represented by a number."[1]

The growing impersonality of economic life was underscored by President Woodrow Wilson in 1913. Railing against the tyranny of big corporations and monopolistic trusts, he pointed to a fundamental shift in social relations. "We have changed our economic conditions absolutely, from top to bottom; and, with our economic society, the organization of our life," he declared. "Today, the everyday relationships of men are largely with great impersonal concerns, with organizations, not with other individual men. Now this is nothing short of a new social age, a new era of human relationships, a new stage setting for the drama of life."[2] Wilson, to be sure, did not have credit bureaus or credit departments in mind. Yet the estrangement of employers and laborers that he condemned ran parallel to that of creditors and consumers.

Six months after Wilson's address, proof of such impersonality was provided in a Cleveland department store, where, as related in the introduction to this book, John D. Rockefeller was subjected to the indignity of a credit check. Rockefeller's creditworthiness was beyond reproach. He was the world's richest man and one of the nation's best-known personalities. Still, the store's young clerk failed to recognize either Rockefeller's name or his appearance even as he stood directly before her. Of course, the Rockefeller incident could all be chalked up to the ignorance of a lowly clerk, one who was perhaps sealed in the bubble of youth and oblivious to the wider world. But I have made much of this now forgotten story, a story that amounted to little more than catty celebrity gossip even in 1913, because it is emblematic of the profound shift in economic relationships that Wilson and many others, before and after, commented on. New "mechanical" ways of knowing one's fellow citizens—via credit reports, credit records, and, later, credit scores—were disturbing because they suggested that economic relationships were losing their human scale and personal touch. Americans were not just estranged from their neighbors and community in everyday life. They were becoming faceless accounts and dollar signs in the ledgers of corporate employers, creditors, insurance companies, retailers, and other business concerns.

This, ultimately, was the darker subtheme beneath the comedy of Rockefeller's department store interrogation. When it came to judging creditworthiness, a quality rooted in trust and integrity, no one was beyond the objectifying gaze of capitalism. Had Rockefeller been recognized by the clerk, he might have been waved through with a grand show of deference. But this would not have changed the fact that he still had a file in the store's credit department and at the local credit bureau. Rockefeller, like everyone else, from the middle-class office professional to the grease-faced mechanic, was just another consumer, "good" or "bad" depending on his or her financial performance. Rockefeller's life and fortune, though spectacular, were just as easily drained of social meaning and summarized in a formulaic credit file or credit rating. It was doubly ironic, and poetic justice perhaps, that the iconic industrialist was temporarily an anonymous cog in the capitalist machine he had helped to build.

As a historical benchmark, the Rockefeller incident illustrates the ordinariness of consumer credit surveillance at the turn of the twentieth century. By the late 1920s a national credit reporting infrastructure was in place. With credit records for fifty million Americans at its disposal, it was a domestic surveillance regime of unprecedented proportions. To put this number in perspective, compare it to one of the most ambitious state surveillance programs during the same period: the collection of fingerprint identification cards. Coordinated by the Justice Department's Bureau of Investigation under the leadership of J. Edgar Hoover, the man who would become the epitome of investigatory overreach, the fingerprinting program was introduced as a system of positive identification for all American citizens. This was not a surreptitious or even particularly controversial plan at the time. In one display of civic duty, "200 business and financial leaders" gathered in New York to submit their own fingerprints to the bureau's collection. At the head of the line was John D. Rockefeller Jr., the oil tycoon's son.[3] By the end of the 1920s, Hoover's agency had gathered around a million fingerprints. A decade later this number had climbed to eleven million.[4] These figures, while remarkable, paled in comparison to the massive accumulations of personal data in the files of the nation's credit bureaus before World War II.

Until the late 1960s, the American public was untroubled by credit reporting. Contrary to sensational press coverage of the time, credit surveillance was no dark conspiracy unmasked by Congress in 1968. Americans had always known that their lives were held under a microscope when they applied for credit. They just did not care. Consumer groups had long fought for safer products, better labeling, and ethical advertising, but the one thing they did not demand was privacy. Such silence on the issue is difficult to fathom from the vantage of our own privacy-conscious age. In the absence of evidence, we can only speculate as to why. Perhaps the lingering stigma of borrowing and the uncertain legitimacy of "the consumer," a new concept in the early twentieth century, was enough to keep dissent at bay. More realistically, consumers probably acquiesced then for the same reason they do today: they wanted the borrowed goods or money more than they cared about their privacy. Even the famously reserved Rockefeller accepted this tradeoff as the price of convenience.

The modern freedom to buy now and pay later would be a dubious one, to say the least. Surcharges and interest payments were not the only hidden costs. In return for the trust of retail creditors and institutional lenders, Americans surrendered the intimate details of their lives. This exchange, personal information for access and convenience, may have seemed a fair trade to credit-hungry Americans during the early twentieth century, but it set a precedent with profound implications for the future of commercial data gathering and privacy. When asking for a merchant's trust, credit customers relinquished their right to withhold information about their personal and financial circumstances. Mass credit not only trapped Americans in the bondage of debt; it also ensnared them in bonds of institutional surveillance. Applying for credit was the original sin of modern consumer surveillance.

By the time that credit bureaus began to computerize in the 1960s, they already had a long history. The significance of this history has been overshadowed by the rise of databases and the transformation of late twentieth-century consumer surveillance. The sudden importance of credit scores and digital financial identities suggested a radical break from the past.[5] Our economic reputations are not only disembodied and impersonal now; they are also continuously monitored by remote systems, animated by data processing, and governed by esoteric algorithms. This new regime of credit surveillance has fostered peculiar forms of self-consciousness and social control, as a number of scholars have noted.[6] Yet the history of credit surveillance reveals the deep roots of financial objectification in the United States. The modern concept of financial identity emerged more than a century ago in the handwritten ledgers, credit rating books, and customer records of credit reporting organizations. It was in these nineteenth-century texts that personal identity was reduced to economic indicators and reconstituted as an information commodity. The history of these developments connects twenty-first-century financialization to the calculating ethos and surveillance regimes of nineteenth-century American capitalism.

The history of credit surveillance is also a reminder that all credit relationships—indeed, all economic relationships—are irreducibly social. Since the 1960s, the quantification of credit information and, ironically, legal regulations to make it "fair" and "equal" have effaced its social nature. Credit reports are institutional data, stripped of personal context or contingency, and credit scores circulate as empirical truths. We are no longer "judged" by human credit managers; we are computed. Yet despite efforts to cordon off the social from the economic, to push credit into the denatured world of risk, the moral valence of creditworthiness continues to reappear. It is encoded in the language of "good" and "bad" credit, and it is implicit in the use of credit scores to make inferences about our honesty and responsibility. To possess a poor credit score is a mark of shame—a sign of incompetence, extravagance, weakness, or, at best, a susceptibility to misfortune. This message is reinforced in advertising that casts low-scoring individuals as immature young men and balding serial killers.[7] Credit scores, thus presented, are more than an amoral reflection of economic risk. They are the reification of character and our "goodness" as consumers, workers, and citizens.

If there is any doubt that character still matters, one need only refer to the Fair Credit Reporting Act. Originally passed in 1970 and revised over more than four decades, the document spells out the legal definition of a credit report. According to the current version of the law, a consumer report is "any written, oral, or other communication of any information by a consumer reporting agency bearing on a consumer's credit worthiness, credit standing, credit capacity, *character, general reputation, personal characteristics, or mode of living*," which may be used to determine an individual's "eligibility" for credit, insurance, or employment.[8] This definition makes it perfectly clear that creditworthiness is concerned with much more than economic facts. Financial identity is still very much a form of moral identity.

Since the late 1960s lawmakers have struggled to define the legal parameters of creditworthiness and to ensure the quality of credit bureau data. Fair and accurate credit information is in everyone's interest, of course. Yet these concerns may soon be eclipsed by much larger and more troubling trends. The three leading bureaus are no longer primarily concerned with credit information. They are multibillion-dollar consumer data brokers with many competitors. Aided by powerful computers and lax privacy policies, twenty-first-century data brokers have been able to compile vast troves of personal information—including detailed financial and health information—from Internet traffic, consumer transactions, retailers, and public records. This data is used to construct marketing lists, consumer profiles, and predictive models. Experian, for instance, offers a "consumer classification solution" that segments American households into seventy-one distinct categories, including "American Royalty," "Blue Collar Comfort," and "Tight Money."[9]

This type of household profiling is no substitute for individual credit reports or credit scores, but it points to broader forces shaping the future of consumer surveillance. In the age of big data, businesses are able to make increasingly sophisticated inferences about our economic status, health, lifestyle, and interests by connecting a disparate array of data points, from motor vehicle records to social media content. An error in one's credit report, in the end, might be less important than how one is modeled in a data broker's secret algorithm. To be listed as "Blue Collar Comfort" might be enough to signal one's undesirability and exclusion from preferential pricing or services. Marketing programs like these threaten to produce—and reproduce—new data-driven classes of "socially and economically powerful 'haves' and disempowered 'have-nots.'"[10] Because these noncredit forms of consumer profiling and scoring are constructed with aggregate data, rather than individual-level information, they fall beyond the purview of existing regulations.[11]

The growing influence of data brokers has only recently begun to attract serious attention. In 2012 an FTC report on consumer privacy criticized their "invisibility" and recommended new legislation to rein in their activities.[12] Later that year a Senate investigation was launched, and the nation's leading data brokers were issued letters of inquiry about their business practices. Among the nine firms singled out for scrutiny were all three major credit bureaus—Equifax, Experian, and TransUnion. The investigation was spearheaded by a senior lawmaker with a famous namesake. He was Senator John (Jay) D. Rockefeller IV, the oil tycoon's great-grandson.

In 2013 Rockefeller convened a hearing to address the findings of his data broker study and to interrogate industry representatives. The proceedings took place just months after Edward Snowden's National Security Agency leaks revealed the shocking reach of the nation's intelligence-gathering apparatus. Though outrage over clandestine state surveillance was fresh in the air, Rockefeller warned that government was not the only threat to freedom. "What has been missing from this conversation so far is the role that private companies play in collecting and analyzing our personal information."[13] To make the point, he observed that the data broker industry produced $156 billion in revenue during the previous year. This was not just a staggering number. It was more than double what the U.S. government allocated to its own intelligence budget.

A century after Senator Rockefeller's great-grandfather exchanged his privacy for credit in a Cleveland department store, consumer surveillance had crept into nearly every facet of everyday life. It is embedded in the technologies we depend upon for communication, work, commerce, and entertainment. No digital presence goes untracked; no digital profile goes unmined. This is by design. In our data-driven economy, personal information is the coin of the realm. It is the commodity we use to pay for "free" content, memberships, and services. This quid pro quo—information for access—has fueled innovation and built new industries, but it has also eroded the boundaries of privacy and, more significantly, opened the doors to new forms of social classification and economic objectification. The history of credit surveillance is the history of this Faustian bargain and the starting point for understanding the monetizing logic of digital capitalism in our own time.

Notes

INTRODUCTION

1. "No Rockefeller Credit," *New York Times*, November 22, 1913, 1.
2. For seminal studies of consumer credit in the United States, see Lendol Calder, *Financing the American Dream: A Cultural History of Consumer Credit* (Princeton, N.J.: Princeton University Press, 1999); Daniel Horowitz, *The Morality of Spending: Attitudes toward the Consumer Society in America, 1875–1940* (Baltimore, Md.: Johns Hopkins University Press, 1985); Martha Olney, *Buy Now, Pay Later: Advertising, Credit, and Consumer Durables in the 1920s* (Chapel Hill, N.C.: University of North Carolina Press, 1991); Louis Hyman, *Debtor Nation: A History of America in Red Ink* (Princeton, N.J.: Princeton University Press, 2011); and Wendy Woloson, *In Hock: Pawning in America from Independence to the Great Depression* (Chicago: University of Chicago Press, 2010). See also Rowena Olegario, *The Engine of Enterprise: Credit in America* (Cambridge, Mass.: Harvard University Press, 2016); and Claire Lemercier and Claire Zalc, "For a New Approach to Credit Relations in Modern History," *Annales: Histoire, Sciences Sociales* 4 (2012): 661–691.
3. Calder, *Financing the American Dream*, 13.
4. For a historiographic review of personal finance research and a plea for further inquiry, see Lendol Calder, "Saving and Spending," in *The Oxford Handbook of the History of Consumption*, ed. Frank Trentmann (New York: Oxford University Press, 2012), 348–375.
5. Though consumer credit reporting has attracted much critical attention since the 1960s, including journalistic exposés and legal and policy analysis, there is no comprehensive history of the industry. This void can no doubt be attributed to the absence of any publicly available archives or major historical collections related to the consumer reporting industry. For scholarly studies of credit reporting and credit scoring during

the 1960s and after, see Hyman, *Debtor Nation*; Donncha Marron, *Consumer Credit in the United States: A Sociological Perspective from the Nineteenth Century to the Present* (New York: Palgrave Macmillan, 2009); and James B. Rule, "Consumer Credit Reporting in America," in *Private Lives and Public Surveillance* (London: Allen Lane, 1973), 175–222. For histories of individual firms, see William A. Flinn, "History of Retail Credit Company: A Study in the Marketing of Information about Individuals" (PhD diss., Ohio State University, 1959); and William Simon, *Pioneers of Excellence: A History of the Chilton Corporation* (Dallas: Chilton Corporation, 1986). More generally, see Mark Furletti, "An Overview and History of Credit Reporting" (discussion paper, Payment Cards Center, Federal Reserve Bank of Philadelphia, June 2002), 1–16; Robert M. Hunt, "The Development and Regulation of Consumer Credit Reporting in the United States," in *The Economics of Consumer Credit*, ed. Giuseppe Bertola, Richard Disney, and Charles Grant (Cambridge, Mass.: MIT Press, 2006), 310–345; and Consumer Financial Protection Bureau, *Key Dimensions and Processes in the U.S. Credit Reporting System: A Review of How the Nation's Largest Credit Bureaus Manage Consumer Data*, December 2012, http://files.consumerfinance .gov/f/201212_cfpb_credit-reporting-white-paper.pdf (accessed July 1, 2016).

6. On the corporatization of consumer debt, see Hyman, *Debtor Nation*.

7. Unlike the consumer reporting industry, the history of American commercial credit reporting is well documented. See Rowena Olegario, *A Culture of Credit: Embedding Trust and Transparency in American Business* (Cambridge, Mass.: Harvard University Press, 2006); Olegario, "Credit Reporting Agencies: A Historical Perspective," in *Credit Reporting Systems and the International Economy*, ed. Margaret J. Miller (Cambridge, Mass.: MIT Press, 2003), 115–159; Scott A. Sandage, *Born Losers: A History of Failure in America* (Cambridge, Mass.: Harvard University Press, 2005); and James D. Norris, *R. G. Dun & Co., 1841–1900: The Development of Credit-Reporting in the Nineteenth Century* (Westport, Conn.: Greenwood Press, 1978).

8. In addition to evaluating creditworthiness, credit managers were typically responsible for collecting customer debts. Many consumer credit bureaus also offered collection services. In reality, credit and collections were two sides of the same coin. The history of collections, as a specialized practice and an emergent industry, is a fascinating and largely ignored subject that deserves its own recounting. It is therefore omitted from this book.

9. Richard R. John, "Recasting the Information Infrastructure for the Industrial Age," in *A Nation Transformed by Information: How Information Has Shaped the United States from Colonial Times to the Present*, ed. Alfred D. Chandler Jr. and James W. Cortada (New York: Oxford University Press, 2000), 55–105.

10. See David Lyon, *Surveillance after September 11* (New York: Polity, 2003), and Richard V. Ericson and Kevin D. Haggerty, eds., *The New Politics of Surveillance and Visibility* (Toronto: University of Toronto Press, 2007).

11. Scholarly inattention to pre-twentieth-century surveillance is doubly curious given the field's theoretical and historical grounding in the works of Max Weber and Michel Foucault, both of whom locate the development and rationality of modern surveillance in nineteenth-century institutions. See Weber, "Bureaucracy," in *Economy and Society*, vol. 1, ed. Guenther Roth and Claus Wittich (Berkeley: University of California Press, 1978), 956–1005; and Foucault, *Discipline and Punish: The Birth of the Prison*, trans. Alan Sheridan (New York: Vintage, 1995).

12. For a critique of presentism in surveillance scholarship, see Josh Lauer, "Surveillance History and the History of New Media: An Evidential Paradigm," *New Media & Society* 14, no. 4 (2011): 566–582.

13. See, for example, Toni Wells, "The Information State: An Historical Perspective on Surveillance," in *Routledge Handbook of Surveillance Studies*, ed. Kirstie Ball, Kevin D. Haggerty, and David Lyon (New York: Routledge, 2012), 57–63. The development of state recordkeeping practices, identification papers, criminal profiling, and policing is well documented in a number of exemplary works. See Jane Caplan and John Torpey, eds., *Documenting Individual Identity: The Development of State Practices in the Modern World* (Princeton, N.J.: Princeton University Press, 2001); Christopher Dandeker, *Surveillance, Power, and Modernity: Bureaucracy and Discipline from 1700 to the Present Day* (New York: St. Martin's Press, 1990); John Torpey, *The Invention of the Passport: Surveillance, Citizenship, and the State* (New York: Cambridge University Press, 2000); Craig Robertson, *The Passport in America: The History of a Document* (New York: Oxford University Press, 2010); Simon Cole, *Suspect Identities: A History of Fingerprinting and Criminal Identification* (Cambridge, Mass.: Harvard University Press, 2001); and Pamela Sankar, "State Power and Record keeping: The History of Individualized Surveillance in the United States, 1790–1935" (PhD diss., University of Pennsylvania, 1992).

14. This chronology, as well as the central role of the nation-state and capitalists, is conventionally attributed to Anthony Giddens. See Giddens, *A Contemporary Critique of Historical Materialism*, vol. 1 (Berkeley: University of California Press, 1981).

15. See Oscar H. Gandy Jr., *The Panoptic Sort: A Political Economy of Personal Information* (Boulder, CO: Westview, 1993); David Lyon, *The Electronic Eye: The Rise of Surveillance Society* (Minneapolis: University of Minnesota Press, 1994); Joseph Turow, *Breaking Up America: Advertisers and the New Media World* (Chicago: University of Chicago Press, 1997); and Mark Andrejevic, *iSpy: Surveillance and Power in the Interactive Age* (Lawrence: University Press of Kansas, 2007).

16. See Shoshana Zuboff, "Big Other: Surveillance Capitalism and the Prospects of an Information Civilization," *Journal of Information Technology* 30 (2015): 75–89.

17. Karl Marx, *Capital: A Critical Analysis of Capitalist Production*, vol. 1, trans. Samuel Moore and Edward Aveling (New York: International, 1992), 400. See also Christian Fuchs, "Political Economy and Surveillance Theory," *Critical Sociology* 39, no. 5 (2012): 671–687; and Mark Andrejevic, "Surveillance and Alienation in the Online Economy," *Surveillance & Society* 8, no. 3 (2011): 278–287.

18. Frederick W. Taylor, *The Principles of Scientific Management* (Mineola, N.Y.: Dover, 1998). See also Mark Andrejevic, "The Work of Being Watched: Interactive Media and the Exploitative Work of Self-Disclosure," *Critical Studies in Media Communication* 19, no. 2 (June 2002): 230–248; and Kevin Robins and Frank Webster, "Cybernetic Capitalism: Information, Technology, Everyday Life," in *The Political Economy of Information*, ed. Vincent Mosco and Janet Wasko (Madison: University of Wisconsin Press, 1988), 44–75. On Taylor and scientific management, see Harry Braverman, *Labor and Monopoly Capital: The Degradation of Work in the Twentieth Century* (New York: Monthly Review Press, 1998).

19. Robert H. Wiebe, *The Search for Order: 1877–1920* (New York: Hill and Wang, 1967).

20. Richard Popp, "Information, Industrialization, and the Business of Press Clippings, 1880–1925," *Journal of American History* 101, no. 2 (2014): 427–453; and Popp,

"Addresses and Alchemy: Mailing Lists and the Making of Information Commodities in Industrial Capitalism" (unpublished conference paper, Histories of American Capitalism, Cornell University, November 7, 2014).

21. See Hartmut Berghoff, Philip Scranton, and Uwe Spiekerman, "The Origins of Marketing and Market Research: Information, Institutions, and Markets," in *The Rise of Marketing and Market Research*, ed. Hartmut Berghoff, Philip Scranton, and Uwe Spiekerman (New York: Palgrave Macmillan, 2011), 1–26; Susan Strasser, *Satisfaction Guaranteed: The Making of the American Mass Market* (Washington, D.C.: Smithsonian Institution Press, 1989); and Pamela W. Laird, *Advertising Progress: American Business and the Rise of Consumer Marketing* (Baltimore, Md.: Johns Hopkins University Press, 1998).

22. My understanding of surveillance and its disciplinary function is informed by the theoretical insights of Michel Foucault. See Foucault, *Discipline and Punish*; and Foucault, *Power/Knowledge: Selected Interviews and Other Writings, 1972–1977*, ed. Colin Gordon (New York: Pantheon, 1980). It is impossible to understate the continuing impact of Foucault's work on the field of surveillance studies. Despite the limitations of the panoptic model and his historical arguments, Foucault's basic assertions about the nature of modern surveillance—its total visibility, continuous monitoring, unverifiable gaze, normalizing force, and biopolitical ambitions—retain much analytical power. For critiques of Foucault, see Gilles Deleuze, "Postscript on the Societies of Control," *October* 59 (1992): 3–7; Kevin D. Haggerty and Richard V. Ericson, "The Surveillant Assemblage," *British Journal of Sociology* 51, no. 4 (2000): 605–622; and Kevin D. Haggerty, "Tear Down the Walls: On Demolishing the Panopticon," in *Theorizing Surveillance: The Panopticon and Beyond*, ed. David Lyon (Portland, Ore.: Willan, 2006), 23–45.

23. "Credit Men," *Time* 27, no. 25 (22 June 1936), 66, 68, 70.

24. Ibid., 66.

25. Robert Wallace, "Please Remit," *Life*, December 21, 1953, 42.

26. On the history of Fair Isaac, see Martha Poon, "Scorecards as Devices for Consumer Credit: The Case of Fair, Isaac & Company Incorporated," in *Market Devices*, ed. Michael Callon, Yural Millo, and Fabian Muniesa (Malden, Mass.: Wiley-Blackwell, 2007), 284–306; and Poon, "Historicizing Consumer Credit Risk Calculation: The Fair Isaac Process of Commercial Scorecard Manufacture, 1957–circa 1980," in *Technological Innovation in Retail Finance: International Historical Perspectives*, ed. Bernardo Batiz-Lazo, J. Carles Maixé-Altés, and Paul Thomes (New York: Routledge, 2011), 221–245.

27. Pam Dixon and Robert Gellman, "The Scoring of America: How Secret Consumer Scores Threaten Your Privacy and Your Future," World Privacy Forum, April 2, 2014, http://www.worldprivacyforum.org/wp-content/uploads/2014/04/WPF_Scoring_of_America_April2014_fs.pdf (accessed July 20, 2016); Amy J. Schmitz, "Secret Consumer Scores and Segmentation: Separating 'Haves' from 'Have-Nots.'" *Michigan State Law Review*, no. 5 (2014): 1411–1473; and Federal Trade Commission, *Data Brokers: A Call for Transparency and Accountability* (May 2014), https://www.ftc.gov/system/files/documents/reports/data-brokers-call-transparency-accountability-report-federal-trade-commission-may-2014/140527databrokerreport.pdf (accessed August 7, 2016).

28. For critical studies of algorithms, see Frank Pasquale, *The Black Box Society: The Secret Algorithms That Control Money and Information* (Cambridge, Mass.: Harvard

University Press, 2015); Danielle Keats Citron and Frank Pasquale, "The Scored Society: Due Process for Automated Predictions," *Washington Law Review* 89, no. 1 (2014): 1–33; John Cheney-Lippold, "A New Algorithmic Identity: Soft Biopolitics and the Modulation of Control," *Theory, Culture & Society* 28, no. 6 (2011): 164–181; Tarleton Gillespie, "The Relevance of Algorithms," in *Media Technologies: Essays on Communication, Materiality, and Society*, ed. Tarleton Gillespie, Pablo Boczkowski, and Kirsten Foot (Cambridge, Mass.: MIT Press, 2014), 167–194; and Cathy O'Neil, *Weapons of Math Destruction: How Big Data Increases Inequality and Threatens Democracy* (New York: Crown, 2016).

29. This perspective is best articulated by Marron, who draws upon neoliberal critique and Foucault's theory of governmentality to explain the institutionalization of contemporary credit risk and its function as a technology of economic governance. See Marron, *Consumer Credit in the United States*. My analysis of late twentieth-century risk scoring agrees with Marron's, though I attribute its development and larger significance to different historical themes and antecedents. For related Foucauldian studies of economic rationalization and governmentality, see Colin Gordon and Peter Miller, eds., *The Foucault Effect: Studies in Governmentality* (Chicago: University of Chicago Press, 1991); and Peter Miller and Nikolas Rose, *Governing the Present* (Cambridge, UK: Polity, 2008).

30. See Randy Martin, *Financialization of Daily Life* (Philadelphia: Temple University Press, 2002); Marron, *Consumer Credit in the United States*; and Paul Langely, "Equipping Entrepreneurs: Consuming Credit and Credit Scores," *Consumption Markets & Culture* 17, no. 5 (2014): 448–467. On the origins and transformation of contemporary finance capitalism, see Greta R. Krippner, *Capitalizing on Crisis: The Political Origins of the Rise of Finance* (Cambridge, Mass.: Harvard University Press, 2011); and Costas Lapavitsas, "The Financialization of Capitalism: Profiting without Producing," *City* 17, no. 6 (2013): 792–805.

31. Sandage, *Born Losers*.

32. Jonathan Levy, *Freaks of Fortune: The Emerging World of Capitalism and Risk in America* (Cambridge, Mass.: Harvard University Press, 2012).

33. François Ewald, "Insurance and Risk," in *The Foucault Effect: Studies in Governmentality*, ed. Colin Gordon and Peter Miller (Chicago: University of Chicago Press, 1991), 197–210. On insurance "risk making" and its historical relationship to credit reporting, see Dan Bouk, *How Our Days Became Numbered: Risk and the Rise of the Statistical Individual* (Chicago: University of Chicago Press, 2015).

34. Bruce G. Carruthers, "From Uncertainty toward Risk: The Case of Credit Ratings," *Socio-Economic Review* 11 (2013): 525–551. On commensuration, see Wendy Nelson Espeland and Mitchell L. Stevens, "Commensuration as Social Process," *Annual Review of Sociology* 24 (1998): 313–343.

35. On the make-or-break seriousness of personal reputation among financiers in Rockefeller's milieu, see Susie J. Pak, *Gentleman Bankers: The World of J. P. Morgan* (Cambridge, Mass.: Harvard University Press, 2014).

36. David F. Jordan, *Managing Personal Finances: How to Use Money Intelligently* (New York: Prentice-Hall, 1936), 56–57.

37. Robert Bartels, *Credit Management* (New York: Ronald Press, 1967), 312.

38. Clyde William Phelps, *Retail Credit Fundamentals,* 4th ed. (St. Louis, MO: International Consumer Credit Association, 1963), 67.

39. See Matt Fellowes, "Credit Scores, Reports, and Getting Ahead in America," Brookings Institution, May 2006, http://www.brookings.edu/~/media/research/files/reports/2006 /5/childrenfamilies%20fellowes/20060501_creditscores.pdf (accessed January 15, 2014); and Board of the Governors of the Federal Reserve System, *Report to the Congress on Credit Scoring and Its Effect on the Availability and Affordability of Credit*, August 2007, http://www.federalreserve.gov/boarddocs/RptCongress/creditscore/creditscore.pdf (accessed May 26, 2015). On the stratifying effects of algorithmic classification, see Marion Fourcade and Kieran Healy, "Classification Situations: Life-Chances in the Neoliberal Era," *Accounting, Organizations, and Society* 38 (2013): 559–572.

40. The social embeddedness of economic life is a key insight from contemporary economic sociology. See Mark Granovetter, "Economic Action and Social Structure: The Problem of Embeddedness," *American Journal of Sociology* 91, no. 3 (1985): 481–510; Greta A. Krippner, "The Elusive Market: Embeddedness and the Paradigm of Economic Sociology," *Theory and Society* 30 (2001): 775–810; and the work of Viviana A. Zelizer, notably *Morals and Markets: The Development of Life Insurance in the United States* (New York: Columbia University Press, 1979) and *The Social Meaning of Money: Pin Money, Paychecks, Poor Relief, and Other Currencies* (New York: Basic, 1994).

41. See David J. Seipp, *The Right to Privacy in American History* (Cambridge, Mass.: Harvard University, Program on Information Resources Policy, 1978).

42. Benjamin Franklin, "The Way to Wealth," in *The Papers of Benjamin Franklin*, vol. 7, edited by Leonard W. Labaree (New Haven, CT: Yale University Press, 1963), 340–350.

43. See Marc Flandreau and Gabriel Geisler Mesevage, "The Untold History of Transparency: Mercantile Agencies, the Law, and the Lawyers (1851–1916)," *Enterprise & Society* 15 (2014): 213–251.

44. On the consumer movement, see Lawrence Glickman, *Buying Power: A History of Consumer Activism in America* (Chicago: University of Chicago Press, 2009); Lizabeth Cohen, *A Consumers' Republic: The Politics of Mass Consumption in Postwar America* (New York: Knopf, 2003); Daniel Horowitz, *The Anxieties of Affluence: Critiques of American Consumer Culture, 1939–1979* (Amherst: University of Massachusetts Press, 2004); and Charles F. McGovern, *Sold American: Consumption and Citizenship, 1890–1945* (Chapel Hill: University of North Carolina Press, 2006).

45. Weare Holbrook, "The Confessions of a Goldfish," *Los Angeles Times*, November 3, 1929, F14, 23. On American attitudes to survey research, see Sarah E. Igo, *The Averaged American: Surveys, Citizens, and the Making of a Mass Public* (Cambridge, Mass.: Harvard University Press, 2007).

46. Vance Packard, *The Hidden Persuaders* (New York: David McKay, 1957), 266.

1. "A BUREAU FOR THE PROMOTION OF HONESTY": THE BIRTH OF SYSTEMATIC CREDIT SURVEILLANCE

1. Francis J. Grund, *The Americans in Their Moral, Social, and Political Relations* (London: Longman, Rees, Orme, Brown, Greene, and Longman, 1837), 111–117. On Grund, see Holman Hamilton and James L. Crouthamel, "A Man for Both Parties: Francis J. Grund as Political Chameleon," *Pennsylvania Magazine of History and Biography* 97, no. 4 (October 1973): 465–484.

2. The concept and chronology of the market revolution are topics of ongoing debate, but historians generally agree that the early decades of the nineteenth century marked a watershed moment in the development of American capitalism. See Michael Zakim and Gary J. Kornblith, eds., *Capitalism Takes Command: The Social Transformation of Nineteenth-Century America* (Chicago: University of Chicago Press, 2012); John Lauritz Larson, *The Market Revolution in America: Liberty, Ambition, and the Eclipse of the Common Good* (New York: Cambridge University Press, 2010); Melvyn Stokes and Stephen Conway, eds., *The Market Revolution in America: Social, Political, and Religious Expressions, 1800–1880* (Charlottesville: University of Virginia Press, 1996); and Charles Sellers, *The Market Revolution: Jacksonian America, 1815–1846* (New York: Oxford University Press, 1991).

3. Bruce H. Mann, *Republic of Debtors: Bankruptcy in the Age of American Independence* (Cambridge, Mass.: Harvard University Press, 2002).

4. Daniel Webster, "The Continuance of the Bank Charter," in *The Writings and Speeches of Daniel Webster*, vol. 7 (Boston: Little, Brown), 89, 92.

5. "The Principles of Credit," *Hunt's Merchant's Magazine* 2, no. 3 (March 1840): 194.

6. The problem of trust (and its obverse, risk) as a defining feature of modernity occupies much of contemporary sociological theory, particularly in connection with the mediating role of institutions and technical expertise. See Anthony Giddens, *The Consequences of Modernity* (Stanford, CA: Stanford University Press, 1990), and Ulrich Beck, *Risk Society: Towards a New Modernity*, trans. Mark Ritter (London: Sage, 1992). The risk management perspective is dominant among economists, who generally view credit reporting as a solution to the problem of imperfect or asymmetrical information in lending situations (see Margaret J. Miller, introduction to *Credit Reporting Systems and the International Economy*, ed. Margaret J. Miller [Cambridge, Mass.: MIT Press, 2003], 1–21).

7. Jessica M. Lepler, *The Many Panics of 1837: People, Politics, and the Creation of a Transatlantic Crisis* (New York: Cambridge University Press, 2013).

8. "Mercantile Agency," *New-York City and Co-Partnership Directory for 1843 & 1844* (New York: John Doggett Jr., [1843]), n.p.

9. For histories of nineteenth-century American credit reporting, see Olegario, *A Culture of Credit*; Sandage, *Born Losers*; Norris, *R. G. Dun & Co., 1841–1900*; James H. Madison, "The Evolution of Commercial Credit Reporting Agencies in Nineteenth-Century America," *Business History Review* 48 (1974): 164–186; Bertram Wyatt-Brown, "God and Dun and Bradstreet, 1841–1851," *Business History Review* 40 (1966): 432–450; Lewis E. Atherton, "The Problem of Credit Rating in the Ante-Bellum South," *Journal of Southern History* 12 (1946): 534–556; and R. W. Hidy, "Credit Rating Before Dun and Bradstreet," *Bulletin of the Business Historical Society* 13 (1939): 81–88. Useful company-sponsored histories include Edward Neville Vose, *Seventy-Five Years of the Mercantile Agency R. G. Dun & Co., 1841–1816* (Brooklyn, N.Y.: R. G. Dun, 1916); and Roy A. Foulke, *The Sinews of American Commerce* (New York: Dun and Bradstreet, 1941).

10. Quoted in Max Weber, *The Protestant Ethic and the Spirit of Capitalism*, trans. Talcott Parsons (New York: Charles Scribner's Sons, 1958), 49.

11. See Edward J. Balleisen, *Navigating Failure: Bankruptcy and Commercial Society in Antebellum America* (Chapel Hill, N.C.: Duke University Press, 2001).

12. For more on the communication of reputation, see Kenneth Lipartito, "Mediating Reputation: Credit Reporting Systems in American History," *Business History Review* 87 (2013): 655–677.

13. On recommendation letters and their connection to bookkeeping, clerical writing, and notions of moral accountability, see Thomas Augst, *The Clerk's Tale: Young Men and Moral Life in Nineteenth-Century America* (Chicago: University of Chicago Press, 2003). On the crisis of social identity in nineteenth-century America, articulated in advice manuals that promoted "'transparency' of character," see Karen Haltunen, *Confidence Men and Painted Ladies: A Study of Middle-Class Culture, 1830–1870* (New Haven, Conn.: Yale University Press, 1982).

14. Atherton, "Problem of Credit Rating," 536.

15. Ibid., 535–536.

16. Another freelance correspondent, Sheldon P. Church, provided credit reports for several New York City dry goods wholesalers as early as 1827 and served as a traveling reporter in the South in the 1840s; see *The Commercial Agency: Its Origin, Growth, &c.* (New York: McKillop & Sprague, 1874), 3–4; Thomas F. Meagher, *The Commercial Agency "System" of the United States and Canada Exposed* (New York: n.p., 1876), 5; and Foulke, *Sinews of American Commerce*, 333–334, 366–368.

17. Hidy, "Credit Rating Before Dun and Bradstreet," 84.

18. Quoted in Foulke, *Sinews of American Commerce*, 363.

19. On legibility as a technique of state control and social engineering, see James Scott, *Seeing Like a State: How Certain Schemes to Improve the Human Condition Have Failed* (New Haven, Conn.: Yale University Press, 1998).

20. Between 1841 and 1890, Tappan and his successors filled more than 2,500 volumes of credit reports (preserved in the R. G. Dun Archive, Baker Library, Harvard Business School, Cambridge, Mass.). Many nineteenth-century agencies, including Tappan's, reported the credit standing of individuals outside the United States, notably in Canada. This chapter addresses the mercantile agency's primary operations in the United States.

21. Quoted in Norris, *R. G. Dun & Co.*, 22.

22. Wyatt-Brown, "God and Dun and Bradstreet," 444, 447.

23. *The Mercantile Agency: Its Claims Upon the Favor and Support of the Community* (New York: Edward Russell, 1872), 6.

24. Jesse R. Sprague, *The Romance of Credit* (New York: D. Appleton-Century, 1943), 111.

25. "The Mercantile Agency," *Hunt's Merchant's Magazine*, January 24, 1851, 47–48.

26. Peter P. Wahlstad, *Credit and the Credit Man* (New York: Alexander Hamilton Institute, 1917), 106–115.

27. "The Mercantile Agencies: They Have Grown Indispensable to Business," *Chicago Tribune*, March 15, 1896, 6.

28. Alfred D. Chandler, *The Visible Hand: The Managerial Revolution in American Business* (Cambridge, Mass.: Harvard University Press, 1997); James Beniger, *The Control Revolution: Technological and Economic Origins of the Information Society* (Cambridge, Mass.: Harvard University Press, 1986); and JoAnne Yates, *Control Through Communication: The Rise of System in American Management* (Baltimore, Md.: Johns Hopkins University Press, 1989).

29. Sandage, *Born Losers*, 149.

30. See Sankar, "State Power and Recordkeeping."

31. Craig Robertson, "A Documentary Regime of Verification: The Emergence of the U.S. Passport and the Archival Problematization of Identity," *Cultural Studies* 23, no. 3 (May 2009): 329–354.

32. Madison, "Evolution of Commercial Credit Reporting Agencies," 171.

33. New York, vol. 189, p. 242, R. G. Dun & Co. Collection, Baker Library, Harvard Business School.

34. For detailed analysis of character and capacity, see Olegario, *A Culture of Credit*, 80–118.

35. "The Mercantile Agency," 50.

36. C. W. Steffler, "The Evolution of the Commercial Agency: The Story of Bradstreet's," *Commerce and Finance*, February 22, 1928, 426.

37. "Beauties of the Credit System," *Circular* [Brooklyn, N.Y.], August 14, 1856, 120.

38. *The Mercantile Agency*, 5.

39. "The Mercantile Agency System," *Banker's Magazine and Statistical Register*, January 7, 1858, 547.

40. "Magnetic Communication for Individual Purposes," *Scientific American*, February 28, 1857, 197; see also "The Telegraph," *DeBow's Review and Industrial Resources, Statistics, Etc.* 16 (1854): 165–169.

41. Initially, tissue-paper copies were pasted into the handwritten ledgers, but their fragility soon led to their being pasted onto sheets of manila paper; these were sent to the various branches, which arranged them alphabetically and by location, and placed them in special binders. See Vose, *Seventy-Five Years*, 125–132; and Norris, *R. G. Dun & Co.*, 138–139.

42. *The Centennial of the Birth of Impartial Credit Reporting—An American Idea* (New York: Dun and Bradstreet, 1941), 30.

43. "Agencies," *Brooklyn Eagle*, November 15, 1873, 2.

44. "Business Credits," *Philadelphia Inquirer*, March 28, 1879, 7.

45. Pennsylvania, vol. 131, p. 101, R. G. Dun & Co. Collection, Baker Library, Harvard Business School.

46. New York, vol. 189, p. 240, R. G. Dun & Co. Collection, Baker Library, Harvard Business School.

47. "Traits of Trade—Laudable and Iniquitous," *Hunt's Merchant's Magazine and Commercial Review*, July 1853, 51.

48. Meagher, *Commercial Agency "System,"* 18.

49. Vose, *Seventy-Five Years*, 36–38. Presidents Chester Arthur, Grover Cleveland, and William McKinley also worked as correspondents.

50. P. R. Earling, *Whom to Trust: A Practical Treatise on Mercantile Credits* (Chicago: Rand, McNally, 1890), 32.

51. "Commercial Credit," *Chicago Tribune*, September 1, 1883, 5.

52. "'Statements' as an Aid in Determining Credit," *The Mercantile Agency Annual for 1873* (New York: Dun, Barlow and Co., 1873), 2; and Foulke, *Sinews of American Commerce*, 374.

53. "The Mercantile Agency System," 547.

54. See "First Annual Convention: National Association of Credit Men [1896]," reprinted in *Golden Anniversary Credit Congress, Souvenir Program* (New York: National Association of Credit Men, 1947), 222–223. For reports presented at the association's annual conventions, see *Business: The Office Paper* 17 (June 1897): 213; 18 (June 1898): 379; and 19 (June 1899): 375–376. See also Olegario, *A Culture of Credit*, 190–196.

55. F. J. Hopkins, "Suggestions on Mercantile Agency Reports," *Business: The Office Paper* 17 (November 1897): 331.

56. "Improvement of Mercantile Agency Service," *Business: The Office Paper* 20 (July 1900): 337–338.

57. "The Mercantile Agency," 49.

58. Hidy, "Credit Rating Before Dun and Bradstreet," 85.

59. Norris, *R. G. Dun & Co.*, 26.

60. *Reports of the Four Leading Cases Against the Mercantile Agency for Slander and Libel* (New York: Dun, Barlow & Co., 1873), 1–125. For a more detailed account of the Beardsley case, see Sandage, *Born Losers*, 164–178.

61. *Reports of the Four Leading Cases Against the Mercantile Agency*, 183–186.

62. For a summary of this legal debate, see Louis M. Greeley, "What Publications of Commercial Agencies Are Privileged," *American Law Register* 35 (November 1887): 681–693. During the 1890s at least four bills—two in the Illinois General Assembly, one in North Dakota, and another in the U.S. Congress—were proposed to check the activities of the mercantile agencies. See "Aimed at the Agencies," *Chicago Tribune*, March 11, 1891, 6; "It Affects Commercial Agencies," *Chicago Tribune*, March 7, 1895, 12; and H.R. 3355, 55th Cong., 1st sess., *Congressional Record*, 30 (1897): 1307.

63. Steffler, "Evolution of the Commercial Agency," 427.

64. Norris, *R. G. Dun & Co.*, 51.

65. Vose, *Seventy-Five Years*, 83.

66. Preface to *The Mercantile Agency's Reference Book*, reprinted in Vose, *Seventy-Five Years*, 84–85.

67. Capital ratings consisted of A1+($1 million or more), A1 ($500,000–$1 million), 1 ($250,000–$500,000), 1½ ($100,000–$250,000), 2 ($50,000–$100,000), 2½ ($25,000–$50,000), 3 ($10,000–$25,000), and 3½ ($5,000–$10,000); see "Key to Markings," in *The Mercantile Agency's Reference Book* [1864], reprinted in Vose, *Seventy-Five Years*, 92.

68. Norris, *R. G. Dun & Co.*, 87.

69. Quoted in ibid., 93.

70. Meagher, *Commercial Agency "System,"* 29–30.

71. Ibid., 6, 7.

72. Vose, *Seventy-Five Years*, 98.

73. "Traits of Trade—Laudable and Iniquitous," 52.

74. "The Mercantile Agency," 50.

75. "Solid Facts," *Business: The Office Paper* 19 (April 1899): 228.

76. Atherton, "Problem of Credit Rating," 542. For more on how nineteenth-century credit reports were used—or, rather, not used—see Claire Brennecke, "Information Acquisition in Antebellum U.S. Credit Markets: Evidence from Nineteenth-Century Credit Reports," Working paper, Federal Deposit Insurance Corporation, September 2016.

77. "The Mercantile Agency," 51.

78. "The Mercantile Agencies: They Have Grown Indispensable to Business," *Chicago Tribune*, March 15, 1896, 6.

79. "The Dry Goods Trade," *New York Daily Times*, March 8, 1856, 10.

80. George G. Foster, *New York Naked* (New York: DeWitt & Davenport, 1850), 119.

81. "Checks Upon Over-Trading," *New York Times*, October 29, 1859, 4.

82. Flandreau and Mesavage, "The Untold History of Transparency."

83. "Agencies," 2.

84. "Commercial Credit," *Chicago Tribune*, September 1, 1883, 5.

85. Mary Poovey, *A History of the Modern Fact: Problems of Knowledge in the Sciences of Wealth and Society* (Chicago: University of Chicago Press, 1998). A similar process of financial objectification was at work in the nineteenth-century life insurance industry; see Zelizer, *Morals and Markets*, and Bouk, *How Our Days Became Numbered*.

86. See Patricia Cline Cohen, *A Calculating People: The Spread of Numeracy in Early America* (New York: Routledge, 1999); Theodore M. Porter, *Trust in Numbers: The Pursuit of Objectivity in Science and Public Life* (Princeton, N.J.: Princeton University Press, 1995); and Ian Hacking, *The Taming of Chance* (Cambridge, UK: Cambridge University Press, 1990).

87. Frederick B. Goddard, *Giving and Getting Credit: A Book for Business Men* (New York: Baker & Taylor, 1895), 39.

88. There are rich parallels between the development of nineteenth-century credit reporting and the history of accounting as a technology of economic objectification. See Peter Miller and Ted O'Leary, "Accounting and the Construction of the Governable Person," *Accounting, Organization, and Society* 12 (1987): 235–265; Peter Miller, "Accounting and Objectivity: The Invention of Calculating Selves and Calculable Spaces," *Annals of Scholarship* 9 (1992): 61–86; and Keith Hoskin and Richard Macve, "Writing, Examining, Disciplining: The Genesis of Accounting's Modern Power," in *Accounting as Social and Institutional Practice*, ed. Anthony G. Hopwood and Peter Miller (New York: Cambridge University Press, 1994), 67–97. On accounting as a rhetoric of objectivity, see Bruce G. Carruthers and Wendy Nelson Epseland, "Accounting for Rationality: Double-Entry Bookkeeping and the Rhetoric of Economic Rationality," *American Journal of Sociology* 91 (1991): 31–69; Porter, *Trust in Numbers*, 89–98; and Poovey, *History of the Modern Fact*, 29–90.

2. COMING TO TERMS WITH CREDIT: THE NINETEENTH-CENTURY ORIGINS OF CONSUMER CREDIT SURVEILLANCE

1. Calder, *Financing the American Dream*, 26. See also Jonathan Prude, *The Coming of Industrial Order: Town and Factory Life in Rural Massachusetts, 1810–1860* (New York: Cambridge University Press, 1983); Thomas D. Clark, *Pills, Petticoats and Plows: The Southern Country Store* (New York: Bobbs-Merrill, 1944); and Balleisen, *Navigating Failure*, 60–64. See Horowitz, *The Morality of Spending*, 1–29, for discussion of nineteenth-century attitudes toward consumption.

2. "The Moral of the Crisis," *United States Magazine, and Democratic Review*, October 1, 1837, 108. The ubiquity of retail credit in Jacksonian America is also noted in B. F. Foster, *The Merchant's Manual, Comprising the Principles of Trade, Commerce and Banking* (Boston: Perkins and Marvin, 1838), 46–48.

3. Nathan S. S. Beman, "Punctuality in the Repayment of Debts," *American National Preacher* 11, no. 11 (April 1837): 172.

4. "Cash and Credit," *Workingman's Advocate*, March 15, 1843, 1.

5. "A Domestic Story: Just Charge It," *The Agitator* [Wellsborough, Tioga County, Pa.], December 7, 1854, 1.

6. "Evils of the Credit System," *Chicago Tribune*, May 8, 1867, 2.

7. "Unpaid Bills," *Daily Constitution* [Middletown, Conn.], January 21, 1874, [1].

8. John J. Cummins, "Retail Credits from Moral and Financial Points of View," *Business: The Office Paper* 19, no. 1 (January 1899): 47.

9. Campbell Gibson, "Population of the 100 Largest Cities and Other Urban Places in the United States: 1790–1990," Population Division Working Paper No. 27 (Washington, D.C.: U.S. Bureau of the Census, June 1998).

10. Terry was forced out of retirement in 1872 thanks to a bad investment. He went to work for A. T. Stewart and took over its silk department for himself when the landmark department store closed in 1876. "Publishers' Notice" in Samuel E. Terry, *How to Keep a Store: Embodying the Conclusions of Thirty Years' Experience in Merchandising*, 17th ed. (New York: Fowler & Wells, 1891), iii–iv.

11. Samuel H. Terry, *The Retailer's Manual: Embodying the Conclusions of Thirty Years' Experience in Merchandising* (Newark, N.J.: Jennings Brothers, 1869), 15.

12. Ibid., 150.

13. Ibid., 179.

14. Ibid., 159.

15. Ibid., 162.

16. "The Other Side," *Chicago Tribune*, April 21, 1874, 10.

17. "New Business Methods," *Chicago Tribune*, October 23, 1886, 9.

18. On nineteenth-century personal loans, including those from pawnbrokers and loan sharks, see Woloson, *In Hock;* Calder, *Financing the American Dream,* 42–55; and Hyman, *Debtor Nation,* 6–25. See also Louis N. Robinson and Rolf Nugent, *Regulation of the Small Loan Business* (New York: Russell Sage Foundation, 1935); and John P. Caskey, "Pawnbroking in America: The Economics of a Forgotten Market," *Journal of Money, Credit, and Banking* 23, no. 1 (February 1991): 85–99.

19. "Blacklisting Poets," *New York Times*, July 1, 1888, 4.

20. "Corsicana," *Dallas Weekly Herald*, March 12, 1885, [4].

21. A. T. Scott, "Newspaper Credit," *The Free Enquirer,* June 15, 1834, 265.

22. "A Typographical Pillory," *Workingman's Advocate*, August 21, 1830, 3.

23. *The Commercial Agency: Its Origin, Growth, &c.* (New York: McKillop and Sprague Company, 1874), 7.

24. Unless specified, the term *credit reporting*, used throughout the remainder of this chapter, refers generically to blacklists, written reports, and credit ratings that organizations published for the use of their subscribers and members.

25. J. R. Truesdale, *Credit Bureau Management* (New York: Prentice-Hall, 1927), 13. After a series of mergers and acquisitions, the original Selss firm became part of what is now Equifax in 1934 (Flinn, *History of Retail Credit Company*, 256–260). There is evidence to suggest that retail credit information-sharing organizations may have existed even earlier. An 1855 announcement, for example, indicates that Washington, D.C., shopkeepers at least planned an association to "circumscribe the retail credit system within limits, and to mutually interchange information respecting the reliability of customers" ("The Cash Principle," *Baltimore Sun*, February 15, 1855, [4]).

26. *Lain's Brooklyn Directory*, 1878 (Selss is misspelled Sells); "At a Meeting Held on Thursday," *Brooklyn Eagle*, April 20, 1882, 2.

27. Advertisement, *Brooklyn Eagle*, February 18, 1869, 2.

28. "The Dead Beats," *Brooklyn Eagle*, March 8, 1870, 2.

29. "Reform in Debt Collection in Brooklyn," *New York Times*, March 8, 1870, 5.
30. H.P., "The Dealers' Credit System—The Wages Lien Law in the Old Countries," *Brooklyn Eagle*, March 14, 1870, 2; and "The New York Citizen Reformers," *Brooklyn Eagle*, March 15, 1870, 2.
31. "People Who Are in Debt," *Brooklyn Eagle*, August 18, 1871, 2.
32. "Bankruptcy Proceedings," *New York Times*, May 14, 1931, 44; and "Bankruptcy Proceedings," *New York Times*, May 27, 1931, 51.
33. New York, vol. 390, p. 2402, R. G. Dun & Co. Collection, Baker Library, Harvard Business School.
34. Truesdale, *Credit Bureau Management*, 13–14. Other agencies predate or do not appear in Truesdale's chronology, such as the American Mercantile Union in Lowell, Massachusetts, and the Retail Merchants' Credit Company in New Haven, Connecticut (the former existed by 1878, the latter by 1889). See American Mercantile Union, *Confidential Reference Book, Compiled in the Interest of the Retail Trade* (Lowell, Mass., 1878); and "Articles of Association of the Retail Merchants' Credit Company," *New Haven* (Conn.) *Register*, April 12, 1889, [4]. The majority shareholder, C. B. Matthewman, published a "Confidential Guide for Retail Merchants" containing 15,000 names a year earlier ("Attorney Matthewman's List," *New Haven* [Conn.] *Register*, March 27, 1888, [1]).
35. American Mercantile Union, Preface to *Confidential Reference Book for San Francisco, Oakland and Vicinity* (San Francisco, 1886), n.p.
36. "The Business Booms," *Sunday Herald* (Syracuse, N.Y.), May 5, 1895, 8.
37. Truesdale's account is confined to private agencies, overlooking the development of trade organizations. Significantly, trade organizations often competed directly with private agencies and large merchant-run associations, thus undermining their centralizing efforts. In 1927 some grocers and meat dealers still maintained their own separate credit information services, which Truesdale criticizes (*Credit Bureau Management*, 208). On the parallel development of trade associations among wholesalers, manufacturers, and distributors, see Olegario, *A Culture of Credit*, 185. On the role of credit information interchanges, see also *Trade Associations: Their Economic Significance and Legal Status* (New York: National Industrial Conference Board, 1925), 149–161.
38. "Merchant Tailors' Exchange," *Philadelphia Inquirer*, October 17, 1871, 3. See also "Milk Dealers," *Philadelphia Inquirer*, June 3, 1871, 2; and "Retail Coal Dealers," *Philadelphia Inquirer*, November 30, 1871, 3.
39. "Green Grocers," *Chicago Tribune*, September 30, 1874, 5.
40. Untitled, *New Orleans Times*, February 12, 1878, 4.
41. "New York," *New York Times*, May 23, 1882, 8. On the prevalence of credit granting among grocers, see Strasser, *Satisfaction Guaranteed*, 67–72.
42. "The Other Side," 10.
43. "Green Grocers," 5.
44. "The Los Angeles Protective Association," *Daily Evening News* (San Francisco), September 26, 1879, n.p.
45. "A Retail Grocer's Association," *Aberdeen* (N.D.) *Daily News*, March 18, 1888, [3].
46. "New England Grocers," *Boston Globe*, January 9, 1883, 6.
47. "Retail Grocers," *Chicago Tribune*, August 24, 1881, 5; "Retail Grocers Combining," *New York Times*, June 19, 1882, 8; "Grocers' Association," *Brooklyn Eagle*, June 9, 1882, 4; "A Protective Association," *St. Louis Globe-Democrat*, January 15, 1882, 3; *Constitution*

and Rules, Richmond Retail Dealers' Association (Richmond, Va.: Carlton, McCarthy & Co., 1883); "The Buffalo Grocers," *New York Times*, April 25, 1886, 1; and "Retail Grocers Organizing," *Philadelphia Inquirer*, April 22, 1886, 3.

48. "The Butchers Organized," *Charlotte* (N.C.) *News*, January 3, 1889, [1]; and "A Grocers' Union," *Charlotte* (N.C.) *News*, March 30, 1892, [4].

49. "Fees of Physicians," *Boston Medical and Surgical Journal*, January 29, 1840, 404.

50. R.C., "Medical Fees," *Boston Medical and Surgical Journal*, February 12, 1840, 13.

51. "Black Lists," *Philadelphia Medical Times*, December 21, 1872, 185.

52. "Doctors," *Brooklyn Eagle*, February 19, 1873, 1.

53. "A Good Move," *Medical and Surgical Reporter* (Philadelphia), February 13, 1869, 136.

54. *For Reference: Published for the Benefit of Physicians, Dentists & Retail Dealers, by the Manhattan Collecting Company* (New York: E. V. Armstrong, 1873).

55. Untitled news item, *San Jose* (Calif.) *Mercury*, February 27, 1886, [4].

56. The confidentiality of rating books was emphatically stated in most volumes, and contracts governing their use often stipulated that they were loaned to members and therefore could not be resold.

57. For examples of racial identification, see *The Credit Guide* 1, no. 2 (Boston: n.p., 1872), in the collection of the Massachusetts Historical Society; *Black List* (Oshkosh, Wis.: n.p., [1872?]); American Mercantile Union, *Reference Book, Compiled in the Interest of the Retail Trade* (Lowell, Mass.: n.p., 1878); *M'Cready's Credit Register, for Retail Dealers, and Country Store Merchants*, 2nd New England ed. (Boston: Alfred Mudge & Son, 1884); and Credit Reporting Company of Newark, New Jersey, *Trust Book* (n.p., [1898]).

58. Though I have drawn a hard distinction between blacklists and rating books, some organizations published hybrids that listed ratings (based on affirmative-negative reporting) along with sums of unsettled accounts for each individual (see, for example, *M'Cready's Credit Register*), while others published modified blacklists that rated graduations of slow- and nonpaying debtors. There was also slippage in the popular use of the term *blacklist*, which might technically refer to an affirmative-negative rating system (for example, the Landlords' Protective Association described in "A Norwich Black List," *New Haven Evening Register* [June 6, 1881], [1]).

59. *Retail Mercantile Agency* ([Brooklyn, N.Y.]: n.p., [1874–1875]), n.p.

60. The practice of fulfilling special inquiries was common, and most agencies encouraged their members to take advantage of this service. By 1880, for example, the RDPA was answering 20,000 special inquiries per year ("To Our Members," Retail Dealer's Protective Association, *Commercial Register*, 1881–1882, 9th ed. [New York, 1881], n.p.)

61. *The Union Credit Co. of Cleveland, Ohio*, rating book (Cleveland, [1895]).

62. "A Norwich Black List."

63. Retail Dealers' Protective Association, letter dated May 1873, *Register for New York, Brooklyn, & Vicinity*, 1873–1874 (New York, 1873), n.p.

64. "Explanatory," in *Commercial Report of Union Credit Reporting Co. of Minneapolis* (Minneapolis, 1894), n.p.

65. Commercial Credit Co., "To Our Patrons," in *Credit Reference Book of St. Joseph, Mo.* (St. Joseph, Mo., 1895), n.p.

66. On the development of ledger information sharing among late nineteenth-century commercial reporting organizations, see Olegario, *A Culture of Credi*, 182–190.

67. "Gentlemen," *Commercial Register,* 1882–1883, 10th ed. (New York Retail Dealers' Protective Association, 1882), n.p.

68. The practice of hiding the identities of merchant contributors is noted in the Brooklyn-based Retail Mercantile Agency's 1874–1875 rating book: "It is not necessary for subscribers to sign their names to the 'Reports,' as they are all numbered, and the number is known only to the officers of the Association."

69. "Terms and Conditions of Membership in the Retail Dealers' Protective Association," *Commercial Register,* 1880–1881, 8th ed. (New York, 1880), n.p. Subscriptions to the RDPA's register were prorated based on a subscriber's annual business volume. In 1880, for example, subscribers with annual volumes above $100,000 were charged $100 per year, while those making between $25,000 and $100,000 paid $100, and those doing less than $25,000 paid $50.

70. Commercial Credit Co., *Credit Reference Book of St. Joseph, Mo.* (St. Joseph, Mo., 1894), 5.

71. Retail Dealers' Protective Association, letter dated June 1872, *Register for New York, Brooklyn, & Vicinity* (New York, 1872), n.p.

72. Retail Dealers' Protective Association "Gentlemen," *Commercial Register,* 1883–1884, 11th ed. (New York, 1883), n.p.; italics in original.

73. See Theodore M. Porter, "Information, Power, and the View from Nowhere," in *Information Acumen: The Understanding and Use of Knowledge in Modern Business,* ed. Lisa Bud-Frierman (London: Routledge, 1994), 217–230.

74. *Confidential Reference Book of the Retail Dealers' Mutual Protective Association* (Nashville, Tenn.: Retail Dealers' Mutual Benefit Protective Association, 1885), n.p.

75. "To Our Members," *Commercial Register,* 8th ed., n.p.

76. New York, vol. 390, p. 2402, R. G. Dun & Co. Collection, Baker Library, Harvard Business School.

77. "To Our Members," *Commercial Register,* 1886–1887, 14th ed. (New York: Retail Dealers' Protective Association, 1886), n.p.

78. "Mercantile Union," *Philadelphia Inquirer,* July 8, 1881, 3; "Failed to Protect," *Chicago Tribune,* September 6, 1884, 8.

79. "Gentlemen," *Commercial Register,* 11th ed., n.p.

80. George Conway, "Financial Information," *Business: The Office Paper* 18, no. 1 (January 1898): 52.

81. Terry, *The Retailer's Manual,* 250.

82. Ibid., 245.

83. James G. Cannon, *Individual Credits: Address Delivered Before the National Association of Credit Men at Kansas City, Missouri* (New York: J. S. Babcock, 1897), 6–7. On the lax bookkeeping practices of small retailers, see Strasser, *Satisfaction Guaranteed,* 72–73.

84. "The Other Side," 10. On the unprofitability of credit granting for small late nineteenth-century retailers, see Louis Hyman, *Borrow: The American Way of Debt* (New York: Vintage, 2012), 8–10. As Hyman notes, consumer debt would not become profitable until "networks of finance" existed to support it. Organized credit surveillance was one of these critical networks.

85. R. Hamilton, "Troubles of the Retail Grocers," *Chicago Tribune,* September 25, 1873, 2.

86. "The Credit System," *Waynesboro* (Penn.) *Village Record,* April 4, 1872, 1.

87. "The Retail Credit Question," *Brooklyn Eagle*, March 15, 1870, 2.
88. "New Business Methods," *Chicago Tribune*, October 23, 1886, 9.
89. Hamilton, "Troubles," 2.
90. John J. Cummins, "The Evil of Retail Credits," *Business: The Office Paper* 18, no. 11 (November 1898): 698.
91. "Retail Grocers," *Atlanta Constitution*, February 10, 1876, 4.
92. "The Grocery Trade," *Boston Globe*, February 9, 1885, 1.
93. "The Barbers Book-Keeping," *Washington Post*, July 5, 1882, 2.
94. "The Abuse of Credit," *Bankers Magazine* 55, no. 1 (July 1897): 13.
95. The early development of the Chilton Corporation, for example, grew out of J. E. R. Chilton's close relationship with the credit manager of Sanger Brothers, a Dallas department store (Simon, *Pioneers of Excellence*, 12–18). See also "Pocket Notebook Forerunner to Multifold Credit Service," *Dallas Morning News*, January 17, 1960, 6.
96. J. E. R. Chilton, "Improved Systems of Handling Retail Credit," *Chicago Tribune*, June 17, 1904, A4.

3. CREDIT WORKERS UNITE: PROFESSIONALIZATION AND THE RISE OF A NATIONAL CREDIT INFRASTRUCTURE

1. "New Business Methods," *Chicago Tribune*, October 23, 1886, 9.
2. Fred W. Smith, "Our Larger Opportunities," *Business: The Office Paper* 20, no. 8 (August 1900): 376.
3. "Commercial Credit," *Chicago Tribune*, September 1, 1883, 5.
4. Quoted in Earling, *Whom to Trust*, 200–201.
5. See, for example, Freeman Hunt, *Worth and Wealth: A Collection of Maxims, Morals, and Miscellanies for Merchants and Men of Business* (New York: Stringer & Townsend, 1856).
6. Earling, *Whom to Trust*, 15.
7. "Keeping Credit Accounts," *Washington Post*, November 4, 1900, 22.
8. "Means of Stopping Failures," *Chicago Tribune*, June 25, 1893, 13.
9. Minutes of First Convention of Credit Men, Toledo, Ohio, June 23, 1896, in *Golden Anniversary Credit Congress, National Association of Credit Men, Souvenir Program* (New York: National Association of Credit Men, 1947), 208.
10. F. R. Boocock, "Practical Realization of Intelligent Theories," *Business: The Office Paper* 17, no. 12 (December 1897): 373.
11. W. G. Sluder, "How and Why I Became a Credit Man," *Credit World* 8, no. 5 (January 1920): 12.
12. W. A. H. Bogardus, *The Strength of the Credit Man Is Knowledge* (New York: National Association of Credit Men, 1902), 3–4.
13. Harlow N. Higinbotham, "Tales of the Credit Man," *Saturday Evening Post* 172, no. 52 (June 23, 1900): 1198.
14. Samuel L. Sewall, "The Ideal Credit Man," *Business: The Office Paper* 2, no. 6 (June 1896): 53.
15. Higinbotham, "Tales of the Credit Man," 1199.
16. F. F. Peabody, "The Man for the Credit Desk," in *Credits, Collections and Finance: Organizing the Work, Correct Policies and Methods; Five Credit and Collection Systems* (Chicago: A. W. Shaw, 1917), 27.

17. James G. Cannon, *Credit, Credit-Man, Creditor* (New York: J. S. Babcock, 1896), 10. Lewis and Arthur Tappan were similarly hailed for their acute memories. See C. W. Steffler, "The Evolution of the Mercantile Agency," *Commerce and Finance* 17, no. 12 (March 21, 1928): 637.

18. "Commercial Credit," *Chicago Tribune*, September 1, 1883, 5.

19. Donald Scott, "Credit Man Has Difficult Work; Requirements for Position Many," *Chicago Tribune*, June 19, 1913, D3.

20. H. Victor Wright," Qualifications of an Ideal Credit Man," *Credit World* 6, no. 1 (June 1915): 33.

21. Higinbotham, "Tales of the Credit Man," 1199.

22. On the history of the American department store, see Vicki Howard, *From Main Street to Mall: The Rise and Fall of the American Department Store* (Philadelphia: University of Pennsylvania Press, 2015); William Leach, *Land of Desire: Merchants, Power, and the Rise of a New American Culture* (New York: Vintage, 1993); Susan Porter Benson, *Counter Cultures: Saleswomen, Managers, and Customers in American Department Stores, 1890–1940* (Champaign: University of Illinois Press, 1986); and A. Chandler, *The Visible Hand*, 224–239.

23. "Selling Goods on Time," *Quincy* (Mass.) *Daily Whig*, September 17, 1889, 3.

24. See Godfrey M. Lebhar, *Chain Stores in America*, 3rd ed. (New York: Chain Store Publishing, 1963); and T. F. Bradshaw, "Superior Methods Created the Early Chain Store," *Bulletin of the Business Historical Society* 17, no. 2 (April 1943): 35–43.

25. Robert W. Twyman, *History of Marshall Field & Co., 1852–1906* (Philadelphia: University of Pennsylvania Press, 1954), 129.

26. "Selling Goods on Time."

27. Irving C. Brown, "Forty Years of Credit Granting," *Credit World* 16, no. 3 (November 1927): 8.

28. "References Are Required," *Chicago Tribune*, December 31, 1894, 12.

29. "The Installment Plan," *Chicago Tribune*, August 28, 1887, 3.

30. For historical accounts of nineteenth-century installment selling, see Robert A. Lynn, "Installment Selling Before 1870," *Business History Review* 31, no. 4 (1957): 414–424; Edwin R. A. Seligman, *The Economics of Instalment Selling: A Study in Consumers' Credit*, vol. 1 (New York: Harper, 1927), 1–117; and Calder, *Financing the American Dream*, 156–183.

31. See, for example, "Plundering the Poor," *New York Times*, April 30, 1875, 6; and "Glimpses of Gotham," *National Police Gazette*, September 6, 1879, 14. On the stigma of installment selling, see Calder, *Financing the American Dream*, 166–183.

32. See "Retail Furniture Dealers," *Boston Globe*, April 14, 1887, 2; and "Piano and Organ Men Combine," *Chicago Tribune*, September 18, 1889, 6.

33. John J. Cummins, "The Evil of Retail Credits," *Business: The Office Paper* 18, no. 11 (November 1898) 698.

34. "For Protection," *Los Angeles Times*, April 19, 1898, 11.

35. J. R. Truesdale, "Agency Men Organize," *Mercantile Monthly* (1906), n.p., quoted in Flinn, "History of Retail Credit Company," 352.

36. "Fake Agencies," *Courier-Journal* (Louisville, Ky.), August 15, 1907, 8.

37. William Sherman Rauch, "For the Good and Welfare of the Association: The Scope of Mercantile Agency Work," *Bulletin of the National Association of Mercantile Agencies* 1, no. 6 (October 1911): 282.

38. G. Norris Shuman, "The Shuman System and Business Extension," *Bulletin of the National Association of Mercantile Agencies* 1, no. 2 (September 1909): 19.

39. "Sherman Gilfillan, Credit Field Leader," *New York Times*, October 2, 1938, 22. See also "S. L. Gilfillan," *Credit World* 7, no. 7 (March 6, 1919): 25; and "A Few Remarks About Our Treasurer, Mr. S. L. Gilfillan," *Credit World* 8, no. 4 (December 1919): 19.

40. S. L. Gilfillan, "The Early Beginnings of the National Association," *Credit World* 25, no. 7 (April 1937): 22.

41. C. J. Allen, "Historical Sketch," *Credit World* 5, no. 3 (February 1915): 8–10.

42. "Cut the Gordian Knot of Abuses, Woodlock Urges Credit Men," *Credit World* 7, no. 1 (September 3, 1918): 9; see also *Credit World* 17, no. 12 (1929): 22.

43. "Credit Men Form Association Here," *Spokesman-Review* (Wash.), August 22, 1912, 7.

44. S. L. Gillfillan, "President's Annual Report," *Credit World* 4, no. 5 (October 1914): 8.

45. "Membership," *Credit World* 18, no. 10 (June 1930): 40.

46. Report of President Blanford, *Credit World* 8, no. 2 (October 1919): 12; and Report of Secretary Crowder, *Credit World* 8, no. 2 (October 1919): 14–15.

47. Ben F. Gray, "Advantages of Forming Associations," *Credit World* 6, no. 1 (June 1915): 82.

48. A. J. Kruse, "Report from the Secretary," *Credit World* 7, no. 2 (October 1918): 12.

49. "We Want All Grantors of Retail Credit to Join Our Association," *Credit World* 6, no. 2 (July 1915): 33.

50. E. G. Bly, "Letter to Editor of the *New England Grocer*, November 23, 1891," in *United States and Canada Abstract of Unsettled Account of Migratory Debtors* (Chicago: Merchants Retail Commercial Agency, January 1892), 10.

51. The histories of specific retail credit reporting organizations are recorded in a number of early accounts. See, for example, John Blocker, *Retail Credit Bureaus in Kansas* (Lawrence: University of Kansas School of Business, 1927); A. V. Storer, *A Narrative Report, 1916–1938* (Pomona, Calif.: Associated Credit Bureaus of California, 1938); C. E. Cormier, "Nearly Half a Century of Efficient Credit Service," *Credit World* 27, no. 9 (June 1939): 14, 31 [Bay City, Mich.]; and *Cooperative Credit in Cleveland: Fiftieth Anniversary, 1898–1948* ([Cleveland, Ohio:] Credit Bureau of Cleveland, 1948).

52. See Truesdale, *Credit Bureau Management*, 14.

53. Storer, *A Narrative Report, 1916–1938*, 10.

54. *The Credit Man and His Work* (Detroit: Book-Keeper Publishing, 1904), 208. For a description of early retail reporting procedures, including the use of ledger experience, see 209–219.

55. *Seaman's United States Directory of Retail Credit Rating Agencies and Associations* (Denver: Seaman Publishing, 1912). My calculations exclude Michigan, which is an outlier, with more than 140 listings for individuals and partnerships (perhaps attorneys).

56. Willis V. Sims, "Credit Reporting in a Town of Thirty Thousand," *Credit World* 5, no. 1 (December 1914): 6.

57. Frank Field, "Rural Credit Bureau Problems," *Credit World* 10, no. 2 (October 1921): 56.

58. E. B. Heller, "Welding the Weakest Link," *Credit World* 15, no. 6 (February 1927): 30.

59. "Calling a Halt on Their Credit," *New York Times*, November 11, 1917, 92.

60. D. J. Woodlock, "Report of the Executive Secretary," *Credit World* 9, no. 1 (September 1920): 16.

61. "Ideas Swapped by Credit Men," *Los Angeles Times*, May 23, 1920, 16.

62. "Miss E. M. Fleming," *Credit World* 10, no. 12 (August 1922): 3.

63. "Following the Retail Credit Men's Convention," *Women's Wear*, August 30, 1918, 27.

64. Helen L. Croul, "A Credit Reporting Association Successfully Conducted by Women," *Credit World* 9, no. 1 (September 1920): 71.

65. "Position Wanted," *Credit World* 14, no. 10 (June 1926): 24.

66. Avadana Cochran, "Credit Women's Breakfast Clubs—Objects and Purposes," *Credit World* 24, no. 11 (August 1936): 8.

67. "Miss Edith Shaw of the Portland Credit Bureau," *Credit World* 19, no. 3 (November 1930): 5; and Ethel M. Dopp, "The Future of Credit Women's Breakfast Clubs," *Credit World* 25, no. 11 (August 1937): 26–28.

68. David J. Woodlock, "Our Responsibilities," *Credit World* 16, no. 2 (October 1927): 3. By comparison, women who worked at Retail Credit Company (now Equifax), one of the largest national credit reporting firms and a non-RCMNA affiliate, enjoyed far less responsibility or upward mobility during the same period. See Maureen A. Carroll, "'What an Office Should Be': Women and Work at Retail Credit Company," *Atlanta History* 40, nos. 3–4 (1996): 16–29.

69. The organization underwent several additional name changes and is presently the Consumer Data Industry Association; hereafter it is referred to simply as the "national association."

70. M. G. Lieberman, "How Local Associations and Reporting Agencies May Be Coordinated with the National Association as a Great Working Unit," *Credit World* 8, no. 2 (October 1919): 73.

71. William Loewi, "The Credit Bureau in a Community," *Credit World* 10, no. 10 (June 1922): 11.

72. "Maxims of a Credit Man, After Twenty Years' Experience," *Credit World* 8, no. 3 (November 1919): 25.

73. *Credit World* 15, no. 4 (1926): 20. The service division was also responsible for vetting bureau membership applications and reviewing the quality of bureau service; see G. C. Morrison, "Report of the Service Department Committee," *Credit World* 18, no. 10 (June 1930): 32.

74. Ralph W. Watson, "The President's Message," *Credit World* 14, no. 6 (February 1926): 11.

75. Truesdale, *Credit Bureau Management*, 158.

76. Credit manager to L. S. Ayres & Co., April 8, 1908, scrapbook, folder 4, John Wanamaker Collection, Historical Society of Pennsylvania, Philadelphia.

77. H. Orrin Jones, "The Interdependence and Interrelation of All Lines of Credit," *Credit World* 15, no. 7 (March 1927): 24.

78. "Credit Decree," *Business Week*, October 21, 1933, 11.

79. William Henry Blake, "History of the International Credit Association," *Credit World* 75, no. 3 (January–February 1987): 29–30.

80. Howard Haines, "A Credit Policy for the Small Business Man," *Barron's*, June 27, 1938, 12.

81. U.S. Department of Commerce, *National Retail Credit Survey* (Washington, D.C.: GPO, 1930).

82. Stephen H. Talkes, "The Value of the Credit Bureau to the Retailer," *Credit World* 15, no. 11 (July 1927): 5.

83. "S. L. Gilfillan, Our Retiring President," *Credit World* 4 no. 5 (November 1914): 3.

84. Arthur H. Hert, "Bureau Manager—Yesterday, Today, and Tomorrow," *Service Bulletin* [of the National Consumer Credit Reporting Corporation] 10, no. 9 (20 May 1937): 6.

4. RUNNING THE CREDIT GANTLET: EXTRACTING, ORDERING, AND COMMUNICATING CONSUMER INFORMATION

1. Robert O. Bonner, "What Kind of a Credit Manager Are You?," *Credit World* 17, no. 5 (January 1929): 8.

2. James Wilson, "Credit Co-operation a Vital Factor in Reducing the Bad Debt Loss," *Credit World* 7, no. 4 (December 9, 1918): 15.

3. William H. J. Taylor, "Credit Office Efficiency," *Credit World* 8, no. 12 (August 1920): 10.

4. On the "paperization of identity," see Craig Robertson, "Paper, Information, and Identity in 1920s America," *Information & Culture* 50, no. 3 (2015): 392–416.]

5. Harry Jeffrey, "The Credit Man and His Department," *Credit World* 17, no. 10 (June 1929): 30.

6. Jonas Howard, "Man's Credit Bump Sensitive; Department Store Knows It," *Chicago Tribune*, January 19, 1908, E3.

7. As Olegario has observed, the persistence of character as the key criterion of creditworthiness gives the development of nineteenth-century credit assessment a remarkable sense of uniformity. "Analyzing the credit reports and business literature from the 1830s to the end of the century leaves one with a striking impression of continuity: a merchant in 1830 would have had little trouble grasping the method for assessing risk that credit manuals began to formalize and codify only toward the end of the century." Olegario, *A Culture of Credit*, 7.

8. U.S. House, *Report of the Committee Appointed Pursuant to House Resolutions 429 and 504 to Investigate the Concentration of Control of Money and Credit*, 62d Cong., 3d sess., 1913, 136.

9. "To Our Members," *Commercial Register*, 1886–1887, 14th ed. (New York: Retail Dealers' Protective Association, 1886), n.p.

10. David J. Woodlock, "Our Responsibilities," *Credit World* 16, no. 2 (October 1927): 2.

11. James G. Cannon, *Character the Basis of Credit* (New York: J. S. Babcock, 1898), 9.

12. Ibid., 10.

13. Fred C. Kelly, "The Kinds of People to Trust in Money Matters," *American Magazine* 86 (August 1918): 51.

14. Edward M. Skinner, "Essentials in Credit Management," in *Credits, Collections and Finance: Organizing the Work, Correct Policies and Methods, Five Credit and Collection Systems* (Chicago: A. W. Shaw, 1917), 10.

15. "The Credit Man," *Credit World* 14, no. 6 (November 1914): 10.

16. John J. Cummins, "The Evil of Retail Credits," *Business: The Office Paper* 18, no. 11 (November 1898), 698.

17. P. R. Earling, *Whom to Trust: A Practical Treatise on Mercantile Credits* (Chicago: Rand, McNally, 1890), 242.

18. Frank Batty, "Taking the Application and Declining the Account," *Credit World* 15, no. 12 (August 1927): 12.

19. J. W. McConnell, "Handling the Credits of a Retail Store," *System* 10, no. 11 (August 1906): 184.

20. Louis Sinclair Grigsby, "That Credit Application," *Credit World* 15, no. 6 (February 1927): 6.

21. Edgar McComb, "The Credit Man," *Credit World* 4, no. 6 (November 1914): 10.

22. Batty, "Taking the Application and Declining the Account," 12.

23. David J. Woodlock, "The Structure of the Credit Department," *Credit World* 18, no. 3 (November 1929): 27.

24. "Mapping a Credit Department for 3 Types of Customers," *Credit World* 19, no. 5 (January 1931): 31–32.

25. G. C. Driver, "Opening an Account," *Credit World* 9, no. 7 (March 1921): 13.

26. John T. Bartlett and Charles M. Reed, *Credit Department Salesmanship and Collection Psychology* (New York: Harper, 1932), 25.

27. Louis Sinclair Grigsby, "That Credit Application," *Credit World* 15, no. 6 (February 1927): 7.

28. E. F. Horner, "Originating Accounts," *Credit World* 18, no. 2 (October 1929): 13.

29. Batty, "Taking the Application and Declining the Account," 24.

30. Skinner, "Essentials in Credit Management," 10.

31. F. Churchill Crouch, "The Watchman at the Gate," *Credit World* 15, no. 2 (October 1926): 28.

32. M. Stevens, "Difficulties of a Woman Credit Manager," *Credit World* 7, no. 9 (May 1919): 10.

33. Minnie Lee Beal, "Woman's Value in the Credit Department," *Credit World* 5, no. 4 (March 1915): 21.

34. Q. B. Leithead, "The Woman Credit Manager," *Credit World* 9, no. 11 (July 1921): 15.

35. R. S. Martin, "The Use of the Central Credit Bureau," *Credit World* 17, no. 5 (January 1929): 24.

36. William Nelson Taft, "The Biggest Problem in Retailing Today," *Credit World* 17, no. 11 (July 1929): 21.

37. Frank B. Morriss, "Is It Pig Headed, Hard Headed—Or—?," *Credit World* 9, no. 8 (April 1921): 29.

38. C. F. Jackson, "A Little 'Shop Talk' on Department Store Credits," *Credit World* 5, no. 6 (May 1915): 18.

39. Frank C. Hamilton, "The Public Appeal Publicly Made Will Help Retail Credit," *Credit World* 18, no. 9 (May 1930): 28.

40. JoAnne Yates, "From Press Book and Pigeonhole to Vertical Filing: Revolution in Storage and Access Systems for Correspondence," *Journal of Business Communication* 19, no. 3 (1982): 20; see also Yates, *Control Through Communication*, 56–63; and Yates, "For the Record: The Embodiment of Organizational Memory, 1850–1920," *Business and Economic History* 19 (1990): 172–182.

41. C. O. Hanes, *The Retail Credit and Adjustment Bureaus* (Columbia, Mo.: C. O. Hanes, 1915), 11.

42. A member survey conducted by the Retail Credit Men's National Association in 1924 found that only 22 percent of respondents published credit guides (Truesdale, *Credit Bureau Management*, 28).

43. "Cash Customers and Credit Ones," *New York Times*, September 20, 1914, 10.

44. "As to Granting Retail Credits," *New York Times*, September 27, 1914, 10.

45. Memorandum, November 9, 1916, scrapbook, folder 5, John Wanamaker Collection, Historical Society of Pennsylvania, Philadelphia. The "U" code, which also stipulated a $15 credit limit, reveals the persistence of personal interaction and case-by-case flexibility despite the movement toward depersonalization in credit departments.

46. "Cash Customers and Credit Ones," 10.

47. J. Frank Quinn, "A Glimpse Into the Operating Methods of the Merchants Service Bureau of Grand Rapids," *Credit World* 14, no. 9 (May 1926): 8. See also *Commercial Organization Credit Bureaus* (Washington, D.C.: U.S. Chamber of Commerce, 1922), 17.

48. John G. Blocker, *Retail Credit Bureaus in Kansas* (Lawrence: University of Kansas School of Business, 1927), 29.

49. George Koelle, "What Constitutes My Business," *Bulletin of the National Association of Mercantile Agencies* 1, no. 5 (October 1910): 206.

50. James D. Hays, "Principles of Credit Reporting," *Service Bulletin* [of the National Consumer Credit Reporting Corporation] 10, no. 5 (March 20, 1937): 6–7. On the use and broader significance of newspaper clippings, see Popp, "Information, Industrialization, and the Business of Press Clippings."

51. Edith M. Stern, "They've Got Your Number," *Reader's Digest* 32 (February 1938): 80.

52. See *Kardex* (Towanda, N.Y.: Kardex Company, [192?]); *The Age of Vision in Business Affairs* (Towanda, N.Y.: Rand Kardex Service Corporation, 1926); and *Visible Records: Their Place in Modern Business* (Buffalo, N.Y.: Remington Rand, 1930). See also Frederick W. Walter, *The Retail Charge Account* (New York: Ronald Press, 1922), 158–166.

53. James Wilson, "The Necessity for an Efficient System of Limiting Accounts," *Credit World* 9, no. 2 (October 1920): 9. See also S. E. Blandford, "The Service Station in a Modern Retail Store," *Credit World* 8, no. 11 (July 1920): 21; James Wilson, "Keeping Accounts Within Limits by Control in Authorization," *Credit World* 10, no. 10 (June 1922): 5–6; and John T. Bartlett and Charles M. Reed, *Retail Credit Practice* (New York: Harper, 1928), 122–123.

54. Peter P. Wahlstad, *Credit and the Credit Man*, (New York: Alexander Hamilton Institute, 1917), 214.

55. Ingrid Jeacle and Eammon J. Walsh, "From Moral Evaluation to Rationalization: Accounting and the Shifting Technologies of Credit," *Accounting, Organizations and Society* 27 (2002): 737–761.

56. B. H. Poindexter, "To the Members of the Retail Credit Men's Association," *Credit World* 9, no. 2 (October 1920): 7.

57. W. F. Jantzen, "How to Refuse a Customer Credit and Still Retain His Good Will," *Credit World* 6, no. 1 (June 1915): 38.

58. Robert H. Cantley, "A Uniform Information Blank," *Credit World* 6, no. 1 (June 1915): 79. See also C. J. Allen, "The Opening of the Account and the Fraudulent Buyer," *Credit World* 7, no. 11 (July 6, 1919): 15.

59. A. N. Fraser, "The Use and Abuse of Credit Forms," *Credit World* 11, no. 2 (October 1922): 7.

60. Ben H. Blanton, *Credit, Its Principles and Practice* (New York: Ronald Press, 1915), 13.

61. Guy H. Hulse, "The Secretary's Page," *Credit World* 17, no. 4 (December 1928): 9.

62. G. L. Harris, "What Progress in Management?," *Executive* 1, no. 5 (November 1927): 10.

63. Hanes, *The Retail Credit and Adjustment Bureaus*, 21.
64. Storer, *A Narrative Report, 1916–1938*, 41.
65. Raymond T. Fiske, "A Model Credit Bureau," *Proceedings of the Controllers' Congress* (New York: National Retail Dry Goods Association, 1930), 183.
66. Bartlett and Reed, *Retail Credit Practice*, 92.
67. "Omaha Has Successful Bureau," *Credit World* 14, no. 5 (January 1926): 21; and Louis Sinclair Grigsby, "Washington, Capital of Credit," *Credit World* 14, no. 6 (February 1926): 15.
68. See, for example, descriptions of telephone systems in St. Louis, Missouri: "Service Spells Success in Any Credit Bureau," *Credit World* 16, no. 5 (January 1927): 15, 27; in Hartford, Connecticut: Alfred C. Moreau, "Promptness in Credit Reporting," *Credit World* 16, no. 3 (November 1927): 27; and in Columbus, Ohio: M. C. Bonnar, "Credit Protection," *Executive* 2, no. 2 (February 1928): 19–20.
69. A. B. Buckeridge, "Pittsburgh Retailers Have Perfect Credit Protection," *Credit World* 15, no. 5 (January 1927): 6–7; and Buckeridge, "Made to Order Telephone Equipment and Telephone Typewriters, Now in Use in the Pittsburgh Credit Bureau," *Credit World* 17, no. 4 (December 1928): 18–19.
70. "Ft. Worth Has Up-to-Date Bureau," *Credit World* 14, no. 9 (May 1926): 15.
71. Kenneth Lipartito, "When Women Were Switches: Technology, Work, and Gender in the Telephone Industry, 1890–1920," *American Historical Review* 99, no. 4 (October 1994): 1075–1111; and related, Jennifer S. Light, "When Women Were Computers," *Technology & Culture* 40, no. 3 (1999): 455–483.
72. R. S. Martin, "Mechanical Aids to Credit Reporting," *Credit World* 17, no. 12 (August 1929): 17.
73. Fred S. Krieger, "Milwaukee Credit Bureau Important Force in Community Life," *Credit World* 11, no. 2 (October 1922): 4.
74. James D. Hays, "Profitable Telephone Reporting," *Credit World* 16, no. 8 (April 1928): 12. See also Truesdale, *Credit Bureau Management*, 237–239.
75. On telautograph technology, see also "Charge and Take in the Credit Man's Office," *Credit World* 18, no. 6 (February 1930): 27–28.
76. Buckeridge, "Made to Order Telephone Equipment and Telephone Typewriters," 18–19.
77. Advertisement, Telautograph Corporation, *Credit World* 18, no. 4 (December 1929): 1.
78. C. F. Jackson, [Pneumatic tube system for charge authorizing], *Credit World* 9, no. 1 (September 1920): 62.
79. Milton J. Solon, [Telephone system for charge authorization], *Credit World* 9, no. 1 (September 1920): 61–62.
80. For description of the Lamson Tube System, see *Credit Control: A Textbook on Charge Authorization* (Boston: Lamson Company, [1917]). See also Holly Kruse, "Pipeline as Network: Pneumatic Systems and the Social Order," in *The Long History of New Media: Technology, Historiography, and Contextualizing Newness*, ed. Nicholas Jankowski, Steve Jones, and David Park (New York: Peter Lang, 2011), 211–230.
81. Lamson Company, "Present Day Business Requirements Demand Stricter Credit Control," *Credit World* 8, no. 12 (August 1920): 12.
82. Jackson, [Pneumatic tube system for charge authorizing], 64.
83. Ibid.

84. "Customers Like the Quiet Dignity of Lamson Authorizing," *Credit World* 18, no. 1 (September 1929): 23.

85. Krieger, "Milwaukee Credit Bureau Important Force," 4.

86. James Wilson, "Fifty Years in Retail Credit," *Credit World* 23, no. 11 (August 1935): 5.

5. "YOU ARE JUDGED BY YOUR CREDIT": TEACHING AND TARGETING THE CONSUMER

1. Sidney E. Blanford, "National Unity in Business," *Credit World* 7, no. 4 (December 1918): 19.

2. "The Dallas Pay Prompt Campaign," *Credit World* 17, no. 7 (March 1929): 23.

3. Robert S. Lynd and Helen Merrell Lynd, *Middletown: A Study in American Culture* (New York: Harcourt, Brace, 1929), 47. Though commenting specifically about commercial rather than consumer credit, their observations are relevant to both.

4. Guy Hulse, "Helping the Retail Trade Through Credit Organizations," *Credit World* 16, no. 1 (September 1927): 21.

5. "One Day to Collect Bills," *New York Times*, 10 September 1920, 24.

6. "Good Publicity," *Credit World* 14, no. 6 (February 1926): 20.

7. H. P. Van Vianen, "Credit as a Moral Issue," *Credit World* 16, no. 9 (May 1928): 24.

8. Frederick W. Walter, ed., *The Retail Charge Account* (New York: Ronald Press Company, 1922), 8.

9. *Federal Reserve Charts on Consumer Credit* (Washington, D.C.: Board of Governors of the Federal Reserve System, 1947), 3.

10. Peter P. Wahlstad, *Credit and the Credit Man* (New York: Alexander Hamilton Institute, 1917), 6.

11. Evans Clark, *Financing the Consumer* (New York: Harper, 1930), 5.

12. M. R. Neifeld, *The Personal Finance Business* (New York: Harper, 1933), 3–4.

13. William J. Fisher, "Reaction to Installment Buying," *Credit World* 18, no. 8 (April 1930): 7.

14. "Is the Average Man Honest?," *Washington Post*, December 1, 1901, 18.

15. See, for example, William R. Basset, "In Every 100 Men 99 Are Honest," *Collier's* 72 (November 10, 1923): 17–18; Earl Chapin May, "Adventures of the Credit Man," *American Magazine* 107, no. 1 (January 1929): 32; and Edith M. Stern, "They've Got Your Number," *Reader's Digest* 32 (February 1939): 81.

16. John J. Raskob, "The Development of Installment Purchasing," *Proceedings of the Academy of Political Science in the City of New York* 12, no. 2 (January 1927): 623.

17. H. J. Burris, "Instructions in Opening and Handling Charge Accounts," *Credit World* 14, no. 7 (March 1926): 9.

18. "Report of the Committee on Resolutions," *Credit World* 7, no. 2 (October 1918): 98–99.

19. "Prompt Payment of Bills Urged," *New York Times*, July 14, 1918, 19; and "Local Association Notes," *Credit World* 7, no. 4 (December 1918): 21–22.

20. Edward A. Filene, "Address by Mr. Filene, of Boston," *Credit World* 7, no. 2 (October 1918): 81.

21. Robert Adams, "Address by Mr. Adams," *Credit World* 7, no. 2 (October 1918): 29.

22. "Is Credit Expansion to Be the New Order of the Day?," *Credit World* 7, no. 5 (January 1919): 10 (reprinted from Indianapolis trade journal *Heart o' Trade* [published by the Indianapolis Chamber of Commerce]).

23. See Truesdale, *Credit Bureau Management*, 35–39. For description of prompt pay and other consumer education campaigns, see John T. Bartlett and Charles M. Reed, *Retail Credit Practice* (New York: Harper, 1928), 344–357.

24. "Run Ads to Stimulate Quick Paying of Bills," *Credit World* 8, no. 5 (January 1920): 8.

25. "Minneapolis Credit Men Tell Benefits of Prompt Payments," *Credit World* 9, no. 3 (November 1920): 29.

26. A. D. McMullen, "A Letter on 'Pay-Up Time,'" *Credit World* 7, no. 7 (March 1919): 30.

27. "National 'Pay-Your-Bills' Day," *Credit World* 7, no. 12 (August 6, 1919), 7–9; C. W. Hurley, Report of Y.M.C.A. Committee, *Credit World* 8, no. 2 (October 1919): 84–86; and "Eight Days for the Middle Class," *Outlook*, January–April 1920, 10.

28. Robert R. Sesline, "Soliciting Accounts Under Present Day Conditions," *Credit World* 11, no. 3 (November 1922): 19.

29. Geo. L. Myers, "The Pay Prompt Campaign Report," *Credit World* 15, no. 7 (March 1927): 5.

30. "Pay Your Bills Promptly Day, January 22," *Credit World* 9, no. 4 (December 1920): 21.

31. Guy S. Hulse, "Our Goal Is a National Consumer Credit Conscience," *Credit World* 18, no. 12 (August 1930): 23.

32. "Keeping Tabs on Credit in the Workshop of the World," *Credit World* 19, no. 3 (November 1930): 37; and "'Lum 'n' Abner' Adopt a *Credit Policy* for Their 'Jot 'Em Down Store,'" *Credit World* 27, no. 4 (January 1939): 3. For the transcript of an Altoona, Pennsylvania, radio broadcast, see Ralph F. Taylor, "Thrift—The Basis of Good Credit," *Credit World* 14, no. 6 (February 1926): 9–10.

33. "For Economic Immorality Education," *Credit World* 18, no. 11 (July 1930): 31. By the late 1920s, retailers in large cities were apparently turning away from prompt pay campaigns, which struck them as "small town stuff." See Milton J. Solon, "A Message from Our Pay Promptly Advertising Campaign," *Credit World* 17, no. 4 (December 1928): 12.

34. "Parading the Bureau on Gala Occasions," *Credit World* 19, no. 3 (November 1930): 23.

35. W. H. Gray, "The Cleveland Retail Credit Organization," *Credit World* 17, no. 7 (March 1929): 20.

36. Clyde William Phelps, *Retail Credit Fundamentals* (St. Louis: National Retail Credit Association, 1941), 78.

37. Frank E. Morris, "Live Problems for Discussion," *Credit World* 9, no. 10 (June 1921): 12.

38. William E. Koch, "Selecting Charge Accounts," *Credit World* 15, no. 12 (August 1927): 28.

39. Bartlett and Reed, *Retail Credit Practice*, 346.

40. Frank C. Hamilton, "Keeping Up with the Jones," *Credit World* 18, no. 5 (January 1930): 32.

41. Frank C. Hamilton, "The Public Appeal Publicly Made Will Help Retail Credit," *Credit World* 18, no. 9 (May 1930): 29.

42. "For Economic Immorality Education," 31. For another reference to Listerine, see Stanley Latshaw, "You Can Do What You Want—If You Know What You Want to Do," *Credit World* 18, no. 11 (July 1930): 30.

43. See, for example, John T. Bartlett and Charles M. Reed, *Credit Department Salesmanship and Collection Psychology* (New York: Harper, 1932), chap. 7; Bryant W. Griffin and H. C. Greene, *Installment Credits and Collections and the Installment Market* (New York: Prentice-Hall, 1938), chaps. 9–12; and Waldo J. Marra, *Streamlined Letters* (St. Louis: National Retail Credit Association, 1940).

44. "Credit-Education Inserts to the Tune of Two Million," *Credit World* 14, no. 10 (June 1926): 2.

45. "Three New 'Pay Promptly' Inserts," *Credit World* 26, no. 2 (November 1937): 32.

46. Antonio Gramsci, *Selections from the Prison Notebooks*, trans. Quinton Hoare and Geoffrey Nowell Smith (New York: International, 1971).

47. J. E. Morrison, "The Characteristics of a Credit Man," *Credit World* 5, no. 3 (February 1915): 6–7.

48. Sidney E. Blanford, "Credit Education," *Credit World* 10, no. 2 (October 1921): 54.

49. Joe Arena, "Framing an Ideology of Information: Retail Credit and the Mass Media, 1910–1930," *Media, Culture & Society* 18 (1996): 423–445.

50. "The San Diego Daily In Its May 4, Sunday Edition, Carried the Following Editorial," *Credit World* 18, no. 10 (June 1930)], 7–8.

51. Peter R. Earling, "The General Function and Work of a Credit Department," in *Credits and Collections: The Factors Involved and the Methods Pursued in Credit Operations; and A Practical Treatise by Eminent Credit Men*, ed. T. J. Zimmerman, 2nd ed. (Chicago: System Company, 1904), 1.

52. Samuel H. Terry, *The Retailer's Manual: Embodying the Conclusions of Thirty Years' Experience in Merchandising* (Newark, N.J.: Jennings Brothers, 1869), 161–162.

53. Harris Copenhaver, "The Significance of Credit Ratings," *Credit World* 18, no. 8 (April 1930): 9.

54. James G. Cannon, *Individual Credits: Address Delivered Before the National Association of Credit Men at Kansas City, Missouri* (New York: J. S. Babcock, 1897), 6.

55. Joseph B. Auerbach, "The Influence of Installment Selling on Open Credit Business," *Credit World* 14, no. 1 (September 1925): 14.

56. "Do You Know What Class of People Cause Losses?," *Credit World* 18, no. 2 (October 1929): 21.

57. Arthur H. Hert, *An Analysis of Credit Extensions in Twenty-Three Texas Department Stores by Occupational Groups* (Austin: University of Texas, 1930), 23.

58. Ibid., 41.

59. Paul D. Converse, "Occupation and Credit," *Personal Finance News* 17, no. 2 (August 1932): 5.

60. Dean Ashby, "Credit Sales Promotion and Customer Control," mimeograph (St. Louis: National Retail Credit Association, [1936]), 45.

61. Ibid., 47.

62. John T. Bartlett and Charles M. Reed, *Methods of Installment Selling and Collection* (New York: Harper, 1934), 87–88.

63. P. D. Converse, "The Occupational Credit Pattern," *Opinion and Comment* 38, no. 51 (August 12, 1941): 1.

64. *Proceedings of the Controllers' Congress, Eleventh Annual Convention* (New York: National Retail Dry Goods Association, 1930), 62.

65. Bartlett and Reed, *Retail Credit Practice*, 106.

66. "The Effect of Credit," *Washington Post*, December 23, 1888, 10.

67. Cromwell Childe, "Why the Retailer Is Willing to Trust You," *Chicago Tribune*, October 23, 1910, E3. See also Thaddeus S. Dayton, "Trusting John Doe," *Harper's Weekly* (February 20, 1912), 21.

68. Bartlett and Reed, *Retail Credit Practice*, 101.

69. Martha L. Olney "When Your Word Is Not Enough: Race, Collateral, and Household Credit," *Journal of Economic History* 58, no. 2 (June 1998): 408–430. Several early university-affiliated studies document the exclusion of African Americans from credit markets and their substandard credit risk classification. See Arthur H. Hert, "An Analysis of Accounts Charged Off to Profit and Loss by Retail Merchants in Texas," *Credit World* 19, no. 11 (July 1931): 28–31; Paul K. Edwards, *The Southern Urban Negro as a Consumer* (New York: Prentice-Hall, 1932); and Dwight A. Stewart, *Factors Affecting Credit Ratings of Consumers Located in Franklin County, Ohio* (Columbus, OH: Bureau of Business Research, Ohio State University, 1942).

70. On the use of "colored" or "col." to identify African Americans in credit bureau files, see C. O. Hanes, *The Retail Credit and Adjustment Bureaus* (Columbia, Mo.: C. O. Hanes, 1915), 23.

71. "Plan Local Credit Reference Service," *Chicago Defender*, June 20, 1914, 4.

72. Ibid.

73. Walter, *The Retail Charge Account*, 126.

74. Bartlett and Reed, *Retail Credit Practice*, 106.

75. "What Nationality Is the Most Honest?," *Credit World* 14, no. 9 (May 1926): 23. On American nativism and racial ideology during the early twentieth century, see Matthew Frye Jacobson, *Barbarian Virtues: The United States Encounters Foreign Peoples at Home and Abroad, 1876–1917* (New York: Hill and Wang, 2000); and John Higham, *Strangers in the Land: Patterns of American Nativism, 1860–1925* (New Brunswick, N.J.: Rutgers University Press, 2008).

76. *Commercial Organization Credit Bureaus* (Washington, D.C.: Chamber of Commerce of the United States, 1922), 7.

77. Walter, *The Retail Charge Account*, 19.

78. H. Paul Kegley, "Psychology for Credit Men—The Matter of Relative Intelligence," *Credit World* 21, no. 3 (November 1932): 32.

79. H. Paul Kegley, "Psychology for Credit Men—Occupation as a Measure of Intelligence," *Credit World* 21, no. 4 (December 1932): 8–9, 28.

80. Cromwell Childe, "Why the Retailer Is Willing to Trust You," *Chicago Tribune*, October 23, 1910, E3.

81. "The Ways of Women," *Observer-Journal* (Dunkirk, N.Y.), January 7, 1889, [1].

82. See, for example, "To the Retail Merchant and Store Owner," *Credit World* 8, no. 7 (March 1920): 5.

83. Fred E. Kunkle, "The Buyer's Strike and the Credit Manager," *Credit World* 9, no. 10 (June 1921): 21; and L. M. Crosthwaithe, "Constructive Credit Granting," *Credit World* 9, no. 5 (January 1921): 10–11.

84. David J. Woodlock, "A Dual Responsibility," *Credit World* 14, no. 10 (June 1926): 3.

85. Daniel J. Hannefin, "Building Prospect Lists—A Continuous Process," *Credit World* 17, no. 6 (February 1929): 12.

86. Mark Lansburgh, "Promoting New Business," *Credit World* 16, no. 1 (September 1927): 9.

87. "Watching the Individual Customer," *Business: The Office Paper* 19, no. 8 (August 1899): 488–489.

88. Unsigned memo to Rodman Wanamaker, February 26, 1902, scrapbook, folder 2, John Wanamaker Collection, Historical Society of Pennsylvania, Philadelphia.

89. Kunkle, "The Buyer's Strike and the Credit Manager," 22.

90. Advertisement for Elliott-Fisher, *Credit World* 8, no. 12 (August 1920): 5.

91. J. G. Pattee, "The Value of Retail Credit as Viewed by a Retail Merchant," *Credit World* 14, no. 7 (March 1926): 6.

92. For an early overview of customer control that details the mechanics of various systems, see Orville Wendell O'Neal, "A Study of Customer Control from the Standpoint of Sales Promotion" (M.B.A. thesis, University of Texas, Austin, 1933).

93. Robert Ross, "Why a Charge Account?," *Credit World* 15, no. 11 (July 1927): 28.

94. Bartlett and Reed, *Credit Department Salesmanship and Collection Psychology*, 245.

95. Robert B. Gile, "Developing the Retail Store's Best Market," *Credit World* 18, no. 4 (December 1929): 5.

96. *Getting More Business from Store Customers: A Study of Retail Customer Control Plans*, Report No. 1037 (Chicago: Dartnell Corporation, [1932]), 5–6. See also Bartlett and Reed, *Credit Department Salesmanship and Collection Psychology*, 224–227.

97. *Getting More Business from Store Customers*, 5.

98. "Hails White-Collar Buyer," *New York Times*, May 20, 1931, 49.

99. *Getting More Business from Store Customers*, [2].

100. Robert B. Gile, "Developing the Retail Store's Best Market," *Credit World* 18, no. 5 (January 1930): 14.

101. Glass, "Sales Promotion Thru the Credit Department," 9.

102. *Getting More Business from Store Customers*, 12.

103. Glass, "Sales Promotion Thru the Credit Department," 27.

104. See Gile, "Developing the Retail Store's Best Market" (January 1930), 5–6; and Dean Ashby, "More Business from Present Customers," *Credit World* 23, no. 10 (July 1935): 30.

105. "Credit Sales Promotion," *Bulletin of the National Retail Dry Goods Association* 19, no. 6 (June 1937): 99.

106. George D. Adams, "New Methods of Account Promotion," *Credit World* 17, no. 7 (March 1929): 16.

107. Gile, "Developing the Retail Store's Best Market" (January 1930), 6–7.

108. Ashby, "Credit Sales Promotion and Customer Control," 19.

109. Robert B. Gile, "Customer Control," *Retail Ledger* (July 1930), 8.

110. Ashby, "Credit Sales Promotion and Customer Control," 32.

111. Gile, "Customer Control," 8.

112. Ashby, "More Business from Present Customers," 10.

113. Gile, "Customer Control," 8.

114. Bartlett and Reed, *Credit Department Salesmanship and Collection Psychology*, 248.

115. *Getting More Business from Store Customers*, 21.

116. O'Neal, "A Study of Customer Control from the Standpoint of Sales Promotion," 82.

117. Hart Vance, "Catering to Human Feeling," *Credit World* 19, no. 4 (December 1930): 33.

118. "Credit Sales Promotion," 98.

119. Katherine G. Cohen, "Needed: More Credit Bureaus," *Independent Woman* 13 (July 1934): 224.

6. "FILE CLERK'S PARADISE": POSTWAR CREDIT REPORTING ON THE EVE OF AUTOMATION

1. Robert Wallace, "Please Remit," *Life*, December 21, 1953, 42–43.
2. "Credit Bureaus Get Bigger Role," *Business Week*, March 8, 1958, 52, 54. See also A. B. Buckeridge, "Credit Information Is Important Again," *Journal of Retailing* 23, no. 3 (October 1947): 99–102.
3. Harold A. Wallace, *Starting and Managing a Small Credit Bureau and Collection Service* (Washington, D.C.: Small Business Administration, 1959), 35.
4. Hillel Black, *Buy Now, Pay Later* (New York: William Morrow, 1961), 41–42.
5. Sam Rees, "Microfilming Reduces Personnel Costs 15 Percent," *Credit World* 48, no. 3 (December 1957): 11–12; "A Business Getter and Time Saver in the Space Age," *Credit World* 50, no. 11 (August 1962): 21; Elmer L. Kestle, "Electronic Servants Aid Credit Bureau Reporting," *Credit World* 56, no. 4 (January 1968): 18–19; "Copying Credit Card Reports Speeds Bureau Service," *Credit World* 55, no. 6 (March 1967): 19–20; and J. J. Boxberber, "Mechanized Files for Credit Bureaus," *Credit World* 48, no. 4 (January 1960): 8–9.
6. The rarity of credit rating is noted by Rule, *Private Lives and Public Surveillance*, 197. For exceptions, see C. A. Wildes, "Home of the Yellow Book," *Credit World* 42, no. 12 (September 1954): 3; and Simon, *Pioneers of Excellence*, 144. For additional discussion of rating guides, see *Credit Bureau Fundamentals: A Manual of Credit Bureau Procedures* (St. Louis: Associated Credit Bureaus of America, 1951), sec. 9, pp. 21–25; and "Question: Every Credit Bureau Should Have a Credit Guide," *Management Monthly* 3, no. 4 (April 1955): 6–7, 24.
7. J. Gordon Dakins, *Retail Credit Manual: A Handbook of Retail Credit* (New York: Credit Management Division, National Retail Dry Goods Association, 1950), 437–438; and Clyde William Phelps, *Retail Credit Fundamentals*, 4th ed. (St. Louis: International Consumer Credit Association, 1963), 66. On the use of teletype by banks, see Black, *Buy Now, Pay Later*, 43.
8. *Credit Bureau Fundamentals*, sec. 6.
9. Clyde William Phelps, *Retail Credit Fundamentals* (National Retail Credit Association, 1941), 96; Dakins, *Retail Credit Manual*, 427; *Credit Bureau Fundamentals*, sec. 6, p. 6; and H. Wallace, *Starting and Managing a Small Credit Bureau*, 87.
10. *Credit Bureau Fundamentals*, sec. 6, p. 10.
11. Phelps, *Retail Credit Fundamentals*, 4th ed., 67.
12. For Dallas sample report, see, Dakins, *Retail Credit Manual*, 427. Charles F. Sheldon, *Investigations: Manual of Operation* (Philadelphia: Philadelphia Credit Bureau, May 1961), 60 (unpublished document in author's personal collection).
13. Howard A. Clarke, "The Evolution of Consumer Credit," *Credit World* 41, no. 1 (October 1952): 7.
14. Flinn, *History of Retail Credit Company*, 238–239.
15. Ibid., 255–260.
16. Ibid., 237.
17. On the introduction of the Character Credit Report, see ibid., 251–255.
18. A sample Character Credit Report (Individual) is reproduced in Cole, *Consumer and Commercial Credit Management*, 3rd ed. (Homewood, Ill.: Richard D. Irwin, 1968), 252. See also Character Credit Report (Individual), U.S. Senate, Committee on

Banking and Currency, *Fair Credit Reporting*, Hearing, May 19–23, 1969 (Washington, D.C.: GPO, 1969), 52–53.

19. On the history of insurance reporting, see Sharon Ann Murphy, *Investing in Life: Insurance in Antebellum America* (Baltimore, Md.: Johns Hopkins University Press, 2010); and Bouk, *How Our Days Became Numbered*.

20. W. Lee Burge, "What Retail Credit Co. Is and Does," *Insurance Management Review*, August 10, 1968, 15–16.

21. U.S. Senate, Committee on the Judiciary, *The Credit Industry*, Hearing, December 10–11, 1968 (Washington, D.C.: GPO, 1969), 99, 105–106.

22. Ibid., 105–106. The RCC also relied upon the Retail Commercial Agency, which had offices in more than sixty of the nation's largest cities. However, its reports, like those of the RCC, were based on direct investigation rather than ledger data. See ibid., 99, 107.

23. Factbilt advertisement, *Credit World* 52, no. 6 (March 1964): [33].

24. "Credit Bureaus Get Bigger Role," *Business Week*, March 8, 1958, 54.

25. *Credit Bureau Fundamentals*, sec. 3, p. 2.

26. Sheldon, *Investigations*, 51. On telephone interviewing, see also *Credit Bureau Fundamentals*, sec. 5, pp. 7–11. An extensive library of directories, including medical college yearbooks and U.S. Navy handbooks, was similarly maintained at the Philadelphia Credit Bureau (Sheldon, *Investigations*, 75–80).

27. Sheldon, *Investigations*, 43.

28. Bureau investigators were also forbidden to reveal to the applicant the identity of the business on whose behalf it was calling, unless the business also gave permission to do so (*Credit Bureau Fundamentals*, sec. 5, p. 5).

29. Sheldon, *Investigations*, 56.

30. Rudoph M. Severa, "The World's Largest Credit Bureau," *Credit World* 40, no. 9 (June 1952): 5.

31. *Credit Bureau Fundamentals*, sec. 5, p. 12.

32. Rule, *Private Lives and Public Surveillance*, 193. See also Furletti, "An Overview and History of Credit Reporting," 3–4.

33. Quoted in Black, *Buy Now, Pay Later*, 40. See also Rudolph M. Severa, "Credit Bureau Services—Today and Tomorrow," in *Credit Management Year Book, 1958–1959*, vol. 25 (New York: Credit Management Division, National Retail Merchants Association, 1958), 260–262.

34. Rudolph M. Severa, quoted in E. M. Arthur, *Checking and Rating the New Account* (New York: Credit Management Division, National Retail Merchants Association, 1960), 13–14.

35. H. Wallace, *Starting and Managing a Small Credit Bureau*, 62–64.

36. Cole, *Consumer and Commercial Credit Management*, 237.

37. "Your Responsibility for Prompt Credit Bureau Service," in *Credit Management Year Book, 1963–1964*, vol. 30 (New York: Credit Management Division, National Retail Merchants Association, 1963), 287.

38. "Cooperation—The Key to Improved Credit Reporting Service," in *Credit Management Year Book, 1958–1959*, 275–276.

39. Hal Higdon, "The Credit Keepers," *Chicago Tribune*, November 19, 1967, I34.

40. Helen Davis, "The Credit Bureau in a Small Community," *Credit World* 47, no. 12 (September 1959): 9.

41. "How Minneapolis Does It," *Credit World* 38, no. 4 (January 1950): 19.

42. H. Wallace, *Starting and Managing a Small Credit Bureau*, 72.

43. Ibid., 90–91.

44. Harold A. Wallace, "Successful? Mediocre? or Sick?," *Credit World* 41, no. 9 (June 1953): 29.

45. *Credit Bureau Fundamentals*, sec. 6, pp. 11–30; and H. Wallace, *Starting and Managing a Small Credit Bureau*, 86–89. On secondary reporting services and the intersection of credit and "investigative" reporting, see also Rule, *Private Lives and Public Surveillance*, 182–183.

46. Paul D. Green, "They Get All the Credit," *Nation's Business* 33, no. 3 (March 1945): 68.

47. Advertisement for Factbilt Personnel Reports, *Credit World* 50, no. 7 (April 1962): inside front cover.

48. *Credit Bureau Fundamentals*, sec. 1, p. 8.

49. H. Wallace, *Starting and Managing a Small Credit Bureau*, 103–104.

50. James D. Hays, "Principles of Credit Reporting," *Service Bulletin* [of the National Consumer Credit Reporting Corporation] 10, no. 5 (March 20, 1937): 6–7.

51. Charles F. Sheldon, "Problems of the Large Credit Bureaus," *Credit World* 39, no. 8 (May 1951): 30.

52. *Credit Bureau Fundamentals*, sec. 9, pp. 1–3.

53. Ibid., sec. 9, p. 3.

54. Severa, "The World's Largest Credit Bureau," 5.

55. "The Credit Bureau of Hawaii," *Credit World* 47, no. 10 (July 1959): 4.

56. U.S. Senate, Committee on Banking and Currency, *Fair Credit Reporting*, 162.

57. Ibid., 175.

58. Dakins, *Retail Credit Manual*, 415.

59. John L. Spafford, "Using Credit Reports to Sell Consumer Durables," *Credit World* 56, no. 9 (June 1968): 20.

60. John K. Althaus, "The ACB of a Transfer Plan," quoted in Arthur, *Checking and Rating the New Account*, 50.

61. *Credit Bureau Fundamentals*, sec. 9, pp. 21, 26.

62. "Your Personal Credit Rating," *Changing Times* 4, no. 6 (June 1950): 15.

63. Rufus Jarman, "Four Thousand Women Ringing Doorbells," *Saturday Evening Post*, September 8, 1951, 40–41, 59, 62, 65–66.

64. Elaine M. Brand, "Your Credit Bureau Should Have a Newcomer Service," *Credit World* 45, no. 10 (July 1957): 6.

65. "Pocket Notebook Forerunner to Multifold Credit Service," *Dallas Morning News*, January 17, 1960, 6.

66. Howard G. Chilton, "Welcome, Newcomer," *Management Monthly* 3, no. 10 (October 1955): 5.

67. On Charga-Plate, see Lewis Mandell, *The Credit Card Industry: A History* (Boston: Twayne, 1990), 18; Hyman, *Debtor Nation*, 117–118, 120–128; Dakins, *Retail Credit Manual*, 218–223; and Charles F. Sheldon, "The New Way—'Charga-Plate It, Please,'" *Credit World* 23, no. 4 (January 1935): 26–27, 31.

68. Brand, "Your Credit Bureau Should Have a Newcomer Service," 6.

69. See Simon, *Pioneers of Excellence*, 114–115; "The Credit Bureau of Cincinnati," *Credit World* 46, no. 7 (April 1958): 11; [on Pittsburgh] "Your Responsibility for

Prompt Credit Bureau Service," 282; and [on Seattle] E. (Pete) DeWitt, "A Complete Credit Service," *Credit World* 40, no. 12 (September 1952): 7.

70. Arthur, *Checking and Rating the New Account,* 47–48.

71. John K. Althaus, "Credit Approval Service," in *Credit Management Year Book, 1961–1962,* v. 28 (New York: Credit Management Division, National Retail Merchants Division, 1961), 215–217.

72. "New Credit Card Offered by MRCA," *Dallas Morning News,* November 13, 1963, 2; and Simon, *Pioneers of Excellence,* 121–122.

73. Simon, *Pioneers of Excellence,* 154–155; and "New Firm Manages 40 Credit Bureaus," *Dallas Morning News,* March 21, 1963, 2.

74. Rudy Rochelle, "Credit Where Credit's Due," *Dallas Morning News,* March 11, 1962, 1; and "Credit Firm Adopts New Name; Moves into Million Dollar Home," *Dallas Morning News,* January 16, 1966, 37.

75. Rochelle, "Credit Where Credit's Due," 1.

76. See Harold A. Wallace, "Good Public Relations," *Credit World* 40, no. 5 (February 1952): 29; and Clyde William Phelps, *Important Steps in Retail Credit Operation* (St. Louis: National Retail Credit Association, 1947), 20–21.

77. *Credit Reporting Fundamentals,* sec. 9, p. 4; emphasis in original.

78. "Code of Ethics," *Credit World* 16, no. 2 (October 1927): 31.

79. H. Wallace, *Starting and Managing a Small Credit Bureau,* 47.

80. *Credit Reporting Fundamentals,* sec. 2, p. 2.

81. Ibid., sec. 7, p. 7.

82. "Credit Agencies Offer Reports to U.S. Gov't," *Women's Wear,* August 13, 1918, 38.

83. "United States Department of Justice Agrees to Buy Credit Information," *Service Bulletin* [of the National Consumer Credit Reporting Corporation] 10, no. 13 (August 5, 1937): 1.

84. Storer, *A Narrative Report, 1916–1938,* 82.

85. Black, *Buy Now, Pay Later,* 41. See also *Credit Reporting Fundamentals,* sec. 11, p. 4; and Rule, *Private Lives and Public Surveillance,* 199.

86. U.S. House, Committee on Government Operations, *Commercial Credit Bureaus,* Hearing, March 12–14, 1968 (Washington, D.C.: GPO, 1968), 133–134.

87. "Hamilton Directs Major Attack at Social Security in Speech Here," *Boston Globe,* November 1, 1936, B21.

88. On the encroachment of Social Security numbers in business and objections to universal identification, see Robert N. Anthony and Marian V. Sears, "Who's That?," *Harvard Business Review* 39, no. 3 (May–June 1961): 65–71.

89. Carolyn Puckett, "The Story of the Social Security Number," *Social Security Bulletin* 69, no. 2 (2009): 55–74.

7. ENCODING THE CONSUMER: THE COMPUTERIZATION OF CREDIT REPORTING AND CREDIT SCORING

1. John Diebold, "Automation—The New Technology," *Harvard Business Review* 31, no. 6 (November–December 1953): 63–71.

2. James F. Benton, "Challenging Credit Management," *Credit World* 55, no. 10 (July 1967): 15.

3. Stephen P. Coha, "Automated Credit Reporting," *Bankers Monthly* 84 (February 15, 1967): 20.

4. James W. Cortada, *Information Technology as Business History: Issues in the History and Management of Computers* (Westport, Conn.: Greenwood Press, 1996); and James W. Cortada, *The Digital Hand: How Computers Changed the Work of American Manufacturing, Transportation, and Retail Industries* (New York: Oxford University Press, 2004).

5. Vannevar Bush, "As We May Think," *Atlantic Monthly*, v. 176, n. 1 (July 1945): 106.

6. On the cashless society, see Bernardo Bátiz-Lazo, Thomas Haigh, and David L. Stearns, "How the Future Shaped the Past: The Case of the Cashless Society," *Enterprise & Society* 15, no. 1 (March 2014): 103–131. On electronic payment systems, see David L. Stearns, *Electronic Value Exchange: Origins of the VISA Electronic Payment System* (London: Springer, 2011).

7. Allan H. Anderson et al., *An Electronic Cash and Credit System* (New York: American Management Association, 1966), 15.

8. William D. Smith, "The Checkless Society: Human Beings Causing the Chief Delays," *New York Times*, May 21, 1967, F1, F14.

9. Walter Mathews, "Credit Checking System Takes Aim at Deadbeats," *Electronic News* 13 (September 23, 1968): 35.

10. Ultronic Systems Corporation, advertisement for Validator, *Credit World* 53, no. 7 (April 1965); and "Computerized Systems for Credit Authorization Are in the News," *Credit World* 54, no. 5 (February 1966): 31. See also Ronald J. Ostrow, "Telecredit, Inc., Unveils Check Verifying Unit," *Los Angeles Times*, December 16, 1965, B10.

11. "Computer to Control Hot Checks," *Dallas Morning News*, April 7, 1963, 1. On Chilton's subsequent acquisitions of check verification services, see Ledgerwood Sloan, "Chilton Corp Makes Effective Use of Computer to Expand, Diversify," *Dallas Morning News*, August 24, 1969, 13.

12. "The Computer and Credit Information," *Burroughs Clearing House* 52, no. 4 (January 1968): 4.

13. Joanne Knoch, "An Electronic Credit Plan? Galvin Says It's Possible," *Chicago Tribune*, March 23, 1961, D7.

14. For Jordan's biography, see "New Service Uses Computers to Supply Fast Credit Checks," *New York Times*, July 10, 1966, 99; and obituary for Norman D. Jordan, *Detroit Free Press*, July 4, 1956, 16.

15. H. C. Jordan, "The Centralization and Automation of Credit Information," *Bulletin of the Robert Morris Associates* 48 (August 1966): 698–699. For more on the development of CDC and credit bureau computerizations, see Rule, *Private Lives and Public Surveillance*, 205–212; and Hyman, *Debtor Nation*, 211–212.

16. Jordan, "The Centralization and Automation of Credit Information," 699.

17. Ernest A. Schonberger, "Computer Helps Speed Credit Checking Process," *Los Angeles Times*, November 27, 1967, B11.

18. "New Service Uses Computers to Supply Fast Credit Checks," *New York Times*, July 10, 1966, 1; and Ronald J. Ostrow, "Computerized Credit Bureau to Be Opened," *Los Angeles Times*, September 15, 1965, 10–11; on oil company participation, see "New: Instant Credit Reports," *National Petroleum News* 58 (June 1966): 139.

19. "New Service Uses Computers to Supply Fast Credit Checks," 41.

20. On CDC's files, see Jordan, "The Centralization and Automation of Credit Information," 700; on CDC's Southern California expansion, see Gilbert H. Bryn,

"New Developments in Credit Reporting," *Consumer Finance News* 52, no. 2 (August 1967): 28.

21. "New Service Uses Computers to Supply Fast Credit Checks," 41.

22. "New: Instant Credit Reports," 138.

23. "New Service Uses Computers to Supply Fast Credit Checks," 41; "Credit Data Extends Automated Operations to Detroit Area," *Management Services* 3, no. 4 (July–August 1966): 11; and Bryn, "New Developments in Credit Reporting," 3.

24. "Credit Data Moves Into East; Office Based in New York City," *Management Services* 4, no. 6 (November–December 1967): 11.

25. Bryn, "New Developments in Credit Reporting," 28.

26. On New York's credit files, see "Credit Data Moves Into East," 11. On New York to Los Angeles connection, see "Credit Reporting System," *Datamation* 15 (March 1969): 149. For additional description of CDC and its operation under TRW, see Rule, *Private Lives and Public Surveillance*, 205–212.

27. James L. McKenney and Amy Weaver Fisher, "Manufacturing the ERMA Banking System: Lessons from History," *IEEE Annals of the History of Computing* 15, no. 4 (1993): 7–26.

28. Cortada, *Information Technology as Business History*, 166. For tables of computer diffusion by industry, see Cortada, *The Digital Hand*, 55.

29. Jordan, "The Centralization and Automation of Credit Information," 704.

30. William M. Carley, "Careless Checking?," *Wall Street Journal*, August 9, 1963, 7.

31. Edward M. Donohue, address before the International Consumer Credit Conference, National Retail Credit Association, Spokane, WA, June 21–26, 1962; published as "Credit Bureaus of the Future," *Credit World* 50, no. 12 (September 1962): 9.

32. William H. Westrup, "Needed: A Central Source for Consumer Credit Data," *Burroughs Clearing House* 51, no. 3 (December 1966): 68.

33. C. W. Fishbaugh, "Confidentially: This is How We Handle Credit Reports," *Banking* 56, no. 9 (March 1964): 100.

34. Ibid.

35. "Bank Keeps Borrower's Record," *Washington Post*, June 5, 1910, MS2.

36. Westrup, "Needed: A Central Source for Consumer Credit Data," 67–68.

37. Associated Credit Bureau study cited in Rule, *Private Lives and Public Surveillance*, 196.

38. "New Service Uses Computers to Supply Fast Credit Checks," 41.

39. Schonberger, "Computer Helps Speed Credit Checking Process," B9.

40. "The Computer and Credit Information," *Burroughs Clearing House* 52, no. 4 (January 1968): 4. For reference to American Express, see U.S. House, Committee on Government Operations, *Commercial Credit Bureaus*, Hearing, March 12–14, 1968 (Washington, D.C.: GPO, 1968), 78.

41. "Credit Data Moves Into East," 11.

42. "Credit Reporting System," 149.

43. U.S. House, Committee on Government Operations, *Commercial Credit Bureaus*, 87.

44. Ibid., 88.

45. Schonberger, "Computer Helps Speed Credit Checking Process," B11.

46. Coha, "Automated Credit Reporting," 22.

47. "Consumer Business Trends," *Credit World* 54, no. 1 (October 1965): 34.

48. Robert Pinger, "ACBofA's 'Year of Action,'" *Credit World* 53, no. 9 (June 1965): 13.

49. Ibid., 14.
50. "Nationwide Computerized Credit-Rating System Set," *Wall Street Journal*, June 3, 1966, 28; "Competition Quickens in Credit Reporting as More Firms Enter the Race," *Management Services* 3, no. 5 (September–October 1966): 9; and Michael J. Kelly, "The Credit Index," in *Credit Management Year Book, 1964–1965*, vol. 31 (New York: Credit Management Division, National Retail Merchants Association, 1964), 172–176.
51. A. J. McGill, "A Program for the Automation of Credit Bureaus," in *Credit Management Year Book, 1965–1966*, vol. 32 (New York: Credit Management Division, National Retail Merchants Association, 1965), 165–175; and John L. Spafford, "Facts about ACBofA's Project 'CB-360,'" *Credit World* 55, no. 1 (October 1966): 11–12.
52. "New Firm Manages 40 Credit Bureaus," *Dallas Morning News*, March 21, 1963, 2.
53. "Credit Association Building Announced," *Dallas Morning News*, August 9, 1964, 1. For cost of new office, see "Credit Firm Adopts New Name; Moves Into Million Dollar Home," *Dallas Morning News*, January 16, 1966, 37.
54. Rosalie McGinnis, "Dallas Firm Pioneers Computerized Credit," *Dallas Morning News*, November 3, 1964, 5.
55. Rosalie McGinnis, "New Credit Office Open," *Dallas Morning News*, January 21, 1966, 3.
56. Alan Drattell, "Corralling Credit Data," *Business Automation* 15, no. 2 (February 1968): 40.
57. U.S. House, Committee on Government Operations, *Commercial Credit Bureaus*, 131.
58. Schonberger, "Computer Helps Speed Credit Checking Process," B11.
59. U.S. House, Committee on Government Operations, *Commercial Credit Bureaus*, 131.
60. Drattell, "Corralling Credit Data," 49.
61. Leo P. Hardwick, "Problems of Consolidation," *Burroughs Clearing House* 52, no. 9 (June 1968): 37.
62. Clarke N. Newlin Jr., "The Credit Bureau of Tomorrow," *Credit World* 56, no. 1 (October 1967): 12; emphasis in original.
63. Robert K. Pinger, "The Credit Bureau of Tomorrow," in *Credit Management Year Book, 1965–1966*, 183.
64. "Computerized Credit Shown," *Dallas Morning News*, September 15, 1966, 14; see also "Dallas: Credit Bureau Putting Records on Computer," *New York Times*, September 25, 1966, 159.
65. John L. Spafford, "A New Common Language for Communicating Credit Information," *Credit World* 54, no. 3 (December 1965): 6–8; and "Let's Talk the Same Language," *Banking* 58, no. 8 (February 1966): 40–41, 136. For additional description of the standard language, see "Credit Bureau Adopts Common Language," *Banking* 61, no. 8 (February 1969): 96.
66. Nathan Ensmenger, *The Computer Boys Take Over: Computers, Programmers, and the Politics of Technical Expertise* (Cambridge, Mass.: MIT Press, 2010), 91–101.
67. Spafford, "A New Common Language for Communicating Credit Information," 6.
68. Duane O. Watkins, "Let's All Talk the Same Language," in *Credit Management Year Book, 1965–1966*, 190.
69. For sample form, see Cole, *Consumer and Commercial Credit Management*, 228.

70. Robert K. Pinger, "Credit Bureaus of the Future," *Credit World* 53, no. 3 (December 1964): 19.
71. *Commercial Credit Bureaus*, 89.
72. On the problem of identification systems, see A. Anderson et al., *An Electronic Cash and Credit System*, 46–50.
73. Jordan, "The Centralization and Automation of Credit Information," 703.
74. Anthony and Sears, "Who's That?," 65.
75. "Your Responsibility for Prompt Credit Bureau Service," in *Credit Management Year Book, 1963–1964,* vol. 30 (New York: Credit Management Division, National Retail Merchants Association, 1963), 292.
76. "Bankers Group Urges Use of Social Security Number for Records," *Wall Street Journal*, March 8, 1968, 8.
77. Hardwick, "Problems of Consolidation," 72.
78. Allen Hall, "Chilton Corp. Shifting Sights to Small Cities," *Dallas Morning News*, February 9, 1973, 11.
79. Robert Bartels, *Credit Management* (New York: Ronald Press, 1967), 391.
80. Frank Batty, "California's Growth and the Credit Education Aspect," *Credit World* 40, no. 2 (November 1951): 4.
81. Albert L. Kraus, "Scoring System Begun on Credit," *New York Times*, July 9, 1961, F1.
82. Henry L. Wells, "New Customer Credit Pointing System," in *Numerical Pointing Plans for Evaluating Consumer Credit Risks*, Second Consumer Credit Symposium, University of Pennsylvania, January 10, 1963, 5.
83. Henry L. Wells, "Discussion," in *Numerical Pointing Plans for Evaluating Consumer Credit Risks*, 63.
84. H. L. Dunham, "A Simple Credit Rating for Small Loans," *Bankers Monthly* 55, no. 6 (June 1938): 332.
85. Joseph M. Greenberg, "A Formula for Judging Risks Accurately," *Credit World* 28, no. 9 (June 1940): 20, 22.
86. Jennifer Light, "Discriminating Appraisals: Cartography, Computation, and Access to Federal Mortgage Insurance in the 1930s," *Technology & Culture* 52 (July 2011): 489.
87. Greenberg, "A Formula for Judging Risks Accurately," 20.
88. David Durand, *Risk Elements in Consumer Instalment Financing*, technical ed. (New York: National Bureau of Economic Research, 1941), 84.
89. Ibid., 100.
90. Ibid., 7.
91. John T. Rose, "Scientific Evaluation of Credit Risks," in *Credit Management Yearbook, 1946–47*, vol. 13 (New York: National Retail Dry Goods Association, 1947), 168–169.
92. See Poon, "Scorecards as Devices for Consumer Credit" and Poon, "Historicizing Consumer Credit Risk Calculation."
93. "William R. Fair—A Credit Industry Pioneer," *Credit World* 84, no. 4 (March–April 1996): 44.
94. R. J. Zaegel, "Experience with a Credit Scoring System," in *Numerical Pointing Plans for Evaluating Consumer Credit Risks*, 25. On AIC, see also Poon, "Historicizing Consumer Credit Risk Calculation," 226.
95. Zaegel, "Experience with a Credit Scoring System," 27–28.

96. Earl J. Isaac, "Statistical Problems in the Development of Credit Scoring Systems," in *Numerical Pointing Plans for Evaluating Consumer Credit Risks*, 44.
97. On AIC, see Albert L. Kraus, "Scoring System Begun on Credit," *New York Times*, July 9, 1961, F11. On GECC, see Charles G. Klock, "Credit Risk Selection Through Statistical Evaluation," in *Credit Management Yearbook, 1964–1965*, vol. 31 (New York: Credit Management Division, National Retail Merchants Association, 1965), 164.
98. G. A. Wilt and J. M. Tierney, "Progressive Risk Analysis Through Credit Scoring," *Credit World* 56, no. 6 (March 1968): 10–11.
99. Al Kutnik, "Consumer Credit in the Electronic Age," *Credit World* 51, no. 1 (October 1962): 8.
100. Wells, "New Customer Credit Pointing System," 8.
101. Ibid., 17.
102. Jeremy Main, "A New Way to Score with Lenders," *Money* 6, no. 2 (February 1977): 73–74.
103. Paul D. Smith, "Measuring Risk on Consumer Instalment Credit," *Management Science* 11, no. 2 (November 1964): 327–340.
104. Klock, "Credit Risk Selection through Statistical Evaluation," 163.
105. Justin Davidson and Joseph Buchan, "Management Sciences and the Computer" *Papers Presented at the Retail Research Institute's 6th Annual EDP Conference for Retailers*, Long Island, NY, August 31–September 4, 1964 (New York: National Retail Merchants Association, 1964), 5.
106. R. A. Biborosch, "Numerical Credit Scoring," *Credit World* 53, no. 9 (June 1965): 7.
107. Robert A. Morris, "Credit Analysis: An O.R. Approach," *Management Services* 3 (March–April 1966): 54.
108. Ibid., 54.
109. Poon, "Historicizing Consumer Credit Risk Calculation," 221–245.
110. Biborosch, "Numerical Credit Scoring," *Credit World* 53, no. 9 (June 1965): 8.
111. H. Martin Weingartner, "Concepts and Utilization of Credit-Scoring Techniques," *Banking* 58, no. 8 (February 1966): 52. On the relationship between automation and workplace surveillance, see Shoshana Zuboff, *In the Age of the Smart Machine: The Future of Work and Power* (New York: Basic Books, 1988).
112. William P. Boggess, "Screen-Test Your Credit Risks," *Harvard Business Review* 45, no. 6 (November–December 1967): 117.
113. Zaegel, "Experience with a Credit Scoring System," 37.
114. H. J. H. Roy and Edward M. Lewis, "Credit Scoring as a Management Tool," *Consumer Credit Leader* 1, no. 4 (November 1971): 12.
115. Nicolas Johnson, "How Point Scoring Can Do More to Help Make Loan Decisions," *Banking* 64, no. 2 (August 1971): 41.
116. William D. Buel and Gilbert L. Lewis, "Credit Scoring—and Beyond," *Banking* 61, no. 8 (February 1969): 43.
117. Durand, *Risk Elements in Consumer Instalment Financing*, 92.
118. Ibid., 8.
119. O. D. Nelson, "Credit Scoring—Outlook for the 80's," *Credit World* 67, no. 5 (April–May 1979): 36.

8. DATABASE PANIC: COMPUTERIZED CREDIT
SURVEILLANCE AND ITS DISCONTENTS

1. David Blair, "The Credit Bureau as a Vital Force in Your Community," *Management Monthly* 2, no. 11 (November 1954): 19.

2. U.S. House, Committee on Government Operations, *Commercial Credit Bureaus*, Hearing, March 12–14, 1968 (Washington, D.C.: GPO, 1968), 120.

3. U.S. Senate, Committee on Banking and Currency, *Fair Credit Reporting*, Hearing, May 19–23, 1969 (Washington, D.C.: GPO, 1969), 13.

4. H. J. H. Roy, "Why Credit Scoring," *Burroughs Clearing House* 56, no. 7 (April 1972): 27.

5. Report of the Committee on the Preservation and Use of Economic Data to the Social Science Research Council, April 1965, in U.S. House, Committee on Government Operations, *The Computer and Invasion of Privacy*, Hearing, July 26–28, 1966 (Washington, D.C.: GPO, 1966), 195–253.

6. Ibid., 2. For an overview of government computerization and congressional investigations during the 1960s, see Alan F. Westin, *Privacy and Freedom* (New York: Atheneum, 1967), chap. 12.

7. U.S. House, Committee on Government Operations, *The Computer and Invasion of Privacy*, 122.

8. Black, *Buy Now, Pay Later*, 37.

9. See John Brooks, "There's Somebody Watching You," *New York Times*, March 15, 1964, BR1; Robert R. Kirsch, "Individual Privacy Loss: With Us Here, Now," *Los Angeles Times*, March 15, 1964, D18; Charles Poore, "Now Everybody Wants to Know What's on Your Mind," *New York Times*, March 17, 1964, 33; Glendy Culligan, "Brothers of Assorted Sizes Are Kibitzing on Our Lives," *Washington Post*, March 18, 1964, A4; Frederick H. Guildry, "Big Brother Is Watching," *Christian Science Monitor*, March 19, 1964, 9; Robert C. Moore, "Is Big Brother 'Bugging' You?," *Boston Globe*, March 22, 1964, 27; Edmund Fuller, "A Pair of Indictments of Privacy-Invaders," *Wall Street Journal*, March 26, 1964, 14; and Lewis Nichols, "Still Naked," *New York Times*, April 26, 1964, BR45.

10. Joseph W. Bishop Jr., review of *The Naked Society*, by Vance Packard, *Yale Law Journal* 74, no. 1 (November 1964): 196.

11. "The Credit Bureau as an Aid to Profitable Credit Selling," *Small Business Aids*, no. 434 (Washington, D.C.: U.S. Department of Commerce, 19 February 1948), 1.

12. Stanford N. Sesser, "Prying for Pay," *Wall Street Journal*, February 5, 1968, 16.

13. U.S. House, Committee on Government Operations, *Commercial Credit Bureaus*, 40–41.

14. William M. Carley, "Careless Checking?," *Wall Street Journal*, August 9, 1963, 1.

15. Ibid.

16. Three separate hearings were held, one in the House (March 12–14, 1968) and two in the Senate (December 10–11, 1968, and May 19–23, 1969). For a summary, see Robert M. McNamara Jr., "The Fair Credit Reporting Act: A Legislative Overview," *Journal of Public Law* 22 (1973): 67–101.

17. U.S. House, Committee on Government Operations, *Commercial Credit Bureaus*, 136.

18. U.S. Senate, Committee on the Judiciary, *The Credit Industry*, Hearing, December 10–11, 1968 (Washington, D.C.: GPO, 1969), 1.

19. Ibid., 136.

20. U.S. House, Committee on Government Operations, *Commercial Credit Bureaus*, 120.

21. Ibid., 7–9.
22. *Fair Credit Reporting*, 165–167.
23. U.S. House, Committee on Government Operations, *Commercial Credit Bureaus*, 135.
24. Ibid., 115.
25. U.S. Senate, Committee on the Judiciary, *The Credit Industry*, 110.
26. Ibid., 118. For an economist's defense of the credit bureau's "surgically-precise gossip," see Daniel B. Klein, "Promise Keeping in the Great Society: A Model of Credit Information Sharing," *Economics and Politics* 4, no. 2 (July 1992): 117–136.
27. U.S. Senate, Committee on Banking and Currency, *Fair Credit Reporting*, 204.
28. Ibid., 206.
29. Ibid., 212.
30. Cornelius E. Gallagher, "The ACB's Guidelines for Protection of Privacy," *Credit World* 57, no. 5 (February 1969): 6.
31. U.S. House, Committee on Government Operations, *Commercial Credit Bureaus*, 61.
32. Ibid., 85.
33. Ibid., 100.
34. Ibid., 62–101.
35. U.S. Senate, Committee on the Judiciary, *The Credit Industry*, 64.
36. U.S. House, Committee on Government Operations, *Commercial Credit Bureaus*, 51.
37. Ibid., 95. On computing and workplace surveillance, see Zuboff, *In the Age of the Smart Machine*.
38. U.S. House, Committee on Government Operations, *Commercial Credit Bureaus*, 86.
39. Ibid.
40. Ibid., 69; and U.S. Senate, Committee on the Judiciary, *The Credit Industry*, 75–76.
41. Leo P. Hardwick, "Problems of Consolidation," *Burroughs Clearing House* 52, no. 9 (June 1968): 73.
42. Allen Hall, "Chilton Corp. Shifting Sights to Small Cities," *Dallas Morning News*, February 9, 1973, 11.
43. U.S. Senate, Committee on Banking and Currency, *Fair Credit Reporting*, 142–147, 173, 230.
44. U.S. House, Committee on Government Operations, *Commercial Credit Bureaus*, 94.
45. Fair Credit Reporting Act of 1970, 15 U.S.C. 1681.
46. U.S. Senate, Committee on Banking and Currency, *Fair Credit Reporting*, 232.
47. Sheldon Feldman, "The Fair Credit Reporting Act—From the Regulators Vantage Point," *Santa Clara Law Review* 14, no. 3 (1974): 474–475.
48. Ibid., 482–485. For additional critique of the FCRA, see Vern Countryman, "Computers and Dossiers," *The Nation*, August 30, 1971, 134–149, esp. 135–138, 147–149.
49. This observation is made in Arthur R. Miller, "Personal Privacy in the Computer Age: The Challenge of a New Technology in an Information-Oriented Society," *Michigan Law Review* 67, no. 6 (April 1969): 1148.
50. Davis Dyer, *TRW: Pioneering Technology and Innovation Since 1900* (Boston: Harvard Business School Press, 1998), 279. For cashless society remarks, see "Thumb-Print Economics," *Time* magazine, November 27, 1964, 64.
51. See, for example, Thomas Whiteside, "Anything Adverse," *New Yorker*, April 21, 1975, 45–50, 53–54, 56, 59, 61–64, 69–71, 74–76, 80–82, 84–86, 89–92, 95–101.
52. U.S. Senate, Committee on Banking and Currency, *Fair Credit Reporting*, 319.

53. Ibid., 323.
54. Edward M. Lewis, *An Introduction to Credit Scoring* (San Rafael, Calif.: Athena Press, 1992), 11.
55. Paul F. Smith, "Measuring Risk on Consumer Instalment Credit," *Management Science* 11, no. 2 (1964): 327.
56. John L. Spafford, "Let's Quit Talking and Do Something," *Credit World* 50, no. 11 (August 1962): 12.
57. Gerald J. Glasser, "Statistical and Mathematical Applications in Consumer Credit Management, Part Two: Statistical Decision Theory," *Credit World* 55, no. 2 (November 1966): 18.
58. U.S. House, Committee on Government Operations, *Commercial Credit Bureaus*, 60.
59. Justin Davidson and Joseph Buchan, "Management Sciences and the Computer" *Papers Presented at the Retail Research Institute's 6th Annual EDP Conference for Retailers,* Long Island, NY, August 31–September 4, 1964 (New York: National Retail Merchants Association, 1964), 1.
60. For more on managerial conflict, see Josh Lauer, "The End of Judgment: Consumer Credit Scoring and Managerial Resistance to the Black Boxing of Creditworthiness," in *The Emergence of Routines: Entrepreneurship, Organization, and Business History,* ed. Daniel M. G. Raff and Philip Scranton (New York: Oxford University Press, 2017), 269–287.
61. H. J. H. Roy and E. M. Lewis, "The Credit Manager's Uncomfortable Position," *Credit World* 59, no. 7 (April 1971): 10–11.
62. E. S. Amazeen Jr., "Credit in a Recession Economy—Back to Basics," in U.S. House, Committee on Banking, Currency and Housing, *To Amend the Equal Credit Opportunity Act of 1974,* Hearing, April 22–23, 1975 (Washington, D.C.: GPO, 1975), 102.
63. U.S. House, Committee on Government Operations, *Commercial Credit Bureaus*, 31.
64. On gender and racial credit discrimination, see Hyman, *Debtor Nation,* chap. 6; and L. Cohen, *A Consumer's Republic.*
65. U.S. Senate, Committee on Banking and Currency, *Fair Credit Reporting,* 256.
66. For legal analysis of the ECOA's provisions, see Earl M. Maltz and Fred H. Miller, "The Equal Credit Opportunity Act and Regulation B," *Oklahoma Law Review* 31, no. 1 (Winter 1978): 1–62.
67. National Commission on Consumer Finance, *Consumer Credit in the United States* (Washington, D.C.: GPO, 1972), 155.
68. U.S. House, Committee on Banking, Currency and Housing, *To Amend the Equal Credit Opportunity Act of 1974,* Hearing, April 22–23, 1975, 86.
69. U.S. Senate, Committee on Banking, Housing, and Urban Affairs, *Credit Card Redlining,* Hearing, June 4–5, 1979 (Washington, D.C.: GPO, 1979), 149, fn16.
70. U.S. Senate, Committee on Banking, Housing, and Urban Affairs, *Credit Card Redlining,* 183–236. Statistical justifications were similarly used to defend racial discrimination in the insurance industry; see Bouk, *How Our Days Became Numbered.*
71. David C. Hsai, "Credit Scoring and the Equal Credit Opportunity Act," *Hastings Law Journal* 30, no. 4 (November 1978): 382–383.
72. U.S. Senate, Committee on Banking, Housing, and Urban Affairs, *Credit Card Redlining,* 196.
73. Chris Anderson, "The End of Theory: The Data Deluge Makes the Scientific Method Obsolete," *Wired,* June 23, 2008, http://www.wired.com/2008/06/pb-theory/ (accessed August 9, 2016). See also Viktor Mayer-Schönberger and Kenneth Cukier, *Big Data: A*

Revolution That Will Transform How We Live, Work, and Think (Boston: Houghton Mifflin, 2013); and José van Dijck, "Datafication, Dataism, and Dataveillance: Big Data Between Scientific Paradigm and Ideology," *Surveillance & Society* 12, no. 2 (2014): 197–208.

74. Noel Capon, "Credit Scoring Systems: A Critical Analysis," *Journal of Marketing* 46 (Spring 1982): 82–91.

75. Ibid., 85fn3. See also U.S. Senate, Committee on Banking, Housing, and Urban Affairs, *Credit Card Redlining*, 95–183.

76. U.S. Senate, Committee on Banking, Housing, and Urban Affairs, *Credit Card Redlining*, 226–230.

77. U.S. House, Committee on Banking and Currency, *Credit Discrimination*, Hearing, June 20–21, 1974 (Washington, D.C.: GPO, 1974), 112.

78. Hyman, *Debtor Nation*, 192.

79. Roland E. Brandel, "New Dangers Arise in Point Scoring, But You Can't Afford to Be Without It," *Banking* 68, no. 3 (March 1976): 86; emphasis in original.

80. U.S. Senate, Committee on Banking, Housing and Urban Affairs, Markup Session, September 25, 1975, 5–6.

9. FROM DEBTS TO DATA: CREDIT BUREAUS IN THE NEW INFORMATION ECONOMY

1. Federal Trade Commission, "Prescreening," *Federal Register* 38, no. 26 (February 23, 1973): 4947.

2. Kathryn Christensen, "What's in a Name? This Consumer Says Privacy and $35,000," *Wall Street Journal*, April 22, 1980, 1.

3. U.S. Senate, Committee on Banking, Housing, and Urban Affairs, *Fair Financial Information Practices Act*, Hearing, February 21, April 22, 23, and 30, 1980 (Washington, D.C: GPO, 1980), 294.

4. Christensen, "What's in a Name?," 45.

5. U.S. Senate, Committee on Government Operations and Committee on the Judiciary, *Privacy: The Collection, Use, and Computerization of Personal Data*, Joint Hearing, June 18, 19, and 20, 1974 (Washington, D.C.: GPO, 1974), 2252.

6. Privacy Protection Study Commission, *Personal Privacy in an Information Society* (Washington, D.C.: GPO, 1977), 5.

7. The history and significance of late twentieth-century information society is addressed in a massive body of scholarship. See, for example, Manuel Castells, *The Rise of Network Society*, vol. 1, *The Information Age: Economy, Society, and Culture*, 2nd ed. (Malden, Mass.: Blackwell, 2009); Mark Poster, *The Mode of Information: Poststructuralism and Social Context* (Chicago: University of Chicago Press, 1990); and Vincent Mosco and Janet Wasko, eds., *The Political Economy of Information* (Madison: University of Wisconsin Press, 1988).

8. Advertisement, *Wall Street Journal*, January 21, 1976, 36.

9. Lisa Fichensher, "Credit Bureaus Reinvent Themselves for Kinder, Gentler, and Wider Role," *American Banker*, December 29, 1997, 1.

10. U.S. Senate, Committee on Banking, Housing, and Urban Affairs, *Fair Credit Reporting Amendments of 1975*, Hearing, October 22, 23, 29, and November 18, 1975 (Washington, D.C.: GPO, 1985), 119.

11. U.S. Senate, Committee on Banking, Housing, and Urban Affairs, *Fair Financial Information Practices Act*, 881.

12. The firm's name was originally Trans Union. For clarity's sake, the current spelling, TransUnion, is used throughout the text.

13. "Trans Union Forms Credit Unit," *Wall Street Journal*, January 20, 1970, 39.

14. Trans Union Corporation, Annual Report, 1975, p. 44.

15. On the disciplinary effects of corporate data gathering and discriminatory risk classification programs, including the contributions of late-twentieth-century credit bureaus, see Gandy, *The Panoptic Sort*.

16. Statement of Edward J. Brennan Jr., Privacy Protection Study Commission, August 4, 1976, p. 6, in David F. Linowes Papers, University of Illinois Archives.

17. U.S. House, Committee on Banking, Finance, and Urban Affairs, *Fair Credit Reporting Act*, Hearing, September 13, 1989 (Washington, D.C.: GPO, 1989), 47.

18. Christensen, "What's in a Name?"

19. U.S. Senate, Committee on Banking, Housing, and Urban Affairs, *Fair Financial Information Practices Act*, 301.

20. Walter Alexander, "What's the Score?," *ABA Banking Journal*, August 1989, 59.

21. Gary G. Chandler, "Generic and Customized Scoring Models: A Comparison," in *Handbook of Credit Scoring*, ed. Elizabeth Mays (Chicago: Glenlake Publishing, 2001), 23–55.

22. On the implications of FICO as a technology of risk and identity formation, see Marron, *Consumer Credit in the United States*.

23. Lew Sichelman, "A Top Credit Score Involves Strategies, Outwitting 'Black Box,'" *Chicago Tribune*, August 23, 1998, 2.

24. On the disjointed diffusion of automatic underwriting, including resistance to "productivity" claims, see M. Lynne Markus, Andrew Dulta, Charles W. Steinfield, and Rolf T. Wigand, "The Computerization Movement in the U.S. Home Mortgage Industry: Automated Underwriting from 1980 to 2004," in *Computerization Movements and Technology Diffusion: From Mainframes to Ubiquitous Computing*, ed. Margaret S. Elliott and Kenneth Kraemer (Medford, N.J.: Information Today, 2008), 115–144.

25. Janet Sonntag, "The Debate Over Credit Scoring," *Mortgage Banking* 56, no. 2 (November 1995): 46.

26. See David Evans and Richard Schmalensee, *Paying with Plastic: The Digital Revolution in Buying and Borrowing* (Cambridge, Mass.: MIT Press, 2001).

27. Alexander, "What's the Score?," 63.

28. For TransUnion's model, see Deirdre Sullivan, "Math Model Weeds Out Card Prospects," *American Banker*, January 6, 1994, 18; for Equifax's model, see Lisa Fickenscher, "Credit Bureaus Devising Tools to Find Debt-Prone Consumers," *American Banker*, March 29, 1995, 14.

29. Fickenscher, "Credit Bureaus Devising Tools to Find Debt-Prone Consumers," 14.

30. G. Chandler, "Generic and Customized Scoring Models," 23–55.

31. "Card Briefs: TransUnion Exhibits Credit Scoring Tool," *American Banker*, September 29, 1994, 21.

32. Gary Robbins, "Credit Scoring: Dual Approach Yields More Predictive Data," *Stores*, September 1993, 30.

33. Karen Epper, "Equifax Begins Testing Bankruptcy Alert System for Banks and Retailers," *American Banker*, April 27, 1994, 14.
34. Marron, *Consumer Credit in the United States*, 128–129.
35. Equifax, 1996 Annual Report, p. 13.
36. "Trans Union to Supply Its Online Insurance Credit Score to Auto/Property Insurer," *Insurance Advocate*, August 21, 1999, 30.
37. Federal Trade Commission, *Credit-Based Insurance Scores: Impacts on Consumers of Automobile Insurance*, July 2007, https://www.ftc.gov/reports/credit-based-insurance -scores-impacts-consumers-automobile-insurance-report-congress-federal (accessed May 30, 2016).
38. Leslie Scism, "A Bad Credit Record Can Get You Rejected for Automobile Insurance," *Wall Street Journal*, November 6, 1995, A1, A5.
39. Robert Ellis Smith, "TRW Sells Its Conscience for Cash," *Business and Society Review* 71 (Fall 1989): 4–7.
40. Popp, "Addresses and Alchemy."
41. Bettye H. Pruitt, *Donnelley and the Yellow Book: The Birth of an Advertising Medium* (N.p.: Reuben H. Donnelley Corporation, 1986).
42. Advertisement, *Journal of Marketing* 44, no. 4 (Autumn 1980): 138–139.
43. Damon Stetson, "Polk Has Facts on Auto Market," *Wall Street Journal*, January 8, 1960, 33. On Polk and the direct mail industry, see Alan F. Westin and Michael A. Baker, *Databanks in a Free Society: Computers, Record-Keeping, and Privacy* (New York: Quadrangle Books, 1972), 154–167. See also Andrew N. Case, "'The Solid Gold Mailbox': Direct Mail and the Changing Nature of Buying and Selling in the Postwar United States," *History of Retailing and Consumption* 1, no. 1 (2015): 28–46; Lisa Petrison, Robert C. Blattberg, and Paul Wang, "Database Marketing: Past, Present, and Future," *Journal of Direct Marketing* 7, no. 3 (Summer 1993): 27–43; and Eleanor Novek, Nikhil Sinha, and Oscar Gandy Jr. "The Value of Your Name," *Media, Culture & Society* 12 (October 1990): 525–543.
44. Leonard Sloane, "Census of Business," *New York Times*, January 17, 1971, F15. See also Martha Farnsworth Riche, "The Wonderful World of Private Data Companies," *American Demographics* 1, no. 2 (February 1979): 24–27.
45. The social significance of U.S. postal codes, notably their contribution to consumer surveillance, has yet to be fully explored. See U.S. Postal Service Office of Inspector General, "The Untold Story of the ZIP Code," report no. RARC-WP-13-006 (April 1, 2013), https://www.uspsoig.gov/document/untold-story-zip-code (accessed June 22, 2016). See also Anna Clark, "The Tyranny of the Zip Code," *New Republic*, March 8, 2013.
46. Michael J. Weiss, *The Clustering of America* (New York: Harper and Row, 1988). On Claritas and related programs developed by SRI International and A. C. Nielsen, see Turow, *Breaking Up America*, 44–49.
47. Dianne Klein, "You Are Where You Live," *Los Angeles Times*, April 16, 1989, 752.
48. On the postwar shift from mass markets to market segments, see Turow, *Breaking Up America*; and L. Cohen, *A Consumers' Republic*.
49. Kirk Johnson, "New Mail-Order Techniques," *New York Times*, July 30, 1983, 1.
50. Equifax, 1983 Annual Report, p. 9.
51. "Big Business Moving In," *Marketing News*, January 11, 1980, 19.

52. "Marketing Information for Zip + 4 Areas," *ABA Banking Journal,* May 1990, 103; "MicroNames and Direct Marketing," *American Demographics* 12, no. 2 (February 1992): 10; and Equifax, 1987 Annual Report, p. 15.
53. Equifax, 1987 Annual Report, p. 12.
54. U.S. House, Committee on Banking, Finance, and Urban Affairs, *Fair Credit Reporting Act,* 813.
55. Maureen Nevin Duffy, "Rather Than Develop Advanced Software, TRW Bought Producer," *American Banker,* October 28, 1987, 16.
56. Ibid.
57. "Mapping and Matching," *American Demographics* 13, no. 8 (August 1993): 10.
58. Thomas B. Rosenstiel, "Someone May Be Watching," *Los Angeles Times,* May 18, 1994.
59. Robert A. Bennett, "A TRW Twist: Selling a Service That Is Often Free," *New York Times,* May 10, 1987, F9.
60. Dennis Cauchon, "TRW's Credit Plan Sells Despite Critics," *USA Today,* January 25, 1988, 3B.
61. Stuart Diamond, "Credit File Password Is Stolen," *New York Times,* June 22, 1984, D1.
62. Michael Weinstein, "TRW Information Unveils 'Credentials,' a Financial Profile Service," *American Banker,* January 15, 1986, 7.
63. John R. Wilke, "Lotus Product Spurs Fears About Privacy," *Wall Street Journal,* November 13, 1990, B1.
64. Langdon Winner, "A Victory for Computer Populism," *Technology Review* 94, no. 4 (May–June 1991): 66.
65. Elizabeth Corcoran and John Schwartz, "On-Line Databases Draw Privacy Protests," *Washington Post,* September 20, 1996, A1, A7.
66. Wilke, "Lotus Product Spurs Fears about Privacy," B1.
67. Paul Saffo, "Desktop Marketing May Open Your Home to 'Little Brother,' " *InfoWorld,* February 18, 1991, 52.
68. U.S. House, *Fair Credit Reporting Act,* 57.
69. Equifax, 1989 Annual Report, n.p.
70. U.S. Senate, Committee on Banking, Housing, and Urban Affairs, *Fair Financial Information Practices Act,* 157.
71. U.S. Senate, Committee on the Judiciary, *The Credit Industry,* Hearing, December 10–11, 1968 (Washington, D.C.: GPO, 1969), 125.
72. *Fair Credit Reporting Act,* Public Law 91-508, *U.S. Statutes at Large* 84 (1970): 1127–1137.
73. U.S. House, *Fair Credit Reporting Act,* 126. For a critique of corporate informational "needs," see Oscar H. Gandy Jr., "Legitimate Business Interest: No End in Sight? An Inquiry Into the Status of Privacy in Cyberspace," *University of Chicago Legal Forum* (1996): 77–137.
74. John Markoff, "More Threats to Privacy Seen as Computer Links Broaden," *New York Times,* June 1, 1988, C10.
75. *The Equifax Report on Consumers in the Information Age* (Atlanta: Equifax, 1991), 19, 69–70. It is worth nothing that when the question about consumer lists was rephrased in pro-consumer language, the results were reversed—67 percent responded that list selling was "acceptable" (72).

76. Jube Shiver Jr., "Equifax to Stop Renting Mailing Lists to Firms," *Los Angeles Times*, August 9, 1991, D1.

77. Milo Geyelin, "Judge Tells Trans Union to Cease Giving Financial Data to Direct-Mail Marketers," *Wall Street Journal*, September 27, 1993, B2.

78. Consent decree, *FTC vs. TRW, Inc.*, U.S. District Court for the Northern District of Texas, Dallas Division, December 10, 1991; amended, January 14, 1993.

79. See Chris Jay Hoofnagle, *Federal Trade Commission Privacy Law and Policy* (New York: Cambridge University Press, 2016), 277–278.

80. Ibid., 290–291.

81. *Consumer Credit Reporting Reform Act*, Public Law 104-208, *U.S. Statutes at Large* 110 (1997): 3009–3428.

82. On other issues, TransUnion was on much shakier ground. Specifically, some of the bureau's marketing lists targeted individuals with active "tradelines"—credit card accounts or mortgages, for example. The use of such tradeline information, even divulged in generalities, allowed marketers to make inferences about an individual's creditworthiness. For this reason, TransUnion's marketing lists were considered "consumer reports" and therefore constrained by FCRA rules. *In the Matter of Trans Union Corporation*, Opinion of the Commissioner, Federal Trade Commission, March 1, 2000, https://www.ftc.gov/sites/default/files/documents/cases/2000/03/transunionopinionofthecommission.pdf (accessed June 27, 2016).

83. Helen Nissenbaum, *Privacy in Context: Technology, Policy, and the Integrity of Social Life* (Stanford, Calif.: Stanford University Press, 2010), 153–156.

84. Federal Trade Commission, *Privacy Online: A Report to Congress*, June 1998, https://www.ftc.gov/sites/default/files/documents/reports/privacy-online-report-congress/priv-23a.pdf (accessed July 2, 2016).

85. Bruce Horovitz, "Privacy: Do You Have Any Left?," *USA Today*, December 19, 1995, A1. On the broad implications of "interactivity" as a mode of surveillance, see Andrejevic, *iSpy*.

86. John Markoff, "Growing Compatibility Issue: Computers and User Privacy," *New York Times*, March 3, 1999, A1.

87. U.S. Senate, Committee on Banking, Housing, and Urban Affairs, *Fair Financial Information Practices Act*, 292–293.

88. Lisa Fickenscher, "Equifax Reshapes Itself to Leverage Its Strengths," *American Banker*, January 5, 1998, 11.

89. Federal Trade Commission, *Data Brokers: A Call for Transparency and Accountability*, May 2014, p. 6, https://www.ftc.gov/system/files/documents/reports/data-brokers-call-transparency-accountability-report-federal-trade-commission-may-2014/140527databrokerreport.pdf (accessed August 7, 2016).

90. James Rufus Koren, "Beyond Mere Numbers," *Los Angeles Times*, December 20, 2015, C1. See also Joe Deville and Lonneke van der Velden, "Seeing the Invisible Algorithm: The Practical Politics of Tracking the Credit Trackers," in *Algorithmic Life: Calculative Devices in the Age of Big Data*, ed. Louise Amoore and Volha Piotukh (New York: Routledge, 2016), 87–106.

EPILOGUE

1. Frederick B. Goddard, *Giving and Getting Credit: A Book for Business Men* (New York: Baker and Taylor, 1895), 30–31.

2. Woodrow Wilson, "A Declaration of Independence and a New Freedom," *Boston Globe*, June 1, 1913, SM6.

3. "Rockefeller Files His Fingerprints," *New York Times*, February 8, 1935, 23.

4. Sankar, *State Power and Recordkeeping*, 266.

5. On financial identity, see Mark Poster, "Identity Theft and the Media," in *Information Please: Culture and Politics in the Age of Digital Machines* (Durham, N.C.: Duke University Press, 2006), 87–115.

6. Marron, *Consumer Credit in the United States;* Kelly Gates, "The Securitization of Financial Identity and the Expansion of the Consumer Credit Industry," *Journal of Communication Inquiry* 34, no. 4 (2010): 417–431; Dawn Burton, "Credit Scoring, Risk, and Consumer Lendingscapes in Emerging Markets," *Environment and Planning A* 44 (2012): 111–124; and Langley, "Equipping Entrepreneurs," 448–467.

7. Annie McClanahan, "Bad Credit: The Character of Credit Scoring," *Representations* 126, no. 1 (Spring 2014): 31–57.

8. Fair Credit Reporting Act; emphasis added. For a summary, see McNamara, "The Fair Credit Reporting Act," 67–101.

9. Experian, *Mosaic USA: The Consumer Classification Solution for Consistent Cross-Channel Marketing,* http://www.experian.com/assets/marketing-services/brochures /mosaic-brochure-october-2014.pdf (accessed August 9, 2016).

10. Amy J. Schmitz, "Secret Consumer Scores and Segmentation: Separating 'Haves' from 'Have-Nots,'" *Michigan State Law Review*, no. 5 (2014): 1415.

11. See Ed Mierzwinski and Jeff Chester, "Selling Consumers Not Lists: The New World of Digital Decision-Making and the Role of the Fair Credit Reporting Act," *Suffolk University Law Review* 46 (2013): 845–880.

12. Federal Trade Commission, "Protecting Consumer Privacy in an Era of Rapid Change: Recommendations for Business and Policymakers" (March 2012), https:// www.ftc.gov/sites/default/files/documents/reports/federal-trade-commission-report -protecting-consumer-privacy-era-rapid-change-recommendations/120326privacyre port.pdf (accessed October 6, 2016).

13. U.S. Senate, Committee on Commerce, Science and Transportation, *What Information Do Data Brokers Have on Consumers, and How Do They Use It?*, Hearing, December 18, 2013 (Washington, DC: GPO, 2015), 2. See also "A Review of the Data Broker Industry: Collection, Use, and Sale of Consumer Data for Marketing Purposes," Committee on Commerce, Science, and Transportation, Majority Staff Report for Chairman Rockefeller, December 18, 2013, https://www.commerce.senate.gov/public /_cache/files/0d2b3642-6221-4888-a631-08f2f255b577/AE5D72CBE7F44F5BFC846 BECE22C875B.12.18.13-senate-commerce-committee-report-on-data-broker -industry.pdf (accessed October 6, 2016).

Selected Bibliography

ARCHIVAL AND MANUSCRIPT COLLECTIONS

David F. Linowes Papers, University of Illinois Archives, Urbana-Champaign, Ill.
J. C. Penney Archive, Southern Methodist University, Dallas, Tex.
John Wanamaker Collection, Historical Society of Pennsylvania, Philadelphia, Pa.
Massachusetts Historical Society, Boston, Mass.
R. G. Dun Archive, Baker Library, Harvard Business School, Cambridge, Mass.

SECONDARY SOURCES

Anderson, Allan H., et al. *An Electronic Cash and Credit System*. New York: American Management Association, 1966.

Anderson, Chris. "The End of Theory: The Data Deluge Makes the Scientific Method Obsolete." *Wired*. June 23, 2008. http://www.wired.com/2008/06/pb-theory/. Accessed August 9, 2016.

Andrejevic, Mark. *iSpy: Surveillance and Power in the Interactive Age*. Lawrence: University Press of Kansas, 2007.

——. "Surveillance and Alienation in the Online Economy." *Surveillance & Society* 8, no. 3 (2011): 278–287.

——. "The Work of Being Watched: Interactive Media and the Exploitative Work of Self-Disclosure." *Critical Studies in Media Communication* 19, no. 2 (June 2002): 230–248.

Anthony, Robert N., and Marian V. Sears. "Who's That?" *Harvard Business Review* 39, no. 3 (May–June 1961): 65–71.

Arena, Joe. "Framing an Ideology of Information: Retail Credit and the Mass Media, 1910–1930." *Media, Culture & Society* 18 (1996): 423–445.

Atherton, Lewis E. "The Problem of Credit Rating in the Ante-Bellum South." *Journal of Southern History* 12 (1946): 534–556.

Augst, Thomas. *The Clerk's Tale: Young Men and Moral Life in Nineteenth-Century America.* Chicago: University of Chicago Press, 2003.

Balleisen, Edward J. *Navigating Failure: Bankruptcy and Commercial Society in Antebellum America.* Chapel Hill, NC: Duke University Press, 2001.

Bátiz-Lazo, Bernardo, Thomas Haigh, and David L. Stearns. "How the Future Shaped the Past: The Case of the Cashless Society." *Enterprise & Society* 15, no. 1 (March 2014): 103–131.

Beck, Ulrich. *Risk Society: Towards a New Modernity.* Translated by Mark Ritter. London: Sage, 1992.

Beniger, James. *The Control Revolution: Technological and Economic Origins of the Information Society.* Cambridge, Mass.: Harvard University Press, 1986.

Benson, Susan Porter. *Counter Cultures: Saleswomen, Managers, and Customers in American Department Stores, 1890–1940.* Champaign: University of Illinois Press, 1986.

Berghoff, Hartmut, Philip Scranton, and Uwe Spiekerman. "The Origins of Marketing and Market Research: Information, Institutions, and Markets." In *The Rise of Marketing and Market Research*, edited by Hartmut Berghoff, Philip Scranton, and Uwe Spiekerman, 1–26. New York: Palgrave Macmillan, 2011.

Black, Hillel. *Buy Now, Pay Later.* New York: William Morrow, 1961.

Board of the Governors of the Federal Reserve System. *Report to the Congress on Credit Scoring and Its Effect on the Availability and Affordability of Credit*, August 2007. http://www.federalreserve.gov/boarddocs/RptCongress/creditscore/creditscore.pdf. Accessed May 26, 2015.

Bouk, Dan. *How Our Days Became Numbered: Risk and the Rise of the Statistical Individual.* Chicago: University of Chicago Press, 2015.

Bradshaw, T. F. "Superior Methods Created the Early Chain Store." *Bulletin of the Business Historical Society* 17, no. 2 (April 1943): 35–43.

Braverman, Harry. *Labor and Monopoly Capital: The Degradation of Work in the Twentieth Century.* New York: Monthly Review Press, 1998.

Brennecke, Claire. "Information Acquisition in Antebellum U.S. Credit Markets: Evidence from Nineteenth-Century Credit Reports." Working paper, Federal Deposit Insurance Corporation, September 2016.

Burton, Dawn. "Credit Scoring, Risk, and Consumer Lendingscapes in Emerging Markets." *Environment and Planning A* 44 (2012): 111–124.

Butler, Nathaniel E., et al. "Equal Credit Opportunity Act." *Business Lawyer* 33 (1978): 1073–1123.

Calder, Lendol. *Financing the American Dream: A Cultural History of Consumer Credit.* Princeton, N.J.: Princeton University Press, 1999.

——. "Saving and Spending." In *The Oxford Handbook of the History of Consumption*, edited by Frank Trentmann, 348–375. New York: Oxford University Press, 2012.

Campbell, Gibson. "Population of the 100 Largest Cities and Other Urban Places in the United States: 1790–1990." Population Division Working Paper No. 27. Washington, D.C.: U.S. Bureau of the Census, 1998.

Caplan, Jane, and John Torpey, eds. *Documenting Individual Identity: The Development of State Practices in the Modern World.* Princeton, N.J.: Princeton University Press, 2001.

Capon, Noel. "Credit Scoring Systems: A Critical Analysis." *Journal of Marketing* 46 (Spring 1982): 82–91.

Carroll, Maureen A. "'What an Office Should Be': Women and Work at Retail Credit Company." *Atlanta History* 40, nos. 3–4 (1996): 16–29.

Carruthers, Bruce G. "From Uncertainty Toward Risk: The Case of Credit Ratings." *Socio-Economic Review* 11 (2013): 525–551.

Carruthers, Bruce G., and Wendy Nelson Epseland. "Accounting for Rationality: Double-Entry Bookkeeping and the Rhetoric of Economic Rationality." *American Journal of Sociology* 91 (1991): 31–69.

Case, Andrew N. "'The Solid Gold Mailbox': Direct Mail and the Changing Nature of Buying and Selling in the Postwar United States." *History of Retailing and Consumption* 1, no. 1 (2015): 28–46.

Caskey, John P. "Pawnbroking in America: The Economics of a Forgotten Market." *Journal of Money, Credit, and Banking* 23, no. 1 (February 1991): 85–99.

Castells, Manuel. *The Rise of the Network Society.* Vol. 1, *The Information Age: Economy, Society, and Culture.* 2nd ed. Malden, Mass.: Blackwell, 2009.

Chandler, Alfred D. *The Visible Hand: The Managerial Revolution in American Business.* Cambridge, Mass.: Harvard University Press, 1997.

Chandler, Gary G. "Generic and Customized Scoring Models: A Comparison." In *Handbook of Credit Scoring,* edited by Elizabeth Mays, 23–55. Chicago: Glenlake Publishing, 2001.

Cheney-Lippold, John. "A New Algorithmic Identity: Soft Biopolitics and the Modulation of Control." *Theory, Culture & Society* 28, no. 6 (2011): 164–181.

Citron, Danielle Keats, and Frank Pasquale. "The Scored Society: Due Process for Automated Predictions." *Washington Law Review* 89, no. 1 (2014): 1–33.

Clark, Evans. *Financing the Consumer.* New York: Harper, 1930.

Clark, Thomas D. *Pills, Petticoats and Plows: The Southern Country Store.* New York: Bobbs-Merrill, 1944.

Cohen, Lizabeth. *A Consumers' Republic: The Politics of Mass Consumption in Postwar America.* New York: Knopf, 2003.

Cohen, Patricia Cline. *A Calculating People: The Spread of Numeracy in Early America.* New York: Routledge, 1999.

Cole, Robert H. *Consumer and Commercial Credit Management.* 3rd ed. Homewood, Ill.: Richard D. Irwin, 1968.

Cole, Simon. *Suspect Identities: A History of Fingerprinting and Criminal Identification.* Cambridge, Mass.: Harvard University Press, 2001.

Consumer Financial Protection Bureau. *Key Dimensions and Processes in the U.S. Credit Reporting System: A Review of How the Nation's Largest Credit Bureaus Manage Consumer Data.* 2012. http://files.consumerfinance.gov/f/201212_cfpb_credit-reporting -white-paper.pdf. Accessed July 1, 2016.

Cortada, James W. *The Digital Hand: How Computers Changed the Work of American Manufacturing, Transportation, and Retail Industries.* New York: Oxford University Press, 2004.

——. *Information Technology as Business History: Issues in the History and Management of Computers.* Westport, Conn.: Greenwood Press, 1996.

Dandeker, Christopher. *Surveillance, Power, and Modernity: Bureaucracy and Discipline from 1700 to the Present Day.* New York: St. Martin's Press, 1990.

Deleuze, Gilles. "Postscript on the Societies of Control." *October* 59 (1992): 3–7.

Deville, Joe, and Lonneke van der Velden. "Seeing the Invisible Algorithm: The Practical Politics of Tracking the Credit Trackers." In *Algorithmic Life: Calculative Devices in the Age of Big Data*, edited by Louise Amoore and Volha Piotukh, 87–106. New York: Routledge, 2016.

Dixon, Pam, and Robert Gellman. "The Scoring of America: How Secret Consumer Scores Threaten Your Privacy and Your Future." World Privacy Forum, 2014. http://www.worldprivacyforum.org/wp-content/uploads/2014/04/WPF_Scoring_of_America_April2014_fs.pdf. Accessed July 20, 2016.

Durand, David. *Risk Elements in Consumer Instalment Financing*. Technical ed. New York: National Bureau of Economic Research, 1941.

Dyer, Davis. *TRW: Pioneering Technology and Innovation Since 1900*. Boston: Harvard Business School Press, 1998.

Ensmenger, Nathan. *The Computer Boys Take Over: Computers, Programmers, and the Politics of Technical Expertise*. Cambridge, Mass.: MIT Press, 2010.

Ericson, Richard V., and Kevin D. Haggerty, eds. *The New Politics of Surveillance and Visibility*. Toronto: University of Toronto Press, 2007.

Espeland, Wendy Nelson, and Mitchell L. Stevens. "Commensuration as Social Process." *Annual Review of Sociology* 24 (1998): 313–343.

Evans, David, and Richard Schmalensee. *Paying with Plastic: The Digital Revolution in Buying and Borrowing*. Cambridge, Mass.: MIT Press, 2001.

Ewald, François. "Insurance and Risk." In *The Foucault Effect: Studies in Governmentality*, edited by Colin Gordon and Peter Miller, 197–210. Chicago: University of Chicago Press, 1991.

Federal Reserve Charts on Consumer Credit. Washington, D.C.: Board of Governors of the Federal Reserve System, 1947.

Federal Trade Commission. *Data Brokers: A Call for Transparency and Accountability* (May 2014). https://www.ftc.gov/system/files/documents/reports/data-brokers-call-transparency-accountability-report-federal-trade-commission-may-2014/140527databrokerreport.pdf. Accessed August 7, 2016.

Feldman, Sheldon. "The Fair Credit Reporting Act—From the Regulators Vantage Point." *Santa Clara Law Review* 14, no. 3 (1974): 459–490.

Fellowes, Matt. "Credit Scores, Reports, and Getting Ahead in America." Brookings Institution, May 2006. http://www.brookings.edu/~/media/research/files/reports/2006/5/childrenfamilies%20fellowes/20060501_creditscores.pdf. Accessed January 15, 2016.

Flandreau, Marc, and Gabriel Geisler Mesevage. "The Untold History of Transparency: Mercantile Agencies, the Law, and the Lawyers (1851–1916)." *Enterprise & Society* 15 (2014): 213–251.

Flinn, William A. "History of Retail Credit Company: A Study in the Marketing of Information About Individuals." Ph.D. diss., Ohio State University, 1959.

Foucault, Michel. *Discipline and Punish: The Birth of the Prison*. Translated by Alan Sheridan. New York: Vintage, 1995.

——. *Power/Knowledge: Selected Interviews and Other Writings, 1972–1977*. Edited by Colin Gordon. New York: Pantheon, 1980.

Foulke, Roy A. *The Sinews of American Commerce*. New York: Dun and Bradstreet, 1941.

Fourcade, Marion, and Kieran Healy. "Classification Situations: Life-Chances in the Neoliberal Era." *Accounting, Organizations, and Society* 38 (2013): 559–572.

Fuchs, Christian. "Political Economy and Surveillance Theory." *Critical Sociology* 39 (2012): 671–687.

Furletti, Mark. "An Overview and History of Credit Reporting." Discussion paper. Payment Cards Center, Federal Reserve Bank of Philadelphia (June 2002): 1–16.

Gandy, Oscar H., Jr. *The Panoptic Sort: A Political Economy of Personal Information.* Boulder, Colo.: Westview, 1993.

——. "Legitimate Business Interest: No End in Sight? An Inquiry Into the Status of Privacy in Cyberspace." *University of Chicago Legal Forum* (1996): 77–137.

Gates, Kelly. "The Securitization of Financial Identity and the Expansion of the Consumer Credit Industry." *Journal of Communication Inquiry* 34, no. 4 (2010): 417–431.

Giddens, Anthony. *A Contemporary Critique of Historical Materialism.* Vol. 1. Berkeley: University of California Press, 1981.

——. *The Consequences of Modernity.* Stanford, Calif.: Stanford University Press, 1990.

Gillespie, Tarleton. "The Relevance of Algorithms." In *Media Technologies: Essays on Communication, Materiality, and Society,* edited by Tarleton Gillespie, Pablo Boczkowski, and Kirsten Foot, 167–194. Cambridge, Mass.: MIT Press, 2014.

Glickman, Lawrence. *Buying Power: A History of Consumer Activism in America.* Chicago: University of Chicago Press, 2009.

Gordon, Colin, and Peter Miller, eds. *The Foucault Effect: Studies in Governmentality.* Chicago: University of Chicago Press, 1991.

Granovetter, Mark. "Economic Action and Social Structure: The Problem of Embeddedness." *American Journal of Sociology* 91 (1985): 481–510.

Hacking, Ian. *The Taming of Chance.* Cambridge, UK: Cambridge University Press, 1990.

Haggerty, Kevin D. "Tear Down the Walls: On Demolishing the Panopticon." In *Theorizing Surveillance: The Panopticon and Beyond,* edited by David Lyon, 23–45. Portland, Ore.: Willan, 2006.

Haggerty, Kevin D., and Richard V. Ericson. "The Surveillant Assemblage." *British Journal of Sociology* 51 (2000): 605–622.

Halttunen, Karen. *Confidence Men and Painted Ladies: A Study of Middle-Class Culture, 1830–1870.* New Haven, Conn.: Yale University Press, 1982.

Hamilton, Holman, and James L. Crouthamel. "A Man for Both Parties: Francis J. Grund as Political Chameleon." *Pennsylvania Magazine of History and Biography* 97, no. 4 (October 1973): 465–484.

Hidy, R. W. "Credit Rating Before Dun and Bradstreet." *Bulletin of the Business Historical Society* 13 (1939): 81–88.

Higham, John. *Strangers in the Land: Patterns of American Nativism, 1860–1925.* New Brunswick, N.J.: Rutgers University Press, 2008.

Hoofnagle, Chris Jay. *Federal Trade Commission Privacy Law and Policy.* New York: Cambridge University Press, 2016.

Horowitz, Daniel. *The Anxieties of Affluence: Critiques of American Consumer Culture, 1939–1979.* Amherst: University of Massachusetts Press, 2004.

——. *The Morality of Spending: Attitudes Toward the Consumer Society in America, 1875–1940.* Baltimore, Md.: Johns Hopkins University Press, 1985.

Hoskin, Keith, and Richard Macve. "Writing, Examining, Disciplining: The Genesis of Accounting's Modern Power." In *Accounting as Social and Institutional Practice,* edited by Anthony G. Hopwood and Peter Miller, 67–97. New York: Cambridge University Press, 1994.

Howard, Vicki. *From Main Street to Mall: The Rise and Fall of the American Department Store*. Philadelphia: University of Pennsylvania Press, 2015.

Hsai, David C. "Credit Scoring and the Equal Credit Opportunity Act." *Hastings Law Journal* 30, no. 4 (November 1978): 382–383.

Hunt, Robert M. "The Development and Regulation of Consumer Credit Reporting in the United States." In *The Economics of Consumer Credit*, edited by Giuseppe Bertola, Richard Disney, and Charles Grant, 310–345. Cambridge, Mass.: MIT Press, 2006.

Hyman, Louis. 2012. *Borrow: The American Way of Debt*. New York: Vintage.

——. *Debtor Nation: A History of America in Red Ink*. Princeton, N.J.: Princeton University Press, 2011.

Igo, Sarah E. *The Averaged American: Surveys, Citizens, and the Making of a Mass Public*. Cambridge, Mass.: Harvard University Press, 2007.

Jacobson, Matthew Frye. *Barbarian Virtues: The United States Encounters Foreign Peoples at Home and Abroad, 1876–1917*. New York: Hill and Wang, 2000.

Jeacle, Ingrid, and Eammon J. Walsh. "From Moral Evaluation to Rationalization: Accounting and the Shifting Technologies of Credit." *Accounting, Organizations and Society* 27 (2002): 737–761.

John, Richard R. "Recasting the Information Infrastructure for the Industrial Age." In *A Nation Transformed by Information: How Information Has Shaped the United States from Colonial Times to the Present*, edited by Alfred D. Chandler Jr. and James W. Cortada, 55–105. New York: Oxford University Press, 2000.

Klein, Daniel B. "Promise Keeping in the Great Society: A Model of Credit Information Sharing." *Economics and Politics* 4, no. 2 (July 1992): 117–136.

Krippner, Greta A. "The Elusive Market: Embeddedness and the Paradigm of Economic Sociology." *Theory and Society* 30 (2001): 775–810.

——. *Capitalizing on Crisis: The Political Origins of the Rise of Finance*. Cambridge, Mass.: Harvard University Press, 2011.

Kruse, Holly. "Pipeline as Network: Pneumatic Systems and the Social Order." In *The Long History of New Media: Technology, Historiography, and Contextualizing Newness*, edited by Nicholas Jankowski, Steve Jones, and David Park, 211–230. New York: Peter Lang, 2011.

Laird, Pamela W. *Advertising Progress: American Business and the Rise of Consumer Marketing*. Baltimore, Md.: Johns Hopkins University Press, 1998.

Langley, Paul. "Equipping Entrepreneurs: Consumer Credit and Credit Scores." *Consumption Markets & Culture* 17 (2014): 448–467.

Lapavitsas, Costas. "The Financialization of Capitalism: Profiting Without Producing." *City* 17 (2013): 792–805.

Larson, John Lauritz. *The Market Revolution in America: Liberty, Ambition, and the Eclipse of the Common Good*. New York: Cambridge University Press, 2010.

Lauer, Josh. "The End of Judgment: Consumer Credit Scoring and Managerial Resistance to the Black Boxing of Creditworthiness." In *The Emergence of Routines: Entrepreneurship, Organization, and Business History*, edited by Daniel M. G. Raff and Philip Scranton, 269–287. New York: Oxford University Press, 2017.

——. "Surveillance History and the History of New Media: An Evidential Paradigm." *New Media & Society* 14 (2011): 566–582.

Leach, William. *Land of Desire: Merchants, Power, and the Rise of a New American Culture*. New York: Vintage, 1993.

Lebhar, Godfrey M. *Chain Stores in America.* 3rd ed. New York: Chain Store Publishing, 1963.

Lemercier, Claire, and Claire Zalc. "For a New Approach to Credit Relations in Modern History." *Annales: Histoire, Sciences Sociales* 4 (2012): 661–691.

Lepler, Jessica M. *The Many Panics of 1837: People, Politics, and the Creation of a Transatlantic Crisis.* New York: Cambridge University Press, 2013.

Levy, Jonathan. *Freaks of Fortune: The Emerging World of Capitalism and Risk in America.* Cambridge, Mass.: Harvard University Press, 2012.

Lewis, Edward M. *An Introduction to Credit Scoring.* San Rafael, Calif.: Athena Press, 1992.

Light, Jennifer S. "When Women Were Computers." *Technology & Culture* 40, no. 3 (July 1999): 455–483.

——. "Discriminating Appraisals: Cartography, Computation, and Access to Federal Mortgage Insurance in the 1930s." *Technology & Culture* 52, no. 3 (July 2011): 485–522.

Lipartito, Kenneth. "Mediating Reputation: Credit Reporting Systems in American History." *Business History Review* 87 (2013): 655–677.

——. "When Women Were Switches: Technology, Work, and Gender in the Telephone Industry, 1890–1920." *American Historical Review* 99, no. 4 (October 1994): 1075–1111.

Lynd, Robert S., and Helen Merrell Lynd. *Middletown: A Study in American Culture.* New York: Harcourt, Brace, 1929.

Lynn, Robert A. "Installment Selling Before 1870." *Business History Review* 31, no. 4 (1957): 414–424.

Lyon, David. *The Electronic Eye: The Rise of Surveillance Society.* Minneapolis: University of Minnesota Press, 1994.

——. *Surveillance After September 11.* New York: Polity, 2003.

Madison, James H. "The Evolution of Commercial Credit Reporting Agencies in Nineteenth-Century America." *Business History Review* 48 (1974): 164–186.

Maltz, Earl M., and Fred H. Miller. "The Equal Credit Opportunity Act and Regulation B." *Oklahoma Law Review* 31, no. 1 (Winter 1978): 1–62.

Mandell, Lewis. *The Credit Card Industry: A History.* Boston: Twayne, 1990.

Mann, Bruce H. *Republic of Debtors: Bankruptcy in the Age of American Independence.* Cambridge, Mass.: Harvard University Press, 2002.

Markus, M. Lynne, Andrew Dulta, Charles W. Steinfield, and Rolf T. Wigand. "The Computerization Movement in the U.S. Home Mortgage Industry: Automated Underwriting from 1980 to 2004." In *Computerization Movements and Technology Diffusion: From Mainframes to Ubiquitous Computing,* edited by Margaret S. Elliott and Kenneth Kraemer, 115–144. Medford, N.J.: Information Today, 2008.

Marron, Donncha. *Consumer Credit in the United States: A Sociological Perspective from the 19th Century to the Present.* New York: Palgrave Macmillan, 2009.

Martin, Randy. *Financialization of Daily Life.* Philadelphia: Temple University Press, 2002.

Marx, Karl. *Capital: A Critical Analysis of Capitalist Production.* Vol. 1. Translated by Samuel Moore and Edward Aveling. New York: International, 1992.

Mayer-Schönberger, Viktor, and Kenneth Cukier. *Big Data: A Revolution That Will Transform How We Live, Work, and Think.* Boston: Houghton Mifflin, 2013.

McClanahan, Annie. "Bad Credit: The Character of Credit Scoring." *Representations* 126 (Spring 2014): 31–57.

McGovern, Charles F. *Sold American: Consumption and Citizenship, 1890–1945.* Chapel Hill: University of North Carolina Press, 2006.

McKenney, James L., and Amy Weaver Fisher. "Manufacturing the ERMA Banking System: Lessons from History." *IEEE Annals of the History of Computing* 15, no. 4 (1993): 7–26.

McNamara, Robert M., Jr. "The Fair Credit Reporting Act: A Legislative Overview." *Journal of Public Law* 22 (1973): 67–101.

Mierzwinski, Ed, and Jeff Chester. "Selling Consumers Not Lists: The New World of Digital Decision-Making and the Role of the Fair Credit Reporting Act." *Suffolk University Law Review* 46 (2013): 845–880.

Miller, Arthur R. "Personal Privacy in the Computer Age: The Challenge of a New Technology in an Information-Oriented Society." *Michigan Law Review* 67, no. 6 (April 1969): 1089–1246.

Miller, Margaret J. Introduction to *Credit Reporting Systems and the International Economy*, edited by Margaret J. Miller, 1–21. Cambridge, Mass.: MIT Press, 2003.

Miller, Peter. "Accounting and Objectivity: The Invention of Calculating Selves and Calculable Spaces." *Annals of Scholarship* 9 (1992): 61–86.

Miller, Peter, and Ted O'Leary. "Accounting and the Construction of the Governable Person." *Accounting, Organization, and Society* 12 (1987): 235–265.

Miller, Peter, and Nikolas Rose. *Governing the Present.* Cambridge, UK: Polity, 2008.

Mosco, Vincent, and Janet Wasko, eds. *The Political Economy of Information.* Madison: University of Wisconsin Press, 1988.

Murphy, Sharon Ann. *Investing in Life: Insurance in Antebellum America.* Baltimore, Md.: Johns Hopkins University Press, 2010.

National Commission on Consumer Finance. *Consumer Credit in the United States.* Washington, D.C.: GPO, 1972.

Neifeld, M. R. *The Personal Finance Business.* New York: Harper 1933.

Nissenbaum, Helen. *Privacy in Context: Technology, Policy, and the Integrity of Social Life.* Stanford, Calif.: Stanford University Press, 2010.

Norris, James D. *R. G. Dun & Co., 1841–1900: The Development of Credit-Reporting in the Nineteenth Century.* Westport, Conn.: Greenwood Press, 1978.

Novek, Eleanor, Nikhil Sinha, and Oscar Gandy Jr. "The Value of Your Name." *Media, Culture & Society* 12 (October 1990): 525–543.

Olegario, Rowena. "Credit Reporting Agencies: A Historical Perspective." In *Credit Reporting Systems and the International Economy*, edited by Margaret J. Miller, 115–159. Cambridge, Mass.: MIT Press, 2003.

——. *A Culture of Credit: Embedding Trust and Transparency in American Business.* Cambridge, Mass.: Harvard University Press, 2006.

——. *The Engine of Enterprise: Credit in America.* Cambridge, Mass.: Harvard University Press, 2016.

Olney, Martha L. *Buy Now, Pay Later: Advertising, Credit, and Consumer Durables in the 1920s.* Chapel Hill: University of North Carolina Press, 1991.

——. "When Your Word Is Not Enough: Race, Collateral, and Household Credit." *Journal of Economic History* 58, no. 2 (June 1998): 408–430.

O'Neal, Orville Wendell. "A Study of Customer Control from the Standpoint of Sales Promotion." M.B.A. thesis, University of Texas, Austin, 1933.

O'Neil, Cathy. *Weapons of Math Destruction: How Big Data Increases Inequality and Threatens Democracy.* New York: Crown, 2016.

Pak, Susie J. Pak. *Gentleman Bankers: The World of J. P. Morgan.* Cambridge, Mass.: Harvard University Press, 2014.

Pasquale, Frank. *The Black Box Society: The Secret Algorithms That Control Money and Information*. Cambridge, Mass.: Harvard University Press, 2015.

Petrison, Lisa, Robert C. Blattberg, and Paul Wang. "Database Marketing: Past, Present, and Future." *Journal of Direct Marketing* 7, no. 3 (Summer 1993): 27–43.

Poon, Martha. "Historicizing Consumer Credit Risk Calculation: The Fair Isaac Process of Commercial Scorecard Manufacture, 1957–circa 1980." In *Technological Innovation in Retail Finance: International Historical Perspectives*, edited by Bernardo Batiz-Lazo, J. Carles Maixé-Altés, and Paul Thomes, 221–245. New York: Routledge, 2011.

——. "Scorecards as Devices for Consumer Credit: The Case of Fair, Isaac & Company Incorporated." In *Market Devices*, edited by Michael Callon, Yural Millo, and Fabian Muniesa, 284–306. Malden, Mass.: Wiley-Blackwell, 2007.

Poovey, Mary. *A History of the Modern Fact: Problems of Knowledge in the Sciences of Wealth and Society*. Chicago: University of Chicago Press, 1998.

Popp, Richard. "Addresses and Alchemy: Mailing Lists and the Making of Information Commodities in Industrial Capitalism." Unpublished conference paper, Histories of American Capitalism, Cornell University, 2014.

——. "Information, Industrialization, and the Business of Press Clippings, 1880–1925." *Journal of American History* 101 (2014): 427–453.

Porter, Theodore M. "Information, Power, and the View from Nowhere." In *Information Acumen: The Understanding and Use of Knowledge in Modern Business*, edited by Lisa Bud-Frierman, 217–230. London: Routledge, 1994.

——. *Trust in Numbers: The Pursuit of Objectivity in Science and Public Life*. Princeton, N.J.: Princeton University Press, 1995.

Poster, Mark. "Identity Theft and the Media." In *Information Please: Culture and Politics in the Age of Digital Machines*, 87–115. Durham, NC: Duke University Press, 2006.

——. *The Mode of Information: Poststructuralism and Social Context*. Chicago: University of Chicago Press, 1990.

Prude, Jonathan. *The Coming of Industrial Order: Town and Factory Life in Rural Massachusetts, 1810–1860*. New York: Cambridge University Press, 1983.

Pruitt, Bettye H. *Donnelley and the Yellow Book: The Birth of an Advertising Medium*. N.p.: Reuben H. Donnelley Corporation, 1986.

Puckett, Carolyn. "The Story of the Social Security Number." *Social Security Bulletin* 69, no. 2 (2009): 55–74.

Raskob, John J. "The Development of Installment Purchasing." *Proceedings of the Academy of Political Science in the City of New York* 12, no. 2 (January 1927): 619–639.

Robertson, Craig. "A Documentary Regime of Verification: The Emergence of the U.S. Passport and the Archival Problematization of Identity." *Cultural Studies* 23, no. 3 (May 2009): 329–354.

——. "Paper, Information, and Identity in 1920s America," *Information & Culture* 50, no. 3 (2015): 392–416.

——. *The Passport in America: The History of a Document*. New York: Oxford University Press, 2010.

Robins, Kevin, and Frank Webster. "Cybernetic Capitalism: Information, Technology, Everyday Life." In *The Political Economy of Information*, edited by Vincent Mosco and Janet Wasko, 44–75. Madison: University of Wisconsin Press, 1988.

Robinson, Louis N., and Rolf Nugent. *Regulation of the Small Loan Business*. New York: Russell Sage Foundation, 1935.

Rule, James B. *Private Lives and Public Surveillance*. London: Allen Lane, 1973.

Sandage, Scott A. *Born Losers: A History of Failure in America*. Cambridge, Mass.: Harvard University Press, 2005.

Sankar, Pamela. "State Power and Recordkeeping: The History of Individualized Surveillance in the United States, 1790–1935." Ph.D. diss., University of Pennsylvania, 1992.

Schmitz, Amy J. "Secret Consumer Scores and Segmentation: Separating 'Haves' from 'Have-Nots.'" *Michigan State Law Review*, no. 5 (2014): 1411–1473.

Scott, James. *Seeing Like a State: How Certain Schemes to Improve the Human Condition Have Failed*. New Haven, Conn.: Yale University Press, 1998.

Seipp, David J. *The Right to Privacy in American History*. Cambridge, Mass.: Harvard University, Program on Information Resources Policy, 1978.

Seligman, Edwin R. A. *The Economics of Instalment Selling: A Study in Consumer's Credit*. Vol. 1. New York: Harper, 1927.

Sellers, Charles. *The Market Revolution: Jacksonian America, 1815–1846*. New York: Oxford University Press, 1991.

Simon, William. *Pioneers of Excellence: A History of the Chilton Corporation*. Dallas: Chilton Corporation, 1986.

Smith, Robert Ellis. "TRW Sells Its Conscience for Cash." *Business and Society Review* 71 (1989): 4–7.

Stearns, David L. *Electronic Value Exchange: Origins of the VISA Electronic Payment System*. London: Springer, 2011.

Stokes, Melvyn, and Stephen Conway, eds. *The Market Revolution in America: Social, Political, and Religious Expressions, 1800–1880*. Charlottesville: University of Virginia Press, 1996.

Strasser, Susan. *Satisfaction Guaranteed: The Making of the American Mass Market*. Washington, D.C.: Smithsonian Institution Press, 1989.

Taylor, Frederick W. *The Principles of Scientific Management*. Mineola, N.Y.: Dover, 1998.

Torpey, John. *The Invention of the Passport: Surveillance, Citizenship, and the State*. New York: Cambridge University Press, 2000.

Truesdale, J. R. *Credit Bureau Management*. New York: Prentice-Hall, 1927.

Turow, Joseph. *Breaking Up America: Advertisers and the New Media World*. Chicago: University of Chicago Press, 1997.

Twyman, Robert W. *History of Marshall Field & Co., 1852–1906*. Philadelphia: University of Pennsylvania Press, 1954.

U.S. Department of Commerce. *National Retail Credit Survey*. Washington, D.C.: GPO, 1930.

U.S. Senate. Committee on Commerce, Science, and Transportation. 2013. "A Review of the Data Broker Industry: Collection, Use, and Sale of Consumer Data for Marketing Purposes." Staff Report for Chairman Rockefeller (December 18, 2013), https://www.commerce.senate.gov/public/_cache/files/0d2b3642-6221-4888-a631-08f2f255b577/AE5D72CBE7F44F5BFC846BECE22C875B.12.18.13-senate-commerce-committee-report-on-data-broker-industry.pdf. Accessed October 6, 2016.

Van Dijck, José. "Datafication, Dataism, and Dataveillance: Big Data Between Scientific Paradigm and Ideology." *Surveillance & Society* 12, no. 2 (2014): 197–208.

Vose, Edward Neville. *Seventy-Five Years of the Mercantile Agency R.G. Dun & Co., 1841–1816*. Brooklyn, N.Y.: R. G. Dun, 1916.

Weber, Max. *Economy and Society*. Vol. 1. Edited by Guenther Roth and Claus Wittich. Berkeley: University of California Press, 1978.

——.*The Protestant Ethic and the Spirit of Capitalism*. Translated by Talcott Parsons. New York: Charles Scribner's Sons, 1958.

Wells, Toni. "The Information State: An Historical Perspective on Surveillance." In *Routledge Handbook of Surveillance Studies*, edited by Kirstie Ball, Kevin D. Haggerty, and David Lyon, 57–63. New York: Routledge, 2012.

Westin, Alan F., and Michael A. Baker. *Databanks in a Free Society: Computers, Record-Keeping, and Privacy*. New York: Quadrangle Books, 1972.

——. *Privacy and Freedom*. New York: Atheneum, 1967.

Wiebe, Robert H. *The Search for Order: 1877–1920*. New York: Hill and Wang, 1967.

Woloson, Wendy. *In Hock: Pawning in America from Independence to the Great Depression*. Chicago: University of Chicago Press, 2010.

Wyatt-Brown, Bertram. "God and Dun and Bradstreet, 1841–1851." *Business History Review* 40 (1966): 432–450.

Yates, JoAnne. *Control Through Communication: The Rise of System in American Management*. Baltimore, Md.: Johns Hopkins University Press, 1989.

——. "For the Record: The Embodiment of Organizational Memory, 1850–1920." *Business and Economic History* 19 (1990): 172–182.

——. "From Press Book and Pigeonhole to Vertical Filing: Revolution in Storage and Access Systems for Correspondence." *Journal of Business Communication* 19, no. 3 (1982): 5–26.

Zakim, Michael, and Gary J. Kornblith, eds. *Capitalism Takes Command: The Social Transformation of Nineteenth-Century America*. Chicago: University of Chicago Press, 2012.

Zelizer, Viviana A. *Morals and Markets: The Development of Life Insurance in the United States*. New York: Columbia University Press, 1979.

——. *The Social Meaning of Money: Pin Money, Paychecks, Poor Relief, and Other Currencies*. New York: Basic Books, 1994.

Zuboff, Shoshana. "Big Other: Surveillance Capitalism and the Prospects of an Information Civilization." *Journal of Information Technology* 30 (2015): 75–89.

——. *In the Age of the Smart Machine: The Future of Work and Power*. New York: Basic Books, 1988.

Index

Page numbers in *italics* refer to illustrations.

accounting industry, history, 50, 287n88
actuarial methods, 17, 201, 202–203, 209–210, 236–237
Acxiom, 256, 267
advertising: consumer credit education and sales, 12, 131–133, 134–135, *135*, 145, 147–148, 150–151, 301n33; consumer manipulation, 12, 25, 134–135; credit ratings, 131–132, 134–135, *170*; credit surveillance, 13, 127, 136; credit workers, 97
affirmative-negative system (consumer credit reporting), 57, 59–60, 137, 166; blacklist terminology and, 290n58; labor needed, 72
African Americans, 67, 141, 236, 303n69, 303n70
age, in credit ratings, 237
algorithms: consumer credit, 15–16, 211, 250–253, 266–267, 272, 274; critical studies, 280–281n28
American Bankers Association, 82, 199, 229, 232–233

American Economic Association, 214
American Express, 190, 248
American Investment Company (AIC), 204–205, 209, 230
American Mercantile Union, 63, 289n34
The Americans (Grund), 26–27
antecedent reports (consumer credit reports), 160–163
antitrust issues, credit reporting, 99–100, 216, 218, 245–246, 260–261
appearance. *See* physical appearance
assets. *See* income and wealth
Associated Credit Bureaus of America (ACB of A), 100, 140, 192, 215, 218; antitrust injunctions, 216, 218; banking income, 190; computerization, 192–194, 195–196, 245; consumer information sales, 219–220; consumer reports, forms, and standardization, 161–165, 168–169, *170*, 171, 173, 196–197, 199; credit report inquiries, 178, 218–219; credit risk study, 140; investigations and oversight, 216,

Associated Credit Bureaus (*continued*)
218, 222; membership, 156, 245;
self-regulation, 225–226
Associated Credit Services of Houston, 246
"As We May Think" (Bush), 184
authorization. *See* credit authorization or
rejection
automation: authorization systems, 167,
184, 191, 192, 193–194, 200, 250; clerical
functions, 183–184, 200; computer
functions, 182; consumer credit
surveillance and reporting, 182–183,
185–200, 225, 230–233, 250; data
reduction, 194–199; employment effects,
194–195, 207–208, 210, 213–214, 229,
230–233, *231*; societal effects, 270

Bain Capital, 246
balance sheets and financial statements,
40–41, 73–74
banking industry: associations, 82, 199,
217, 229, 232–233; credit data
subscribers, 190–191, 245; credit
marketing, 242–243, 247–249, 263;
credit review elements, 201, 229, 231,
264; data storage confidentiality,
189–190, 190–191, 220; national banks,
28; regulation legislation, 263–264;
technologies and automation, 185–186,
188, 189, 191, 213, 232–233, 249
Bank of America: automation, 203;
consumer data, 190, 229; credit
card marketing, 242–243, 248,
249, 266
Bank of New York, 191
bankruptcies, business, 39
bankruptcies, personal: economic panics,
29; reporting, 224, 225
Bankruptcy Act (1841), 30
Baran, Paul, 214–215
barbers, 76
Baring Brothers & Company, 31, 42
"Barry's Book," 33–34
Baxter, C. H., 62
Beardsley, John and Horace, 42

Bellamy, Edward, 184
Beman, Nathan S.S., 52
Biden, Joseph, 241
bill paying: affirmative-negative system, 59,
137; avoidance methods, 62, 65–66;
credit bureaus' disciplinary influence,
127; credit scoring delinquency models,
249, 252; cycles and schedules, 47,
52, 131, 196–197; non-payment and
blacklisting, 57–60, 63–64, 65;
promptness, character, and credit
rating, 47, 52, 68, 69, 70–71, 131–132,
137–138, 196–197; promptness and
available capital, 130–131
Binet, Alfred, 143
Black, Hillel, 215
blacklists (consumer credit reporting), *57,*
57–60; ratings-blacklists hybrids,
290n58; trade organizations and
independent retailers, 63–64, 65, 66, 78
Bloomingdale's, 138, 148
bookkeeping systems: retailers, 73–74;
technological tools, 146–147, 195–196
Borg-Warner Corporation, 177
Bradstreet, Edward Payson, 36–37
Bradstreet, John M., 33, 37
Bradstreet Company, 33, 37, 38, 41; rating
reference books, 43, 66; subscriptions
profits, 92
*Bradstreet's Improved Commercial Agency
Reports* (rating reference book), 43
Briggs, Thomas W., 173–174
bureaus. *See* commercial credit reporting
organizations; consumer credit
bureaus
Burge, W. Lee, 220, 221–222
Burr, William H., 91
Bush, Vannevar, 184
business failures, 39
Buy Now, Pay Later (Black), 215

Calder, Lendol, 4
Cannon, James G., 74, 85–86, 105–106, 138
capitalism: consumer capitalism and
culture, 3–4, 5–6; language and

vocabulary, 16; 19th century, and credit surveillance, 10, 11, 16–17, 25, 27, 34–35, 50, 51, 272, 279n14

Capon, Noel, 239–240

Capper and Capper (clothier), 148, 150

cash: cash-only businesses, 55, 74, 75–77, 87–88; end of use, 184–185; loans, 56–57; payments, and credit ratings, 68, 133–134; scarcity, 51; spending habits, vs. credit, 53, 74–76, 76–77, 143–144, 146–147

catalog businesses, 200–201

CCN Group, 251

census data and database marketing, 254–259, 260

centralized credit and databases: barriers to centralized data, 188, 192–193, 217; credit prescreening, 248–253, 266–267; credit reporting industry, 212–213, 214–241, 243–245, 248–249, 257, 259–260; database marketing, 242–243, 247, 253–259, 261; government data and databases, 214, 243–244, 260; government investigations, 214–215, 217–223; linking, 260; privacy issues, 212–213, 214–217, 218–219, 223–225, 243–244, 257–265, 274

character and reputation: affirmative-negative system, 59, 137, 166; character as financial identity, 46–47, 105–107, 172, 296n7; charity and social supports, 64; consumer investigations and reports, 161–168, 169, 171, 221–222, 228–229; credit flattery, 147–148, 153; credit workers' discernment, 86, 105, 106–107, 115, 136, 199–200, 203; debt collection, 30, 66, 131–132; derogatory information, 167–168, 177, 219; hearsay and opinion, 35, 39, 46, 47, 203, 221; libel and slander, 42–43; medical patients, 65–66; morality and creditworthiness, credit rating, 19–22, 26–27, 28, 30, 35–36, 39, 81, 105–107, 115, 126, 134–135, 167–168, 191, 201–202,

205, 296n7; morality and creditworthiness, U.S. system characteristics, 26–27, 28, 91, 105, 127–128, 129–130, 135, 135–136, 199–200, 203, 214, 273; reference letters, 30–31, 284n13. See also personal identity; personal information

Charga-Plate, 175–176

Chase Manhattan, 191, 248, 249

chattel mortgages, 89–90

check clearing technologies, 188

Chicago Grocers', Butchers', and Marketmen's Exchange, 64–65

Chicago World's Fair (1893), 82–83

Chilton, Bob, 193

Chilton, J.E.R., 77, 95, 176

Chilton Company/Corporation, 95, 292n95; computerization projects, 193–194; consumer credit surveillance and reporting, 77, 159, 162, 176–177, 227, 246; electronic credit check systems, 185; personnel reporting, 172

Choicepoint, 252

Claritas Corporation, 254–255, 256

classification. See social classification

COBOL (programming language), 196

commercial credit reporting organizations: information standardization, control, and dissemination, 38–43, 196–197; financial identity concept, 6–7, 32, 35–36, 47; history, 6–7, 17, 22–23, 29–30, 35, 278n7; mergers and acquisitions, 33; methods and technology, 14–15, 35–38, 43–46; modern-day, 35; nonparticipation and consequences, 48–49; size and scope, 34, 38; vs. consumer, 90, 173, 218. See also commercial credit ratings; consumer credit bureaus; mercantile agency system

commercial credit investigations, 23, 31, 32, 35–36

commercial credit ratings: code/rating examples, 17, 32–33, 36, 42, 43–46, 68; information control and

commercial credit ratings (*continued*)
dissemination, 38–43; nonparticipation
effects, 48–49; reference books, 43–46,
44; narrative examples, 35, 36, 39, 43.
See also credit rating reference books
Commercial Publishing Company, 63
communication systems: credit agencies,
history, 37, 42–43, 119–125, 157–158,
160; telegraph correspondence, 37,
122, 160
Computer Reporting Systems, Inc. (CRS),
192
Computer Sciences Corporation (CSC),
246
computer technology: code, and
credit information, 159, 183, 196;
computerization of credit reporting/
scoring, 182–186, 192–199, 204–205,
210–211, 223, 225, 227–228, 230–233;
computerized surveillance and
consumer rights, 212–241; credit
reporting industry history, 14–15, 21,
158–159, 176–177, 182–183, 210, 225, 253;
market, 182, 183–184; security,
224–225, 257
confidentiality: banks, 189, 190–191, 220;
credit bureaus, 177–181, 218–219,
264–265; credit rating reporting codes,
42, 70, 114; list brokers and database
marketers, 264–265
Congress of Mercantile Credits (1893),
82–83
consent, information sharing, 262–264,
265
consumer behavior: bill payment and
patriotism, 130–131; credit and
spending amounts, 53, 143–144,
146–147, 152–153, 209; credit card
marketing and rejection, 242–243,
248; credit education, 127–128,
130–136, 301n33; credit surveillance and
collection, 18–19, 20–21, 59, 86, 88,
106–107, 117, 125, 127, 143, 169, 211,
215–216, 221–222, 267, 274; customer
control, 147–148, *149*, 150–155, 304n92;

lifestyles and target marketing,
254–259, 267, 274; online tracking, 9,
265, 275; privacy attitudes, 23–24, 25,
117, 136, 212, 215–216, 256–259, 261–262,
265, 266, 271–272; purchasing habits,
143, 146–147, 148, 150, 152
consumer credit bureaus: automation and
computer age, 182–211, 223, 233,
244–247; 'big data,' 244–245, 247,
273–274; bureaucratic challenges,
71–74, 90, 91–92, 94, 99, 157;
computerized/centralized credit
surveillance, 212–241, 253–265,
266–267, 273–274; credit prescreening
systems, 248–253, 266–267; data and
records, 7, 10, 13–14, 25, 32–33, 57–60,
104, 112–119, *116*, 158–159, 173, 183,
191, 194–199, *198*; government
investigations and oversight, 215,
217–226, 260, 262; history, 5, 7–8, 9,
10, 12–13, 17, 25, 51–77, 78–80, 94–95,
103–125, 156–168, 294n51; in
information economy, 242–267;
infrastructure 1900–1940, 90–102,
126; infrastructure, postwar, 156–159,
164, 173; mergers and acquisitions,
14–15, 77, 177, 183, 227–228, 245,
246–247, 251, 255–256, 260–261;
methods and technology, 10–11, 14–15,
15–16, 17–18, 20–21, 60–62, 66–71, 85,
88, 99, 113–125, 157–159, 173–177,
187–194, 199–211, 212–213; office
environments, 133, *158*; privacy
protections, 223–225; repurposing
information and data marketing,
168–181, 223; self-regulation, 223,
225–226; size and scope, 7, 13–14, 25,
80, 93–94, 96, 100, 102, 103, 113, 157,
164, 167, 192, 225, 243, 245, 246, 257,
262, 271; supplemental consumer
record collection, 18–19, 168–169, 219;
vs. commercial, 90, 173, 218; vs. store
credit departments, 154, 173; welcome
associations, 173–177, 219. *See also*
commercial credit reporting

organizations; consumer credit ratings; Equifax (consumer credit bureau); Experian (consumer credit bureau); TransUnion (consumer credit bureau)
Consumer Credit Protection Act (1968), 226, 236
consumer credit ratings: alternative/future scoring systems, 267, 274; automation and updating, 194–195, 224, 252; blacklists and affirmative-negative system, 57–60, 79, 137, 166; code/score examples, 15, *67*, 68–69, 70–71, 114–115, 119, 125, 141–142, 183, 196–197, *198*, 233, 249, 298n45; consumer awareness and maintenance, 16, 88–89, 111, 131–132, 133, 156–157, 212, 225–227, 234–235, 237, 249–250, 256–257; credit flattery, retail, 147–148, 153; credit management, 7–8, 12–13, 158–168, 228, 273; credit rejection and shame, 131–132, 134–135, 250, 273; credit reporting laws, 264; credit workers' roles, 79–102, 111; data marketing, 168–181; errors and consumer rights, 16, 71, 72, 123, 178, 213, 222–223, 226, 266; forms, 142, 161–163, 164–165, 168–169, *170*, 171, 221–222; generic scoring models, 248–249, 250–251; mortgage lending, 249–250; narrative examples, 119, 156, 162, 168; reference books, 66–71, 88, 114, 145–146; report types, 160–161, 196; statistical and risk scoring, 15–16, 17, 21–22, 25, 183, 200–211, 213–214, 229, 230–241, 245, 247–253, 266–267; subprime lending, 209–210; visual examples, *3*, *67*; vs. financial identity, 160. See also consumer credit bureaus; credit rating reference books
Consumer Data Industry Association, 295n69
consumer loyalty: cash customers, 143–144; preferred credit/customer control, 152–153, 154
Converse, Paul D., 138–140

Cottrell Clothing Company, 150–151
Credentials (identity management service), 257–258
credit authorization or rejection: automation and speed, 167, 184, 191, 192, 193–194, 200, 205, 207; charge cards, 176; communication flows, 177–178; consumer occupations, 18, 128, 137, 138; credit bureaus shifts, 159, 169, 173, 176–177, 231–233, 240–241, 244–245, 247–253, 273–; Credit Data Corporation processing, 190–191; credit democratization, 130, 232, 234–235, 240; credit managers and applicants, 111, 128, 133–134; forms, 117–118, 142, 168–169, 197, 199; geography and judgement, 140–141; rejection consequences and shame, 131–132, 134–135, 250, 273; screening systems, 18, 19, 200–201, 205–206, 228–229, 247–253, 267; telegraph/phone, 37, 121, 122–124
Credit Bureau Incorporated of Georgia, 246
Credit Bureau Management, 193–194
Credit Bureau of Greater Boston, 195, 225
Credit Bureau of Greater New York, 157, *158*, 165, 172, 179–180, 218–219
Credit Bureau of Houston, 180, 193, 194–195, 197
credit bureaus. See commercial credit reporting organizations; consumer credit bureaus; Equifax (consumer credit bureau); Experian (consumer credit bureau); TransUnion (consumer credit bureau)
Credit Bureaus, Inc. (CBI), 192
credit cards: credit information and reporting, 190–191, 193, 197, 264; direct marketing and mailing, 242–243, 247–248, 247–253, 266; issuing companies, 190, 248; predecessors and history, 148, 175–176, 184–185, 186; security, 257
credit consciousness, 132–135

credit databases. *See* centralized credit and
databases
Credit Data Corporation (CDC), 186–193,
197–199, *198,* 218; acquisitions, 227–228;
clients, 229; operations, ethics, and
privacy, 223–226
credit departments, stores. *See* department
stores; store credit
credit limits: automation, 167, 184, 207,
252; consumer credit forms, 118;
consumer credit systems, 114–115, 117,
252, 298n45
credit managers. *See* credit workers
credit monitoring services, 256–258
credit rating reference books: consumer
awareness, 133; history and industry:
commercial, 43–46, *44,* 66, 73;
history and industry: consumer,
66–71, 72, 73, 88, 114, 133, 145–146,
159–160, 305n6; ledger experience,
69–71; labor in creation, 72, 146,
290n60; medical trades, 66;
plagiarism and theft, 73; retail trades'
own, 66, 146
credit scores. *See* commercial credit
ratings; consumer credit ratings
Credit Service Exchange Division,
National Retail Credit Association, 98
Credit Women's Breakfast Clubs of North
America, *97,* 98
credit workers: associations, 41, 83–84,
90–100, 102; automation effects,
194–195, 207–208, 210, 213–214, 229,
230–233, *231;* bureau filing and
technology, *116,* 120–125, *124;* credit
"correspondents" and reporters, 32,
36–37, 40–41, 82, 111, 164–166, 169;
credit education, 127–128, 133–135;
credit managers: consumers' privacy
rights, 24, 177–179, 212, 213, 224; credit
managers: debt collector duties, 278n8;
credit managers: industry history, 7–8,
9, 14, 21, 69–70, 78–102; credit
managers: professionalization, 7–8, 41,
77, 79–102, 108, 144–145, 178–179, 232;

credit managers: social classification, 18,
128; credit reporting specialization,
40–41, 80, 87; earnings, 80; guides and
literature, 18, 81–82, 107, 117, 129,
139–140, 141–142, 178, 200, 270, 296n7;
personality descriptions, 108, 109, 110,
165; skills and methods, 85–87,
106–107, 108–110, 112–113, 115, 118, 128,
135, 141, 164–165, 199–200, 203,
207–208, 230–231, *231;* welcome
associations, 173; women, 14, 96–98, *97,*
110–111, 121–122, 295n68; workforce size
and scope, 38, 63, 80, 93–94, 100, 103,
157, 164, 230. *See also* department stores
Credit World (industry journal), 93
"Cs" of creditworthiness, 20, 35–36, 172,
201, 229
customer behavior. *See* consumer behavior

database marketing, 242–243, 247,
253–259, 261; consumer backlash,
242–243, 258–259, 266; "desktop
marketing," 258–259
databases. *See* centralized credit and
databases
data mining and selling: consumer and
credit data, 168–169, 168–181, 242–243,
245, 247, 253, 259–265, 267, 273–275;
customer lists sales, 19, 34, 159, 173–177,
227, 253, 256, 258–259, 261–262, 267;
industry history, 19, 128, 201, 227, 245,
260, 267, 273–274, 275; legislation
enabling, 227, 261, 262–264, 273;
mercantile agency as personal
information brokers, 34; personnel
reports, 171. *See also* database
marketing
data reduction via automation, 194–199
Dealers' Mutual Protective Agency, 61–62
debt: blacklist publishing, 58–59; credit
industry defenses, 128–129, 185,
201–202; philosophical and religious
perspectives, 23, 51, 52, 53, 145, 272;
social criticism, 128, 215; vs. freedom,
23, 272. *See also* bill paying

debt collection: consumer credit agencies, 61–62, 66; credit managers' duties, 278n8; legal avenues, 30; medical, 66
deferred payment plans. *See* installment selling
delinquency alert models, 249, 252
democratization of credit, 128–130, 232, 234–235, 240
demographic data. *See* census data and database marketing; target marketing
department stores: charge accounts as status, 111–112; charge plates, 175–176; credit departments and credit data collection methods, 103–105, 107–112, 125, 146–147, 148, 153–154; credit departments and credit management, 77, 87–90, 93, 114–117, *116*, 122–123, 126, 135, 138, 146–148, *149*, 150–155; credit office environments, 133; electronic credit check systems, 185; history, 293n22
"derogatory" consumer reports, 166–167, 171, 177, 219
"desktop marketing," 258–259
Dewey, Melvil, 113
Diebold, John, 182
direct mail: consumer credit accounts and control, 145, 147–148, 150–151, 153, 154, 200–201; credit/target marketing, 242–243, 247–253, 253–254, 255–256, 261–262; history, 12
discriminant analysis, 202–203, 204–205, 209–210
Donnelley (list broker), 253–254, 255
Douglass, Benjamin, 42
drinking habits, 156, 171, 221, 222
Dun, Robert Graham, 33, 37, 38, 45, 63
Dun & Bradstreet, 6, 33, 173
Durand, David, 202–203, 209–210

Earling, Peter R., 81–82, 107
Early's Mercantile Agency, *3*
economic panics and crises: 1819, 28; 1837, 17, 28, 29, 51, 82; 1873, 64, 65; 1893, 82

education, consumers: credit consciousness, 132–135; credit counseling, 133–134; credit management, 127–128, 130–136, 301n33; prompt payment, 130–132, 133
electric vs. pneumatic communication systems, 122–124, 194
Electronic Recording Machine Accounting (ERMA), 188
Elrick & Lavidge, 255
employment records. *See* personnel reporting
Equal Credit Opportunity Act (1974), 235–241
Equifax (consumer credit bureau): credit information business, 244–245, 247, 251, 255, 273–274; database marketing and prescreening, 247, 255–256, 258–259, 261–262, 265, 266, 320n75; history, 5, 77, 244, 295n68; lawsuits and regulation, 274; mergers and acquisitions, 77, 255–256, 288n25; risk scoring models, 249, 250–251, 252, 318n28
errors, consumer credit reports/ratings: consumers' lack of power, 16, 222–223, 226; government focus, 266; identification and correction, 72, 178; introduction, 71, 123, 213
ethnicity data, 142, 303n75
Executive Services Companies (list broker), 256
Experian (consumer credit bureau): credit information business, 244–245, 273–274; history, 5, 77, 95, 177, 246; lawsuits and regulation, 227–228, 242–243, 246, 274; risk modeling, 251; TRW history, 227–228, 242–243, 246

"Factbilt" standard forms, 161–163, 164, 169, *170*, 197, 199
Fair, Isaac, and Company, 204; credit scoring, 203–204, *204*, 206, 208, 209, 210–211, 237, 238–240, 249, 252, 280n26; FICO score standard, 15, 249,

Fair, Isaac, and Company (*continued*)
251; PreScore, 248–249; staff, 204, *204,*
208, 238
Fair, William R., 204, 238–239
Fair Credit Reporting Act (1970), 221, 226,
227–229, 235, 259, 260–264, 273
Federal Bureau of Investigation (FBI):
credit surveillance capabilities
compared, 14, 156, 166; credit
surveillance use, 10, 179, 180, 216,
219–220; fingerprinting, 271
Federal Home Loan Mortgage
Corporation (Freddie Mac), 249–250
Federal Housing Administration (FHA),
169, 172, 180, 201, 216–217
Federal National Mortgage Association
(Fannie Mae), 249–250
Federal Reserve Board, 237
Federal Trade Commission (FTC),
226–227, 237, 262, 264–265, 274,
321n82
FICO score standard, 15, 249, 251
Filene, Edward A., 131
filing systems: centralization vs.
dispersion, 217–218, 244;
computerization and automation,
195–196; consumer credit information,
113–125, 157–158, 159, 224; customer
control, 146–147, 148, *149,* 150; digital
vs. paper privacy, 224–225, 244;
ledgers, 285n41; operators, 14, 120–121,
125, 157–158
financial identity: character as, 46–47,
105–107, 172, 273, 296n7; commercial
credit reporting organizations, history,
6–7, 32, 35–36, 46–50; consumer credit
bureaus, history, 5, 7, 9, 13–14, 16–17,
19, 22, 35–36, 47, 60, 104–112, 113–114,
158–160; details tracked, 7, 10, 13–14,
67–68, 115, 137–138, 139, 141–142,
158–160; identification numbers, 181,
198–199; personal identity as, 5, 9,
16–17, 19, 22, 104, 272, 273; risk
computation inputs, 15–16, 21–22; risk
management, computerized, 210–211;

stakes and risk, 2, 9, 10–11, 256–258; vs.
credit ratings, 160
Financial Services Modernization Act
(1999), 263–264
financial statements, 40–41, 73–74
fingerprinting, 271
fiscal education. *See* education, consumers
Fisher, Ronald A., 202
Fleming, E. M., 96
forms: advertisements, *170;* consumer
reports, 161–163, 164–165, 168–169, *170,*
171, 221–222; credit applications and
records, 117–118, 142, 168–169, 197, 199
Foucault, Michel, 135, 278n11, 280n22,
281n29
Franklin, Benjamin, 23, 30, 81
fraternal and trade associations, 63–65, 66,
76, 289n37
freedom: debt vs., 23, 272; vs. surveillance
society, 25, 214, 217, 243–244, 265, 275

Gallagher, Cornelius, 214, 217, 220,
222–223, 226
Galvin, Robert W., 186
Garn, Jake, 241
gender, in credit ratings references, 67–68,
228, 229, 235–238, 240. *See also* women
General Electric Credit Corporation
(GECC), 191, 205, 207
General Motors Acceptance Corporation
(GMAC), 191
generic credit scoring models, 248–249,
250–251
geographical differences. *See* census data
and database marketing; regional
differences, credit reporting; regional
differences, lending industry
Gile, Robert B., 152–153
Gilfillan, Sherman L., *92,* 93, 102
Glass-Steagall Act (1933), 263
Golden Charg-It Card, 176
government data, 214, 254–259, 260
government oversight, credit industry:
credit reporting and privacy, 213,
214–215, 217–227, 231, 235, 243–244,

260, 263–264, 274–275; credit scoring, 241; mercantile agencies, 286n62; trade regulations, 262, 264–265, 274, 321n82

government-sponsored loan organizations. *See* Federal Home Loan Mortgage Corporation (Freddie Mac); Federal Housing Administration (FHA); Federal National Mortgage Association (Fannie Mae); Veterans Administration (VA)

government surveillance, 9–10, 22–23, 179–181, 275; centralized data, potential and fears, 214, 215–216, 217–222, 243–244, 275; programs, 271, 275; use of consumer credit reports, 227

Gramm-Leach-Bliley Act (1999), 263–265

Gramsci, Antonio, 135

Great Universal Stores (GUS), 246

Grocers', Butchers' and Marketmen's Exchange, 64–65

grocers' associations, 64–65, 66, 76

group classification. *See* social classification

Grund, Francis J., 26–27, 233, 282n1

guilds. *See* trade organizations

hacking, computer, 256–257

handwritten ledgers and records, 36, 37, 122

Hart, Philip A., 218

The Hidden Persuaders (Packard), 25

Higinbotham, Harlow N., 82, 85

history, credit industry, 2–4, 5–6; credit surveillance: and end of privacy, 22–25, 50, 136, 212–213, 214–217, 271–272; credit surveillance: birth and rise, 5–8, 9, 11, 12–14, 16–22, 27–31, 137, 270; credit surveillance: information gathering and reporting, 35–36, 57–66, 78–102, 125, 142, 166–181, 182–211, 270–275, 273–274; credit surveillance: mercantile agency system, 29–30, 31–35, 36, 37–43, 46–50, 136, 220–221, 284n20; credit surveillance:

rethinking, 8–11; democratization, 128–130, 232, 234–235, 240; and history of study, 3–5, 9, 18, 22, 24, 34, 35, 127, 206, 277–278n5, 278n11, 279n12. *See also* technological change

honesty: democratization of credit and, 128–130, 232; as unquantifiable, 205. *See also* character and reputation; morality

Hoover, J. Edgar, 271

House of Representatives, U.S. *See* U.S. Congress, industry investigations and oversight

IBM, 182, 187, 192, 193

identification systems: fingerprinting, 271; numbers, 181, 198–199, 262, 263, 308n88

identity theft: consumer fears and services, 256–258; credit authorization telephone calls, 124–125; occurrences, 2

impersonality of credit system, 2, 119, 252–253, 258–259, 269–271, 272, 273

inactive customers, 147–148, 150–151

income and wealth: capital estimates, credit rating, 45, 46, 47, 286n67; credit evaluation component, 18, 19, 20, 26, 45, 107, 137, 138–140, 160, 206; customer control, 151–152, 153; targeting desirable credit customers, 151–152, 248, 254, 258

in-file clearances (consumer credit reports), 160

information, personal. *See* personal information

information, public. *See* public information

information economy, 243, 244, 265, 275, 317n7

information industry: computer revolution, 182–183; credit ratings system history, 38, 49, 100, 159, 239, 244–245; data sales opportunities, 49, 159, 227–228, 244–245, 247, 251, 255, 259–265, 275; data security, 256–258; place in information society, 243, 244, 275

installment selling: consumer abuses, 90,
141; consumer credit history, 51–53,
89–90, 129, 141; price inflation,
52–53, 75
insurance: classification systems, 17, 201,
237; credit reporting/ratings, 162–163,
164, 169, 172–173, 220, 227, 228, 252;
government investigation and
oversight, 220, 221–222, 263
intelligence gathering: credit data as
business intelligence, 18, 34–35, 166;
credit data as national intelligence, 10,
14, 156, 179–180; domestic surveillance,
271, 275
intelligence tests, 142–143
interest rates, 209–210, 250, 252
Internal Revenue Service (IRS): credit
surveillance use, 10, 180, 214, 216,
219–220; public opinion, 261; Social
Security numbers, 181
internet, 9, 214, 265
interviews: consumer and insurance
reporting, 164–165, 168–169; consumer
credit, 20–21, 23, 79, 104–112, 133, 144,
178, 200, 230; credit education, 133;
credit forms and, 118, 168–169;
employment, 165, 169, 171
inventory systems, 74
IQ tests, 142–143
Isaac, Earl J., *204,* 204–205

Jackson, Andrew, 28
John W. Barry Company, 33–34
Jordan, Harry C., 186–187, 188, 191,
223–225, 226, 227
journalism coverage: computerization
of credit, 194; consumer credit
reporting, 2, 13, 58–59, 62, 78, 115–116,
187, 189, 206, 215, 219, 230, 240–241,
244, 250, 277n5; credit marketing,
232, 248; credit use, 52–53, 65–66,
75–76, 78, 144; criticism of
surveillance systems, 48, 136, 172, 215;
professional, credit workers, 18, 81–82,
107, 117, 129, 139–140, 141–142, 178,

200, 270, 296n7; retail commercial
agencies, 56; retail credit support,
144; unpaid debt, publishing, 58–59.
See also advertising
Juran, Joseph M., 153

Kardex and Kard-Veyer, 116, *116,* 157–158
Kresge, S. S., 87

labor and occupations. *See* credit workers;
occupations
labor relations: capitalist surveillance and
regulation, 11, 12; impersonality,
270–272
Lamson Company and tube system,
123–124, 299n80
landlord interviews and tenant data, 165,
168
Larkin, Kenneth V., 229
law enforcement: credit surveillance use,
10, 179–180, 216, 219–220; surveillance
infrastructure, 271
lawsuits: commercial credit reporting, 23,
42; database marketing and lists sales,
242–243, 262, 264–265, 266
The Lawyer and the Credit Man
(periodical), 82
lawyers as credit correspondents, 31, 32,
40, 82
ledger experience: computerized data, 183,
195–196; consumer credit ratings,
69–71, 111, 112, 113, 146, 160; consumer
credit reports, 164, 169, 173, 183,
196–197; copies and filing, 285n41
legislation: bankruptcy, 30; consumer
credit protection, 226, 236, 274; credit
reporting, 25, 212, 213, 221, 226,
227–229, 235, 259, 260–264, 273; equal
credit opportunity, 235–241; finance
industry, 263–264; self-regulation vs.,
225–226, 274
letters of reference, 30–31, 46–47, 284n13
libel: avoidance, consumer credit
reporting, 173; commercial credit
rating/reporting, 41, 42–43, 48, 100

Life (periodical), 14, 156, 157, 159, 168, 180, 215
life insurance industry, 17, 201, 221–222
Lincoln, Abraham, 40
Linowes, David F., 260
Lipartito, Kenneth, 121
list marketing and selling: lawsuits, 242–243, 260, 266; personal information, 19, 34, 159, 173–177, 223, 242–243, 247, 253–254, 256, 258–259, 261–262, 267; reselling, 159, 246, 260, 263, 265
Looking Backward (Bellamy), 184
Lotus Development Corporation, 258
Lotus Marketplace: Households, 258–259
loyalty. *See* consumer loyalty
L. S. Ayres, 103
L. S. Donaldson, 93
lumber industry, 33–34
Lum 'n' Abner (comedy duo), 132–133, 301n32
luxury goods, marketing, 151–152, 248
Lynd, Robert and Helen, 127, 300n3

Macy, R. H., 87
Macy's, 185
Magnetic Ink Character Recognition (MICR), 188
mailing lists. *See* direct mail; list marketing and selling
mail-order businesses, 200–201
Management Decision Systems (MDS), 249, 250, 251
Manhattan Collecting Company, 66
Marcus, Herbert, 126
market research: consumer behavior and credit surveillance, 18–19, 24–25, 127, 128, 228; origins, 12
"market revolution" (19th century U.S.), 27, 283n2
market segmentation: credit customer reach, 176, 209; customer control, 147–155; database tools, 247, 248, 254–259, 261, 266–267
marriage status, and credit, 191, 228

married couples, credit accounts, 109, 111, 151, 235
Marron, Donncha, 252, 281n29
Marshall Field, 88
Marx, Karl, 11
mass consumption/production: advertising and, 12, 25, 132–133, 134; mass production and consumer surveillance, 12, 155; mass production and credit reporting, 32; mass retailers and credit, 77, 87–90, 130, 146, 154–155, 272; mass retailers and customer service, 146, 152–153
Master Charge, 190
Meagher, Thomas, 40, 46
medical professions. *See* physicians, and credit
memory skills, credit workers, 85–86, 112, 141
mental ability, 142–143
Mercantile Agency, 80; business and surveillance, 29–30, 31–35, *33*, 36, 37, 41, 42, 284n20; rating reference books, *44*
mercantile agency system: associations, 91; criticism, 48, 136; history, credit surveillance, 29–30, 31–35, 36, 37–43, 46–50, 136, 220–221, 284n20; nonparticipation and consequences, 48–49; quality improvements and control, 41; rating references, 43–46; retailers' own ratings vs., 69–70
merchants, credit surveillance. *See* commercial credit reporting organizations
Merchants Credit Bureau of Detroit, *120*
Merchants' Protective Union, 69
mergers and acquisitions: commercial credit reporting organizations, 33; consumer credit bureaus, 14–15, 77, 177, 183, 227–228, 245, 246–247, 251, 255–256, 260–261, 288n25; industry legislation, 263
Metromail (list broker), 253–254
Meyers, John, 231

microfilm records, 157, 305n5
Middletown (study), 127
Miller, Arthur R., 218, 260
mistaken identity, 185, 198
monopolies, credit reporting, 99–100, 216, 218, 245–246, 260–261
morality: consumer character and creditworthiness, 19–22, 26–27, 28, 30, 35–36, 39, 81, 115, 128, 134–135, 142, 147, 167–168, 172, 201–202, 205, 228–229, 273; credit surveillance influence, 127–128, 214; credit system failures, 52–53, 142; credit system foundation, 127–128, 129–130; debt aspects, 23, 51, 52, 53, 145, 272; derogatory reports and sensitive information, 166–168, 171, 177, 219; late payments, 52; new technology and, 265; occupations, perceptions, 139–140; physicians' treatment obligations, 65–66
Morgan, John Pierpont, 105
Mortgage Bankers Association of America, 217
mortgage defaults, 2, 216–217
mortgage lending. *See* Federal Home Loan Mortgage Corporation (Freddie Mac); Federal Housing Administration (FHA); Federal National Mortgage Association (Fannie Mae); Veterans Administration (VA)
Motorola, 186

Naked Society, The (Packard), 215–216
names, 142, 151; credit abuses, 62, 124–125; credit report data, 36, 67–68, 72; ethnicity, 142; personal identification numbers, 181, 198–199; store blacklists, 58
National Association of Credit Men (NACM), 41, 83–84
National Association of Mercantile Agencies (NAMA), 91–93, 98, 179
National Association of Retail Credit Agencies, 91
National Bureau of Economic Research (NBER), 202–203, 209–210

National Cash Register Company, 122
National Commission on Consumer Finance, 236
National Consumer Credit Reporting Corporation (NCCRC), 99–100, 179
National Consumer Finance Association, 240
National Decision Systems (NDS), 255–256
nationality data, 142, 303n75
National Retail Credit Association, 98–99, 135, 295n69. *See also* Retail Credit Men's National Association (RCMNA)
National Retail Credit Survey, 101, *101*
National Security Agency (NSA), 275
National Small Business Association, 235
Neifeld, Morris R., 129
Neiman-Marcus, 126, 147
New England Retail Grocers' Association, 65
newspapers. *See* journalism coverage
Nixon, Richard, and administration, 213, 226
nonparticipation, credit systems: commercial/mercantile agencies, 48–49; opt-out clauses, 263, 265; prescreening rejection, 242–243, 260, 266
nonpublic personal information (NPI), 263–265
Norris, James D., 45

objective vs. subjective data: credit policy effects, 205, 208–209, 213–214, 236–237; credit rating methods and challenges, 38–39, 40–43, 46, 47, 107, 125, 202–203, 210, 221–222; modern vs. historic credit reporting, 35–36, 50, 100, 130, 213; perceptions vs. data usage, 138–141, 221–222, 231, 239; records and files systems, 113, 114, 117–119, 125, 196–197; "science" of credit analysis, 80, 86–87, 88, 118–119, 125
occupations: consumer credit risk evaluation, 18, 128, 137, 138–140, 143, 239; intelligence testing, 143

occupations, credit. *See* credit workers

office environments, 38, 133, *158*. *See also* filing systems

office technologies: automation, clerical functions, 183–184, 200; bookkeeping, 146–147, 195–196; communications, 37, 119–125, 157–158; credit reporting industry history, 14, 37; filing systems, 116–117, 157–158. *See also* computer technology

Olney, Martha, 141, 303n69

opt-out clauses, 263, 265

Ormsby, Waterman L., 42

Packard, Vance, 25, 215–216

Panic of 1819, 28

Panic of 1837, 17, 28, 29, 51, 82

Panic of 1873, 64, 65

Panic of 1893, 82

Pareto principle, 153

pawnbrokers and loan sharks, 56–57, 90

payment, bills. *See* bill paying

Penney, J. C., 87

personal identity: credit ratings details, 7, 10, 13–14, 67–68, 115, 137–138, 139, 141–142, 148, *149,* 156, 158–160; credit surveillance and information brokerage, 8–9, 10–11, 34, 100, 168–181, 182, 214, 223, 260; financial identity as, 5, 9, 16–17, 19, 22, 104, 272, 273; identification numbers, 181, 198–199, 308n88; identity theft dangers, 124–125, 256–258; shifts to data/statistics, 2, 119, 252–253, 258–259, 269–271, 272, 273. *See also* character and reputation; financial identity; personal information; physical appearance; privacy

personal information: consumer consent, 262–264, 265; consumer data collection and marketing, 18–19, 20–21, 36, 66–71, 113–114, 117–118, 125, 160–169, 171–181, 182–185, 211, 220–222, 223, 228, 256–259, 260, 261–265, 271–272; Credit Data Corporation protocols, 191; credit

evaluation components, 18, 20–21, 22, 35–36, 67, 70–71, 115, 117, 201–202, 202–203, 209, 216, 228, 235–238, 264; credit interviews, 107–110, 118, 169, 178, 200; lacking, credit evaluations, 74, 197; names lists selling and brokering, 19, 34, 159, 173–177, 223, 227, 242–243, 247, 253–254, 256, 258–259, 261–262, 267; "nonpublic personal information," 263–265; prejudice and credit reporting, 40, 47, 67, 141–142, 229, 232, 235–237, 303n69, 303n70, 303n75; publishing and credit research, 115–116, 145. *See also* character and reputation; personal identity; physical appearance; privacy; public information

personnel reporting, 171; credit records and, 172–173, 227, 228; government investigations and oversight, 220, 222

physical appearance: credit evaluation and, 1, 6, 10, 74, 76, 106, 110, 200, 231, 270

physical storage, credit information. *See* filing systems

physicians, and credit, 64, 65–66

plagiarism, 73

Platt, Jesse, 63

pneumatic vs. electric communication systems, 122–124, 194

Polk (list broker), 253–254, 256

population data, 254–259, 260

population migration, 28–29, 54, 55

predatory lending, 56–57, 89–90, 235

prejudice, credit industry, 40, 47, 67, 141–142, 229, 232, 235–237, 303n69, 303n70, 303n75

PreScore (Fair Isaac prescreening model), 248–249

prescreening, credit, 247–253, 261–262, 266–267

price inflation, credit sales, 52–53, 75

privacy: centralized credit reporting, 212–213, 214–217, 218–219, 223–225, 243–244, 257–265, 274; confidentiality and the public good, 177–181, 189, 220;

privacy (*continued*)
consumer opinions and awareness,
23–24, 25, 88–89, 117, 136, 212,
215–216, 256–259, 261–262, 265, 266,
271–272, 320n75; credit authorization
methods, 124–125, 191, 218–219; credit
correspondents, 36–37, 42, 111; credit
interviews, 107–108, 178; credit
ratings, secret codes, 42, 70, 114;
credit ratings reference books, 43, *44,*
66, 70, 73, 290n56, 291n68; data
gathering and ethics, 9, 10–11, 13–14,
15, 18, 36–37, 189, 191, 212–213, 219,
223–224, 228–229, 275; derogatory
and sensitive information, 167–168,
171, 177–178, 219; digital footprints, 9,
275; digital vs. paper records, 224–225,
244; "end of," via credit surveillance,
22–25, 50, 136, 212–213, 214–217,
271–272; mental/psychological,
24–25; public criticism of surveillance
systems, 48, 136, 214, 215, 280n27;
rights, citizens, 23–24, 172–173,
177–178, 212–241, 258–259, 266,
271–275; studies, 260; unpaid debt,
publishing, 58–59
private consumer credit agencies, 61, 66,
243, 289n37; centralized credit systems,
and investigations, 214–215, 217–233,
244; self-regulation, 223, 225–226
privileged communication, 42–43, 177,
178, 227, 286n62
PRIZM system, 254–255
profitability, consumer credit accounts,
250–252, 275
profit and loss analysis, 208
programming languages, 183, 196
propaganda, credit, 130–136
Protective Association of Grocers, 66
protective associations, 63–65, 66, 76,
289n37
Proxmire, William, 221
psychology: credit surveillance research,
127, 221–222; market research
techniques, 24–25, 256

public information: credit bureau record
collecting, 112, 115–116, 145, 159, 160,
166–167, 171, 223, 260, 262–263,
264–265, 298n50; creditworthiness
evaluation, 216; law enforcement use,
180, 216; list broker record collecting,
12, 254, 260, 264–265
punch card systems, *149,* 150, 154
P$YCLE (database marketing tool), 256

race: credit industry prejudices, 67–68,
141–142, 229, 232, 235, 238, 303n69,
303n70; in credit ratings references,
67–68, 141–142, 162, 229, 235–236, 238,
290n57, 303n70; equal credit
opportunity, 235–236
radio advertising, 132–133, 301n32
Rand Corporation, 116, 117, 158, 214
rating reference books. *See* credit rating
reference books
ratings. *See* commercial credit ratings;
consumer credit ratings
reference letters, 30–31, 46–47, 284n13
regional differences, credit reporting:
active regions, retail, 94–96, 127,
188–189; consumer report/credit
forms, 162, 197; electronic credit
checking, 185, 186–188, 188–189,
192–193, 225; information sharing, 99,
246; urban credit agencies, scope, 63,
96, 157, *158,* 186–188
regional differences, lending industry:
creditworthiness calculations
challenges, 28–29, 38–39, 54, 140–141,
206–207, 239; information sharing
systems, 31, 71–72; predatory lending,
235; targeting desirable credit customers,
209, 239, 248, 254–259, 274, 319n45;
urban credit and trust, 54, 56, 64
rejection. *See* credit authorization or
rejection
Remington Rand Company, 116, 117, 158
reputation. *See* character and reputation
retail business: bookkeeping and financial
statements, 73–74; cash and credit

sales, 55, 74–77, 146–147; mass retailers and credit, 77, 79–80, 87–90; trade associations, 63–65, 66, 76, 289n37
Retail Commercial Agency, 163, 306n22
retail credit. *See* installment selling; store credit
Retail Credit Company (RCC), 162–164, 218; consumer information sales, 219–220; consumer reporting methods and forms, 161, 168–169, 172, 220–222, 225; history/Equifax, 5, 77, 162–163, 244, 295n68; investigations and oversight, 220–222; reports, 306n22; self-regulation, 225–226
Retail Credit Men's National Association (RCMNA), *92*, 92–98, 102
retail credit reporting bureaus. *See* consumer credit bureaus
Retail Dealers' Protective Association, 62–63, 68–69, 69–70, 72–73; labor scope, 290n60; membership, 291n69
Retail Mercantile Agency, *67*, 68, 291n68
R. G. Dun and Company: business history, 33, 37, 38; business industry influence, 37, 126–127; legal troubles, 48; ratings and rating reference books, 41, 43–46, 66, 72–73, 146; subscriptions profits, 92
R. H. Donnelley (list broker), 253–254, 255
risk: calculation methods (consumers), 15–16, 18, 141–142, 201, 202–203, 204–205, 209–210, 210–211, 231–233, 245, 247, 248–249, 250–252, 266–267; credit sales, descriptions, 55–56, 89; industries, 17, 201; occupations and, 138–139, 239; quantification, via credit scoring, 15–16, 17, 18, 21, 38–39, 46, 201–211, 213–214, 229, 234, 238, 241, 250; textualization, 45–46, 49
R. L. Polk (list broker), 253–254, 256
Rockefeller, John D., 1, 2, *3*, 19–20, 22, 130, 270–272, 275
Rockefeller, John D., Jr., 271
Rockefeller, John (Jay) D., IV, 274–275, 322n13
Roosevelt, Franklin D., 181

Rosenthal, Benjamin, 215, 220
Ruggles, Richard, 214
Rule, James B., 166

sales promotions: credit bureau functions, 173, 176–177; loans, 209; local business syndicates, 173–177; target marketing and customer control, 151–154
Sandage, Scott, 16, 34
"science" of credit analysis, 80, 86–87, 88, 118–119, 125
scientific management, 11–12, 13, 153
scores. *See* consumer credit ratings
screening. *See* credit authorization or rejection; prescreening, credit
Sears, 185
seasonal lending, 28–29, 54
Selss, Herman and Conrad, 61, 288n25
Senate, U.S. *See* U.S. Congress, industry investigations and oversight
Severa, Rudolph, 166
sexism, 110–111, 240
Shaw, Edith, 97–98
Singer Sewing Machine Company, 89
slander: avoidance, consumer credit reporting, 173; commercial credit rating/reporting, 42–43, 100
Snowden, Edward, 275
social classification: credit management, 18, 128, 137, 147, 237–238; data collection and grouping, 10–11, 18–19, 274, 275; equality in credit opportunity, 235–236, 237–238; Europe vs. America, 26–27; lifestyles and target marketing, 254–259, 267, 274
social inequality: American society, 238, 240; credit scoring and, 21, 141–142, 236, 238, 240, 274
social media, consumer behavior, 267
Social Science Research Council, 214
Social Security Act (1936) and system, 181
Social Security numbers, 181, *198*, 199, 262, 263, 308n88

social services: business promotions,
173–177; local retailers: grocers, 64,
65, 74–75, 75–76; medical services,
65–66

social trust: breakdown, commercial
lending, 28–29, 54, 55–56; breakdown,
consumer lending, 54, 55–56; prompt
payments, 52, 131–132; U.S. credit
system base, 26–27, 28, 55–56, 64, 91,
104–105, 128, 129–130, 135–136,
233–234, 269, 273

Spafford, John L., 218, 220

Spiegel, 200–201, 201–202, 205, 206

standardized forms. *See* forms

Stanford Research Institute (SRI),
203–204

statistical science history, 50, 202–203

statistical scoring (credit rating):
consumer credit rating, 15–16, 17,
21–22, 25, 183, 200–211, 213–214, 229,
230–241, 247–253, 266–267; credit
policy effects, 208–209, 213–214,
233–234, 236–241; equality
considerations, 236–241; structures
and guides, 201, 202–203, 204–205,
209, 236–237, 240–241, 248–253;
transience, 206–207

status symbols: charge accounts, 111–112;
credit card brands, 248; zip codes,
244–245, 248, 319n45

Steinberg, Bruce, 242–243, 247, 248, 253,
260, 266

Stern, Louis (and Stern Brothers), 87, 88

Stewart, A. T., 87

Stix, Baer & Fuller, *116*

storage, credit files. *See* centralized credit
and databases; filing systems

store credit: cash and credit systems, 53,
74–76, 76–77, 87–88, 146–147; credit
industry history, 3, 5–6, 51, 53; credit
surveillance methods, 20–21, 69,
103–105, 107–112, 146, 200–201; credit
surveillance uses, 18; informal systems,
74–75; retailers' own credit ratings,
69–71, 78–79, 103–104, 114–115, 146,

153–154; selling manuals, 55. *See also*
department stores

study of credit industry history. *See under*
history, credit industry

subjective vs. objective data. *See* objective
vs. subjective data

subprime lending, 2, 209–210

subscription-based reporting:
commercial credit reporting
organizations, 32, 41, 92; consumer
credit ratings, 72–73, 91–92, 160,
171–172, 177, 188–189, 245, 291n69;
fragmentation, 188–189; membership
challenges, 91–92, 93–94

Supreme Court cases, 23, 42

surveillance, credit: affirmative-negative
system, 59–60, 137, 166; computer era
beginnings, 184–211; computerized
surveillance and consumer rights,
212–241, 242–243, 258–259, 266–267,
271–275; consumer awareness or lack
thereof, 16, 24, 111, 131, 133, 212,
215–216, 225–227, 237, 249–250,
256–259, 261–262, 265, 266, 271–272,
320n75; consumer data marketing,
168–181, 242–267; disciplinary
function, 12–13, 24, 46–50, 126–127,
280n26, 318n15; and "end of privacy,"
22–25, 50, 136, 212–213, 214–217,
271–272; future, 9, 266–267, 274;
information economy and society,
242–267, 275; investigations
described (commercial), 23, 31, 32,
35–36; investigations described
(consumer), 85, 160–161, 164–168,
169, 171–172, 221–222, 228–229;
origins/history, consumer, 5, 7–8,
9, 10, 12–13, 17, 25, 51–77, 78–79,
94–95, 113–114, 127, 137, 156–181,
184–185; scholarly attention, 278n11,
279n12. *See also* credit workers;
interviews

surveillance, government, 9–10, 22–23,
179–181, 275; centralized data,
potential and fears, 9, 214, 215–216,

217–222, 243–244, 275; programs, 271, 275; use of consumer credit reports, 227

surveillance state/society, 9, 25, 217, 243–244, 265, 275

surveys: credit bureau education campaigns, 133; credit bureau privacy protection, 261–262, 265, 320n75; credit bureau risk perception, 138–139; retail credit, 101, *101*, 148, 297n42; retailers, on customers, 152–153

switchboards, 121, 124

Tappan, Arthur, 29, 31, 80

Tappan, Lewis, 29–30, 31–35, 36, 41, 42, 49, 59, 80, 220–221

target marketing: consumer backlash, 258–259; credit customer reach, 176, 209, 228, 239; customer activity and tools, 146–147, 150–152, 153–155; database tools, 247, 253–259, 261, 266–267; origins, 12, 128, 255

Taylor, Frederick W., 11, 12

technological change: bookkeeping, 146–147, 195–196; check clearing, 188; computerized credit reporting, 14–15, 21, 158–159, 182–186, 192–199, 204–205, 210–211, 223, 225, 227–228, 230–233; data storage methods, 113, *116*, 116–125, 157–158, 195–196, 305n5; market revolution (19th century U.S.), 27, 283n2; office technologies, 14, 37, *116*, 116–117, 119–125, 157–159, 183–184; past's future visions, 184, 185–186; surveillance methods and ethics, 9, 10–11, 14–15, 189, 212–213, 220, 265

Telecredit, 185

telegraph and teletype communication, 37, 122, 160

telephone communication: computer connections, 187–188; consumer reports interviews, 165, 167, 306n26; credit bureaus and workers, 119–123, *120*, 157–158; credit report transmission, 192, 194

Terry, Samuel H., 54–56, 73–74, 137, 288n10

theft, information: commercial credit reporting organizations, 41; consumer credit authorization process, 124–125; consumer credit data, 256–258; consumer credit ratings, 73, 145–146, 177

Thomas H. Lee, 246

"three Cs" of creditworthiness, 20, 35–36, 172, 201, 229

time-motion studies, 11, 12

trade clearances (consumer credit reports), 160

trade organizations, 63–65, 66, 76, 91–93, 98, 179, 289n37

trade regulation. *See* Federal Trade Commission (FTC)

TransMark (list broker), 256

TransUnion (consumer credit bureau): credit information business, 244–245, 273–274; database marketing, 256, 262, 321n82; history, 5, 246, 318n12; lawsuits and regulation, 262, 264–265, 274, 321n82; risk scoring models, 249, 250–251, 252, 318n28

Truesdale, J. R., 289n34, 289n37

trust. *See* social trust

truth in lending laws, 226

TRW (defense firm), 227–228, 246

TRW Credit Data/Information Systems: credit monitoring, 257–258, 259; credit profitability, 251; database marketing, 227–228, 242–243, 246, 247, 256–257, 261, 262, 264; generic scoring models, 249. *See also* Experian (consumer credit bureau)

Tsongas, Paul, 243, 266

typewriters and typed reports, 37, 122

Union Credit Company, 69

Union Tank Car, 246

United States national characteristics, and credit, 26–27, 28

U.S. Census Bureau, 254, 259, 260

U.S. Congress, industry investigations and oversight: credit data sharing and marketing, 243, 260–261, 263, 266; credit reporting and information privacy, 213, 214–215, 217–227, 231, 235, 243–244, 260, 263–264, 274–275; credit scoring, 241; hearings information, 275, 314n16; mercantile agencies, 286n62
U.S. Department of Commerce, 101, 141, 216
U.S. Department of Justice, 99, 179–180, 216
U.S. Department of State, 216
U.S. Supreme Court, 23, 42, 262

variable interest rates, 209–210
verbal information sharing: consumer credit reports, 160, 192; mercantile agencies/commercial credit reports, 32–33, 33, 41, 43, 45
Veri-Check, 185
Veterans Administration (VA), 161, 172, 180, 216

Wanamaker's, 146
Ward, Thomas Wren, 31, 42
wealth. See income and wealth

Weber, Max, 10, 278n11
Webster, Daniel, 27, 28
Welcome Wagon and welcome associations, 173–177, 175, 219
Westin, Alan F., 218–219, 224, 233, 261
whites, 67, 141, 162
wholesale trade, credit business, 55, 56, 80, 81–82, 85, 90, 92, 127
Whom to Trust (Earling), 81–82, 107
Wilson, Woodrow, 269–270
Winner, Langdon, 258
women: classification and credit use, 144, 148, 151, 236; credit access and ratings, 67, 67–68, 203, 235, 236, 237, 238, 240; credit interviews, 107–108, 109; credit workers, 14, 96–98, 97, 110–111, 121–122, 295n68; sexism, 110–111, 240
Woolford, Cator, 77
Woolworth, F. W., 87
World's Fair, 1893, 82–83

Yates, JoAnne, 113

ZIP codes, 319n45; credit risk by region, 239; database and target marketing, 209, 248, 254–255

Printed and bound by CPI Group (UK) Ltd, Croydon, CR0 4YY

23/01/2024